"New Raiments of Self"

Dress, Body, Culture

Series Editor **Joanne B. Eicher, Regents' Professor, University of Minnesota**

Books in this provocative series seek to articulate the connections between culture and dress which is defined here in its broadest possible sense as any modification or supplement to the body. Interdisciplinary in approach, the series highlights the dialogue between identity and dress, cosmetics, coiffure, and body alternations as manifested in practices as varied as plastic surgery, tattooing, and ritual scarification. The series aims, in particular, to analyze the meaning of dress in relation to popular culture and gender issues and will include works grounded in anthropology, sociology, history, art history, literature, and folklore.

ISSN: 1360-466X

DRESS, BODY, CULTURE

"New Raiments of Self"

African American Clothing in the Antebellum South

Helen Bradley Foster

Oxford • New York

First published in 1997 by
Berg
Editorial offices:
150 Cowley Road, Oxford, OX4 1JJ, UK
70 Washington Square South, New York, NY 10012, USA

Berg is an imprint of Oxford International Publishers Ltd.

Library of Congress Cataloging-in-Publication Data
A catalog record for this book is available from the Library of Congress.

British Library Cataloguing-in-Publication Data
A catalog record for this book is available from the British Library.

Front cover photograph reproduced with kind permission of the J. Paul Getty Museum Malibu, California; artist unknown; title – Portrait of a black man wearing a bow tie, ca. 1856, daguerreotype, 6.4 × 5.2 cm.
Back cover photograph: reproduced with kind permission of the J. Paul Getty Museum, Malibu, California; artist unknown, title – Portrait of a seated black woman, 1855–1860, ambrotype, hand-colored, 6.9 × 5.6 cm.

ISBN 1 85973 184 8 (Cloth)
1 85973 189 9 (Paper)

Typeset by JS Typesetting, Wellingborough, Northants.
Printed in the United Kingdom by WBC Book Manufacturers, Bridgend, Mid Glamorgan.

[The immigrants to the New World had the] opportunity not only to be born again but to be born again in new clothes . . .
The new setting would provide new raiments of self.

Toni Morrison, *Playing in the Dark*

For

Wilhelmina Beatrice Jones Allen

In beloved memory

Contents

Acknowledgements

Partial funding for this research came from a Sullivan Fellowship granted by the Museum of American Textile History for which I am most grateful. The book is enhanced with illustrations of objects in the collections of several institutions. For their permissions, I thank the J. Paul Getty Museum, Malibu, California; Jay Graybeal and the Historical Society of Carroll County, Maryland; and Shadows-on-the-Teche, a museum property of the National Trust for Historic Preservation, New Iberia, Louisiana.

I wish to express my debt to four teachers, Professor John Wright, Dr. Richard Price, and Professor Houston Baker who, early on, acted as my guides into the territory of African American literature, culture, and history, and Professor Roger Abrahams who, at an auspicious moment, directed me to the *Narratives* of the formerly enslaved. My sincere thanks go also to people who read this work as it progressed through various stages of writing. These scholars include Professors Roger Abrahams, John Roberts, and Robert St. George at the University of Pennsylvania; Professor Simon Bronner at Penn State University; Professor Joanne Eicher, University of Minnesota; and three anonymous readers. Each helped give shape to this book with his or her thoughtful critiques.

My husband, Fred Cooper, has been a reader through all the drafts, and I thank him for his continuous, loving support during this endeavor, especially at those frequent intervals when my self-assurance waned.

My children, Berry, Heidi, and Chock Griebel, have given me unending encouragement even as they must have wondered why I began to write a book so late in life.

It began because I wanted to understand. Peter Høeg has written that "to want to understand is an attempt to recapture something that is lost." My loss is Wilhelmina Allen, whom I called Mimi, the earliest, most precious, and longest lasting influence on my life. My attempt to understand and thereby recapture her begins with this book about her ancestors.

Introduction: Warping a Folk History

> Material culture is made up of tangible things crafted, shaped, altered, and used across time and across space . . .. It is art, architecture, food, clothing, and furnishing. But more so, it is the weave of these objects in the everyday lives of individuals and communities.
>
> Simon J. Bronner, *American Material Culture and Folklife*

For the apparel oft proclaims the man (William Shakespeare, *Hamlet* Act 1, Scene 3).

Know first who you are, then deck yourself out accordingly (Epictetus *Discourses* 3.1).

[N]ature . . . has further complicated her task and added to our confusion by providing not only a perfect rag-bag of odds and ends within us . . . but has contrived that the whole assortment shall be lightly stitched together by a single thread. Memory is the seamstress, and a capricious one at that. Memory runs her needle in and out, up and down, hither and thither. We know not what comes next, or what follows after (Virginia Woolf [1928] 1981:49).

. . . your existence will be woven of all the threads in the loom, exactly as are the lives of all men (Carlos Fuentes 1983:29).

But society . . . is not a tapestry to pick threads from and expect to find a new design in one's hand; and assimilation is one of the most subtle and elusive of social processes, which does not reveal itself by plucked threads, by isolated facts . . . (Elsie Clews Parsons 1936:vii).

One's culture is not like a suit of clothes that can be discarded easily . . . (James P. Spradley and David W. McCurdy 1980:4).

Respect, Elspeth Huxley has candidly observed, was, for the European 'an invisible coat of mail . . . the least rent or puncture might . . . split the whole garment asunder and expose its wearer in all his human vulnerability' (Shiva Naipaul 1984:63).

It was open warfare, the inevitable clash of two opposing natures who sought to express themselves in apparel, since clothes, after all, are a form of self-expression (Radclyffe Hall [1928] 1990:73).

[T]he destiny of the Negroes is in some measure interwoven with that of Europeans (Alexis de Tocqueville [1835] 1954:370).

In the South [the Negro] is a perpetual and immutable part of history itself, a piece of the vast fabric so integral and necessary that without him the fabric dissolves . . . (William Styron 1993:8).

You cannot assume a nationality as you would a new suit of clothes (Paul Robeson 1935, quoted in Sterling Stuckey 1994:195).

But [my negroism] was fitting me like a tight chemise. I couldn't see it for wearing it (Zora Neale Hurston [1935] 1978:3).

I am cognizant of the interrelatedness of all communities and states . . .. We are caught in an inescapable network of mutuality, tied in a single garment of destiny. Whatever affects one directly, affects all indirectly (Reverend Martin Luther King, Jr. 16 April 1963).

The Negro is the central thread of American history (W. E. B. DuBois 1924:135).

Images of weaving cloth and images of clothing permeate the literature on human cultures, and nowhere is this symbolism more acute than in the story of the Black experiences in white America (Figure 1).This profound metaphor provides the bulwark for an examination of one item of one American social group's material culture at one historical period – the clothing worn by enslaved Americans in the Southern United States during the thirty years before the Civil War.[1] This folk history takes the perspective of the formerly enslaved and their descendants by underpinning its contents and direction on their testimonies. Vivid, first-person accounts lead to a richer understanding of how clothing fit into the realities of their daily life. What emerges is that clothing played a central part in the enslaved people's consciousness of self: to them clothing was tactile, visual, and metaphoric.

My topic concerns a group of people who were involuntary immigrants to a new world, who descended from people who were not enslaved and whose own descendants are not enslaved. Slavery is only my topic in that it represents a chronological horizon, an historical moment (the years preceding emancipation) that encompasses more than the beginning or ending of racial slavery in the United States. The temporal dimension is the antebellum period with glances backward into earlier times and forward into later times. The spatial boundary is the United States South with comparative expeditions to West Africa.

Figure 1. Threads, weaving, and clothing: metaphors for human culture. Abraham Lincoln "Winding off the Tangled Skein" of the Union. *Harper's Weekly* 30 March 1861:208.

I base this work on those aspects of clothing which the formerly enslaved brought forth as important enough to discuss. For them, clothing provided a context in which to describe the material realities of slavery. By extension, the positive customs, habits, and oral traditions maintained and reinterpreted by a specific group of persons living under the most adverse social conditions, provide insights into the ways by which other individuals and groups respond to different sets of social change in a salubrious manner. Viewing the peculiar institution from the perspective of those who were economically and politically the least powerful, rather than from the usual vantage point of the more powerful, contributes an added depth and necessary balance to our present knowledge about this period in history and to our knowledge about humanity itself.[2]

I have additional objectives: first, to understand how a people who did not even legally own their bodies still manage to reveal themselves as individual and communal human beings by their dress; second, to explore how certain styles and concepts were modifications of both African and European customs, changed because of American experiences; third, to illustrate that specific aesthetic styles and metaphysical outlooks form a spatial bridge with West Africa; and fourth, to demonstrate that the period of enslavement forms a temporal bridge with the present – what happened *then* remains a potent factor in explaining what happens now.

Clothing enables a human being to identify personal self and communal self, and that self in relation to those of other communities; and clothing is the most obvious, silent message by which a person communicates his or her self as an individual to others. Although particular items and styles of dress change over time and from place to place, the meanings that people give to clothes are universal: clothes mark one's age, sex, and status; and clothes are encoded with meanings for particular times, places, and events.[3] But in a broader sense, clothing helps to regulate bodies within a socially constructed order; this was no less so during the time of slavery in the United States. During that period, clothing was meant to mark differences. White people demarcated and enforced this system, but in many instances, Blacks subverted it by purposely marking their difference with personal choices of dress. The enslaved dealt with both their own attitudes about their bodies as well as those attitudes held by whites. For them, clothing became the metaphor to illustrate what it had meant to be a slave. More profoundly, clothing became their way to symbolically qualify humanity – the humanness of others and most especially their own.

Just as the formerly enslaved repeatedly used clothing as a symbolic way to portray the experience of slavery, so also "clothing" becomes the item of material culture by which I attempt to add to our current understanding of racial slavery in the United States. By focusing on the ways in which American materials were used as clothing for and by enslaved African Americans, I seek to better understand how African Americans perceived the institution, and thereby come closer to an understanding of what it was like during white America's most damning historical period.

The *Narratives*

> Will Parker (b. 1842): *I can't 'member ever'thing – my mind twinkles like de sunshine* (S2.8.7:3019 [GA/TX]).

> Elisha Doc Garey (76 years): *I knowed you was comin' to write dis jedgment . . .. I seed your hand writin' and long 'fore you got here I seed you jus' as plain as you is now. I told dese folks what I lives wid, a white 'oman was comin' to do a heap of writin'* (12.2:2 [GA])

From 1936 to 1938, approximately 2,000 formerly enslaved African Americans recounted their experiences and contributed their oral histories to interviewers working state-by-state under the auspices of the Federal Writers' Project (FWP). The result was an abbreviated compendium entitled *Slave Narratives: A Folk History of Slavery in the United States From Interviews with Former Slaves* (B. A. Botkin, Chief Editor, Washington, 1941).[4] Subsequently, George P. Rawick assembled the entire body of material for publication as a forty-volume compilation, *The American Slave: A Composite Autobiography* (Westport, Conn., and London: Greenwood Press, 1972, 1977, and 1979).[5] Hereafter, I refer to the volumes as the *Narratives*, an abbreviation of the original FWP report title. All citation abbreviations refer to the Rawick compilation.[6]

Sometimes a contributor knew his or her birth year; at other times it was possible to work backwards for a birth date from statements such as, "I was six years old when freedom came." Most of the narratives were collected from the mid- to late 1930s; but because the year of collecting is not always given, the age of an informant is relevant only insofar as it offers another personal dimension.

Any scholar quoting from the *Narratives* comes up against the problem of dialectical spelling.[7] Elizabeth Kytle notes in her biography of a Southern Black woman, "The speech in *Willie Mae* is *not* so-called dialect but is idiom common to blacks and whites in the rural south" (1993:xvii). Kytle differentiated between idiom and dialect in this way: idiom is "apt, succinct, expressive" while dialect looks "like nothing more than bad spelling" (ibid.). Kytle opted not to spell badly as she wrote down Willie May's words. Interviewers of the *Narratives* (most of whom were white), however, transcribed their contributors' words into dialectic spelling. In so doing, they adhered to a long tradition in American literature which includes not only nineteenth-century white writers such as Mark Twain, Joel Chandler Harris, and innumerable newspaper cartoonists, but also embraces the first widely recognized African American novelist, Charles W. Chestnutt, in the last century, and Ishmael Reed in the twentieth century. No matter who styled the spelling, the result is a prose difficult for some readers and, in certain cases, downright offensive to many.

Because of these concerns, the dilemma of a scholar quoting from the *Narratives* is whether to leave the spelling as is or to correct it. Changing it might mean making a mistake in interpretation. The other problem with changing the spellings used by the interviewers is that in so doing we erase historic documentation of white perceptions of Blacks at the time. On the basis of these concerns, the quotations used herein remain in the original.[8] That is, while I question the rationale for writing "was"as "wuz," "pretty" as "pritty," or "right" as "rite," I leave the spelling as it appears in the collection and retain the innumerable dangling apostrophes, wishing only that the interviewers could have heard in their own voices the very "dialect" which they heard in the voices of those whose words they were writing down. Or as David Holt, a white interviewer, said of the narrator Abe Whitess' speech, "No effort is made here to use his dialect. In fact, Abe uses fairly good Mississippi" (S1.1:447 [MS]).

My aim to present the many voices in the testimonies led to my decision to compose the text in the following manner. Unless the formerly enslaved people's words are included in a running passage, they are not set off by quotation marks. Their comments are marked, instead, by first giving the contributor's name and age (when known), followed by the statement, and ending with the source abbreviation. A quotation from any person who was enslaved is italicized, whether their words come from the *Narratives* or another source. Where the interviewer writes only a third-person narration, or paraphrases the narrator, I most often avoid using these remarks; when I use them, I indicate this and place them within quotation marks and do not italicize them.

By styling sections in this way, my intent is that the voices of the formerly enslaved, and not mine, will dominate. Nonetheless, I am aware that I still control what is being (con)textualized. I will not, after all, include every statement; nor will all narrators be heard. Furthermore, my own voice intrudes as I introduce and summarize each topic, and as I interject historical evidence from other sources about which the narrators could not have known and with which they could never engage in dialogue. Finally, I, alone, am responsible for the very way in which the text is structured: I control when and where the narrators' voices enter and exit.[9]

The *Narratives* represent the most extensive corpus of oral testimony available from the people who were enslaved and, as such, previous scholars have adopted these materials for one or another purposes.[10] To date, however, only incidentally has the information on clothing from the *Narratives* entered the scholarship on slavery, and that in digested form.[11] To my knowledge, no one has applied the *Narrative* testimony toward development of an extended interpretation of African American clothing.

The *Narratives* contain approximately 1,300 entries indexed under "Clothing."The general category, however, does not specify the variety of topics about which contributors relate information. One of my purposes in doing this research was to find and then organize these subtopics within more narrowly defined frames to provide not only a comprehensive, but also a detailed, forum for analysis. Most often, the formerly enslaved people's statements about clothing are concise, rarely more than a few sentences. In turn, these statements are often contained within longer commentaries about other topics. In spite of an economy of words and the problem of extraneous comments not directly related to clothing, numerous narrators artistically place their statements about clothing within a story. That is, the people give functions for the cloth and clothing, they are not just naming items of dress. Consequently, the details with which they embroider their memories of clothing aid in keeping the data from merely becoming sterile inventories.

FWP guidelines for the *Narratives* project included a suggested list of twenty questions meant to be used as prompts by the interviewers. Of these, just one question dealt explicitly with clothing. From Henry G. Alsberg, director, to the state directors of the Federal Writers' Project, 20 June 1937:

> Question 5. What clothing did you wear in hot weather? Cold weather? On Sundays? Any shoes? Describe your wedding clothes (*Rawick, From Sundown to Sunup* 1972:174, 175).

I must point out here that, as well as addressing these specific inquiries about their own clothing, in numerous instances the contributors also gave accounts of white peoples' dress, something they were not asked to do. This represents one of the ways in which the subjects of the *Narratives* took over the interviews and made others the subjects instead. Another way in which numerous contributors usurped control of the interviews was by using "clothing" as a prevailing image in couching their responses to all other topical questions. As a result of these manipulations by the formerly enslaved, the *Narratives* contain at least 2,000 statements pertaining to clothing.

I did not use every remark made about clothing in the *Narratives* because many of the comments overlap; to have repeated them all would have been both tedious and redundant.[12] But, because a number of people contributed information about more than one aspect of clothing, these people are quoted several times.

As it turned out, the *Narratives* reveal certain patterns regarding the standard types of clothing that were distributed among enslaved people and which they were expected to wear. Within these "ideal,"white-imposed boundaries, however, there emerged other patterns concerning customs and attitudes about dress that showed they evolved distinctly from within the African American communities both as a reflection of the people's Afrocentric craftsmanship and sensibilities and as a reaction to their particular place in American society. Therefore, the many voices which structure the categories that I devised express both individual, functional knowledge as well as community world view.

My purpose is not to inventory everything that has ever been written on the subjects of slavery, dress, or even on the clothing of enslaved Africans in the Americas. Rather, I chose to read and then include those texts which seemed best suited to the task of giving a broad comparative analysis to the information I received from the contributors to the *Narratives*.

A Folkloristic Approach

My scholarly approach is not politics, nor anthropology, but folklore. U.S. history, like all histories, has been told like the tally of a scorecard, a tally of who won and who lost and who was in debt to whom. The error for humanity is that we continue to write our histories in such a way; the tragedy is that we continue to believe them. Our histories contain the stories of mostly men who became powerful and demonstrated their power by "conquering" other men (and thus women). But such a history is not the story of humankind at all. For between each glorious year of war, and even during those few moments of relative peace, most people had other concerns, and it is the cumulative concerns of most people that should be our histories; their stories ought to be the essence of America's national story through space and time.

In order to present such a history, I turned to a group whom I shall label a folk group because they shared perceptions about their life experiences, traditions, and histories. The evidence they offer is residual memory, and I employ it beyond a condemnation of slavery as an institution to provide a profound understanding as to how clothing became the metaphorical term by which the enslaved presented perceptions of self.

Several years before the formal collections made under the auspices of the FWP, John B. Cade enlisted his students at Southern University in Louisiana to interview formerly enslaved people. Thirty-six students reported their interviews with eighty-two people. Cade drew from this material and published an essay "Out of the Mouths of Ex-Slaves" in 1935 in *The Journal of Negro History*. Although Cade knew the precautions advanced against promoting oral narratives as historical "fact," he nevertheless felt they offered a counterbalance to "the story of Negro life" as penned by whites (295). In his introductory notes, Cade summed up the arguments against using oral narratives, and then expressed why he would use them:

> The passing of the years, the early age of witnesses at the time, and the bitterness against the institution of slavery might be arguments against the historical accuracy of everything which follows. Even the love to weave a good story for attentive listeners bids us be cautious. We notice, however, that other authors dealing with American Negro Slavery quote from ex-slaves. If it is a fault, then we feel that we are in good company (295).

Following Cade, a number of historians argue cogently for using the *Narratives* as historical evidence and making them the starting point and heart of their investigations.[13] What makes the *Narratives* so compelling? They maybe compared to what Ralph Ellison has written about the blues: "Their attraction lies in this, that they at once express the agony of life and the possibility of conquering it through sheer toughness of spirit" (1972:94).

In spite of the vast body of scholarship wherein the *Narratives* form the weight of documentary evidence, other historians nevertheless argue against using the *Narratives* as documentation, citing four main problems all having to do with veracity. The issues are: first, the *Narratives* we recollected seventy years after emancipation; second, many of the contributors were too young during the period of enslavement to remember very much;[14]

third, most of the interviewers were Southern whites, which suggests that African Americans self-censored what they said, or that whites heavily edited the final format of the narratives; and fourth, the *Narratives* were collected at the height of the Depression and thus, for certain people, the material reality during the period of enslavement seemed better than the present. My own rationale for using the *Narratives* refutes each of these arguments.

First, one of the outstanding features of memory ("history")is that there is no past without the present.

> Willis Woodsen: *Yes'm talking about it makes me member lots of things dat I had jist about forgot* (S2.10.9:4279 [TX]).

> Aunt Clussey (b. ca. 1844): *Yassuh, white folks, I has seed a lot in my days, an' I ain't a forgittin' none of it . . .. Peoples don't forgits de things dey wants to remember* (S1.1:20, 21 [AL]).

For all human beings, the present acts as a filter for past events. In this sense, there can never be any concept about the past which is absolutely true for all. As a folklorist, my concern is for the truth as individuals believe it to be. Or, as A. R. Burns appraised the material collected by Herodotus (often called "the father" of both history and folklore): ". . . *the fact that these statements were current* is, after all, itself a *historical* fact" (1983:10; original emphasis).[15]

An important point to be made about memory in regard to this particular analysis is that, as well as using the statements made in the FWP *Narratives*, I also incorporate testimony taken from the autobiographies of formerly enslaved people which were published in the nineteenth century. In spite of the fact that nearly a century (or more) often separates these two types of sources, the testimonies are corroborative. That is, although seventy years had elapsed between the end of the American Civil War and the time of the interviews, for many African Americans it was not long enough to erase memories of their enslavement.

Second, wherein another historian might rely on more"official" documents, I rely on folk memory. That is, no matter what the age of the contributors during the period of enslavement, the stories from older people continued to be told within the African American communities, keeping the memories fresh even as time separated them from the events.

Martha Madeline Hinton (b. 1861): *You sees I wuz mighty young an' I members very little 'bout somethings in slavery but from what my mother and father tole me since de war . . .* (14.1:434 [NC]).

Julia Woodberry (age 70–80): *Well, I can speak bout what I used to hear my auntie and my mammy en my grandmammy talk bout what happen in dey day, but I never didn' live in slavery time* (3.4:237 [SC]).

Third, in dealing with the *Narratives*, one can not be concerned with what they do not contain (i.e., negative evidence). Yes, the *Narratives* were edited and, as noted, sometimes written in the third person; but, in actuality, the reader is often jarred by the obvious candidness, coherence, and complexity with which the contributors spoke about their former experiences.

Adline Marshall: *Old Cap'n has a big house, but I jes' see it from de quarters, 'cause we wasn't 'lowed to go up in de yard. I hear 'em say he don't have no wife, but has a black woman what stays at de house. Dat's de reason why dere is so many 'No Nation' niggers 'round now. Some call 'em 'Bright' niggers, but I calls 'em 'No Nation' niggers, 'cause dat's what dey is, – dey ain't all black and dey ain't white, but dey is mixed. Dat comes from slave times and de white folks did de wrong, 'cause de blacks get beat and whipped if dey don't do what de white folks tell 'em to* (S2.7.6:2578 [SC/TX]).

And fourth, in the instances when contributors say their material goods were better during slavery, this does nothing to alter the probable fact that, for some people, the physical conditions during the antebellum period were less adverse than during the Depression. Parker Pool's plaintive, 91-year-old voice spoke for many folks during the 1930s:

No man can make times real good till everybody is put to work. Wid de lan' layin' out dere can't be real good times. Dis is my 'lustration. My horse died las' year. I ain't got no money ter buy nother and can't git one. You see dat lan' lyin' out dere I have farmed it every year fer a long time. Through part o' de year I always had vegetables and sich ter sell, but now my horse is dead an' I can't farm no more. I ain't got nothin' ter sell . . .. I shore hope sumpin' will be done fer me (15.2:191 [NC]).

And yet, Annie Stanton emphatically offset Poole's reality by stating:

Chiles, folks talkin' 'bout de 'pression now and don't know nothin' 'bout hard times. In dem days peoples didn't have nothin' 'ceptin' what dey made. Eben iffen you had a pile of money, dere wuzn't nothin' to buy (S1.1:177 [AL]).

Facts and Histories

> [F]or both black and white American writers, in a wholly racialized society, there is no escape from racially inflected language . . . (Toni Morrison 1992:12–13).

The clothing worn during the period of slavery was not stylistically static; it changed as fashions always do. Although at certain times and in certain locales dress codes were enforced, industrial mechanizations of manufacture allowed for more changes in clothing styles than at any time previously. Just as types of clothing changed, so too the African Americans whose voices rise from the following pages do not all have the same story to tell. All did not share the same experiences, nor did they all react to shared experiences in the same way.

A demographic overview of the contributors reveals that during the final years of racial slavery in the United States, contributors were not all the same age; some were adults, some adolescents, most were children, and some had not yet even been born but could tell the stories of their parents and grandparents who had been enslaved. Rarely did any live on the same plantation or on the same smaller farmstead, or even in the same county or parish; all did not live in the same state, nor under the same geophysical and climatic conditions. A very few lived in urban areas. Far more lived in the settled countryside while others lived on the remote frontier. Some lived all their lives under slavery in the same place, under the same conditions; others lived in more than one place; others lived with changing conditions. Some lived among hundreds of other enslaved peoples, most lived with only a few others or lived alone. Most shared living quarters with other Blacks; some lived with whites. Most toiled for whites in fields, others on lawns and in gardens, blacksmith shops, ginning mills, tanneries, weaving rooms, nurseries, barns, stables, and kitchens, and some few others worked inside the houses of whites. Some possessed a fair amount of material comforts; most did not. Freedom of movement varied but in general was restricted.

What then links their multiple stories into this single history? Two facts bind all these African Americans: once in the United States they did not legally own their own bodies, and they all chose to individualize themselves by describing the cloth and clothing they wore during their time of enslavement.

Although this book takes its form because of statements made by only one segment of the American population and concerns only one aspect of the material world of Southern enslaved people, within these limitations the voices very often conflict. For instance, Caroline Wright was born ca. 1845, and was about 90 years old when interviewed sometime in the mid-1930s. *"Us sho' did come out looking choicesome"* was Wright'sway of expressing her opinion about her people's way of dressing during the last years of racial slavery in the American South (5.4:221 [TX]). What does Caroline Wright mean by "come out"? Does she mean everyday presentation of self or only presentation of self on special occasions? Caroline Wright might ultimately mean coming out of bondage.

And what does Wright mean by "choicesome," a word not found in the dictionary, but one that she fashioned by joining two other proper English words. "Choice" is the act of choosing; the right of choosing; an alternative; the best or preferred part of anything. "Some" is an adjectival suffix, characterized by a (specified) thing, quality or state. "Choicesome" has cognates: "choicer" or "choicest" meaning "excellent; chosen with care."

Indeed, Caroline Wright was talking about qualitative choice, and her words underscore the power of individuals in their decisions about self–definition. But Wright's statement does not reflect the thoughts and feelings of all African Americans who remembered clothing during the time of enslavement. Even when many people address the same topic, their testimonies sometimes appear to conflict. The paramount point is that the cacophony of voices demonstrates that slavery was an individual experience and that it cannot be reduced to a single collective fact. There is no single African American viewpoint on the topic of clothing during that period of their historical past. Rather, there are many pasts, many histories, many facts.

As I analyzed state-by-state what people from a single state were saying about clothing, I became aware that the feelings and memories which survived and were recorded displayed a multi-vocal testimony. From Mississippi, three different men offered three conflicting statements about powerful whites and about clothing. In these statements, "clothing" acts as a metaphorical judgment for the institution of slavery as well as a critique concerning gender and class differences among the white overlords.

> James Lucas (b. 1833): *Yes'm, wives [of "masters"] made a big diffe'ence. Dey was kin' an' went 'bout mongst de slaves a-look-in' after 'em. Dey gives out food an' clo'es an' shoes* (7.3:93).
>
> *Dey [the enslaved] don' know de meanin' of it [freedom]. Slaves like us, what was owned by quality-folks, was sati'fied en' didn' sing none of dem freedom songs* (ibid. 94).

> *Sometimes Marse L. would come down to de place wid a big wagon filled with a thousan' pair o' shoes at one time* (ibid., 95).
>
> *I guess slav'ry was wrong, but I 'members us had some mighty good times* (ibid., 97).

> Charlie Moses (84 years): *When I gits to thinkin' back on them slavery days I feels like risin' out o' this here bed an' tellin' ever'body 'bout the harsh treatment us colored folks was given when we was owned by poor quality folks. My marster was mean an' cruel. I hates him, hates him!* (7.2:113).
>
> *He had two daughters an' two sons. Them an' his poor wife had the work in the house to do, 'cause he wouldn' waste no Nigger help 'em out. His family was as scared o' him as we was. They had all their lives under his whip* (ibid., 114).
>
> *We never had much clothes 'ceptin' what was give us by the marster or the mistis. Winter time we never had 'nough to wear. . .* (ibid., 115).

> Henri Necaise (105 years): *To tell de truf, de fac' o' de business is, my Marster took care o' me better'n I can take care o' myse'f now.*
>
> *Den us didn' have to think whar de nex' meal comin' from, or de nex' pair o' shoes or pants. De grub an' clo' es give us was better'n I ever gits now.*
>
> *Dey didn' give me money, but, you see, I was a slave. Dey sho' give me ever'thing else I need, clo'es an' shoes* (7.2:120).
>
> *I seen good marsters an' mean ones. Dey was good slaves an' mean ones* (ibid., 121).

The following examples, all from North Carolina (15.2) and each on the topic of clothing, best help express my hypothesis that there are many facts concerning our histories.

> Lila Nichols: *We had just a few pieces of clothes an' dey wuz of de wurst kind* (148).

> Jane Lassiter (ca. 80 years): *Our clothes wuz home made but we had plenty shiftin' clothes* (39).

> Patsy Mitchner (84 years): *Our clothes wuz bad . . .* (97).

> Clara Jones (a "married 'oman way 'fore de war"): *[Marse] give us good clothes . . .* (31).

> Parker Pool (91 years): *. . . we had plenty o' clothes, sich as they wuz, but de wuz no sich clothes as we have now* (185).

Tina Johnson (85 years): *[W]e ain't had nothin' but de coarsest food an' clothes . . .* (21).

These remarks express the individual experiences of people who often were isolated from one another in various communities and locations. On the other hand, although each person speaks as an individual, the statements still group under related topics. The vast body of material, however discordant, contains patterns that can best be assimilated by more specific categorization: "clothing" is simply too broad a label. My advantage is in having all the statements available to collate topically.

Keith R. Bradley, exploring slavery in the ancient Roman empire, writes: ". . . there could be no unanimous response to slavery on the part of the enslaved, nor necessarily any unanimous opinion about slavery itself" (1989:43). In my own examination of slavery in a different place and time, I deal with the dilemma posed by Bradley's observation by "not shy [ing] from confusion, contradiction, and complexity"(Henry Glassie 1977:21).

Taken as a whole, the formerly enslaved people's words were the source that enabled me to conclude that certain details, such as the specificity concerning the availability of particular fabrics, the processing of organic fibres into cloth, and the manufacturing of clothing, represent the knowledge of the people; and that their attitudes about clothing and their styles of dress represent their cultural world view. In the end, however, this history is mine alone. It does not represent any single fact. It represents, first, my understanding of the knowledge and attitudes of the people who talked nearly sixty years ago about the lives they had lived seventy years prior to that and, second, it signifies my own knowledge and attitudes as an individual living at this particular time in the United States. This book is not meant to expose a single reality, rather it represents a single interpretation.

My conclusion is that clothing, one aspect of the enslaved people's material culture, was of major significance in enabling them to build and stabilize their own communities as distinctly separate from the ever-present, threatening white communities. Clothing served as a symbolic means by which they could examine and articulate what slavery had meant to themselves, their families, their neighbours, and the white people whom they had known. By self-consciously constructing meaning through their spoken words about clothing, they had found a superlative method of empowerment.

Notes

1. Throughout, I shall refer to an American of whole or partial African descent as either an African American or a Black. Both of these terms will be capitalized. I shall refer to Americans of European descent as whites, and this term will not be capitalized. *The Chicago Manuel of Style*, 1993, section 7.35, allows me this prerogative. When African American is used as a modifier, I will not hyphenate the term.

2. Publications by John Blassingame (1972, 1975, 1977, 1979), Eugene Genovese (1974), Richard Price (1983 and 1990), Houston Baker (1984), Sterling Stuckey (1987) and John Roberts (1990), are among the finest examples of this approach.

3. Mary Ellen Roach and Joanne Bubolz Eicher write: "Personal adornment is characteristic of all societies, whereas coverings that protect are not." They outline and discuss the following as "The Language of Personal Adornment": 1) aesthetic experience, 2) as definition of social role, 3) as statement of social worth, 4) as indicator of economic status, 5) as political symbol, 6) as indicator of magico-religious condition, 6) as a facility in social rituals, 7) as reinforcement of belief, custom, and values, 8) as recreation, and 9) as sexual symbol (1979:8–19).

4. A few states published their own materials: for example, Writers Program, Louisiana, *Gumba Ya-Ya* (1945); Virginia Writers' Project, *The Negro in Virginia* (1940); Georgia Writers' Project, *Drums and shadows* (1972).

5. Volumes 18 and 19 include the material collected under the auspices of another institution, Fisk University.

6. Rawick published the *Narratives* in three sets. The initial set consists of nineteen volumes. The series begins with *From Sundown to Sunup: The Making of the Black Community* (Volume 1), Rawick's critical historical and cultural assessment of the *Narratives* testimony. The remaining contain the actual narratives. Those from some states are contained in more than one volume, while some other volumes contain narratives from more than a single state. I devised the following system for identifying the quoted *Narratives* sources. Abbreviations for states are designated by the two-letter postal code method. A narrative from South Carolina in volume 3, part 4 on pages 147–150 is abbreviated as: (3.4:147–150 [SC]). If a narrative was collected in a state other than where the contributor had been enslaved, the state of enslavement is noted, followed by the state where the narration was collected. For example, the abbreviation for a person enslaved in Alabama who gave information in Ohio is [AL/OH]; the abbreviation for a person enslaved in Kentucky and Texas who gave information in Texas is [KY,TX/TX]. The second set was published in 12 volumes and is designated here by S1 which stands for Supplement Series One. Several volumes are divided into more than one part. A narrative from Virginia in Volume 5, Part 2 in this group is listed: (S1.5.2:378–379 [VA]).The third set of ten volumes is Supplement Series Two, and several

volumes are divided into more than one part. These volumes are designated as: S2.

7. See Zora Neale Hurstson's short passage on "Negro Dialect" in which she notes that "there are so many quirks that belong only to certain localities that nothing less than a volume would be adequate" to fully analyze the "rules" on this subject ([1934] 1988:68).

8. With this decision, I follow other scholars; for example, Vlach (1993:237, n. 8) who follows Levine (1977:xv–xvi).

9. Four scholarly books in particular proved instrumental in my decision to highlight the *Narratives* material: Roger D. Abrahams and John F. Szwed, editors, *After Africa* (1983); John W. Blassingame, editor, *Slave Testimony* (1986); Richard Price, *First Time* (1983), and *Alabi's World* (1990). In each work, by allowing the other voices much more independent space than is usual in academic writing, these scholars give emphasis to the historical voices rather than their own.

10. Scholars have used them to study the oral genres of tales, legends, work songs, and spirituals (e.g., Levine, 1978; Roberts, 1982); to explore the sports, games, dances, and other popular events on plantations (David K. Wiggins, 1979); and to analyze corn shucking, a seasonal plantation event (Roger Abrahams, 1992). Several scholars draw from the *Narratives* for specific categories of the material culture of the enslaved; for instance, Charles Joyner on foodways (1971), Gladys-Marie Fry on quilts (1990), and John Michael Vlach on architecture (1993).

11. For example, in the works of two eminent historians who have made extensive use of the *Narratives* towards other aims: John Blassingame (1972 and 1979) and Eugene Genovese (1974:550–561).

12. All readers of earlier versions of this book suggested that it contained too many quotations from the *Narratives* and that I needed to delete redundant statements; but because each of these statements had become precious to me, I found myself unable to decide whose words should be removed. This final version reflects the work of Bobbie Sunberg who edited out the "too-many voices," for which you, the reader, and I owe a large thanks.

13. For example, Botkin ([1945] 1989), Yetman (1967), Rawick (1972), Blassingame (1972, 1975, 1977), Genovese (1974), Sterling (1984), and Joyner (1984).

14. In 1967, before Rawick's final compilation, Norman R. Yetman quantitatively analyzed the then-available collection. From data available at that time, Yetman found that 64% of the interviewees were between the ages of 6 and 15 in 1865, 16% were age 16–20, 13% were between 21–30 years old, and only 3% were over 30 (534–535).

15. On the other hand, the entry to the *Oxford Classical Dictionary* on Herodotus reads: "Devoid of race-prejudice and intolerance, he venerates antiquity and is fascinated by novelties; and in these things trusts informants overmuch" (1989:509).

1

Beginning in Africa

> Everything will be done to wipe out their traditions, to substitute our traditions for theirs and to destroy their culture without giving them ours (Franz Fanon 1963).

> "America will always mean more to him than Africa, you know that."
> "I don't know" (James Baldwin 1948).

> In an age of political infidelity, of mean passions, and petty thoughts, I would have impressed upon the rising race not to despair, but to seek in a right understanding of the history of their country . . . it is the past alone that can explain the present . . . (Benjamin Disraeli 1845).

> We shall not cease from exploration and the end of all our experiences will be to arrive where we started and know the place for the first time (T. S. Eliot).

> . . . the end is in the beginning . . . (Ralph Ellison 1952:5).

Why Africa?

Whether a folklorist studies a contemporary phenomenon or an historical one, an interest usually develops because a change is perceived as taking place. This underlying fascination leads the folklorist to ask this question: In what way does the change manifest itself? Quite often the answer will be that the change is in the form, but not in the underlying function. Scholars have remarked on this quality. Roger Abrahams writes:

> One of the most remarkable features of folklore is its adaptability and endurance. Man does not give up the results of his creative acts easily. Instead, he is inclined to change either their form or substance, adapting them to new needs and stresses (1968:170).

Speaking directly to this feature as it relates to African retentions, Sidney Mintz and Richard Price write: "But overall, direct formal continuities from Africa are more the exception than the rule in any African-American culture . . ." (1992:60). This concern for recognizable change in usual form, and my interest in the accounts of cloth production and clothing in the *Narratives*, lead to finding out what forms cloth and clothing had taken in Africa and what functions they had served there in order to better understand what changed for Africans brought to the United States.

This chapter will not be a microcosmic study of a single community. My documentation covers large geographical areas of the ancestral continent, just as it does for the sections on the antebellum South. By this, I do not mean to condense all West African social groups nor African American communities into a homogenous whole. Rather, my concern is for a composite view of diverse people who were joined by the fact that they were all of African ancestry whether or not they remained in Africa or descended from Africans who were part of the diaspora. In some instances, West African technologies and attitudes correlate to technologies and attitudes prevalent among African Americans during the antebellum period. The West African data also support my claim that certain West African attitudes were congenial with European and white American attitudes; meaning that in some cases coercion, in whatever manner, was not always necessary – Blacks in America were already thinking along the same lines as white Americans as regards certain assumptions and beliefs about cloth and clothing.

To collate a documentary history of cloth production and clothing in Africa would be a lifetime's work. I view my own research into this topic prefatory to much more in-depth study. My discussion is limited to West Africa, to those regions whose populations formed the greatest proportion of people deported to the Americas. While specific customs associated with the manufacture of cloth and modes of dress varied in Africa, the reasons for making cloth and wearing clothing appear to be the same not only there, but wherever people live.

As with all cultures, ways of making cloth and items of dress change over time. Therefore, West African cloth-making techniques and clothing are not to be seen as static even though the changed forms often continue to serve the same functions. New introductions no doubt occurred during internal trading when various African groups exchanged cloth and clothing among themselves. From historical records, we know that this did occur when Arabs and Europeans began trading in Africa.

The West African trade with Arabs precipitated alterations in African cloth production and distribution, and instigated changes in certain items of clothing. The European trade began in the fifteenth century, and because this trade also coincided with the diaspora of millions of Africans, the ways in which cloth was made and the types of clothing worn would also change for Africans in the Americas. For, no matter if a person moves voluntarily or not, any emigrant will experience some change in adjusting to the new environment.

In the *Narratives* very few people mention Africa or Africans. After 1808, the United States restricted foreign trade in slaves; thereafter, into the 1850s, smuggling of Africans continued, but only sporadically. Under these circumstances, most Southern Blacks were American born and had little or no contact with newly arrived Africans.[1] Occasionally, American-born descendants of Africans remembered what their forebears told them about cloth or clothing, but these accounts are often of an apocryphal nature:

> Mariah Halloway (prob. b. ca. 1852): *My grandfather came directly from Africa and I never shall forget the story he told us of how he and other natives were fooled on board a ship by the white slave traders using red handkerchiefs as enticement* (12. 1:172 [GA]).

> John Brown (b. 1850): *The oldest ones come right from Africa. My Grandmother was one of them. A savage in Africa – a slave in America. Mammy told it to me. Over there all the natives dressed naked. The slaves landed at Charleston. The town folks was mighty mad cause the blacks was driven through the streets without any clothes . . .. Grandmother was one of the bunch. The Browns taught them to work. Made clothes for them. For along time the natives didn't like the clothes and try to shake them off* (7:24–25 [AL]).

> Mary Johnson (half Choctaw): *Clost to where I's born they's a place where they brung the Africy people to tame 'em and they have big pens where they puts 'em after they takes 'em outta they gun ships. They sho' was wild and they have hair all over jus' like a dog and big hammer rings in they noses. They didn't wore no clothes* (4. 2:219–220 [TX]).

Because few contributors to the *Narratives* spoke of Africa, the weight of documentation about cloth and clothing comes from two other sources. First, from Africans themselves who gave testimony to others or who composed their own narratives about enslavement in Europe and the Americas. The second source is comprised of accounts by non-African travelers who observed the customs of the people whom they encountered.

To set the stage for what would happen in the American South, I first present the Arabs' and Europeans' initial impressions of Africans. These outsiders' descriptions of African clothing show that Africans used dress to denote differences in age, gender, prestige, and class hierarchies and that they wore particular body ornamentations and clothing for special events.

My specific interest is in tracing African connections to the common know-how and attitudes possessed by African Americans about cloth and clothing. The technological procedures for making cloth and clothing offer concrete evidence for continuities and changes from Africa to the United States. Attitudes, however, are of a different nature than technical knowledge, and thus make it more difficult to decipher what continued and what changed in regard to West African attitudes about cloth, clothing, and the human body.

James Deetz terms these more deeply ingrained, cultural outlooks "mental templates" (1967:43–52), Monni Adams terms them "models of the mind" (quoted in Eli Leon, 1978:26), and Melville Herskovits calls them "unconscious cultural retentions" or, more specific to this examination, Herskovits labels them "Africanisms" ([1941] 1958). These terms all mean culturally learned ways of doing, seeing, feeling, and perceiving in the world around us. Although cultural world view survives even under constant pressure to change, and even while living in the midst of a more formidable social group, it is a concept not easily grasped. My purpose in the sixth chapter of this book is to determine whether or not the concept of cultural world view is, after all, but an analytical construct or if it really is a significant force for explaining a social group's behaviour.

On Bodies and Civilization: The Clothed and the Unclothed

> The passion for dress is curiously strong in these people, and seems as though it might be made an instrument in converting them, outwardly at any rate, to something like civilization; for, though their own native taste is decidedly both barbarous and ludicrous, it is astonishing how very soon they mitigate it in imitation of their white models . . . (Frances Kemble 1863).

> [N]o white American ever thinks that any other race is wholly civilized until he wears the white man's clothes . . . (Booker T. Washington [1901] 1986:98).

> Many Westerners have judged the civilization of a people by the degree to which they have adopted Western style garments (Ina Corrine Brown 1965).

Nehemia Levtzion extracts from the earliest Arabic sources in which the authors describe the dress or lack of clothing of ordinary Black Africans.

> The rural people in the Sudan, according to Ibn Sa'îd [1240], used to go naked, but the Muslims covered their privy parts. Most of them wore skins, but those who mixed with white men [i. e. , the foreign traders] put on imported clothes of cotton and wool (179).

Using only Arab testimony, Levtzion leaps to the ethnocentric conclusion that: "This suggests that clothing was introduced and diffused through trade and Islam" (ibid.). He proceeds to prove his point with the following evidence:

> In the tenth century Ibn al-Faqîh noted that the Sundanese people of Ghana wore skins. A century later al-Bakrî described the commoners of Ghana wearing robes of cotton, silk, or brocade. Only the king and the crown prince had the right to wear sewn clothes according to the Muslim's fashion. Away from the capital, in the province of Sâma, the people went naked, and women only covered their sexual parts with skins. The people of Malal, in the country of Lamlam, were naked according toal-Idrîsî [1154]. When the king of Mali was converted to Islam he was given a cotton dress. Islam helped in creating a market for clothes and encouraged the increase of imports as well as the expansion of local manufacturing (ibid.).

Throughout the early eye-witness accounts, two distinct West African modes of dress are apparent: indigenous attire and adaptations of Muslim dress. Levtzion, therefore, may be correct in his hypothesis that certain items of clothing, such as *kaftans* and turbans, derive from the Islamic influence in West Africa. The objectionable part of Levtzion's argument is his suggestion that only Islamic forms ("sewn," woven cloths) constitute "clothing", while "skins" (that is, an item of indigenous dress) are not to be considered "clothing."

Eight-hundred years after Ibn al Faqîh recorded the dress and lack of clothing of certain Ghanaian people, Olaudah Equiano published his memoirs (1789). Olaudah Equiano was born in 1745 in the present-day Benin province of Nigeria and lived through European enslavement and eventual freedom. In his autobiography, he includes a proposal to British capitalists on the gains to be made in trading British products ("clothing &c") for African raw materials ("cotton and indigo") instead of relying on the trade in human beings which, at any rate, was about to become illegal.

> *I doubt not, if a system of commerce was established in Africa, the demand for manufactures will most rapidly augment, as the native inhabitants will insensibly adopt the British fashions, manners, customs, &c. In proportion to the civilization, so will be the consumption of British manufactures* (290).

Equiano outlined his plan, noting:

> *A case in point. It cost the Aborigines of Britain, little or nothing in clothing &c. The difference between their forefathers and the present generation, in point of consumption, is literally infinite. The supposition is most obvious. It will be equally immense in Africa. The same cause, viz. civilization, will ever have the same effect . . .. The manufactures in this country [England] must and will . . . have a full and constant employ by supplying the African markets* (291).

Equiano felt that British manufactured items could be traded for the wealth of African raw materials, which he enumerated:

> *Cotton and indigo grow spontaneously in most parts of Africa; a consideration of this of no small consequence to the manufacturing towns of Great Britain. It opens a most immense, glorious and happy prospect – the clothing &c. of a continent ten thousand miles in circumference, and immensely rich in productions of every denomination in return for manufactures* (293).[2]

That is, Equiano unwittingly outlined a system of colonialism; but more importantly, like Levtzion, he equated "civilization" with clothing. In this, Equiano and Levtzion were not alone. Cloth and clothing served as metaphors for the relationships in Africa between Africans and Europeans just, as later, cloth and clothing would serve as metaphors by which the enslaved described how they related to those around them in the United States.

Although we know the reactions of early Arabic travelers to the West Africans they first encountered, records were not kept of the first encounters between Africans and Arabs from the African point of view. For the period of the African-European trade, however, a few accounts exist of African first perceptions about Europeans. Bound together with considerations about the other because of the clothing he or she wears, are notions about the body – particularly the skin color – of the other. In his life story, Charles Ball (a West African captured and forced into slavery in the Southern United States) succinctly summed up what must have been the reaction for many Africans upon seeing Europeans for the first time: "*I had never seen white people before; and they appeared to me the ugliest creatures in the world*" (1854:703).

Alvise da Cadamosta, a Genoese merchant, at the Gambia River mouth, 1482?, gives two similar accounts of African reactions upon first encountering Europeans:

> [He] had one of his interpreters shout after them: 'Why have you greeted us in this unfriendly manner?' And they replied: 'We have heard of your visits to the Senegal and we know that you Christians eat human flesh and buy black men only to make a meal of them' (Forbath, 53).

> The negroes [Bakongo] came stupidly crowding around me, wondering at our Christian symbols, our white color, our dress, our Damascenes, garments of black silk and robes of blue cloth or dyed wool all amazed them; some insisted that the white color of the strangers was not natural but put on (ibid., 74).

Just as the Africans held misconceptions about the Europeans' skin color and wearing apparel, so too did the Europeans often misinterpret these aspects of the Africans. Far more extensive than the African accounts of Europeans, are the European descriptions of West Africans. A few white men were not misled by their own culture's prejudices. One was Leo Africanus who wrote in 1550:

> The language of this region is called Sungai [Songhai] and the inhabitants are black people and most friendly unto strangers.
>
> The inhabitants [of Timbuktu] are people of a gentle and cheerful disposition, and spend a great part of the night in singing and dancing through all the streets of the citie: they keep great store of men and women-slaves . . . (Bovill, ed., 146).

Another unprejudiced observer was Thomas Phillips who made a voyage to Africa in 1693–1694 and reasoned about the people he saw there:

> nor can I imagine why they should be despised for their colour, being what they cannot help, and the effect of the climate it has pleased God to appoint them. I can't think there is any intrinsic value in one colour more than another, nor that white is better than their black, only we think so because we are so, and are prone to judge favourably our own case, as well as the blacks, who in odium of the colour, say, the devil is white, and so paint him ([1746], in Gunther, 1978:16).

In the records outsiders kept about Africans, three thematic elements dominate: 1) the skin color and/or class of people who wear no clothing, 2) detailed descriptions of important men's clothing, or 3) a description of the contrasts between the two. The theme of "unclothed Africans" begins in the earliest accounts and continues into the 1700s.

> Muhammad ibn Abdullah ibn Battuta, Mali, ca. 1352: Women servants, slave women and young girls go about quite naked, not even concealing their sexual parts . . .. Women go naked into the sultan's presence, too, without even a veil; his daughters also go about naked . . . (Davidson, 101).

> Songhay, ca. 1495. One of their evil practices [continued Muhammad] is the free mixing of men and women in the markets and streets and the failure of the women to veil themselves . . . [while] among the people of Djenne it is an established custom for a girl not to cover any part of her body as long as she remains a virgin . . . and all the most beautiful girls walk about naked among the people . . . (Davidson, 106).

> Duarta Pacheco Pereira describing the Jolof/Wolof on the Senegal River, ca. 1505: [A]ll of these people go naked save nobles and notables who wear blue cotton shirts *and serouals* (trousers?) of the same stuff . . . (Davidson, 217).

> Dutch West India Company factor/governor at Elmina, now Ghana, 1700: . . . Negroe-Women naked, except a Cloth wrapped about them to hide what Modesty obligeth (Davidson, 257).

> William Bosman, Dahomey coast, 1705: When these slaves come to Fida they are . . . naked too both Men and Women, without the least Distinction or Modesty (Davidson, 259).[3]

In short, Arabs and Europeans judged Black Africans from Arabic and European world views which, by the time of contact, equated covering certain body parts with being civilized.[4] Testimony proves that Muslim and Christian concepts of "civilized" were in part encoded by one's clothing. Nudity, no matter how much a hindrance and discomfort clothing might be in a tropical climate, would play a major role in outsiders' opinions about the degree of civilization that Africans had achieved. According to these ideas, as suggested by Equiano and perpetrated by Levtzion, animal skins or "unsewn" lengths of cloth, apparently were not considered "clothing."

Thus, nudity or even certain types of clothing and ways of ornamenting the body became a stereotypical way of viewing Black Africans as uncivilized. The far-reaching effect that the European and American trade in African people had on societal norms for judging the differences between "them" and "us" by accentuating differences in bodily attire and ornamentation is dramatically illustrated by Equiano's description of yet another group of people, the Native Americans he encountered in Jamaica.

> The women are ornamented with beads, and fond of painting themselves; the men also paint, even to excess, both their faces and shirts: their favourite color is red (256) . . .. One Owden, the oldest father in the vicinity, was dressed in a strange and terrifying form. Around his body were skins adorned with different kinds of feathers, and he had on his head a very large and high head piece, in the form of a grenadier's cap, with prickles like a porcupine (260).

Equiano's comments about Native Americans may be compared to comments made earlier by Andrew Battell about an important man in the interior from the Angola coast, in 1600 or 1601. The Yaka chief

> hath his hair very long, embroidered with many knots of Banba shells, which are very rich among them, and about his neck a collar of *masoes*, which are also shells, that are found upon the coast, and are sold among them . . . and about his middle he weareth landes, which are beads made of the ostrich eggs. He weareth a palmcloth about his middle, as fine as silk. His body is carved and cut with sundry works, and every day anointed with the fat of men. He weareth a piece of copper across his nose, and in his ears also. His body is always painted red and white. (*The Strange Adventures of Andrew Battell*, reprinted in Forbath, 127).

Such colorful descriptions ("strange and terrifying") and perhaps exaggerations ("anointed his body with the fat of men") led to prejudices and misconceptions regarding the newly encountered people. Of particular interest here are the prejudices about Africans that were held even into this century by many whites as well as by some African Americans. Henry Louis Gates, looking back on his childhood in West Virginia during the 1950s, humorously, but astutely, conveys the long-term effects:

> We accepted Tarzan as King of the Jungle without too many doubts. It was not until much, much later that anything even remotely "political"about Tarzan ever crossed our greased-down, stocking-capped minds. But the *National Geographic*-type documentaries, with bare-chested black women and grass-skirted tribesmen who spoke funny mumbo-jumbo talk, were the source of *real* embarrassment, and I'm sure that we all silently thanked some nameless Dutch sea captain for carting us up and out of the Heart of Darkness into the good ole U. S. A. ("Portraits in Black," 1993:163).

A few years after Gates' childhood, another African American completely turned around the question of biases:

> In that day the black man in Egypt was wearing silk, sharp as a tack, brothers. And those people up in Europe didn't know what cloth was. They admit this.

They were naked or they were wearing skins from animals. If they could get an animal, they would take his hide and throw it around their shoulders to keep warm. But they didn't know how to sew and weave. They didn't have that knowledge in Europe, not then.

Now I'm not talking racism. This isn't racism – this is history, we're dealing with just a little bit of history tonight (Malcolm X, "On Afro-American History," 24 January 1965:22, 34).

In spite of the obvious Arabic and European prejudices against nudity, and penchant for "sewn clothing," many other eye-witnesses recorded quite different variations on the theme; that is, these report that the Africans were fully clothed in standards acceptable to the outsiders' view. But note that in these instances the Africans' clothing is often specifically likened to non-African items of dress:

Duarte Barbosa at Malindi, early 1500s: The folks are both black and white; they go naked, covering only their private parts with cotton and silk cloths. Others of them wear cloths folded like cloaks and waistbands, and turbans of many rich stuffs on their heads (Davidson, 163).

Barbosa on Morrish traders at Sofala, Swahili civilization, early 1500s: These Moors are black, and some of them are tawny; some of them speak Arabic, but the more part use a language of the country. They clothe themselves from the waist down with cotton and silk cloths, and other cloths they wear over their shoulders like capes, and turbans on their heads. Some of them wear small caps dyed in grain in chequers and other woollen clothes in many tints, also camlets and other silks (Davidson, 156).

An account of a 1651–1652 Spanish mission to Benin: When they go to the King's palace or other places, the chiefs dress themselves like the women of Spain: from the waist down they wear cloths resembling sheets and farthingales (Ryder, 314).

John Barbot (the Gambia coast, 1680s): Both men and women generally wear a sort of coat, or vest, made after the manner of a shirt, reaching down to the knees, with wide open sleeves; and under it the men have drawers, after the *Turkish* fashion. (*A Description of the Coasts of Nigritia, vulgarly called North-Guinea* in A. and J. Churchill, eds. , *A Collection of Voyages and Travels*, London, 1746, V, 77–78; reprinted in Fishel and Quarles, 14).

Captain John Adams, in West Africa 1786–1800, among the Fantees: the elders . . . have in their dress some distinguishing marks, and, like Quakers, always wear their hats wherever they may be . . . by which they are as readily

> known in the villages where they reside, as counsellors are by their wigs in Courts of Assize. These hats . . . are probably used to cover pericraniums as naturally acute and sagacious as those immense, powdered, hairy, three-bobbed wigs are, that seem to give importance, and apparent wisdom to the logical nobs of English barristers ([1822] 1966:21–22).

The extant documents show that both the Arabs and Europeans held a particular fascination for the clothing worn by African chiefs and kings. Levtzion suggests that compared to other African rulers "the Diawara kings were exceptional in their simplicity and austerity" and quotes an early Arab source:

> Their kings have not that awe-inspiring appearance of [other] kings. They do not sit [for audience] dressed in a kingly fashion nor do they go out decorated. They never put on a turban nor are they seated on carpets. Their king has only a cap on his head (Levtzion, 109).

As comparison, Levtzion continues: "In eleventh-century Ghana only the king and the crown prince could wear sewn clothes; all other people wore robes of cotton, silk, or brocade, according to their means, made of unstitched lengths of cloth" (ibid.). Through the following centuries, observers continued to describe the sumptuous dress of African rulers:

> Ibn Fadl Allah al Omari, Mali, 1336: [The sultan] wears wide trousers made of about twenty pieces [of stuff] of a kind which he alone may wear. Behind him there stand about a score of Turkish or other pages which are bought for him in Cairo; one of them, at his left, holds a silk umbrella surmounted by a dome and a bird of gold . . . (Davidson, 94).

> Muhammad ibn Abdullah ibn Battuta, Mali, ca. 1352: [Over the platform of the sultan] is raised the umbrella, which is a sort of pavilion made of silk, surmounted by a bird in gold . . .. On [the sultan's] head he has a golden skullcap, bound with a gold band which has narrow ends shaped like knives, more than a span in length. His usual dress is a velvety red tunic, made of the European fabrics called *mutanfas* (Davidson, 98).

> King Iginua, ca. 1473, being very proud and fond of wearing fine clothes . . . was nicknamed 'Iginua the Proud' (Egharevba, 21).

> Andreas Josua Ultzheimer, Benin, 1603: The king . . . rides side-saddle as a woman would, and similarly clad in scarlet cloth, and ornamented not only with red beads but also with other unusual things. A white horsetail hangs over his head and down his back to his heels . . . (Davidson, 235–236).

William Smith, Benin, 1726–1727: The King appears . . . most magnificently dress'd . . . (Davidson, 265).[5]

Captain John Adams, Benin, 1786–1800: The King and his principal courtiers are ostentatious in their dress, wearing damask, taffity, and cuttanee, after the country fashion. Coral is a very favourite ornament in the royal seraglio . . . (115).

Hugh Clapperton on the Muslim Fulani-ruler at Sokoto, Northern Nigeria, 1824: He [the sultan] was dressed in a light blue cotton *tobe*, with a white muslin turban, the shawl of which he wore over the nose and mouth in the Tuareg fashion (Davidson, 381–382).

A. C. P. Gamitto, Central African King's [*Kazembe*] costume, 1831–1832: His head was ornamented with a kind of mitre, pyramidal in shape and two spans high, made of brilliant scarlet feathers; round his forehead was a dazzling diadem of beads of various kinds and colours. Behind his head a band of green cloth, supported by two small ivory needles, fanned out from the back of his neck. Neck and shoulders were covered with a kind of capuchin the upper part of which was covered with upturned cowries; there followed a band of pretty imitation jewels, made of glass, and the lower part had a string of alternately placed little round and square mirrors, in symmetry. This fell round his shoulders and over his chest, and when struck by the sun's rays it was too bright to look upon. Above each elbow was a band of blue feathers four inches wide, edged with what looked like a fringe, but which was in fact very fine strips of hide, the hair of which, four or five inches long, was black and white in colour. This ornament only Kazembe [the king] and his closest relatives may use, for it is a royal emblem. The arm from elbow to wrist was decorated with a string of bright blue beads . . . (Davidson, 345).

From first-hand descriptions, it becomes evident that almost always the African kings were outfitted in ways that marked them from ordinary people. In addition, the kings' royal entourage also dressed as befitted their stations.

Osifekunde, an Ijebu: *In addition to their usual clothing, the Ijebu have official costumes of set form and color for certain professions or certain functions. Thus the dress of priests is white and consists of two large cloths, one wrapped around the chest and the other draped over the head . . .. The soldier's uniform is characterized by a white sling passed around the neck and crossed over the chest like the crossed belting of our own soldiers, and by a red cloth or kerchief rolled like a turban around the head* (Lloyd, ed. , 265).

Thomas Bowdich, Kumasi, (Asante capital), 1817: The dress of the [warrior] captains was a war cap, with gilded rams' horns projecting in front, the sides

> extended beyond all proportion by immense plumes of eagles' feathers . . .. Their vest was of red cloth, covered with fetishes and saphies in gold and silver . . .. They wore loose cotton trousers, with immense boots of a dull red leather, coming half way up the thigh . . ..
>
> At least a hundred large umbrellas, or canopies, which could shelter thirty persons, were sprung up and down by the bearers with brilliant effect, being made of scarlet, yellow, and the most showy cloths and silks, and crowned on the top with crescents, pelicans, elephants, barrels and arms and swords of gold . . . (Davidson, 384).

> Gamitto describes the two principal wives of the *Kazembe*, Central Africa, 1831–1832: The first was to the right and sitting on a stool and mantled in a large green cloth; her arms, neck and forehead were ornamented with differently coloured beads, while on her head was an ornament of scarlet feathers like Kazembe's only smaller. . .. The second wife, who was seated to the left sitting on a lion skin on the ground, was simply dressed in a cloth, without ornament . . .. Behind them stood more than four hundred wives of various ages dressed in Nyandas . . . (Davidson, 346).

Jacob Egharevba (*A Short History of Benin*, first published in 1934) makes extensive use of folk accounts. The following examples define the royal paraphernalia, including clothing, by telling who began these traditions (always kings) and when they began:

> It was Ere [12th century] who introduced the royal throne (*ekete*), the chief's rectangular stool (*agba*), the round leather fan (*ezuzu*), the round box (*ekpokin*) made of bark and leather, the swords of authority (*ada* and *eben*), beaded anklets (*eguen*) and collars (*odigba*), and a simple, undecorated form of crown (Egharevba, 1). The royal beads and scarlet cloths (*ododo*) were introduced by him [Ewuare the Great, ca. 1440] . . . (ibid. , 17).

One way of symbolically humbling those who appeared before the sumptuously dressed monarchs was to enforce a more abbreviated manner of bodily attire for the commoners.

> Battuta, Mali, ca. 1352: The Negroes are of all people most submissive to their king and the most abject in their behaviour before him . . .. If he summons any of them while he is holding an audience in his pavilion, the person summoned takes off his clothes and puts on worn garments, removes his turban and dons a dirty skullcap, and enters with his garments and trousers raised knee-high (Davidson, 99).

> [To salute the king of ancient Mali a man] takes off his gown and wraps himself in it. He then kneels down, beats his breast and scatters dust over himself . . .. No one was allowed into the king's presence with his sandals on; negligence was punished by death . . .. When the king addressed them, the officers of the court removed their headgear and stroked the strings of their bows in approval of the king's words (Levtzion, 108).

> The villages of Mali gave Maghan Sundiata an unprecedented welcome . . .. The women of Mali tried to create a sensation and they did not fail. At the entrance to each village they had carpeted the road with their multi-coloured pagnes ["cloths"] so that Sundiata's horse would not so much as dirty its feet on entering the village . . ..
>
> Sundiata was leading the van. He had donned his costume of a hunter king – a plain smock, skin-tight trousers and his bow slung across his back (Niane, 80).

> James L. Smith (escaped from enslavement in Virginia): *During my stay in Springfield, Mass., I became acquainted with a man by the name of Amos B. Herring, a native of Africa [Liberia] . . .. I used to love to hear him tell of Africa . . .. In passing the king, the white man is obliged to take off his hat. It is necessary, in presenting yourself before a chief or king, to carry a lot of presents to insure a welcome . . . they must be showy, such as bright colored shirts, and red cloth which is worn to adorn the breast pocket. Only a few Africans are able to wear stripes of red cloth. Some are clad entirely in shirts made of leather, which they skillfully prepare* (reprinted in Bontemps, 192–193).

Some African societies ornament the skin by paint, scarification, or other methods. The following account explains when and why this became a practice among the Yoruba; again, a king is credited.

> To prevent any further desertion Ewuare [ca. 1440] sent word to all rulers in the neighbouring states to give no refuge to his deserting subjects, and he began to tattoo their bodies so that they might easily be known and identified amongst the people and other tribes. This was the origin of our tribal marks (Egharevba, 15).

An interesting point to be made about West African leaders is that, from the earliest contact, many of them creatively adopted European textiles and articles of European clothing, mixing them with more traditional African attire. Levtzion quotes from a fourteenth-century source: "In . . . Mali, the king was dressed in a long garment made of European cloth" (109). Often royal personages received European cloth and clothing as presentations or as trade items.

In 1491, Duarte Lopes gave this description of the king at the capital of Soyo, present-day Angola's Santo António do Zaire: [T]he Mani Kongo . . . was draped in beautifully tanned, glossy hides and leopard and civet furs, and around his waist, affixed as a sort of apron over his skirt of palm cloth, he wore a piece of European damask which Diogo Câohad sent him nearly a year before. His arms were laden with bracelets of copper, the tail of a zebra hung from his shoulder, an ironwood baton and a bow and arrows lay across his lap, and on his head he wore a cap of palm cloth resembling velvet and embroidered with the figure of a snake (Forbath, 93–94).

Among other gifts, the Oba of Benin City received from the King of Portugal a big umbrella in 1504 (Egharevba, 27).

Duarte Lopes on the Congo Mani Kongo, Alfonso (reigned 1507–1542/43), and his court: cloaks, capes, scarlet tabards, and silk robes . . .. They also wear hoods and capes, velvet and leather slippers, buskins, and rapiers at their sides . . .. The women also have adopted Portuguese fashions, wearing veils over their heads, and above them black velvet caps, ornamented with jewels, and chains of gold around their necks (Forbath, 108).

At Warré, ca. 1800, Captain John Adams describes the King's attire: A Boy was holding a pink silk umbrella over his head, and another was brushing away flies with an elephant's tail. To our extreme surprise, we found the king rigged out in European style, and wanting nothing to complete the dress but a shirt and a neckcloth.

The king whose name is Otoo, appeared about sixty years of age . . .. He had on a white satin waistcoat trimmed with silver lace, a silk purple coat much embroidered, black satin small-clothes with knee buckles, coarse thread stockings, shoes and buckles, and a large black hat trimmed round the edge with red feathers; all of which appeared to us of Portuguese fabric, except the coat and waistcoat, which, there is little doubt, had, at a former period, been worn by some noble peer or knight at the court of St. James (123–124).

At Lagos, Adams noticed the items spread around the king's audience chamber, among which were cloth items. Adams remarked on the prestige associated not only with the objects but on the symbolic manner of their display:

On each side of the apartment, there were tumbled together, promiscuously, articles of trade, and costly presents, in a state of delapidation; namely, . . . pieces of cloth, of Indian and European manufacture . . .. These, I presume, were placed thus conspicuously, with a view to impress the minds of those persons who were permitted to approach the royal presence, with ideas of the wealth and grandeur

> of his sable Majesty; and politically, might perhaps be considered as something similar to the pageantry with which it is thought necessary to surround royalty in civilized countries, and which have so captivating and imposing an effect on the unthinking and vulgar (101–102).

Mungo Park, a Scots surgeon, made two voyages inland from the Gambia river in 1795–1797 and 1805–1806. His descriptions about the West African people whom he encountered are most objective; and throughout, his accounts show that Park was a traveler imbued with a highly developed curiosity, who did not tint his perceptions about newly encountered societies with a Eurocentric bias. On leaving the Gambia and proceeding to Mali in 1795, Park writes of the king's pleasure with the European gifts he receives:

> When I delivered my presents, he [the king of Bondou] seemed well pleased, and was particularly delighted with the umbrella, which he repeatedly furled and unfurled, to the great admiration of himself and his two attendants, who could not for sometime comprehend the use of this wonderful machine . . .. He next proceeded to an eulogium on my blue coat, of which the yellow buttons seemed particularly to catch his fancy; and he concluded by entreating me to present him with it; assuring me, for my consolation under the loss of it, that he would wear it on all public occasions, and inform every one who saw it of my great liberality towards him (Davidson, 363).

Park's journal from his second expedition provides a "List of Merchandize for purchasing provisions and making the necessary presents to the Kings of the Woolli, Bondou, Kajaga, Fooladoo, Bambarra, and the Kings of the Interior," naming specific types and amounts of cloths and beads as the predominate items needed for trade and gifts (1815:40).

More extensive lists of "goods suitable to barter" at all the important ports and inland appear as an appendix to Captain John Adam's book published in 1822. Adams divides this list into columns which note the types of goods, remarks about them, their English cost, and the African items for which they may be traded. Cloth and cloth items predominate. In a final section of his appendix, Adams' "Remarks on Goods Suitable to Barter in Africa" provide even more detail. Under categories such as "India Trade Goods"and "English Manufactured Cotton Goods," he lists the specific types, patterns, and colors of cloth and cloth goods favored by specific African societies (235ff.). This remarkable document by an English trader to the West African coast at the end of the eighteenth century offers certain proof that Africans carefully chose the imported items on the basis of pronounced regional aesthetics, and that by insisting that their own demands be meant, they helped to control what the Europeans brought in the way of foreign merchandise.

Nevertheless, from the very beginning, the trade resulted in disruptive internal changes. Ryder, for instance, assesses an aspect of the impact which the Portuguese had on one kingdom in particular. By the early sixteenth century:

> . . . the most obvious result of the Portuguese arrival upon the scene must have been the appearance in Benin of many articles previously unknown there. A large proportion of the goods acquired from the Portuguese reflected the preferences of the Oba and court chiefs who controlled European trade, and much of what they received was probably consumed within their own households (39).

By this we may assume that at least during the early period in the European trade, the ordinary folk did not gain possession of these new articles, among which were European and Indian cloth and clothing. Ryder brings home these points, as well as the point that personal adornment was a highly developed notion in Benin royal society:

> The amount of cloth supplied to Fernandez [in 1512] was relatively small, and seems to have been consumed mainly in customary presents to Benin chiefs, interpreters, and other officials who administered trade with the Europeans . . . (40) . . . A present delivered [to the Oba] in the name of King Manuel in 1505 consisted of . . . a piece of printed chintz from Cambay, a *marlota* (a short, close-fitting cloak with hood attached) of orange taffeta and white satin, six linen shirts, and a shirt of blue Indian silk. Such gifts no doubt helped to establish the convention that only the Oba wear silk . . . perhaps the most striking thing about these trade goods and presents is that almost all could serve only for personal ornamentation; strictly utilitarian articles were conspicuously absent (41).

The presentations of cloth and clothing as gifts to important African men continued throughout the centuries of trade. Of his audience with the King of Benin, Captain John Adams remembered, "The day following my arrival, I had the honour of an interview with him; he received me with much politeness, particularly after the fine flashy piece of red silk damask, which I had brought with me as a present for him, had been unfolded" (113). Well into the nineteenth century Europeans continued the custom of presenting important African men with textiles and items of clothing. Among the gifts that Henry Morton Stanley gave to Chief Ngalyema in the Belgian Congo in 1881 were a gold-embroidered coat and pieces of fine cloth, but the chief wanted more goods in exchange for a station at the Stanley Pool. Along with other items he demanded "finer pieces of cloth . . . then Stanley's own best black suit, which the white man wore for ceremonial meetings with great chiefs . . .." The negotiations were broken off by Stanley who refused "to give Ngalyema the suit" which infuriated the chief (Forbath, 351). On palavering for land on the Congo, 1879, Stanley agreed to make a payment of £2 sterling worth of cloth down and £2 sterling worth of cloth per month. In return, the Vivi chiefs agreed to sell him a 20-square-mile tract for his base station . . . (ibid., 344).

One final note should be made concerning presentations to important men: an African precedent appears to overlay the custom of Europeans offering gifts, particularly of cloth and other items of bodily adornment to African kings. Captain John Adams remarked on a visit by African emissaries to the King of Benin:

> It is the practice here for masters of vessels to pay the king a visit soon after their arrival; and such a ceremony is seldom allowed to be dispensed with, as on these occasions the black monarch receives a handsome present, consisting of a piece of silk damask, a few yards of scarlet cloth, and some strings of coral (110).

The travelers give detailed renderings concerning the dress of powerful African men; but in comparison, they appear to have been far less interested in what ordinary people wore, unless they were unclothed. Offsetting this omission, several contemporary West Africans, who had been enslaved in Europe or the Americas, described the common dress of the people of their homelands.

Mahommah Gardo Baquaqua, a Muslim, born ca. mid 1820s, was enslaved in Brazil and escaped to New York. In his narrative (1854), Baquaqua gave an account of the dress of his people in Djougou which lay north of present-day Benin. The description shows the full range of clothing proscribed according to class, sex, and age:

> *It is customary for the Mohammedans [men] to wear a loose kind of trousers, which are made full at the bottom and are fastened round the hips by a cord. A loose robe is worn over this, cut in a circular form, open at the centre, sufficiently large to put over the head, and allowed to rest on the shoulders, with loose sleeves, the neck and breasts being exposed. The women wear a cloth about two yards square, doubled cornerwise, and tied around the waist, the tie being made at the left side. The king's dress is made in a similar style, but of more costly materials. Children do not wear much clothing* (in Austin, 608).

Osifekunde reported about his people, the Ijebu from the Nigerian coast. Again, the clothing is differentiated by the sex and class of the wearer.

> *A simple cloth wrapper, knotted at the waist, is the usual costume for men in the interior of their homes. Outdoors, they wear a kind of wide, short pantaloons, called choukotou* [Yoruba:*Sokoto*]. *And the rich replace the knotted cloth of the common people with a large open gown. Women wear a cloth wrapper as well, but larger, rolled around the body, and held in place below the bust by a knotted kerchief in the form of a belt* (Lloyd, ed., 263–264).

An early European remark on ordinary peoples' dress comes from Duarte Barbosa, at Mombasa in the first decade of the sixteenth century. In this statement, Duarte also makes references to skin color: "The men are in color either tawny, black or white and also their women go very bravely attired with many fine garments of silk and gold in abundance" (Davidson, 160).

Later observers shaded their remarks in other ways, not the least of which was the continuing concern for the dress of important men. For example, when Joseph Dupuis, the British envoy and consul to Ashanti, reported on the Gold Coast (present-day Ghana) and the West Africa interior in 1824, he begins a rich and, by-and-large, objective description of the local, Muslim male clothing by noting the everyday dress of ordinary men. Dupuis then moves on to a description of the clothing worn by upper-class men, and ends with the local chief's attire. His observations show that each group possessed an impetus towards improvisation in the clothes they wore and an apparent eagerness to adopt an astonishing array of clothing styles. Dupuis' statements, however, indicate that a hierarchical concept of class and power constrained each group in just how far it might move towards eclectic dress.

> The dress of these people corresponded better with the costume of Egypt or Tripoli, than it did with that of western Barbary; yet it was a medley of several nations; but the privileged classes were handsomely habited in robes of Turkish or Indian cut silk, called *cofatten*, trousers of native cotton, with turbans of the same, and a small body vest richly braided with silk twist. This was perhaps the prevailing mode of dress, but other fashions, not less graceful, denoted foreign traders; and in some instances, it was a mixture of Indian and Turkish habits, in which loose flowing shirts with long and broad sleeves formed the whole attire. I recognized also the common dress of the Arabs and mountaineers of Atlas: this was simply a sort of tunic without sleeves, falling down to the knee, called in Arabic *kussabi*. The chief, however, was a solitary instance in deviation from

> every national mode. This man, who was far advanced in years, was decorated in yellow damask robes, something of a theatrical cut, although rich in faded embroidery and braiding. A muslim turban, preposterously studded with pieces of looking glass, charms, bits of unwrought coral, and glass beads, enveloped his head, which was covered, besides, with a damask scarf that fell over his shoulders in ample folds, and united with a cumbrous load of apparel of various colours (72).[6]

As well, outsiders noted the differences in dress between Muslims and non-Muslims. Mungo Park, among the Mandingos in the 1790s, gives a rare description of women's clothing:

> The dress of both sexes is composed of cotton cloth, of their own manufacture; that of the men is a loose frock, not unlike a surplice, with drawers that reach half-way down the leg; and they wear sandals on their feet, and white cotton caps upon their heads. The women's dress consists of two pieces of cloth, each of which they wrap round the waist, which, hanging down to the ankles, answers the purpose of a petticoat; the other is thrown negligently over the bosom and shoulders (14–15).

Park's description of the female dress of "Moors" (in this case meaning Black Muslims) may be compared to his description of the non-Muslim Mandingo women's dress above.

> The Moors have singular ideas of Feminine perfection . . .. As the Moors purchase all their clothing from the Negroes, the women are forced to be very economical in the article of dress. In general they content themselves with a broad piece of cotton cloth, which is wrapped round the middle, and hangs like a petticoat almost to the ground; to the upper part of this are sewed two square pieces, one before and the other behind, which are fastened together over the shoulders. The head-dress is commonly a bandage of cotton cloth, with some parts of it broader than others, which serve to conceal the face when they walk in the sun; frequently, however, when they go abroad, they veil themselves from head to foot (116–117).

Another rare description concerning women's self-adornment comes from Captain John Adams who traveled in West African between 1786 and 1800.

> [The Fantee woman's toilette] consists of a large calabash, containing a small mirror, paint(generally white), teeth brushes made of a very fibrous tough wood, a bark which has a powerful musky smell, grease, and soap . . .. She often consumes an hour or two in adorning her person; and in the application of her

> paint, the management of her hair, and the scenting of her person, discovers no inconsiderable degree of skill ([1822] 1966:39).

In Benin, Adams noted "the women, like those of the Heebo nation, wear a profusion of beads, if they can by any means obtain them" (115).

As with women and ordinary male adults, the travelers have little to report about the dress of children. Osifekunde (Ijebu) said that in his country, "Children of both sexes remain absolutely nude to the age of fifteen years, which is that of puberty" (in Lloyd, ed., 255). Roy Sieber, drawing from eighteenth- and nineteenth-century traveler's accounts, notes: " [I]n most areas, some form of body covering was in general use, except among children" (1972:19). Sieber then quotes from John Barbot who traveled along the West African coast in the last quarter of the seventeenth century: "The youngest people of both sexes, about the [Gold] coast, are seldom clothed [*sic*] till eight or ten years of age, but go stark naked, playing, bathing, and swimming together, without any distinction . . ." (19). In many societies, puberty marks a change in dress, and Sieber notes that in modern Africa: "The achievement of adulthood is in part celebrated by the assumption of adult dress. Coming-of-age ceremonies may include the change, symbolically, from nudity to dress" (19).

As has been shown, West African kings and chiefs readily adapted some European clothing items. By comparison, contemporary, early nineteenth-century descriptions of the West African *Amistad* captives offer important insights into the seemingly carefree manner in which ordinary West African men also adopted certain articles of European and American clothing; but in addition, these descriptions also illustrate the instability of these adaptations.

In 1839, Africans illegally captured and brought to the Americas seized the *Amistad*, the ship on which they were being transported after leaving Havana. After sixty-three days at sea, the schooner was brought to harbor in New London, Connecticut; and thereafter, the captives received a great deal of public notice. Mary Cable (1977) bases her history of the *Amistad* case on contemporary eye-witness accounts, throughout which are sprinkled descriptions of the captives' responses to non-African clothing.

On boarding the *Amistad* soon after it arrived in port, a reporter for the New London *Gazette* wrote:

> Here could be seen a negro with white pantaloons and the sable shirt which nature gave him, and a planter's broad brimmed hat upon his head, with a string of gewgaws about his neck; and another with a linen cambric shirt, whose bosom

> was worked by the hand of some dark-eyed daughter of Spain, while his nether proportions were enveloped in a shawl of gauze or Canton crepe (Cable, 9).

No doubt, after several months at sea, the Blacks donned some of the European clothing out of sheer necessity, but from the rest of the information about the captives' stay in New England, it also appears that they well understood that Western-style dress could be used to mark a person's importance.

In the following three years, the captives became sensational news for the northern press. Interest in the Africans included details about their appearance; and of particular interest was the arresting leader of the Africans, "Joseph Cinquez," a Mende, better known as Cinque. At a judicial hearing held at New London within days of the *Amistad* docking, the New Haven *Daily Herald* reported that Cinque wore a red flannel shirt, white duck pants and manacles; " [h]is appearance was neat, and in cleanliness would compare advantageously with any colored dandy of Broadway" (Cable, 13).

Cinque, however, changed back-and-forth between his native dress and that of the country in which he now found himself; he could be equally insistent about wearing American cloth in African style. In jail, awaiting trial in Hartford, the captives had been provided with shirts and trousers. They were visited by Joseph Tappan who said that he found Cinque: "Wholly unclothed – a blanket partly wrapped around him. He does not seem to like the tight dress of this country" (Cable, 29). The other captives apparently had the same reaction to New England garb. The judge ordered that the Africans be relieved of their irons since they should no longer be treated as criminals; however, they were removed to the New Haven county jail to await another trial. Here they were

> . . . supplied with checked cotton shirts, cotton and wool trousers, wool socks, and thick shoes . . ., [but] New England autumn had set in . . .. Joshua Leavitt wrote to the newspapers, saying that . . . the prisoners had no change of shirts; and, because they had no coats, could not go out. A lady had given Cinque a frock coat and a clean shirt, but the jailer had taken them away . . .. Charles Hooker, the physician in charge, added that the Africans seemed to find clothing burdensome and would not wear what they had . . .. An editorial in one of the New Haven newspapers commented sternly, 'There are white men in the prison not so comfortably clad as the Africans? Would it not be well to show a little sympathy for them?'(Cable, 47–48).

The Africans' ordeal ended with a Supreme Court decision that they be returned to Africa. Certain citizens of New England felt this should be prolonged so that they could first "bring light to the Africans," and Cinque and the others were detained in order to be educated. During this period, abolitionists continued to rally behind the Africans' cause, giving both spiritual advice as well as material goods.

> Someone had given Cinque a coat that did not fit him; he gave itto Bar-ma, bought some cloth, and ordered another coat from a tailor, saying that Mr. Williams could pay for it. On being spoken to severely, Cinque offered to pawn his watch and pay the tailor himself (Cable, 122). [Williams owned the Framington barn where the Africans lived at this time.]

In the preceding account, it seems Cinque was well aware of the prestige associated with wearing an American suit. It is important to note, however, that in the 1841 portrait for which Cinque sat while in the United States, he wears African clothing.

Many observers commented on the dress of Cinque and the other Africans involved in the *Amistad* affair; and many travelers wrote descriptions about the clothing of important African men. These observations offer insights into an African worldview that appears to embrace not only the new and unusual, but to retain something of the traditional as well. As will become apparent in the following chapters, the African ability to inventively manipulate and blend the traditional with the novel extended into communities of African Americans in the antebellum South. But even when sometimes adopting Arab-style clothing and, later, items of European dress, West Africans never wholly discarded customary items of clothing. Rather, the new additions were simply added to the older.

The most stable forms of West African dress and other body ornamentation appear to be those worn in ceremonial contexts, such as the clothing worn by kings and chiefs, and the special clothing worn by even ordinary men and women for special events.[7] In these instances, West Africans share with others the concept that the cloth and clothing associated with more unusual secular and sacred happenings serve important purposes, not the least of which are tangible links to ancestors.[8]

In his discussion of the costumes worn for modern Yoruba ceremonies, Saburi O. Biobaku traces older elements as well as modern adoptions and astutely notes that:

> Somehow, in cultural institutions like the festival certain practices are resilient whereas others are subject to constant change, depending on the nature of the sanctions of each festival . . . (104) . . .. For our purposes the significance of all this is that just as the different ceremonies of a Yoruba community usually have their genesis in different eras of the community's history, so do the costumes that are used to give physical expression to such ceremonies. Thus one can get an insight into the artistic life of the community from such an investigation. It will reveal a process from the rough-and-ready raffia threads to the magnificent fabric of today (105).

A very early account provides an insight into the apparent delight with which a leader of the Kongo people received the newer European trade goods, as well as a description of how these West Africans preserved their traditional modes of body ornamentation during a celebration. In 1491, Portuguese traders "brought cloth, clothes, ornaments" to the *mani Sonyo* in the Kongo kingdom (Hilton, 50) and recounted:

> The *mani Sonyo* was overwhelmed by the sight of the gifts . . .. He then organized a festival which was clearly a *nkimba* cult assembly. The people were naked to the waist and their skins were painted white, the colour of the other world. They wore palmcloth from the waist to the ground and feathers in their hair. The *mani Sanyo* wore a hat embroidered with a snake . . . (Hilton, 51).

We learn from this description about the ways in which one group of West Africans decorated their bodies with color and cloth and other adornments for a secular celebratory gathering. Still other accounts give us glimpses into the clothing worn for sacred events for which the West Africans retain more traditional clothing.[9]

Muhammad ibn Abdullah ibn Battuta (1304–1377), in Mali, ca. 1350s remarked: "The negroes wear fine white garments on Fridays. If by chance a man has no more than one shirt or a soiled tunic, at least he washes it before putting it on to go to public prayer" (Davidson, 100). An account of a Spanish mission to Benin in 1651–1652 mentions the following ceremonies in preparation for marriage. Note how body ornamentation figures in these proceedings.

> Before taking a wife, the negro who is to be married has to cover himself completely with a certain white clay, so that he looks like a demon. After going about the city for some days in this livery, he has to wash it off and have his whole head dressed with a white clay paste, giving an effect like Flemish lace. He then goes about the city in great state for several days with a number of

> companions, and afterwards receives his bride from the hand of the King who acts as priest. The woman is fully adorned with coral, brass manillas, glass beads, ivories, and cowries (Ryder, 313–314).

Equiano (b. 1745) described the wedding customs in the province of Benin (in present-day Nigeria), the region of his birth. The bride " . . . *is brought home to her husband, and then another feast is made, to which the relations of both parties are invited: her parents deliver her to the bridegroom, accompanied with a number of blessings, and at the same time they tie round her waist a cotton string of the thickness of a goose-quill, which none but married women are permitted to wear*" (11).

West Africans also associate special cloths and clothing with funerals. And, as in many other societies, in West Africa, cloth and clothing adorn the dead as well as the living.

> In Yoruba society, the burial rite of the *Alagemo* in the Agemo cult . . . the body is dressed up with long raffia threads, the same costume as the deceased person has used in his annual dances. The *eru* (luggage of charms) of the deceased is put on his head . . . (Biobaku, 88).

> Joseph Wright (Yoruba, settled in Sierra Leone): *Perhaps there would be twenty large pieces of costly cloth, besides those with which they lined the wall where the dead man lay. And then they would make a large coffin about five feet high and about four feet wide and properly dressed with all fine and costly things* (originally a hand-written account titled "The Life of Joseph Wright: A Native of Ackoo," June 1839; in Curtin, 328).

More recently, 1925, a witness to the funeral of a Kuba king of Zaire wrote:

> When we arrived it (the coffin) had not yet been closed and we could see the corpse, thickly painted with camwood paste and enveloped in fine cloth . . .. At the king's feet space was reserved for a trunk, in which were laid piece on piece of the rarest examples of the Bakuta art of cloth-weaving and embroidery (quoted in Darish, 129–130).

For West Africans, as well, the colors of cloth and clothing worn by the living during funerals are symbolic. In Asante society, "Mourning robes, for example, were subdued hues of brown, black, or brick red (representing eyes red from grief)" (*Art of West African Kingdoms*, 23). But, in direct opposition to the traditional European and American mourning color, a number of West African groups imbue white as the symbolic color for the dead. Mahommah Gardo Baquaqua (b. ca. mid–1820s, a Muslim from Djougou, north of present-day Benin) said: "*When a person dies, they wrap the body in a white cloth, and bury it as soon as possible*" (in Austin, 607).

Initiation rites may also be considered sacred. Sylvia Boone describes body ornamentation in her study of the Mende women's Sande Society in modern Sierra Leone, offering proof that the customs are quite old. As in the funerary context, the color white plays a significant role during the initiation ceremony when the bodies of the Sande Society girl initiates are first covered in clay "so that they are chalk white" and "they are dressed in white clothes and adorned with white beads" (196). To their black caps, white ribbons are attached (ibid.) which symbolically link the girls to the ruling Sande females who wear white headdresses and often white clothing as one of the honours of their high rank (23). The girls are also linked to the spiritual waters from which the sacred mask of the society comes(196). While not associated with Christian baptizing, the Sande Society suggests how a blending of customs might have occurred in the Southern United States wherein Christian African Americans being baptized traditionally wear white (Figure 2).[10]

The popular conception has been that Africans were unclothed barbarians until Arabs brought them Islam and sewn cloth and until the Europeans brought them Christianity and clothing. From the Arabic and European points of view, nudity was immoral; therefore, some Arabs and Europeans observers dwelled overly on the Africans' lack of dress. More objective testimony from outsiders, as well as from West Africans themselves, however, provides overwhelming evidence that most West African adults wore some form of clothing: the more powerful wearing an excess, the lower classes apparently dressing in a more abbreviated manner. Africans wore not only animals skins, furs and feathers, but cloth items which they had been producing before the beginning of European trade. Out of these they fashioned not only ordinary clothing, but more elaborate, celebratory raiments as well.

Indigenous Cloth Fibers

In their comprehensive examination, *African Textiles*, 1989, John Picton and John Mack define the terms most often used in discussing cloth and clothing construction (15–16). To avoid confusion, I follow their explicit definitions:

Figure 2. White robes worn during a turn-of-the-century Southern baptism, place unknown. *Negro Baptism* photograph, Historical Society of Carroll County, Maryland, Dr. Jacob J. Weaver Collection, gift of Western Maryland College, 1989.

Fabric: the generic term for all fibrous constructions
Textile: refers specifically to woven fabrics
Cloth: all textiles are cloths, but not all cloths are textiles, for they need not be woven
Fabric all cloths are fabrics, but, again, not all fabrics are cloths. Cloth is inherently flexible and is not composed of rigid woven elements [as are, eg. , baskets].
Weaving: the technique of interworking two sets of elements.

Picton and Mack fully describe the raw materials available in Africa for cloth and textile manufacture (23–37). Animals and plants were used to produce clothing and, with few exceptions, these were the same as those available in the Southern United States during the antebellum period.[11]

Wool

From the testimonia, there is scant evidence that West Africans raised goats or sheep for the purpose of using the wool for clothing. Perhaps this is due to climatic conditions which make this warmer type of fabric unnecessary during much of the year.[12] One exception is the following testimony from Salih Bilali (b. ca. 1765) who was an enslaved African Muslim in Georgia. His Parents were Mandingo-Fulbe. In the 1830s, James Hamilton Couper recorded in a letter what Bilali said about his homeland, Massina, 200 miles southwest of Timbuktu.

> *The usual dress of the men, is a large pair of cotton trousers, and a shirt with a conical straw hat, without a rim. They manufacture their own cotton cloth; and dye it of a very fine blue better than any he has seen here. They also wear blankets, made from the long wool of their sheep* (Austin, 324).

Silk

Another animal which produces fibres suitable for clothing is the silkworm. Silk, however, appears to have been a prestige textile in West Africa, just as it was elsewhere. In West Africa silk was apparently a rarity for most. Heinrich Barth wrote in the mid-nineteenth-century, "The people of Timbuktu are very experienced in the art of adorning their clothing with a fine stitching of silk, but this is done on a very small scale, and even these shirts are only used at home" (Davidson, 402).

Animal Skin

Mammal skins were the most oft-described animal parts used by Africans to produce clothing (eg., see above, Lopes' description of the ManiKongo's attire). They wore these as dressed furs and as tanned hides. Leather was fashioned into a number of objects including shoes.

Leo Africanus, in Gobir, ca. 1510: Here are also great stores of artificers and linen weavers: and here are such shoes made as the ancient Romans were woont to weare, the greatest part whereof be carried to Tombuto and Gago (Bovill, 150).

Osifekunde (b. Ijebu) 1810s: *Footwear is not worn by the common people, but restricted to those of the higher orders. There is a kind of sandal or slipper called lagolago; and a more distinguished form of shoe, which looks like our clogs, is called "saka"* (in Lloyd, ed., 264).

African leather workers were considered master craftsmen.

Richard Jordan, Gambia Coast, 1623: They make also Bridles and Saddles, of which I have seen some very neat, hardly to be bettered here: whereby it seemes they have skill to dress and dye their Deeres skins and Goats skins (Davidson, 24).

Thomas Winterbottom, Sierra Leone, 1796: [T]he most ingenious man in the village is usually the blacksmith, joiner, architect, and weaver, the chief trades which they require or exercise . . .. Among the Foolas [Fulani], however, and other nations beyond them, some progress has been made informing distinct occupations or trades. One set of men, *called garrankees* or shoemakers, are exclusively employed in manufacturing leather, and converting it into useful articles, as sandles . . . (Davidson, 288).

Mungo Park described the tanning methods employed in West Africa during the late eighteenth century. He says that the African leather makers:

tan and dress leather with a very great expedition, by steeping the hide first in a mixture of wood ashes and water, until it parts with the hair, and afterwards by using the pounded leaves of a tree called *goo* as an astringent. They are at great pains to render the hide as soft and pliant as possible, by rubbing it frequently between their hands, and beating it upon a stone. The hides of bullocks are converted chiefly into sandals . . .. The only artists which are distinctly acknowledged as such by the Negroes, and who value themselves on exercising appropriate and peculiar trades, are the manufacturers of *leather* and *iron*. The

> first of these . . . [a]re to be found in almost every town, and they frequently travel throughout the country in exercise of their calling (Miller, ed., 1954:216, original emphasis).

Sieber mentions a description of West African footwear given in the 1880s, and writes: "Shoes, when worn, were usually simple sandals of fibre or a piece of leather tied on with thongs . . .. Wooden clogs, reflecting the influence of the Arab world, are known in several parts of east Africa"(80).

Bark Cloth

West Africans made cloth and clothing from a variety of plant materials. In some instances, the exact material cannot be ascertained from the early documents. For instance, Captain John Adams notes in his journal of West African travels between 1786 and 1800 that the people from Ardrah (50 miles from Lagos) chiefly wove cloth from cotton but also wove a cloth of grass([1822] 1966:79). Just what the "grass" was remains unknown.

As some continue to do today, Africans and African Americans used palms and other types of stiff plants to produce hats, as well as baskets. In Central Africa, an unwoven cloth made from bark was produced(Picton and Mack, 42–46), but apparently was never made in the United States. This cloth was sufficiently pliable to be worn as clothing. From a British account of Guinea, 1555–1556: "All their clothes, cordes, girdles, fishing lines, and all such like things, which they have, they make of the bark of certaine trees, and thereof they can worke things very pretily . . ." (Davidson, 231).

Ryder notes that an English merchant crew of 1591 gathered a cargo which may have included:

> 'cloth made of cotton wooll very curiously woven, and cloth made of the barke of the palme trees', samples of which had been gathered on the first voyage. Among other objects of Benin craftsmen which these early crews bought as curios were 'pretie fine mats and baskets that they make' . . . (84).

Bast Fibre

More ordinary than bark cloth in West Africa, are bast fibres which are made by soaking and then removing the fibres from the woody core of stems. Thomas Winterbottom, Sierra Leone, 1790s, describes a bast fibre, although he does not name the specific plant: "They have various substitutes for hemp and flax, of which they make fishing lines and nets equal in strength and durability to those of Europeans . . ." (Davidson, 289).

In tropical Africa, the most important bast fibres come from the raffia palm leaflet. Carol Kroll writes: "The raffia palm is cultivated for its leaves, which are used in thin-dried strips." Noting that it is a coarse fibre, she says that it can be spun nevertheless. Kroll says that in "Madagascar, raffia is used for sacks, baskets, mats, and various types of outerwear" (40). Kongo men wove raffia palm cloth during the 15th and 16th centuries. These cloths were used for clothes, cushions, and coverings and "were so fine that later European observers likened them to damask, velvet, satin, and taffeta" (Hilton, 6).[13]

Cotton

The most common plant fibre used by West Africans to produce cloth was cotton, just as it was in the antebellum South. In her richly detailed study, *Nigerian Handcrafted Textiles* (1976), Joanne Bubolz Eicher gives a brief historical background for cotton and its use in African cloth manufacture.

Cotton grows easily in Africa, and its existence in that continent has been traced back at least 5, 000 years. Africans used and manufactured cotton cloth before the arrival of the Europeans. Reports of African travelers and explorers often include descriptions of indigenous cotton in both plant form and clothing (12).

Eicher notes that as late as the 1890s, one observer estimated "that over ninety-five percent of the Yoruba cloth consumption at that time was handcrafted from locally grown cotton which was handspun and hand-dyed" (1976:32–33). Nevertheless, she writes that "During the last half of the 1800s export of locally woven fabrics to other parts of Nigeria and to other countries was reduced by the large imports of printed cotton cloth from England which could be purchased more cheaply than handwoven fabrics" (33).[14]

Early travelers commented on indigenous African cotton cloth.

> Alvise da Cadamosto (Senegal, 1450s): In this market I perceived quite clearly these people are exceedingly poor, judging from the wares they brought for sale – that is, cotton, but not in large quantities, cotton thread and cloth (Gunther, 1978:12).

> Hans Mayr? (at Kilwa, 1505): There was a large quantity of cotton for Sofala in the town, for the whole coast gets its cotton cloth from here. So the Grand-Captain got a good share of the trade of Sofala for himself. A large quantity of rich silk and gold embroidered clothes was seized . . . (Davidson, 164).

John Barbot (the Gambia coast, 1680s): The weavers make great quantities of narrow cotton-cloth, which from the *Portuguese* name, they call *Panho*, of the same as has been mention'd at *Cabo Verde*. The best sort they call *Panhos Sakes*, being eight narrow slips stitch'd together, generally white, clouded with flames. The second sort is of six narrow slips put together, called *Bontans*, about two yards long, and a yard and a half broad, curiously striped. The third sort is call'd *Barfoel*, of the same size, but coarser (Fishel and Quarles, 14).

Martin R. Delany in Kano, Western Sudan, 1851: The principal commerce of Kano consists in native produce, namely, the cotton cloth woven and dyed here or in the neighboring towns, in the form of tobes or *rigona* (sing. *riga*); *turkedi*, or the oblong piece of dress of dark-blue colour worn by women; the *zenne* or plaid, of various colours; and the *rawani baki*, or black litham (Davidson, 390).

West Africans also noted the use of cotton in the manufacture of clothing in their homelands.

Osifekunde (b. Ijebu), 1810s: *The Ijebu dress themselves, by and large, in textiles which they make themselves. These are cotton cloths whose raw material is furnished by the soil . . . and it is known that a considerable quantity of textiles manufactured and exported, not merely to countries but even to Brazil, whence ships come to Lagos in search of this merchandise so highly esteemed by the peoples of African origin transplanted to those distant lands* (Lloyd, ed., 263).

Gi-la-ba-ru (Fulu, in Mendi country): In his country people . . . wear cotton cloth (evidence taken in 1840, Cable, n. p. n.).

Ba: . . . in his country . . . cotton cloth is manufactured . . . (ibid.).

Cloth and Clothing Production

After the cotton was harvested, the first step in turning the raw fibres into cloth was the removal of seeds. Next the fibres needed to be combed to free them of bits of chaff and to untangle them. Following that, the fibres were spun and formed into hanks of certain lengths in preparation for weaving. Kroll writes: "Some form of hand spinning existed as early as twelve thousand years ago in North Africa . . ." (5). She notes there are several basic methods (ibid.). In Africa, a hand spindle, rather than a wheel, is used (Figure 3).

Figure 3. Woman using a drop spindle. Nyohene, Northern Region, Ghana, 1995. Photograph by the author.

Thomas Winterbottom, Sierra Leone, 1790s: They raise upon most parts of the coast a sufficient quantity of cotton for their own use . . .. They spin the cotton in a very tedious manner, by twirling a spindle, one end of which is loaded with clay, in a large shell or wooden dish, passing the thread between the finger and thumb of one hand (Davidson, 289).[15]

Winterbottom's comment on the African manner of spinning seems to hold a European bias; that is, being more familiar with the spinning wheel, he found the drop spindle a "tedious" spinning method.

All reports on spinning, whether from travelers or from Africans, describe it as a woman's task.

Salih Bilali (b. ca. 1765, 200 miles southwest of Timbuktu), an enslaved Muslim in Georgia, reported that in his homeland, *The women spin, and attend to household duties, but never work in the fields* (Couper letter, 1830s, in Austin, 324).

During the 1790s, in a village near Segu, capital of Bambarra, a woman takes Mungo Park to her home and feeds him:

. . . my worthy benefactress . . . called to the female part of her family, who stood gazing on me all the while in fixed astonishment, to resume their task of spinning cotton; in which they continued to employ themselves [a] great part of the night. They lightened their labor by songs, one of which was composed extempore; for I was myself the subject of it. It was sung by one of the young women, the rest joining in a sort of chorus . . . (Davidson, 372).

Osifekunde said: "*In each [Ijebu] family, the harvest, spinning, weaving, and dyeing are the customary occupations of women . . .*" (Lloyd, ed., 263). Mahommah Gardo Baquaqua, an enslaved West African Muslim, was born in the mid 1820s at Djougou, north of present-day Benin. He said: *The women do the spinning by a very slow process, having to twist the thread with their fingers; the men do the weaving; they weave cloth in narrow strips, and then sew it together. The women also grind the corn* (in Austin, 607). *The women in Africa are considered very inferior to the men, and are consequently held in the most degrading subjection* (ibid., 604).

Bilali, Parke, Osifekunde, and Baquaqua are careful to note that spinning as they knew it in the eighteenth and nineteenth centuries was a task performed by women. And, Baquaqua, from Benin, is equally careful in noting that men were the weavers. On the other hand, Equiano (b. 1745), also from Benin, wrote: *When our women are not employed with the men in tillage, their usual occupation is spinning and weaving cotton, which they afterwards dye, and make into garments* (13). These first-hand observations about who the weavers were seem to be contradictory, but this may be explained by the fact that today African men and women use different types of looms, as they perhaps did in former times (Figure 4). In his 1969 ethnology of the Nigerian Yoruba, William Bascom writes: "Both men and women weave, using different types of looms. Women weave on the vertical 'mat loom,' . . .. Men weave on the horizontal narrow-band treadle loom (100) . . .. Ginning, fluffing, spinning, rewinding, and dyeing are done by women" (101).

Thomas Winterbottom offsets his somewhat Eurocentric comments on the spinning methods he observed in Sierra Leone, in the 1790s, with his more objective and complimentary remarks about West African weaving techniques.

> The looms resemble those used in England to weave shalloons, except in being much narrower, not more then six inches in breadth, seven such pieces, between four and five feet in length, must be joined to forma cloth for a woman; but they are so exact in the pattern, that at a small distance the junctures cannot be easily discovered . . . (Davidson, 289).

Although we do not learn from Winterbottom who the weavers were, other accounts concerning cloth production always describe women as spinners, dyers, and occasionally as weavers, while men are described only as weavers. Picton and Mack give a general outline as to how the taskis delegated today:

> In . . . most of West Africa, Ethiopia, East Africa and Zaire, all weaving is done by men. Elsewhere, for example Berber North Africa and Madagascar, all the weaving is done by women. In other areas, such as Nigeria, Arab North Africa and the Sudan, both men and women weave (19).

Lisa Aronson, who demonstrates the gendered character of who makes which craft items in contemporary Black African societies, includes cloth-production as one such example of the taboos related to craft traditions (1990:119–138 and 1991:551–574). How closely these present-day gendered task patterns relate to past patterns is unknown, but some historical accounts indicate that they are long-standing. Sieber encapsulates the historically known gendered tasks and the rich traditions of cloth production in West Africa:

In many parts of West Africa male weavers, working on narrow horizontal looms, produced cloth as a family industry. Women weavers, using a vertical loom, worked more to meet family needs, although some ritual and some trade weaving existed. The famous Benin cloths used in the early trade may have been made by women. Men produced the fine raffia cloths of western and central Zaire, and women embroidered the famous cut pile designs of the Kuba (230–132).

Figure 4. Man weaving kente cloth on the loom-type used exclusively by West African men. Bonwire, Asante Region, Ghana, 1995. Photograph by the author.

During the 1790s, when Mungo Park recorded the folk life of the peoples whom he came in contact with as he traveled inland from the west coast of Africa along the Senegal and Niger Rivers, he makes it clear that in late eighteenth-century West Africa, the tasks of preparing the fibres for weaving fell to women. What is unclear in his narration, however, is whether or not women actually wove, for he refers to women as "spinning the garments" and he speaks of men as the weavers, but he also says, "almost every slave can weave." Perhaps it is the differences in the looms that caused Park to use the terminology he did. Because of its descriptive detail, I quote Park's late eighteenth-century passage on West African cloth production in full:

> [T]he women are very diligent in manufacturing cotton cloth. They prepare the cotton for spinning by laying it, in small quantities at a time, upon a smooth stone or piece of wood, and rolling the seeds out with a thick iron spindle, and they spin it with the distaff. The thread is not fine, but well twisted, and makes a very durable cloth. A woman with common diligence will spin from six to nine garments of this cloth in one-year . . .. The weaving is performed by the men. The loom is made exactly upon the same principle as that of Europe; but so small and narrow that the web [weft] is seldom more than four inches broad. The shuttle is of the common construction; but as the thread is coarse, the chamber is somewhat larger than the European.
>
> As the arts of weaving, dyeing and sewing, etc., may easily be acquired, those who exercise them are not considered in Africa as following any particular profession, for almost every slave can weave, and every boy can sew (Miller, ed., 1954:215–216).

The end product for the woven cloth was most often clothing. While unsewn cloths might be draped about the body, Mungo Park encountered West Africans in the late eighteenth century who cut and sewed it: "This cloth is cut into various pieces, and sewed into garments with needles of the natives own making" (ibid., 216).

West Africans ornamented the cloth with color and patterns. Most often they applied these decorative additions by dying the fabric with coloring matter extracted from various parts of different plants. (I found no references to mineral dyes.)[16] Sieber quotes John Barbot's late-seventeenth century description of West African dying techniques and says, "This description matches remarkably closely the technique used today in Nigeria" (201). A century later, Equiano (b. 1745) gives an appraisal of dying as he knew it in Benin:

> *The dress of both sexes are nearly the same. It generally consists of a long piece of calico, or muslin, wrapped loosely round the body . . .. This is usually dyed blue, which is our favourite color. It is extracted from a berry, and is brighter and richer than any I have seen in Europe . . .* (12).

Captain John Adams remarks several times about West African dyes and their native locales in his 1822 journal. He mentions "some valuable dyewoods, especially a bright yellow, like turmeric" used in Chambas, north of the Asante kingdom (48); the barwood from Majumba, on the coast of Angola, "is held in high estimation, as containing the greatest quantity of colouring matter" (172); "the dye from it [indigo] is very successfully used by the natives of Ardrah (50 miles from Lagos), Hio, and Jaboo. There are many other dyes, particularly a fine bright yellow, which the Africans cannot render permanent" (173). Of particular interest are Adams' notes on the methods by which the people of Ardrah added color to their fabrics. "Cotton thread is always dyed before it is woven and dressed" (80), while "kidskins are tied all over in knobs, very tight, then soaked for some days in a strong dye, and, when untied, exhibit a pattern resembling a star, or rays of blue and white radiating from round blue spots"(ibid.).

Thomas Winterbottom again pays tribute to the people he observed in Sierra Leone in the 1790s; these remarks concern dying procedures:

> They dye the threads, which are very fine and even, several colours, which are both vivid and permanent, especially blue, of a kind equal or superior to the finest blues in Europe. Upon the Gold Coast, this blue dye is obtained by infusing the leaves of a species of bignonia, and the root of a species of tabernamontana, in a solution of the ashes of palm nut in water . . . (Davidson, 289).

Prominent in the reports is the specific mention of blue dye, usually identified as coming from the indigo plant. A species of indigo, *I. tinctoria*, is native to Africa. Ryder references M. Heyman, a Dutchman, who was in Benin in the early eighteenth century: "In his search for natural products to augment commerce in the Benin region, Heyman met with meagre success" (158). Ryder, however, continues:

> Vegetable dye-stuffs seemed to offer better commercial prospects – especially a plant resembling indigo which produced a fast blue dye, and a stem and root which when ground yielded a green dye. Both plants grew abundantly in Benin where they were in common use for dying locally-woven cloth(159).

About the same time, Mungo Park provides us with a good description of the indigo dye process and evidence that West African cloth dying was a woman's craft.

> The women dye this cloth a rich and lasting blue colour, by the following simple process. The leaves of the indigo, when fresh gathered, are pounded in a wooden mortar, and mixed in a large earthen jar with a strong lye of wood ashes. Chamber-lye [urine] is sometimes added. The cloth is steeped in this mixture, and allowed to remain until it has acquired the proper shade. In Kaarta and Ludamar, where the indigo is plentiful, they collect the leaves, and dry them in the sun; and when they wish to use them they reduce a sufficient quantity to powder, and mix it with the lye, as before mentioned. Either way, the colour is very beautiful, with a fine purple gloss, and equal, in my opinion, to the best Indian or European blue (Miller, ed., 1954:216).

In Park's journal of his 1805–1806 voyage, he gives a longer description of the stages in indigo dying at Jindey, Kajaaga, and Kasson, again noting this to be a woman's occupation (1815:133–135). Park lists the "European Articles" and "African Produce" which he exchanged with the Bambarra. The African "produce" included "*Indigo* leaves beat and dried in lumps larger than one's fist, each 40 [cowries]" (as well as "prime" slaves of each sex and their price in cowries) (ibid., 253).

Although indigo appears to be the most popular dye among West Africans, Heyman located a plant or plants that West Africans used to produce a green color. As well, several Europeans merchants report on other West African dyestuffs that produced a variety of hues. For example, a French trading ship left Benin in 1769 with a cargo that included: "360 slaves and . . . red, blue, violet and yellow dyewoods, . . . cloths" (Ryder, 199); and among African items taken away by another French trader in 1789, were: "1, 000 cloths . . . and red, yellow, blue and violet dyewoods" (ibid., 221–222).

In his 1819 travelogue, George Robertson writes about Ijebu merchants on the Nigerian coast between Oyo and Benin. In an edited version of the work, P. C. Lloyd says that Robertson:

> . . . represented the inhabitants [of Ijebu] as active and industrious . . . making excellent cotton textiles, twelve to fourteen inches wide and very much sought after. Some were white, others of a very stable blue, still others of different colors, quite well dyed, except the yellows (Robertson, *Notes on Africa*, Lloyd, ed., 232–233).

Of his people, Osifekunde (b. Ijebu) reported "*the textiles they manufacture in such large quantities indicate a degree of perfection in the arts of spinning, weaving, and dyeing* . . ." (Lloyd, ed., 254). Using Osifekunde's testimony, d'Avezac writes: "The most common colors, after white and blue, are yellow, red, crimson, and green, some in solid colors, others multicolored" (Lloyd, ed., 263).

In West Africa, certain colors might only be worn by certain personages. For instance, Wargee of Astrakhan (born ca. 1770s), a Tartar from the west shore of the Caspian Sea, commenced on an African journey from the Mediterranean to the Gulf of Guinea around 1817. He gives the following information concerning the dress of Timbuktu royalty, wherein he notes that the very color of clothing was hierarchical:

> The king's wives wear a lower cloth fastened round them, and another thrown over their bodies; these are generally white, but the lower one sometimes blue; indeed, he says, coloured clothes are rarely to be seen; white and blue are the prevailing colours, varying in their quality according to the station in life of the wearer (Wilks, ed., 1963:181).

In addition to dying indigenous cloth, Africans sometimes unravelled European trade cloth and rewove the threads in patterns which more conformed to African aesthetics. Barbosa gives a description of these practices among the Swahili, ca. 1500–1518:

> In this same Sofala now of late they make great store of cotton and weave it, and from it they make much white cloth, and as they know not how to dye it, or have not the needful dyes, they take the Cambay cloths, blue or otherwise colored, and unravel them and make them up again, so that it becomes a new thing. With this thread and their own white they make much colored cloth, and from it they gain much gold . . . and it is here that the Moors have many *almadias* [boats] to convey cloth and much merchandise from Angoya . . .. In [Angoya] dwell many merchants who deal in gold, ivory, silk and cotton cloths and Cambay beads as those of Sofala were wont to do. The Moors of Sofala, Mombasa, Malindi and Kilwa convey these wares in very small craft concealed from our ships . . . (Davidson, 157).

Nearly 300 years later, Captain John Adams noticed that the Ardrah people "frequently weave threads taken from the red Indian silk taffity, having no red dye which they can render permanent" (79–80). Thomas Bowdich at Kumasi (Ashanti capital), 1817, observed:

> The caboceers, as did their superior captains and attendants, wore Ashanti cloths, of extravagant price from the costly foreign silks which had been unravelled to weave them in all the varieties of colour, as well as pattern; [these cloths] were of an incredible size and weight, and thrown over the shoulder exactly like a Roman toga; a small silk fillet generally encircles their temples, and massy gold necklaces, intricately wrought . . . (Davidson, 384–385; cf. *Art of West African Kingdoms*, 23–24).

Along with being highly knowledgeable in the dying arts and in reweaving threads taken from foreign cloths, West Africans also achieved ornamentation by stamping patterns onto the fabric (Figure 5).

> For another type of cloth . . . a pattern was stamped onto plain imported cloth. Stamps were carved from hard calabash shells and dyes were made from tree bark. There were many stamp designs: geometric patterns, stylized plants and animals, and abstract figures representing a proverb or story. Cloth was usually stamped in a bold combination of patterns, but sometimes a chief made a declaration of policy by appearing in a cloth stamped with a single design (*Art of West African Kingdoms*, 23).

Regarding gendered tasks, men as well as women might apply decoration to clothing. In the mid-nineteenth century, Sir Richard Burton described Benin cloth as "'fine cotton work, open and decorated with red worsted – a work confined to the ladies of the palace;' and Punch saw pieces decorated with life-sized figures that had been worked by the Oba's menservants" (Ryder 207). A modern comparison to the latter observation is offered by William Bascom. In 1969, he noted that Nigerian Yoruba "[m]en do embroidery, particularly on the large gowns worn by men and on men's caps [Figure 6]. Men also are tailors and dressmakers, and the ones who use hand-operated sewing machines" (101).

Cable offers a final note on West African cloth decoration which gives another interesting insight into men's contributions. Most important for this examination, it shows one way in which West Africans adapted their own know-how to an American setting.

> At Lowell [the *Amistad* captives] . . . were invited to visit a rug factory . . .. The Africans expressed great interest in the rugs, saying that weaving was a Mende specialty. In aid of their fund, they offered tablecloths and napkins for sale, which they had made by unravelling the edges of squares of linen or cotton and making the ravels into net fringes (121–122).

Figure 5. Master craftsman, Stephan Yaw Boakye, using hand-carved calabash stamp to decorate *adinkra* cloth. Ntonso, Asante Region, Ghana, 1995. Photograph by the author.

Trade Cloth

> Equiano, Benin, 1756: . . . *we have few manufactures. They consist for the most part of calicoes, earthenware, ornaments, and instruments of war and husbandry*. . .. *We also have markets* . . .. *These are sometimes visited by stout mahogany-colored men from the southwest of us: we call them* Oye-Eboe . . .. *They generally bring us* . . . *hats, beads* . . . (Davidson, 286).

Graham Connah suggests that "trading activity was almost as old as West African food production and the beginnings of a trading network could already have been in existence by about three thousand years ago" (1992:100). He goes on to point out that "it seems likely that an extensive

Figure 6. Man wearing smock decorated by male embroiders. Nyohene, Northern Region, Ghana, 1995. Photograph by the author.

trading network existed within West Africa before the Arab trade across the Sahara was developed . . .. After all, what ship would ever visit a port unless there was a chance of a cargo to collect?" (120). In other words, West Africans had a long history of trade among themselves before they exchanged with Arabs and later with Europeans. Among the items of exchange were clothing and, by at least 1,000 years ago, cloth.

> In ancient Mali: Castes of artisans were also respected for the esoteric value of their technological know-how. The *nyamakala* artisans – workers in iron, hide, and wood – maintained a rudimentary industry necessary in the more elaborated political system . . .. One industry, perhaps the most developed of all, was not restricted to the *nyamakala*. Weaving and other branches of the textile industry . . . (Levtzion, 119–120).

> Heinrich Barth, Western Sudan, 1851: The great advantage of Kano is, that commerce and manufactures go hand and hand, and that almost every family has its share in them. There is really something grand in this kind of industry, which spreads to the north as far as Murzuk, Ghat, and even to Tripoli; to the west, not only to Timbuktu, but in some degree even as far as the shores of the Atlantic, the very inhabitants of Arguin dress in the cloth woven and dyed in Kano; to the east . . . and southeast . . ., and is only limited by the nakedness of the pagan sans-culottes, who do not wear clothing (Davidson, 390).

Arguably, the most famous of all cloth produced in West Africa was Kano cloth which was sold from the great markets at Timbuktu. Levtzion reports: "In the seventeenth century there were twenty-six workshops of tailors in Timbuktu, each with fifty to a hundred apprentices" (179).

Africans also traded in Indian goods:

> Duarte Barbosa, Dofala, Swahili civilization, ca. 1500–1518: And the manner of their traffic was this: they came in small vessels . . . from the kingdoms of Kilwa, Mombasa, and Malindi, bringing many cotton cloths, some spotted and others white and blue, also some of silk, and many small beads . . . which things come to the said kingdoms from the great kingdom of Cambay [in Northwest India] . . . (Davidson, 156).

The balance of trade in cloth, however, eventually fell to the Europeans who brought in not only Indian textiles but also those of European manufacture. Leo Africanus reported, ca. 1510: "Here are many shops of artificers and merchants, and especially of such as weave linen and cotton cloth. And hither do the Barbarie merchants bring cloth of Europe" (Bovill, 147). In 1853, Heinrich Barth wrote:

> It was formerly supposed that Timbuktu was distinguished on account of its weaving, and that the export of dyed shirts from hence was considerable; but I have already had an opportunity of showing that this was entirely a mistake, almost the whole clothing of the natives themselves, especially of the wealthier classes, being imported either from Kano or from Sansandi, besides the calico imported from England (Davidson, 402; cf. Bovill, 243).

There were other great trading centers besides Timbuktu where imported cloth was merchandise. Leo Africanus describes the trade at Jenne: "Their cotton they sell unto the merchants of Barbarie, for cloth of Europe, for brazen vessels, for armour, and other such commodities" (Bovill, 149). At Gao, the capital of Askia, Africanus says:

> Here are exceeding rich merchants: and hither continually resort great store of Negroes which buy cloth here brought out of Barbarie and Europe . . .. Here it is likewise a certain place for slaves are to be sold, especially upon such days as the merchants are use to assemble . . . (ibid.).

With the advent of European traders on the African west coast, the indigenous people found another outlet for their cloth products.

> These cloths they sell to the *English* and *Portuguese*; one of the first sort for a bar of iron; three of the second for two bars; and two of the third for one bar; with which those *Europeans* trade at *Sierra Leona*, *Sherbro*, and on the south coast of *Guinea*, and purchase for them elephant teeth (*A Description of the Coasts of Nigritia, vulgarly called North-Guinea*, in A. and J. Churchill, eds., *A Collection of Voyages and Travels*, London, 1746, V:77–78; reprinted in Fishel and Quarles, 14).

Ryder notes that E. Bold (*Merchant's and Mariners' African Guide*, 1819, London) "stressed the importance of Ijebu cloths bought in the Benin River for ships trading to the south where these cloths equalled, in his estimation, the finest Manchester products" (234).

But clearly these examples of the trading importance of indigenous cloth were exceptions by the eighteenth and nineteenth centuries; the demand for imported fabrics are well-documented. Arabs first carried Indian cottons to Africa in exchange for "ivory, or gold, or horses for the warriors of India" (Beer, 9), but " [i]n the middle of the seventeenth century, the Dutch and English became immersed in trade in India." A consequence was "the development of block printing in Holland, England, and France, as a result of these importations" of India chintz (ibid.).

The West African clamor to accumulate articles of European dress was accompanied, very early, by a desire for nonindigenous textiles. Leo Africanus notes the esteem by which the Africans held European cloth in 1550: "There is not any cloth of Europe so coarse, which will not be sold for fower ducates an ell, and if it be anything fine they will give fifteen ducates for an ell: and an ell of the scarlet of Venice or of Turkie-cloath is here worth thirtie ducates" (Bovill, 150).[17]

At first, cloth items were in the form of presentations to local kings in return for trading privileges. At Mina (i.e. , Elmina, Gold Coast), 1482, a representative from Portugal, "sent to the king and his men a good present of many lambres, basins, manillas and other cloth, which was to be given to them first before all else to ensure their goodwill . . ." (from the translation of Ruy de Pina's chronicle of John II, 1792, in J. W. Blake, *Europeans in West Africa*, 1942, reported in Davidson, 215).

That European goods remained prestigious items even for ordinary West Africans 500 years later is suggested in an entry by Mungo Park. In a village near Segu, the capital of Bambarra, a woman takes Park to her home and feeds him: "In the morning I presented my compassionate landlady with two of the four buttons which remained on my waistcoat; the only recompense I could make her" (Davidson, 372).

In 1831–1832, A. C. P. Gamitto reported this about the slave women of the *Kazembe* people of Malawi (Central Africa) who worked the gold mines: "Owners of Bars usually have imported cloths, beads, etc. , at them to sell to their slaves at exorbitant prices; and so these slaves buy from any passing merchant, secretly, what they need . . ." (Davidson, 342).

The vast influx of imported cloth, however, did not mean the end of indigenous production. In his report of the market at Ardrah, fifty miles from Lagos, Captain John Adams demonstrates that the merchandise of West African traders included both imported and indigenous cloth and clothing items. [Their stalls]

> . . . exhibited for sale the manufactures of Europe and India, of various kinds, such as handkerchiefs, both red and blue, from Manchester; silk linens, silesias from Germany, silk handkerchiefs, cuttanees and taffities from Madras . . .. There are also exhibited for sale, cloth from Eyeo and Jaboo, spun cotton, dyed and otherwise; kid skins, dyed and dressed; sandals . . . ([1822] 1966:89–90).

Yet even with their own quality cloth products, their grand markets, and their intricate trading patterns, the Africans' desire for European cloth became enormous: " [T]he imports into Kano . . . [a]part from salt and a coarse silk from Tripoli . . . consisted of a wide range of European goods: Manchester cottons, French silks . . ." (Bovill, 243). D'Avezac, writes that Osifekunde related: "Linen cloth imported from Europe is valued by the Ijebu as having the same superiority over the cotton that we ourselves [i.e., Europeans] recognize. Ordinary or embroidered silk textiles, even our most luxurious, are not unknown to these people, and the rich wear these magnificent clothes on special occasions. Velvet, satin, and brocade are used in the costume of the sovereign" (Lloyd, ed., 264). [For a glossary of trade-cloth terms used by Europeans, see Appendix I.][18]

Numerous traders' and travelers' accounts detail the items that Europeans traded to the Africans; nearly all these lists include cloth and pieces of clothing.

> John Barbot, West African voyages, 1678–1682: The Dutch have Coesveld linen, sleysiger lywat, old sheets. Leyden serges, dyed indigo-blue, perpetuanas, green, blue and purple, Konings-Kleederen, anabas, large and narrow, made at Harlem, Cyprus and Turkey stuffs . . . silk stuffs, blue and white . . . chints . . . cloth of Cabo-Verdo . . .. The English . . . have micanees fine and coarse; many sorts of chints, or Indian callicoes printed . . . many sorts of white callicoes; blue and white linen, China sattins . . . Welsh plain, boysades, rombergs, clouts, gingarus taffeties, amber, brandy, flower, Hamburgh brawls, and white, blue and white, and red chequer'd linen, narrow Guinea stuffs chequer'd, ditto broad, old hats, purple beads (Davidson, 251–252).

In his history of Benin during the time of the European trade, A. C. Ryder cites primary documents which itemize the cloth commodities that Europeans traded to the Africans. I composed the following distilled list to show the rich variety of available cloth types. The items are given as they appear chronologically in merchants inventories in Ryder's text (*passim*). Note that the prevalence of Indian cloth in the early years gives way to luxury European cloths by the early eighteenth century:

> India Cambay (early 1500s), blue India silk(1505), Cambay printed chintz (1505), Bruges green satin (1535), Calicut cloth (1582), painted Calycot (1582), Rouen canvas (white and brown, 1582), Silesian cloth(1623), *kannekens* (late 17th Century), Indian cottons (late 17th century), Ypres cloth (late 17th century), raised Hessian cloth (late 17th century), Indian chintz (flower pattern, 18th century), East Indian muslin or sheeting (18th century), fine East Indian chintz (1715), French linen (1715), Irish tablecloths (1715), rough Irish sheets (1715), French silk (1717), Haarlem cloth (decorated with large flower pattern, early 1770s), Cholet kerchief (early 1770s), Nîmes silk satin (early 1770s), Breton

linen (early 1770s), Rouen cotton (early 1770s), and Nîmes silk kerchief (early 1770s).

In spite of the apparent regard the Africans held for European cloth, the merchandise was not always of the highest standards. In Sierra Leone, Rev. John Newton (1788) remarked:

> Not an article that is capable of diminution or adulteration is delivered genuine or entire . . .. The linen and cotton cloths are opened, and two or three yards, according to the length of the piece, cut off: not from the end but out of the middle, which is not so readily noticed (Davidson, 268) . . .. The natives are cheated in the number, weight, measure or quality of what they purchase in every possible way (269).

Even with these unscrupulous tactics, more and more European cloth and clothing came into Africa. At first, Europeans promoted African cloth both as a local trade item and as an exported one; but in time, trade in African-manufactured cloth would be disrupted by Portuguese merchants and the other Europeans who came later. Although indigenous African cloth continued to be used within the communities of production, the European trade in imported cloth eventually forced a decline in the internal and external trade in West African cloth.

African cloth was of a high quality, and this was not the problem with finding a European market. The foremost problem was that, unlike European trade cloth, West African cloth continued to be hand-made and, therefore, the growing demand could not be met. The mayhem produced by European involvement in African internal trade is highlighted by the circumstances that occurred with the Portuguese presence in Kongo where men produced a highly valued raffia palm cloth. In her history of the Kongo, Anne Hilton reports on the undermining of the Luanda cloth trade in the sixteenth century by the European governors of the Kongo kingdom (167).

The Kongo, of course, was not the only country whose economy was affected by the trade. In his extensive analysis of the European presence in Benin, Ryder notes that "Benin was the most important slave mart west of the Niger" (1969:233). The importance of European cloth in West African culture and its prominence during the slave trade, marks the underlying theme of his detailed social history. Ryder describes the final disintegration of Benin cloth as a viable trading commodity, and in so doing, he also presents the second problem encountered by the Africans in their attempt to market their cloth to Europeans: it was narrower than the customary width of European cloth.[19]

During the period of the slave-trade, Europeans had only a toe hold along the West Coast of Africa. Nevertheless, they could utilize their fortifications and advanced weaponry and, in at least one noteworthy instance, this completely destroyed one African country's ability to trade its cloth.[20]

One way that we express our humanity is the manner in which we adorn our bodies. In many parts of our world, cloth is used as one form of that expression. The culturally specific meaning and importance that cloth came to have for West Africans may be best expressed in a memory that Captain John Adams had of John Africa, a West African trader he met sometime between 1786 and 1800:

> I once observed this African bestow a valuable present on a captain, in so delicate a manner, as would have done honour to an European of refined sentiment. The captain was a great favourite of his; and the ship which he commanded, being on the point of sailing, he went on board to take leave of him. Having done so, and got into his canoe, he dropped astern under the cabin port, and put through it, into the cabin, three elephant's teeth, weighing at least forty pounds each: he then called out to the captain, 'Da something for buy your woman cloth,' (meaning his wife in England); and paddled away as fast as possible (142–143).

Trading Cloth for Human Beings

Societies of Africans made their own cloth for the primary purpose of clothing themselves. They also traded cloth and clothing with other African social groups, sometimes to acquire other Africans.

> Asa-Asa (b. in Bycla, near Egie; narrative published in 1831): *They took away brothers, and sisters, and husbands, and wives; they did not care about this. They were sold for cloth or gunpowder, sometimes for salt or guns* . . . (123). *I was sold six times over [in Africa], sometimes for money, sometimes for cloth, sometimes for a gun* (124).

Cable includes in her Appendix I (n. p. n.) the brief biographical information collected from thirty-six of the captive Africans by John A. Barber (*A History of the Amistad Captives*, 1840). Cloth, presumably indigenous African cloth, and clothing are interwoven in five of the biographies. One account notes that a man was sold for an article of clothing. Two accounts note the purchase of wives: one bought for twenty cloths and an article of clothing, another purchased for ten cloths.

> [Pung-wu-ni's] mother's brother sold him for a coat.
>
> Ndzha-gnwaw-ni: He has a wife and one child; he gave twenty cloths and one shawl for his wife.
>
> Gba-tu (from the country of Tu-ma): was sent by his father to a village to buy clothes; on his return, he was seized by six men, and his hands were tied; was ten days in going to Lomboko.
>
> Ba-u: In his country all have to pay for their wives; for his, he had to pay 10 cloths, 1 goat, 1 gun, and plenty of mats; his mother made the cloth for him.
>
> Gua-kwoi (Balu country): When going to the gold country to buy clothes, he was taken and sold to a Vai-man who sold him to a Spaniard named *Peli.*

Forms of slavery existed on the African continent before the arrival of Europeans, and continued long afterwards.

> Mungo Park, late 1790s: Hired servants, by which I mean persons of free condition, voluntarily working for pay, are unknown in Africa; and this observation naturally leads me to consider the condition of the slaves, and the various means by which they are reduced to so miserable a state of servitude. This unfortunate class are found, I believe, in all parts of this extensive country, and constitute a considerable branch of commerce with the states on the Mediterranean, as well as with the nations of Europe (Miller, ed., 1954:219).

The kings of the various African countries usually controlled this trade which was overseen by middlemen, a practice that continued during most of the European trade period. And from the beginning, in exchange for trading rights, the kings and chiefs demanded tribute from the Europeans, and very often the presentations were in the form of European goods. In 1483, the Portuguese first arrived in Kongo, and the Kongo received "rich gifts" from them. In 1491, the gifts brought for the Kongo included cloth, clothing and ornaments (Hilton, 50).

Another early European account comes from Duarte Pacheco Pereira who writes (probably between 1505 and 1508) from first-hand knowledge of the Yoruba states along the coast. In his discussion of Portuguese and Yoruba trade relations Pereira says: "the trade is mainly in slaves (who are sold for twelve or fifteen copper bracelets each), but there is also some ivory" (Biobaku, 9).

In a very short time, however, cloth became one of the main items of exchange for humans. For instance, Ryder makes clear that early on, European and Indian textiles were part of the standard items of negotiation in trading with the Oba of Benin and other officials for African commodities, notably slaves. Ryder says that in a Portuguese trade in Benin, 1526, while most of the slaves were bought with manillas or cowries,

> . . . 30 slaves were bought from the Oba in exchange for all the cloth in the cargo – a transaction which suggests that the ruler had established rights of pre-emption to certain categories of merchandise. He gave 15 slaves for two and a half pieces of red cloth measuring 81 *covados* (60½ yards), and another 15 for 300 linen "cloths" . . . (63).

> Alonso de Palencia, a Spaniard on "the coasts nearest to Guinea," 1500s: [The king of that region] agreed to the barter [with Spanish traders] of slaves for brass rings, small oval leather shields, clothes of diverse colors, and other objects, which the poverty of the inhabitants caused them to covet greatly (Davidson, 221).

Hilton notes that in the 1630s, the Portuguese made the following demands in the Kongo:

> Luanda slaves that escaped to Kongo were to be returned and Kongo was to pay 900 loads of indigenous cloth as compensation for the Portuguese losses incurred during the occupation [by the Dutch] . . .. At that time 900 loads equalled 1, 000 slaves (164). [In the late eighteenth century] Mbamba sold slaves at Ambriz in exchange for guns, pots, powder, and cloth . . .. They sold the best slaves at Musul in exchange for British and French brandy, glass, and cloth . . . (211) . . .. Nsundi and the people of the River Zaire traded with Kibangu and with the Vili who sold the slaves at Sonyo and Cabinda in exchange for cloth . . . (212).

> John Adams (in West Africa between 1786 and 1800): [T]he Lagos people . . . be themselves traders . . .. They therefore go out in their canoes to Ardrah and Badgry, and to the towns situated at the NE extremity of Cradoo [Ikorodu] lake [i.e. Lagos Lake], where they purchase slaves, Jaboo [Ijebu] cloth, and such articles as are required for domestic consumption (Biobaku, 11).

Levtzion writes that "The most essential commodities of the trade eventually became the medium of exchange" and that "Pieces of cloth were the money in Zawila, in the Sus, on the Gambia, and in Kanem" by the 14th century (120). Ryder reports that when a Portuguese vessel reached Benin in 1526

> . . . the pilot was met by three officials sent there by the Oba; these had to be paid five "cloths" apiece for unspecified services . . .. This is also the first reference to the "cloth" (*pano*) as a standard unit in Benin trade, though in the Forcados River it had been known at least as early as 1522. As used in Benin in 1526 it was a piece of linen two-thirds of a yard in length, and almost certainly equivalent to the earlier 'customary yard' . . .. the 'cloth' was already on the way to becoming

a national measure of value. After visiting the Oba and delivering his present (a piece of Holland cloth, a damask hat trimmed with gold thread and a piece of fine cloth dyed in the grain), the pilot and clerk settled in Benin City to conduct their trade from a house they rented for ten 'cloths' (62–63).

The trade in cloth for human beings eventually reaches an existential level when we consider that the Portuguese term for human beings traded into slavery was "*peca*," literally "piece," "a trade term also employed for metal, beads, cloth, and other items of commerce" (Blier, 395 after Ryder, 293). Similarly, "a piece of India" (cotton goods from India) came to mean "equivalent to the price of a man" (Braudel, 442).[21]

The following is a fragment from the ship's book of the *Sao Miguel* trading to Benin in the year 1522:

ACCOUNT OF THE PIECES WHICH WERE BOUGHT FOR LINEN.

item. The pilot bought one female piece aged 18 years more or less for 24 customary yards of linen.

item. The pilot bought one female piece aged 17 more or less for 24 customary yards of linen. (reprinted in Ryder, 299).

A Slave's Body

The clothing one puts on one's corporeal self helps to mark one's place in humanity. And just as the human being may be embodied through clothing, so too the body may be deprived of its humanness by stripping it of its clothing. In a rare description of the Middle Passage from an African perspective, Mahommah Gardo Baquaqua (from Djougou, north of present-day Benin) said: "*We were thrust into the hold of the vessel in a state of nudity, the males being crammed on one side and the females on the other . . .*" (testimony taken ca. 1820s, biography published in 1854; reprinted in Austin, 624).

Chief factor (or governor) for the Dutch West India Company, 1705: . . . we send them on Board our Ships with the very first opportunity; before which their Masters strip them of all they have on their Backs; so that they come Aboard stark-naked as well Women and Men; In which condition they are obliged to continue, if the Master of the Ship is not so Charitable (which he commonly is) as to bestow something on them to cover their Nakedness (Davidson, 260).

Besides taking away someone's clothing, another way to attempt to dehumanize someone else's body is to mark its skin.

> Chief factor (or governor) for the Dutch West India Company, 1705: In the mean while a burning Iron, with the Arms or Names of the Companies, lyes in the Fire; with which ours are marked on the Breast.
>
> This is done that we may distinguish them from The slaves of the English, French or others; (which are also marked with their Mark) and to prevent the Negroes exchanging them for worse, at which they have a good Hand.
>
> I doubt not but this Trade seems very barbarous to you, but since it is followed by mere necessity it must go on; but we yet take all possible care that they are not burned too hard, especially the Women, who are more tender than the Men.
>
> We are seldom long detained in the buying of these Slaves, because their price is established, the Women being one fourth or fifth part cheaper than the Men (Davidson, 259).

> Theophilus Conneau (*A Slaver's Log Book*, 1854):They are then marked; this is done with a hot pipe sufficiently heated to blister the skin. Some use their initials made of silver wire. The object of this disagreeable operation is done only when several persons ship slaves in one vessel, otherwise when only one proprietor is sole owner it is dispensed with.
>
> This disgusting duty is one of those forcible cruelties which cannot be avoided. When several proprietors ship in one vessel it is indispensable to mark them, in order that on the arrival the consignees may know them. Also, when death takes place in the passage, by the mark it is ascertained whose loss it is, as every Negro thrown over the board during the voyage is registered in the log book.
>
> But in extenuation for this somewhat brutal act, let me assure the reader that it is ever done as lightly as possible, and just enough for the mark to remain only six months; when and if well done, it leaves the skin as smooth as ever. This scorching sign is generally made on the fleshy part of the arm to adults, to children on the posterior([1854] 1977:96).

In West Africa, traders also ordered captive people to groom their bodies in preparation for sale; yet this, too, was but another attempt to devalue the body's humanness. Venture (b. ca. 1729, Guinea), sold into slavery by members of another African tribe, related in his autobiography (1897),

> *. . . our master told us to appear to the best possible advantage for sale. I was bought on board by one Robert Mumford, steward of said vessel, for four gallons of rum and a piece of calico, and called Venture . . .* (11).

Over time and space, the various patterns in these relationships between Africans and Europeans profoundly affected what would happen in the

United States as regards the perceptions Europeans held about the slave's body. As well, these relationships would affect the perceptions Blacks held concerning the body's embodiment through clothing.

The Will to Adorn

Clothing is a material indicator of culture, and the historical accounts contribute evidence for three outstanding patterns about West Africans and their clothing in general. First, West Africans were not conservative in terms of what they wore. Not being bound by constrictions on types of dress, they freely borrowed items of apparel from new peoples with whom they came in contact. Second, they displayed a preference for wearing cloth as is, with little or no additional shaping by sewing and other means. The clothing was loose, it neither bound nor constricted the body. Third, they wore clothing made from a variety of materials woven into a rich assortment of patterns, further decorated with bright hues and added ornamentation. This means that West Africans held a heightened appreciation and fondness for the colorfulness and for the tactile qualities of the clothing they donned.

Zora Neale Hurston wrote that: "The will to adorn is the second most notable characteristic in Negro expression" ([1934] 1988:50). Her remarks about twentieth-century African Americans mirror what others had noted about the West Africans whom they had encountered in earlier centuries. The West Africans who were brought to the New World filtered new ideas about bodily raiments through much older ideas about self-presentation.

Notes

1. In 1958, Rayford D. Logan wrote a historiography of the African American comprehension of Africa during the first half of the twentieth century. He makes evident that the distorted or contradictory views held by many Black Americans resulted from not only isolation from Africa but because of lack of "factual information."

2. Thirty years later, Captain John Smith, after having travelled in West Africa from 1786 to 1800, wrote: "The cotton and the sugar-cane are found growing spontaneously in many parts of Africa; the former might be cultivated with great success, particularly upon the sea-coast from Popo to Lagos, and also at Malemba" (173).

3. In the earliest encounters, Europeans usually describe some segment of each West African social group as wearing some form of bodily attire, while, in contrast,

East, Central, and South Africans often are noted for not wearing any form of clothing:

> Duarte Barbosa (a Portuguese at Monomotapa, Central Africa, essentially in Zimbabwe and western Mozambique, early 1500s): [The Cafres, i.e., heathens to the Moors] are black men and go naked save that they cover their private parts with cotton cloth from the waist down. Some are clad in skins of wild beasts, and some, the most noble, wear capes of these skins with tails which trail on the ground, as a token of state and dignity. They leap as they go, and sway their bodies so as to make these tails fly from one side to the other (Davidson, 180–181).
>
> Duarte Barbosa (on Mozambique Island, ca, 1500): On the mainland . . . [t]he land is inhabited by heathen who are like beasts, going naked and smeared with red clay. Their private parts are wrapped in strips of blue cotton cloth with no other clothing (Davidson, 158).
>
> Ludivico de Varthema on the mainland from Mozambique (originally published 1510): We found some races of people quite black and quite naked, except that the men wore their natural parts in a piece of bark, and the women wore a leaf before and one behind. These people have their hair bristling up and short (John Winter Jones, trans. , 228).

4. Ina Corrine Brown observes: "There is, however, no essential connection between clothing and modesty, since every society has its own conception of modest dress and behaviour" (10).

5. The life story of Osifekunde, an Ijebu (on the Guinea Coast), was taken during the 1810s by the French ethnographer Marie Armand Pascal d'Avezac-Macaya and published in 1845.

6. A contemporary example of similar sumptuary codes comes from modern Asante culture:

> When a chief attends a ceremony, a generous swath of silk, intricately woven in patterns of bright colors, drapes his body. A retinue of specialists accompany him . . .. Those who wear silk follow strict sumptuary laws, which dictate that the weave and pattern of a chief's clothing are to be the finest (National Museum of Art, *Art of West African Kingdoms*, 22).

7. Concerning contemporary Africa, Dale Idiens writes: "The impact of imported European goods has already affected a marked decline in hand weaving although there is still a local demand in many places for handwoven cloth for ritual use, in funerals, for example, and for dress wear on important occasions (the latter sometimes reinforced by nationalist feelings)" (1980:20).

8. Corresponding Western examples might include the crown and coronation robe worn by British monarchs, the costume of Greek Orthodox priests, the white veil and gown of a bride, and the dark-colored funeral clothes of mourners.

9. William Leo Hansberry offers a cautionary note concerning early European accounts of African sacred ceremonies. He writes that most religions are distinguished by two aspects: "first, their spiritual or esoteric aspects and, second, their outward or exoteric elements, including the dogmas, rites and ceremonies

which are vehicles designed to provide ways and means through which allegiance and nominal allegiance to the spirit and inner teachings of the religions may be expressed. Hence, though there were notable exceptions, a number of Portuguese, Dutch, and English explorers who visited Africa in the fifteenth, sixteenth and seventeenth centuries allowed themselves to be impressed almost wholly by the often unique and colorful, though grossly misunderstood, externals of African religions and generally overlooked or missed entirely their inner teachings and spiritual essences" (97).

10. Water also links the Sande ceremony and that of Christian baptism.

11. Cheryl Plumer gives an extensive, regional, and historical overview of African textile production and trade in cloth in *African Textiles: An Outline of Handcrafted Sub-Saharan Fabrics* (1971). Barbara Nordquist offers a more compact essay on modern African traditional textiles and dress, including fibre types, weaving styles, and applied decoration in "African Traditional Dress and Textiles: Material Form" (1990:19–38); also, see Lydia Wares, "African Dress" (1990:39–47).

12. Renée Boser-Sarivaxevanis notes:

> The African wool-bearing sheep is very delicate and fragile. Apart from the fact that it succumbs to numerous diseases, its survival is only assured by proximity to a relatively abundant water source. Outside of Upper Senegal, the Niger Bend, several islands downstream of the river and the Fulani Liptako, it is unknown in West Africa (n. 3, p. 27).

13. Anne Hilton notes that raffia cloth was used as currency in the northeastern part of the middle zone of Zaire. She says that the cloth was not only valued in Africa, but "raffia cloth was a luxury item in the west" as well (7). Hilton traces the Kongo trade routes for this cloth and notes that even though it was known for its poor durability, it nevertheless held a high intrinsic value. Raffia cloth remained a popular and prestigious item even after the Portuguese disrupted the traditional trade routes for the raffia cloth by expanding the trade to the south (106–107, 164).

14. Eicher goes on to make the important point that: "Despite this competition, the demand for locally woven cloth continued. Even today handwoven cloth remains important for many traditional ceremonies and events. It grew in popularity with the rising spirit of nationalism generated by independence in 1960" (ibid.).

15. Carol Kroll describes this as the common method used in India (6).

16. Picton and Mack document the types of dyes and the traditional techniques for dying cloth in their encompassing work on contemporary *African Textiles* (37–42). They make particular note of indigo and other vegetable dyes.

17. Levtzion summarizes the earliest descriptions concerning the importation of European cloth and clothing into West Africa:

> The development of a local textile industry did not reduce the volume of cloth imports. These were mainly luxurious clothes such as the Egyptian dress of wealthy people in Walata and the European imported clothes of the king of Mali. Silk products were exported to the Sudan from Tunisia and Granada. About 1470 Bendetto Dei reported an active trade

of European cloth in Timbuktu. Leo Africanus met the same in Gao. These European products reached the entrepóts of the Sahel across the desert. By that time the Portuguese on the Atlantic coast had begun to trade in cloth, responding to a great demand by the local traders. On the Casamance, where the people wove fine cloth, the Portuguese exchanged their cloth for the local woven cloth. In Elmira the Portuguese met with a demand for Moroccan cloth, as the people there developed a taste for this cloth, which had reached them for some time through the Dyula commercial network (180).

The Mande-speaking Muslim traders, with whom the Portuguese negotiated on the Gambia, were the Diakhanke (168) . . .. The Diahanke traders brought down the Gambia river slaves, hides, local cotton, and gold which they exchanged for horses and fancy clothes (169).

18. Levtzion notes:

The most essential commodities of the trade eventually became the media of exchange. In the eleventh-century commercial centre of Siliá on the Senegal there were millet, salt, copper rings, and small strips of cotton . . .. Pieces of cloth were the money in Zawíla, in the Sús, on the Gambia, and in Kanem (120).

When Europe gradually recovered from its long economic recession [in the eleventh and the twelfth centuries] its exports – mainly cloth – paid for the imports and even attracted a growing amount of gold(130) . . .. In the twelfth and thirteenth centuries Italian merchants established factories (*fundúgs*) in the principal coast towns of the Maghrib, from Tripoli to Ceuta on the Mediterranean, and as far as Mássaon the Atlantic. Varieties of European cloth were in great demand in the Maghrib because of their quality and durability . . .. The most important imports on record were skins, leather goods and alum, needed for the dying industry (130–131).

19. Ryder says:

[In 1717] the [Dutch] company made one more effort to find a profitable outlet for Benin cloth – this time in the European market. The factor was to look into the possibility of having cloths made larger, and sent samples to Europe, together with 6, 000 pounds of local cotton yarn. Nothing would come of this project because the looms on which Benin cloths were woven could not produce the broad, long cloth suited to a European market (159–160).

20. Hilton writes:

The Portuguese used this [indigenous] cloth as the official general purpose currency in Luanda and as the most important means of exchange in the slave trade south of Kongo . . .. The Dutch occupation in Luanda, and more especially the Portuguese blockade of the interior, had drastically reduced the slave trade and with it the demand for Kongo cloth . . .. When the Portuguese restored Luanda the cloth currency was in tatters, and 'nearly extinguished' (166). [T]he Portuguese experienced considerable difficulty in re-establishing trade, and the demand for cloth remained relatively low. As demand increased, Luanda imported cloth from Loango rather than from Kongo (167).

21. Joanne Eicher says that the modern Kalabari of Nigeria refer to India madras as "real India" (personal communication, March 1994).

2

Constructing Cloth and Clothing in the Antebellum South

. . . the making of a piece of cloth is never just the making of a piece of cloth . . . (John Picton 1995:13).

Commercial Goods

African Americans and whites in the nineteenth century shared the same two sources for their clothing: they either produced it at home or they purchased commercially manufactured items. The bulk of commercial fabric was manufactured in New England. After the American Revolution, the New England textile industry grew enormously, fed in large part by the boom in Southern cotton production (Hollen, et al. , 1988:24). The first power mill for spinning cotton in the United States went into operation in 1790; wool was not carded and spun by power until 1801 (Morris, 494). These machines developed in New England, the center of commercial textile production through the nineteenth century. Lowell, Massachusetts, became the most important site for the manufacture of factory-made cloth.[1] Particular terms denote commercially manufactured cloth; for example, many narrators refer to "lowell cloth," a textile produced in the mills in Lowell.

Charlie Davenport (ca. 100 years):*Us wore lowell-cloth shirts. It was a coarse tow-sackin'* (7. 2:37 [MS]).

I found few instances in the *Narratives* where the contributors were aware of local mills, and the mills which they mentioned only processed wool, but did not weave the actual cloth. In some cases, "mill" and "gin" or "factory" were synonymous terms meaning a commercial processing establishment.

Rachel Cruze (b. 1856): *Yes, we raised sheep – by the hundreds. The raw wool was first sent to the mill to be carded, then we would spin it* (S1. 5. 2:297 [TN/OH]).

Sina Banks (86): *The sheep were sheared in May. The wool was washed, picked apart and combed and taken to the factory to be made into rolls* (S1. 12. 17 [MO/OK]).

Whites might wear both homemade and store-bought clothing.

Zek Brown (80 years): *Many days Ise watched my mammy wo'k de loom makin' cloth. 'Twas a tudder woman dat made all de clothes. All de clot an' clothes am made right thar by de cullud fo'k. De Marster's family had store clothes fo' de nice dresses but hom spun fo' everyday* (S2. 3. 2:496 [TN/TX]).

Mollie Dawson (b. 1852): *Of course, Marser Newman and his folks wore a little bettah clothes den de slaves did, but de clothes dat dey wore fer every day on de farm was jest like ours, but de clothes dat dey had fer special occasions was made outten de best cotton and was bettah made den ours, and sometimes dey would buy cloth at de sto' and makes der clothes to wear away from home* (S1. 4. 3:1127 [TX]).

Commercially manufactured cloth also evidently reached a few plantations for the purpose of making the African Americans' clothing.

Della Mun Bibles (b. ca. 1856): *Everybody wore the clothes made of cloth and made at home. When the cotton was hauled by ox waggons [sic] to them places [Austin and Houston] and sold, the wagons always brought back a full load of supplies . . . some different kinds of cloth* (S. 2. 2. 1:291 [TX]).

Louis Hughes (b. 1843, enslaved in Mississippi and Virginia):*Each piece of [homemade] cloth contained forty yards, and this cloth was used in making clothes for the servants. About half of the whole amount required was this made at home; the remainder was bought, and as it was heavier it was used for winter clothing* (41).

Martha Everette (b. ca. 1852) reported that some clothes were made on her cotton plantation, but other times *"Master'd send us clothes from Savannah"* (S1. 3. 1. :240 [GA]). The next contributor noted that although the enslaved people's clothing was far from adequate, in her case, the clothes were both commercially produced as well as homemade.

Emma Knight (b. ca. 1845): *We didn't have hardly any clothes and most of the time they was just rags. We went barefoot until it got real cold . . .. Late in the Fall master would go to Hannibal or Palmyra and bring us shoes and clothes. We got those things only once a year. I had to wear the young master's overalls for underwear and linseys* [apparently homemade] *for a dress* (S1. 2. 4:202 [MO]).

Evidently both male and female enslaved people held machine-made cloth and store-bought clothing in esteem; for, if money came their way, they often spent it on cloth and clothing.[2]

Peter Randolph (b. 1820, enslaved in Virginia) noted differences between people enslaved on plantations and those enslaved in cities: "*The slaves in the cities . . . have the privilege of hiring themselves out, by paying their owners so much, at stated times . . .. They do very well, . . . All can dress well . . .*" (1855:58). The narrators who had been enslaved in rural areas, nevertheless, show an equal regard for commercially produced clothing:

Mandy Jones (80 years): *Yes, chile, we had Sunday close. Once I 'member my daddy bought my mammy a beautiful blue dress, an' paid $7. 00 for it. Yes, he had ample money. Marse Stewart let him make cotton baskets at night and paid him good money for 'em* (S1. 8. 3:1230 [MS]).

Lucy Lewis: *When we all real good, Marsa John used to give us small money to buy with. I spent mos' mine to buy clothes* (5. 3:15 [TX]).

Betty Brown: *My mamma could hunt good ez any man. Us'tuh be a coup'la pedluh men come 'round' wuth they packs. My mammy'd a'ways have a pile o' hides tuh trade with 'em fer calico prints n' trinkets, n' sech-like, but mos'ly fo' calico prints* (11. 8:53 [MO]).

Nan Stewart (b. 1850): *I us' tu gather de turkey eggs an' guinea eggs an' sell 'em. I gits ten cents dozen fo' de eggs . . .. What I do with my money? Chile I saved it to buy myself a nackeen [?] dress* (16. 4:87 [WV/OH]).

Susan McIntosh (b. 1851): *Marse Billy let the slaves raise chickens, and cows, and have cotton patches too. They would sell butter, eggs, chickens, brooms, made out of wheat straw and such like. They took the money and bought calico, muslin and good shoes, pants, coats and other nice things for their Sunday clothes* (13. 3:81 [GA]).

Thomas Cole (b. 1845): *Den each family have some chickens and sell dem and de eggs and maybe go huntin' and sell de hides and git some money. Den us buy what am Sunday clothes with dat money, such as hats and pants and shoes and dresses* (4. 1:227 [AL/TX].

Cicely Cawthon (78 years): *Pore white folks used to hang around the quarters, and if they could beat you out of anything they did. They'd trade the slaves out of their rations for calico and stuff* (S1. 3. 1:183 [GA]).

Calvin Moye (b. 1842): *Every Christmas morning Maser Ingram would come around and gives ever family a present of $25. and tells dem dat was their Christmas present and to spend it for things dey needed worse . . . de rest of de folks bought shoes and clothes for Sunday with their money. We didn't needs to buy no groceries nor work clothes either . . . cause Maser Ingram furnished all dat. So we all bought Sunday clothes 'ceptin Uncle Zeke and he just wore de clothes dat was made in de plantation. He said we better save all de money dat we can gits our hands on cause we was going to be free some day and we would needs it cause we would has to hustle for ourselves and we would needs money* (S2. 7. 6:2842–2843 [GA, TX/TX]).[3]

James L. Smith, while enslaved in Virginia, kept some of the earnings he was supposed to give to his "master" for Smith's work in a shoe-making shop. That whites viewed well-dressed Blacks as an affront is evident in the episode:

In this way, I saved at one time fifteen dollars; I went to the store, bought a piece of cloth, carried it to the tailor and had a suit made . . .. You can imagine how I looked the following Sunday; I was very proud and loved to dress well . . ..

The first Sunday that I was arrayed in my new suit, I was passing the court house bounds, when I saw my master and a man named Betts standing near by. Betts caught sight of me; says he: 'Lindsey, come here.' Not knowing what he wanted, I went to him; whereupon he commenced looking first at me, then at my master; then at my master, then at me; finally he said: 'Who is the master; Lindsey or you, for he dresses better than you do? Does he own you, or do you own him?' (reprinted in Bontemps, 164).

The potential for enslaved people to purchase (or trade for) their own cloth and clothing probably was not the norm, but as they gave detailed descriptions of the more well-to-do white people's dress, the African Americans exhibited in another way their appreciation of commercially produced clothing.

Rebecca Jane Grant: *Old times, they'd make underbodies with whalebone in it. There was something they'd put over the whoop they call, 'Follow me, boy'.*

Used to wear the skirts long, with them long trains that trail behind you. You'd take and tuck it up behind on some little hook or something they had to fasten it up to (2. 2:184 [SC]).

Nancy Smith (ca. 80 years): *Mist'ess' dresses had full, ruffled skirts and, no foolin', her clothes was sho'ly pretty. De white menfolks wore plain britches, but dey had bright colored coats and silk vests dat warn't lak de vests de men wears now. Dem vests was more fancy had fancy coats dat didn't have no sleeves'* (13. 3:298 [GA]).

Home-Grown and Home-Made

The *Narratives* provide strong evidence that in spite of the availability of commercially produced fabric during the nineteenth century, the fibres for enslaved people's and whites' clothing were usually home-grown and the clothing was homemade.[4]

Henry Probasco (79 years): *In de days w'en I's a boy, 'twarnt lak now. No, Sar, w'at weuns have, 'twas made or raised on de place* (S2. 8. 7:3185 [TX]).

Tildy Moody ("six years old when freedom came"): *I never see' a bought material 'til I was 'bout 13 year' ol'* (S2. 7. 6:2727 [TX]).

Ike Derricotte (78 years): *Most everybody wore clothes made out of homespun cloth and jeans, and dey didn't know nothin' 'bout ready-made, store-bought clothes. Dem clothes what dey made at home didn't cost very much* (12. 1:279 [GA]).

Frank Hughes (78 years): *Wasn't no buyin out de store in dem days* (S1. 8. 3:1060 [AL/MS]).

Rachel Adams (78 years): *Ma's job was to weave all de cloth for de white folks. I havè wore many a dress made out of de homespun what she wove* (12. 1:3 [GA]).

James Bolton (85 years): *I never seed no store bought clothes twel long atter freedom done come!* (12. 1:94 [GA]).

Amanda Jackson: *De white folks clothes an' all de slaves clothes wuz all made on de plantation. De marster's wife could sew an' she an' her mother an' some of de slaves done all o' de spinning an' weaving on de place* (12. 1:290 [GA]).

In the North, machine-manufactured textiles may have been the norm by mid-century,[5] but in other areas of the nation, machine-made cloth and store-bought clothing were distinct rarities for most.[6]

In the late 1820s, a white farm wife in Ohio outlined for Frances Trollope the tasks she and her sister performed. Besides caring for her husband and three little children, preparing all the food, and tending to chickens and cows,

> The woman told me that they spun and wove all the cotton and woollen garments of the family, and knit all the stockings; her husband, though not a shoemaker by trade, made all the shoes. She manufactured all the soap and candles they used . . . (42).

Before the turn of the nineteenth century, the majority of the Southern U. S. population lived in rural areas on self-sufficient farms where the raw materials were raised and processed into the useful articles. In contrast to a scarcity of statements about commercially produced textiles, time and again, both male and female African Americans reported on homemade clothing.[7] The *Narratives* give overwhelming evidence that most cloth and clothing was homemade, and the evidence for this mode of manufacture comes from every slave-holding state.

> Georgia Baker (87 years): *Chillun what was big enough done de spinnin' and Aunt Betsey and Aunt Tinny, dey wove most evvy night 'til dey rung de bell at 10:00 o'clock for us to go to bed. Us made bolts and bolts of cloth evvy year* (12. 1:41 [GA]).

> William Branch (b. 1850): *Marster's clothes? We makes dem for de whole fam'ly. De missis send de pattren and de slaves makes de clothes* (4. 1:144 [TX]).

> Julia Woodberry (age 70–80, born after slavery): . . . de cloth wear better too, in dem days den dey do now. You see, mostly, de people would make dey own provisions at home (3. 4:234 [SC]).

> Aaron Carter (80 years): *Mos everythin' we wears is made right on de plan'tation. All out clothes, an everythin'* (S1. 9. 4:358 [MS]).

> Andy Anderson (94 years): *[Massa Haley's plantation] was sort of like de small town, 'cause everything we uses am made right there. There am de shoemaker and he is de tanner and make de leather from de hides. Den massa has 'bout a thousand sheep and gits de wool, and de niggers cards and spins and weaves it, and dat make all de clothes* (4. 1:14 [TX]).

Henry Lewis (b. 1835): *That was one plantation what was run 'sclusively by itself. Massa Rimes have a commissary or sto' house, whar he kep' whatnot things – then what made on the plantation and things the slaves couldn' make for themselves. That wasn't much, 'cause we make us own clothes and shoes . . .* (5. 3:13 [TX]).

Charles Crawley: *The white folks or you slave owners would teach dem who could catch on easy an' dey would teach de other slaves, an' dats how dey kept all slaves clothed* (16. 5:10 [VA]).

Tap Hawkins (94 years): *All de close wuz wove on de plantation, en us didn't have none too many of 'em* (S1. 5. 2:358 [NC/OH]).

The interviewer paraphrased Amanda McDaniel (b. 1850): "None of the clothing that was worn on this plantation was bought as everything necessary for the manufacture of clothing was available on the premises" (13. 4:73 [GA]).

George McAlilloy (84 years): *All of our clothes was made from wool and cotton dat was made right dere on de plantation. Wool was sheared from de sheep. Cotton was picked from de field. De cotton was hand-carded, took to de spinn' wheels, made into thread, loomed into cloth, sewed into clothes, or knitted into socks and stockin's* (3. 3:143–144 [SC]).

Morris Sheppard (b. 1852): *De clothes wasn't no worry neither. Everything we had was made by my folks* (7:286–287 [OK]).

Charley Williams (b. 1843): *Everything boughten we got come from Shreveport, and was brung in by the stage and the freighters, and that was only a little coffee or gunpowder, or some needles for the sewing . . .. We made and raised everything else we needed right on the place* (7:332 [LA/OK]).

Gendered Tasks

In West Africa, certain craft-making procedures were gendered and some of these divisions of labor remained stable for Africans brought to the American South. For instance, men traditionally were leather-workers in Africa, and they remained so in the South. On the other hand, in the United States, women were weavers, while in several African societies, men were the weavers and continue to be so at present. Until recently, tasks were gender-related throughout the United States, with women's craft performance relegated to domestic production.[8] In the Southern United States, although both women and men might be found working in the fields during the day, once back at the quarters, the chores were decidedly gendered.

> James Williams (b. 1805, enslaved in Virginia and Alabama):*There was little leisure for any of the hands on the plantation. In the evenings, after it was too dark for work in the field, the men were frequently employed in burning brush, and in other labors until late at night. The women, after toiling in the field all day, were compelled to card, spin, and weave cotton for their clothing, in the evening* (n. d. :47).

The concept that some tasks will be done by men and some by women was culturally constructed in both West Africa and the United States, and it appears that in the United States, certain tasks were gendered by African custom, some by European.[9]

A particularly compelling aspect of the *Narratives* is the complimentary way in which daughters, sons, and brothers remembered their female relatives' abilities, never once questioning whether or not the work was "gender appropriate."

> Linley Hadley (age 77): *Mama was born same year as papa [1832]. She was field hand and a cook. She could plough good as any man. She was a guinea woman. She weighed ninety-five pounds. She had fourteen children* (9. 3:125 [MS/AR]).

> Richard Orford (b. 1842): *Women in dem days could pick five-hundred pounds of cotton a day wid a child in a sack on dere backs* (13. 3:150 [GA]).

> Monroe Brackins (b. 1853): *I remember they tasked the cotton pickers in Mississippi . . .. My sister there, she had to bring in 900 pounds a day. Well, cotton was heavier then. Most of 'em could pick 900 pounds. It was heavier and fluffier* (4. 1:125 [MS, TX/TX]).

African American women also worked at the demanding jobs associated with cloth manufacture. A very early account, *A Perfect Description of Virginia*, shows African American women already involved in cloth production by 1649 (cited in Jernegan, 227). More than 200 years later, Black women continued to be manufacturers of textiles as well as field laborers.

> Ellen Thomas (81 years): *I was still a young girl, but I plowed, grubbed and hauled water . . .. I used to know how to spin and weave. I could make a pair of sox in two nights* (S2. 9. 8:3792 [TX]).

Myra Jones (b. 1849): *[W]hen I growed up big 'nuf I wuz sont to de plantation to Wauk in de feel's an' 'round de overseers house. I wuz taught to spin an' weave an' knit an' to help dye de cloth. We had to make de dye we used an' mos' every thing else, sich as candles from tallow, soap, lard, and' shoes an' socks* (S1. 8. 3:1247–1248 [MS]).

Mary Woolridge (ca. 103 years): *My Massa has his nigger gals to lay fence worms, mak fences, shuck corn, hoe corn en tobacco, wash, iron, and de missus try to teach de nigger gals to sew and knit* (16. 2:107 [KY]).

Regarding the tasks related to textile production, only one man was found who disparaged the women's work. His young age during the period of enslavement ("*I's too lil' to wo'k much . . .*") perhaps accounts for his particular view:

C. B. McKay (b. 1861): *The Nigger women spinned and weaved the cloth. I 'spec' dat.'s the onlies' place in Jasper whar you could go any time of day and see a parlor full of nigger woman, sittin' up dare fat as dey could be and with lil' to do* (5. 3:41 [TX]).

The letters to Sarah Childress Polk from her plantation overseers make evident that keeping the enslaved people clothed was a constant worry (Bassett, 1925). The letters written during the 1840s concerning Polk's Mississippi plantation also make evident that Black women became capable weavers and might be self-taught. One of the enslaved, Maria, appears in several letters of the 1830s as sickly. Yet when overseer Isaac H. Dismukes of the Mississippi plantation wrote to Mrs. Polk in 1841, that the new "spining masheane" (i.e., loom) had arrived, he said that "marier sais she thinkes that she can put in a web now herself and weave it out without enny assistance" (Bassett, 150–151). In his letter, dated just five months later, a local friend of Polk writes:

I had the Winter Clothing measured, and Mariah says there will be about 10 yds., perhaps 15 wanting, which, if wanting I can supply upon as good terms as it can be had for. Mr. Dismukes informed me that the Winter Shoes for the Negroes were all made . . .. Mariah wished me to inform her mistress that she is worth at least $30 more than when she left Tennessee. She can spool, warp, and *weave* with a little more practice thinks she will made a first rate weaver . . . (157).

By the next month, Dismukes wrote: "Clothing for the negrows wear have anuff with the exception of a fiew yardes . . ." (159); and by the early months of the following year, Dismukes could report: "I am having 7 yardes of cloth wove ady [a day] . . ." (161).

Although spinning and weaving were women's crafts in the United States, several men expressed a communal bond in the making of clothing when they used the first-person plural pronoun.

> Joe Rutledge (b. ca. 1849): *We card and spin and weave our own clothes on mistress's spinning wheel* (3. 4:57 [SC]).

> Clayton Holbert (86 years): *There was no such thin as going to town to buy things. All our clothing was homespun . . .. We always wore yarn socks for winter, which we made. It didn't get cold, in the winter in Tennessee, just a little frost was all. We fixed all our clothes and wool ourselves* (16:1 [TN/KS]).

> Bill Simms (b. 1839): *We made our own clothes, had spinning wheels and raised and combed our own cotton, clipped the wool from our sheep's backs, combed and spun it into cotton and wool clothes. We never knew what boughten clothes were* (16:8–9 [MO/KS]).

In 1863, Elizabeth Hyde Botume arrived in Beaufort, South Carolina, one of the first of the Northern teachers to volunteer to teach Black refugees during the "Port Royal Experiment." In *First Days Among the Contrabands* (1893), Botume wrote of her experiences among the newly "freed" people, and her descriptions offer invaluable, first-hand reports of the customs of a people who were on the cusp between one way of life and a different one. Because these first teachers found the people to be nearly destitute, teaching them to make clothing became one of the Northerners' most immediate missions. Concerning this, Botume noted:

> Most of the women around us had always been field-hands, and they knew nothing of any other kind of work.
>
> One of the old men came to me to signify his approbation of his wife's learning to sew. He apologized for her deficiency by saying, 'Him ain't much on de needle, but him's great on de hoe' (220–221).[10]

Botume offers her view of the women as she found them in a particular place, but from other areas of South, different voices indicate that many, many enslaved women possessed the necessary knowledge to produce clothing. From each state, the testimony demonstrates that the African Americans had a full knowledge of cloth and clothing production, beginning with the types of plants and animals used, to growing, harvesting, and processing the raw fibres, through refining these by spinning, dying, weaving and knitting, cutting patterns, and sewing.

Fibres for Cloth

On many plantations there were several sources of domestic fibre.

Animal Sources

Wool. In the United States, sheep were the most important domestic source of animal fibres for clothing. Wool was sometimes purchased.[11]

> Sally Murphy (b. 1855): *Dey made our own cloth. Our mammas wove long dresses, bought de wool and made flannels to our knees and wool pantalets long too, dey wus wool, us wore home made homespun, some er hit was dyed and some checked* (S1. 1:267 [AL]).

At other times, the wool might come from another plantation.

> Martha Mays (84 years): *[W]hen shearing time came around him [Old Marster] an Old Miss would sen' Miss Ann big sacks of wool. Den dey would set women to spinnin' and makin' cloth. Hit was good cloth. A sight better dan we kin buy today* (S1. 9. 4:1468 [GA/MS]).

Often the sheep were raised on the home farms and plantations. Wool, of course, served particularly as the fibre for winter clothing.

> Lottie Jones ("age 14 at freedom"): *Master raised sheep of different colors, dere wuz white, black and yellow, and so we didn't dye de wool* (S2. 6. 5:2128 [AL/TX]).

> Morris Sheppard (b. 1852):*Old Master bought de cotton in Ft. Smith because he didn't raise no cotton, but he had a few sheep and we had wool-mix for winter* (7. 287 [OK]).

> Mary James: *[W]e had about 150 sheep on the farm, producing our own wool. The old women woved clothes; we had woolen clothes in the winter and cotton clothes in the summer* (16. 3:38 [VA/MD]).

> Cicely Cawthon (78 years): *Marster had sheep. In cold weather, women wore woolen dresses and coats; they called 'em jackets, and woolen stockings, and*

the men wore woolen socks and britches too; everything they had was woven and made on the place (S1. 3. 1:181 [GA]).

Nicey Pugh (b. 1852): *De men wud shear de sheep and us chilluns wud pick de burrs out ob de wool and den wash it* (S1. 1:301 [AL]).

Rachel Cruze (b. 1856): *Yes, we raised sheep – by the hundreds. The raw wool was first sent to the mill to be carded, then we would spin it into thread, to be dyed just as the cotton was. The wool, too, would be woven into jeans for the heavier winter clothin for the men and into linsey-woolsey for the women's warmer dresses* (S1. 5. 2:297 [TN/OH]).

Thomas Johns (b. 1847): *We wore some cotton clothes in de summer, but we was tol' dat wool clothes was better in dat country as it would help keep de heat out. In de winter, we wore wool clothes* (S2. 6. 5:1961 [AL/TX]).

Silk. Sallie Paul (79 years) reported that enslaved African Americans wore silk clothes. Although she was born after emancipation, she carefully explained how they obtained this fabric before freedom:

Oh, dey have de finest kind of silk in slavery times. Colored people wore just as much silk in dem days as dey do now cause when dey had a silk dress den, it been a silk dress. Won' no half cotton en half silk. All de colored people, dat been stay on white folks plantation, had dey own little crop of corn en fodder bout dey house en when a peddler come along, dey would sell dey crop en buy silk from de peddler(3. 3:244–245 [SC]).

The interviewer paraphrased Amanda McCray (a house servant and "a grownup during the Civil War"): "At Christmas time . . . there was always some useful article of clothing included, something they were not accustomed to having. One little Mandy received a beautiful silk dress from her young mistress, who knew how much she liked beautiful clothing" (17. 1:213–214 [FL]).

But silk clothing was obviously used almost solely for special articles of clothing worn by whites and was a rarity for most Blacks. Although silk production in the South was not wide-spread, Margaret Davis Cate reports:

Mulberry Grove at the South End of St. Simons . . . took its name from the fact that here were planted thousands of mulberry trees. These were to feed the silk worms of the industry which was planned in the early days of the Colony [Georgia](149).

A contributor to the *Narratives* offers first-hand evidence of silk manufacture in Texas:

> Rebecca Thomas (b. 1825): *Mistress Sukie raised what yo' called coccoons [sic]. She had 'im on her place and she made her own silk f'om 'em, and made her own silk dresses. She never did let me help wide dis work. She had a lot of mulberry trees and she fed the leaves to dem coccoons* (S2. 9. 8:3821 [TX]).

James W. C. Pennington (b. ca. 1816, enslaved in Maryland) used the image of a skein of silk as a metaphor for slavery.

> *There lies a skein of silk upon a lady's work-table. How smooth and handsome are the threads. But while that lady goes out to make a call, a party of children enter the apartment, and in amusing themselves, tangle the skein of silk, and now who can untangle it? The relation between master and slave is even as delicate as a skein of silk; it is liable to be entangled at any moment* (reprinted in Katz, v).[12]

Animal Skins. Wild mammal skins and furs were a source of clothing material for some Americans, particularly those living on the frontier.

> Lucendy Griffen (80 years): *We have clothes made out of deerskin* (S2. 5. 4:1608 [NC/TX]).

By the second quarter of the nineteenth century, domestic cattle hides were the more usual source for leather. Cattle skins were converted into certain articles of clothing, such as belts and footwear. Chapter 4 examines in detail leather processing and leather footwear on antebellum plantations.

Plant Sources

Bast Fibres. Carol Kroll writes that nearly every American farmer had a flax patch, attributing this to the power of the English woolen interests who curtailed the American colonists from raising sheep (36). Flax, thus, became an alternative source of cloth fibres. The comments made by numerous contributors to the *Narratives* demonstrate that even after the American Revolution, when the United States turned to domestic production of woolen cloth, flax continued to be grown by many country people.[13]

As noted, the important bast fibre in West Africa came from the raffia palm; in the United States South, the counterpart plant was flax which produces linen. Raffia palm and flax are processed in a similar manner.

When Rachel Cruze (b. 1856) described the growing and harvesting of flax, she produced one of the most poetic passages in the *Narratives*:

> *We grew flax, too, and made plough lines out of it. I reckon that was before the leather harnesses had come in. The flax field was so pretty. The long shoots, no thicker than a pencil, would bloom – the purtiest little pink and white flowers – and when the wind would sweep over the field it would ripple and wave like silk. When the seed appeared it was carefully picked – flax seed seemed to be precious – then, the flax would be cut down and left to dry where it fell. When the sun dried it the outside skin would crack, and then they'd scutch it and it would fly out like feathers. Then they'd wind it on a big ball, and it would then be spun into thread by a flax wheel* (S1. 5:298 [TN/OH]).

Sina Banks (age 86) offered the precise details about the tools and manner of processing flax:

> *Flax grew about two feet high . . .. The hands would go through and cut it down and let it lay there till it rotted. It was then gathered up and placed in brakes. A brake was a frame on a stand with a slatted floor about three feet long and three or four feet high. The flax was laid across these slats and a lever was pressed down to break the chaff from the coarse thread like skin. The chaff fell to the ground and the skins were placed in piles to be run through the heckles. Heckles were comb-like things made of wood with teeth like a comb or brush* (S1. 12:18 [MO/OK]).

Parker Pool (91) explained what happened after the carding:

> *Den dey clean an' string it out till it looks lak your hair. Dey flax when it came from de hackles wuz ready for de wheel whur it wuz spun into thread. I tell you, you couldn't break it either. When it wuz spun into thread dey put it on a reel. It turned 100 times and struck, when it struck it wuz called a cut. When it come from de wheel it wuz called a broach. De cuts stood fer so much flax. So many cuts made a yard, but dere wuz more ter do, size it, and hank it before it wuz weaved. Most of the white people had flax clothes* (15. 2:186–187 [NC]).

Refined flax processing produces quality linen fibres. Less concern for processing results in a much coarser fibre and final woven product.

> Sina Banks (age 86): *The flax was combed through three or four heckels each one a little finer than the other. The product was called tow. This made coarse linen. Finer tow made finer linen for dresses* (S1. 12:18 [MO/OK]).

Figure 7. Hoeing and Planting Cotton Seeds. *Frank Leslie's Popular Monthly* May 1880:564.

Figure 8. Carrying Cotton From the Fields. *Frank Leslie's Popular Monthly* May 1880:565.

The roughly-finished fabric, "tow," was used for work clothes, often those of enslaved people.[14] In a memorable passage, Booker T. Washington (1856–1915) described what it was like to wear clothing made of this poorer-grade cloth:

The most trying ordeal that I was forced to endure as a slave boy, however, was the wearing of a flax shirt. In the portion of Virginia where I lived it was common to use flax as part of the clothing for the slaves. That part of the flax from which our clothing was made was largely refuse, which of course was the cheapest and roughest part. I can scarcely imagine any torture, except, perhaps, the pulling of a tooth, that is equal to that caused by putting on a new flax shirt for the first time. It is almost equal to the feeling that one would experience if he had a dozen or more chestnut burrs, or a hundred small pin-points, in contact with his flesh. Even to this day I can recall accurately the tortures that I underwent when putting on one of these garments (11).

Hemp provides another important bast fibre, processed in much the same manner as flax. Two people noted that hemp sometimes served as clothing fibre.

Sina Banks (86 years):*A coarse cloth was made from hemp and this was made into summer work clothes as it was very cool* (S1. 12:18 [MO/OK]).

Bert Mayfield (1852): *The flax and hemp were raised on the plantation. The younger slaves had to 'swingle it' with a wooden instrument, somewhat like a sword, about two feet long, and called a swingler. The hemp was heckled by the older slaves. The heckle was an instrument made of iron teeth, about four inches long, one-half inch apart and set in a wooden plank one and one-half feet long, which was set on a heavy bench. The hemp stalks were laid in piles and taken to the work shops where it was twisted and fed [?] then woven, according to the needs. Ropes, carpets, and clothing were made from this fibre* (16. 2:13 [KY]).

This is what Topsy wears when Harriet Beecher Stowe first presents her to the reader: "She was dressed in a single filthy ragged garment, made of bagging . . ." (351). William Green (enslaved in Maryland) said of his master: "*He half clothed and fed his people. He gave each man two shirts, two pair of pantaloons made of coarse sacking, such as grocers keep salt in*" (1853:7). Likewise, the contributors to the *Narratives* mentioned wearing clothing made from various types of sacking material. Some sacks were made of cotton.

Adline Marshall: *All we got to wear is jes' a plain cotton slip with a string 'round de neck, jes' de same kind of stuff what dey make de picking sacks of* (S2. 7. 6:2578 [SC, TX/TX]).

Jute is another plant used to produce bast fibre, but it is used mainly to weave ropes and burlap sacks. Most of the clothing made from sacks appears to be of burlap.

Albert Todd (86 years): *My clothes was a long shirt, made out of a meal sack* (5. 3:106 [TX]).

Charles Crawley: *Underclothes [were] made out of sacks and bags* (16. 5:10 [VA]).

William Mathews (b. 1848): *De clothes we wear den was made out of 'dyed lows'. Dat's de stuff dey make sacking out of. Dey dyed 'em brown an' black an' dark green an' made pants an' jumpers out of 'em* (S2. 7. 6:2612 [LA/TX]).

George Harmon (b. 1854): *If they didn't have any [home-made cotton] cloth they would take a crocus sack and cut holes in each corner for armholes and the center for the head and wear that* (S1. 12. 1:141 [TX/OK].

The interviewer paraphrased George Womble (b. 1843): "Once the master had suffered some few financial losses the slaves had to wear clothes that were made of crocus material" (13. 4:184 [GA]).

Often the sacking cloth, called "lowerings", was the same as that used to make cotton-picking sacks.

Horace Overstreet (b. 1852): *Dey gimme a shu't t' wear. It was made'n outer lowers. Day w'at dey make cotton sack outer* (S2. 8. 7:2997 [TX]).

Cato Carter (b. 1836): *I wore lowerin's like the rest of the niggers. That was things made from cotton sackin'* (4. 1:204 [AL/TX]).

Cotton. Cotton was the main plant source for cloth fibre in the United States for all people during the nineteenth century.

Octavia George (b. 1852): *We didn't know nothin' about any clothes other than cotton; everything we wore was made of cotton, except our shoes . . .* (7:112 [LA/OK]).

Celia Henderson (b. 1849): *We weahs cotton cloths when ah were young. Jes plain weave it were; no collar nor cuffs, n' belt like store cloths* (16. 4:44 [KY/OH]).

Elsie Pryor (b. 1856): *The first dress I remember having besides croker sacks, was cotton homespun. They gave us dresses for Christmas. It was plain white. Later we got striped ones. They made our dresses for Christmas. They didn't waste any sheep wool on us little niggers* (S1. 12:262 [OK]).

In the following section, I detail the processing of cotton because in the Deep South and throughout the cotton-growing belt, most cloth was manufactured from home-grown cotton.

Cloth Manufacture

Producing clothing from raw fibres involved many steps.[15] Here, I use cotton to illustrate these procedures and the technological know-how of the workers involved in the production of cloth in the antebellum South.

Rachel Cruze (b. 1856) outlined the entire process of producing clothing from cotton:

The material for the cotton clothes worn on the farm in summer was woven right in our own kitchen. We bought the raw cotton usually, but sometimes we would grow a small patch. Then we would card it, spin it and weave on the big loom in the kitchen. I have spun many a brooch. They take it off and wind it on a reel, and make a great hank of thread – there would-be four cuts in a hank. They would first size the thread by dipping it in some solution, and then, when it was dry, they would dye it (S1. 5. 2:297 [TN/OH]).

In the Field

Cotton first had to be planted, then tended during the growing season, and picked at harvest time (Figures 7 and 8). In the narrative of his life, James Williams, born 1853 and enslaved in Virginia and Alabama, outlined the cotton season:

In March we commenced ploughing, and on the first of April began planting seed for cotton. The hoeing season commenced the last of May. At the earliest dawn of day, and frequently before that time, the laborers were roused from their sleep by the blowing of the horn (n. d. :46).[16]

A poetic description of cotton cultivation is offered by

> Aunt Clussey (b. ca. 1844): *I remembers de way de slaves looked when dey walked fum de cabin at de break of day while it wuz still dark an' dere figures moved slowly . . . . I can see raght now dem niggers a-sweatin' in de field an' de roustabouts a-loadin' cotton. I can hear de voices of de tired folks a comin' home singing atter de sun done sunk behin' de mountain* (S1. 1:21 [AL]).

Other formerly enslaved people remembered the songs sung for each of these tasks. Harriet Jones (93 years) related a song sung early in the day on the way to the fields:

It's a cold an frosty mornin'
And de niggers goes to work,
With hoes upon dey shoulders,
Without a bit o' shirt (4. 2:233 [NC/TX]).

Lydia Parrish interviewed formerly enslaved people living on the Georgia Sea Islands between 1915 and 1940 (*Slave Songs of the Georgia Sea Islands*, 1942). Two of Parrish's contributors, Janey Jackson and Floyd Wilson, reported that "*June month was a ha'd month*" for hoeing the cotton crop because "*the weeds grew fast and the sun was hot.*" Wilson then sang several variations on a song that proved their point. The lyrics also include an item of clothing:

What y'u gwine t'do fo' June month? Jerusalem Jerusalem.
Pull off y'u coat an' go t' work – Jerusalem Jerusalem.
June month's a ha'd month – Jerusalem Jerusalem.

Jerusalem in de mornin' – Jerusalem Jerusalem (245).

The following are partial lyrics to a cotton-picking song that Parrish recorded:

Way down in the bottom – whah the cotton boll's a rotten
Won' get my hundred all day
. . . .
Befo'e I'll be beated – befo'e I'll be cheated
I'll leave five finguhs in the boll . . . .

> [When Parrish] asked Josephine what the words 'five fingers in the boll' meant, she explained that in the shade at the bottom of the stalk of cotton the bolls are likely to be rotten; they come off in the hand, and *'y'u can't make any time grabbin' de cotton out uv 'em.'* 'Fingers' are the compartments holding the white fibre. The song has reference to the variety that has five in a boll . . . (247).

"My hundred" refers to the number of pounds a hand should pick in a day.

Annie Little (b. 1856) described the context for cotton-picking singing:

> *How did dey sing? Well mos' like dey do now, only dey sang more in de cotton patch dan now, and dey would all sing togedder as dey picked de cotton an keep time to de song with the motion of dere bodies bending low ober de stalks wen de song went low den up high, wen de song would go high. Dey don' do dat way no more* (S2. 6. 5:2397 [MS/TX]).

Others remembered all too well cotton-picking as an arduous (and detested) task:

> Mary Reynolds (over 100 years): *The times I hated most was pickin' cotton when the frost was on the bolls. My hands would get so sore that they would crack open and bleed. We would have a little fire in the fields and iffen the ones with tender hands couldn't stan' it no longer we would run and warm our hands a little bit* (S2. 8. 7:3288 [LA/TX]).

> Steve Robertson (79 years): *De cotton dat am growed on de place a ma sight fo' sho. Ise can 'most see de white fields now. Deys picks de cotton an' outs it in big wickah baskets. Ise can see dem old fo'ks comin' in f'om de field now, wid de big basket dat am tallah dan some ob de chilluns on top de head. Sometimes youse sees de baskets befo' youse sees de fo'ks totin' dem w'en deys am walkin' in de tall river bottom cotton* (S2. 8. 7:3334–3335 [TX]).

> Vina Moore (b. 1845): *We picked cotton in sacks, I can't membah any of us pickin in baskets, hit was too much trouble. Master Smiley did not have no gin and he had ter haul hit off ter have it ginned. Hit would allus be late in de fall when we'd git through picking cotton and when they'd finish dey would all throw der sacks up in der air and holler til everybody in de country would know what was happenin'* (S2. 7. 5:2757 [MS, TX/TX]).

> Adeline Hedge: *I jes hates to hab to weigh any thing today, 'cayse I 'members so well dat each day dat de slaves war given a certain number ob pounds of cotton to pick an' when weighin-up time cum an' you didn't hab de number ob pounds,*

set hit aside, an' you may be sho' dat you war goin' to be whippe (S1. 1:184 [MS/AL]).

Seeding and Pressing

After the cotton was picked, the seeds had to be removed. The invention of the cotton gin, credited to Eli Whitney in 1793, cheapened "the most costly process in refining cotton" (Morris, 1953:535) and "promoted the rapid expansion of the cotton kingdom [and] firmly established the plantation system" (ibid., 514). After that time, cotton for home use could be either mechanically ginned or the seeds continued to be removed by hand. An influential southern, agricultural journal, *The Commercial Review of the South and West*, began publication in 1846. In 1850, it became *De Bow's Review* and, in that year, illustrated, commercial advertisements first appeared on its pages. The following year, the journal began running such advertisements for cotton gins. Figure 9 is the advertisement that, significantly, shows a Black man operating the machine. Mechanical gins operated on some plantations, especially when the cotton was a commercial crop.

Sarah Benjamin (82 years): *De women had to run de gin in de daytime and de man at night. Dey fed de old gin from baskets and my mammy fed from dose baskets all day with de high fever and died dat night* (4. 1:71 [LA/TX]).

Bob Maynard (79 years): *He [master] saw to it that the cotton was took to the gin. They used oxen to pull the wagons full of cotton. There was two gins on the plantation. Had to have two for it was slow work to gin a bale of cotton as it was run by horse power* (7:224 [TX/OK]).

Josh Hadnot (in his 80s): *Dey hab a great big ol' wooden gin on de place. De han's haul de cotton on big ox wagon an hab a boy to pass us de cotton to de man feedin' de gin. It mek such a noise you could hear it a mile. Dey run it by hitchin' mules and hosses to de lever, I calls it* (S2. 5. 4:1622 [TX]).

Most cotton was raised to be sold, in which case it had to be pressed into compact bales for hauling. The first illustrated ad in *DeBow's Review* was for a cotton press(1850), sometimes called a "pit screw" (Figure 10).

Josh Hadnot (in his 80s): *Dey had a cotton press too, It was like dis. Dey hab a box w'at dey put de cotton in. Den dey hab a piece of hebly lumber w'at come down and press de cotton in a hole. Den dey tek it out wid cotton hooks. Dat piece w'at press it was on a big hebly piece of timber wid places 'roun 'it like a big screw. Dey was a li'l shed ober it. Dey hole long t'ings down from dat. I calls*

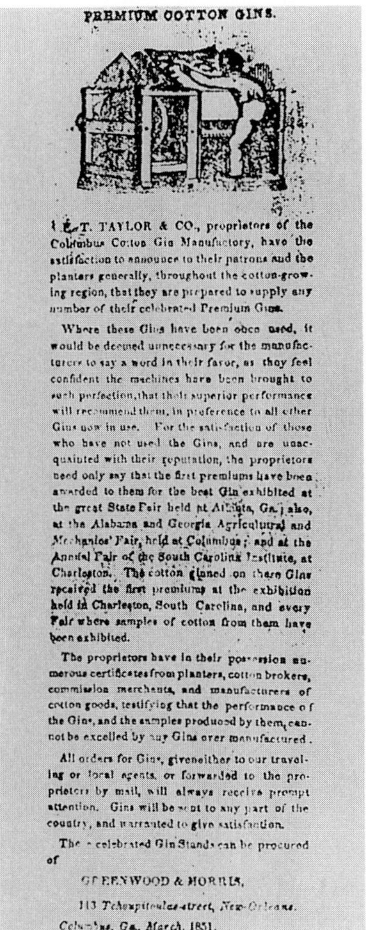

PREMIUM COTTON GINS.

J. E. T. TAYLOR & CO., proprietors of the Columbus Cotton Gin Manufactory, have the satisfaction to announce to their patrons and the planters generally, throughout the cotton-growing region, that they are prepared to supply any number of their celebrated Premium Gins.

Where these Gins have been once used, it would be deemed unnecessary for the manufacturers to say a word in their favor, as they feel confident the machines have been brought to such perfection, that their superior performance will recommend them, in preference to all other Gins now in use. For the satisfaction of those who have not used the Gins, and are unacquainted with their reputation, the proprietors need only say that the first premiums have been awarded to them for the best Gin exhibited at the great State Fair held at Atlanta, Ga.; also, at the Alabama and Georgia Agricultural and Mechanics' Fair, held at Columbus; and at the Annual Fair of the South Carolina Institute, at Charleston. The cotton ginned on these Gins received the first premium at the exhibition held in Charleston, South Carolina, and every Fair where samples of cotton from them have been exhibited.

The proprietors have in their possession numerous certificates from planters, cotton brokers, commission merchants, and manufacturers of cotton goods, testifying that the performance of the Gins, and the samples produced by them, cannot be excelled by any Gins ever manufactured.

All orders for Gins, given either to our traveling or local agents, or forwarded to the proprietors by mail, will always receive prompt attention. Gins will be sent to any part of the country, and warranted to give satisfaction.

These celebrated Gin Stands can be procured of

GREENWOOD & MORRIS,

113 Tchoupitoulas-street, New-Orleans.

Columbus, Ga., March, 1851.

Figure 9. Advertisement for a cotton gin with image of a Black man operating the machine. *DeBow's Southern and Western Review*, 1851.

dem levers and dey hitch two mules or hosses to de en' of each and dey go 'roun' and 'roun' and press dat cotton. You don' see no mo' of dem now. Befo de gin and de compress was run by hosses or mules. Mos' od de haulin' was done by ox team cause dey ain' hab much wuk team in slav'ry time (S2. 5. 4:1622 [TX]).

Moses Roper, enslaved in North Carolina, illustrated how he was tortured on such a machine:

This is a machine used for packing and pressing cotton. By it he hung me round the screw c, and carrying it up and down, and pressing the block c into the box

Figure 10. Pit Screw or Cotton Press. *Frank Leslie's Popular Monthly* May 1880:572.

d, into which the cotton is put. At this time he hung me up for a quarter of an hour. I was carried up ten feet from the ground, when Mr. Gooch asked me if I was tired. He then let me rest for five minutes, then carried me round again, after which he let me down and put me into the box d, and shut me down in it for about ten minutes (1838:48).

Carding

In the next stage, all types of raw fibres needed to be separated and then carded or combed to untangle them in preparation for spinning (Figure 11).

> Sarah Graves (b. 1850): *Sometimes we had it carded at a mill, an' sometimes we carded it ourselves. But when we did it, the threads were short, which caused us to have to tie the thread often, makin' too many knots in the dress* (11. 7. 8:131 [MO]).

The following statements from formerly enslaved people show the problem with assuming that all men and women filled separate spheres of work. In the early stages of cloth production, we do not find an easy distinction between women's and men's work as children of both sexes remembered helping to do tasks related to carding and spinning. We are not told at what age men stopped helping with tasks associated with preparing the fibres for textile production, but many clearly remembered helping as youngsters (Figure 12). A rare, early account comes from a northern male. Venture, who was born ca. 1729 and enslaved in Rhode Island wrote: "*The first of the time of living at my master's own place, I was pretty much employed at the house, carding wool and other household business*" (12).

According to many Southern experiences during the following century, the tasks associated with fibre processing often took place in the family cabin at night.

> Bert Luster (b. 1853): *Us darkies would stay up all night sometimes sep'rating cotton from seed* (7:203–204 [TN/OK]).

> Peter Mitchell (ca. 76 years): *Many a night I hatter sit up an' spin, an' card an' spin out t'ree reaches befo' I could go to bed. I kin card an' spin to dis day, but I hopes it won' happen no mo'*(S2. 7. 6:2718 [LA?/TX]).

> Charlie Meadow (83 years): *I's 'bout ten years old when I could card and spin good* (3. 3:177 [SC]).

Figure 11. "Separating White Cotton from Yellow". *Frank Leslie's Popular Monthly* May 1880:569.

Alice Hutcheson (b. 1862): *Us had to cyard, spin and real cotton. Missy give us chillun six cuts of thread for a days wuk and if us wokked hard and fas' us got done in time to go chestnut and chinquapin huntin'* (12. 2:285 [GA]).

Spinning and Winding

Two additional steps preceded weaving. First, the fibres were spun. As noted, West Africans used a drop spindle. In the United States, a spinning wheel was employed; early on, however, African American women mastered the European wheel. A colonial Virginia will, dated 1774, and probated in 1812, supports this assumption:

Figure 12. Child Helps to Wind Yarn. In David Hunter Strother, *Virginia Illustrated*, [1857] 1871:225.

I desire, that all the wool which may be yearly produced from my sheep, may be delivered to her [my wife], and that she will have the same spun up by her house servants, or with the occasional assistance of one of the negro women who may work out; and that it be wove and appropriated to the clothing of the slaves which are set apart for her use, as well as for clothing my other slaves . . . (Catterall, 1924:123).

Betty Cofer (b. 1856): *All our spinnin' wheels and flax wheels and looms was hand-made by a wheel wright, Marse Noah Westmoreland . . .. Those old wheels are still in the family. I got one of the flax wheels. Miss Ella done give it to me for a present* (14. 1:169 [NC]).

Unidentified man (b. 1842): *You never seed a spinning wheel, I reckon, is you? Well, they would take sheep wool and card it and would make a bat, and they would start that spinning wheel running . . .. Well, this spinning wheel would be just turning over and over and you could hear that wheel whip from here to long ways, and it would roar louder than it did when they were spinning. The cloth they used to make would-be stout and thick. They would get the cloth spun during the time they were having prayer meeting* (18. 149 [TN or KY]).

The interviewer paraphrased Mariah Halloway (prob. b. 1852): "When The women come home from the fields they had to spin 7 cuts, so many before supper and so many after supper. A group of women were then collected to weave the cuts of thread into cloth" (12. 1:173 [GA]).

The interviewer paraphrased Rias Body (b. 1849): "Many spinning wheels and looms were operated on the Body plantation by expert female spinners and weavers who made practically all the cloth for the slaves' clothes. This cloth was of four kinds – cotton, mixed cotton and flax, mixed cotton and wool, and all-wool" (S1. 3. 1:73 [GA]).

Rebecca Thomas (b. 1825): *I used to work de spinnin' wheel, and I wove my own clothes on de loom, I used one of dem big, hummin' wheels fo' my work, dat I had to turn by hand; but Mistress Sukie had a little black spinnin' wheel dat she worked wide her feet* (S2. 9. 8:3821 [TX]).

To pass the time, singing might accompany spinning.[17]

Wade Glenn *("I was only a baby slave . . . I've just heard them tell about it."): Mammy sang a lot when she was spinning and weaving. She sing an' that big wheel a turnin': When I can read my title clear/Up yonder, Up yonder, Up yonder! – and another of her spinning songs was a humin The Promise of God Salvation free to give* (16. 4:38 [SC/OH]).

A formerly enslaved Virginian remarked: "*Mother said dey would always spin in pairs – one would treadle whilst de other one would wind the ball. You got to wind fast, too, an' take de thread right off de spindle, else it get tangled up. An' mamma tole me dey would all pat dey feet an' sing*"

> *Wind de ball, wind de ball*
> *Wind de ball, lady, wind de ball*
> *Don't care how you wind de ball*
> *Wind de ball, lady, wind de ball*
> *Ding, ding, ding, – wind de ball*
> *Wind de ball, lady, wind de ball*
> (*The Negro in Virginia*, 1969:90).

Dorothy Scarborough collected this spinning song:

> *Spin ladies, spin all day*
> *Sheep, Skill corn,*
> *Rain rattles up a horn . . .*
> (*On the Trail of Negro Folksongs*, Cambridge: Harvard University Press, 1925:215; cited in Jackson-Brown, 390).

From the Freedmen's Bureau files, a contract between a Georgia freedwoman, Dianna Freedwoman and her employer, James Alvis, states that: "he further agrees to furnish her with Cards Spinning wheel and Cotton to Spin for herself as much as she shall Spin at night after having performed her said Service for said Alvis . . ." (Sterling, 327).

The enslaved subverted the system of enforced servitude in numerous ways including working at a slow pace or shirking duties. Textile workers were counted among those who offered resistance to bondage.

> The interviewer paraphrased Adeline Hedge: "She was the house girl, and had certain tasks to perform . . . and after finishing that work, she had to spin thread, and each day she would have to spin so many cuts, and if she did not finish the required number, she was punished. She said that her mistress kept the finished work on top of a large wardrobe, and 'Aunt' Adeline said that many times she would steal a cut of thread off that wardrobe to complete a certain task given her to keep from being punished" (S1. 1:183–184 [MS/AL]).

> Mollie Dawson (b. 1852): *At the end of the day Marser Newman would counts dem to see dat each woman was doin' what she was sposed to, but lots of de*

womens could do lots mo' den dey was sposed to, but dey knew jest about how fast ter work ter gits what dey was tasked to do, so dey jest gits a few mo' den dey was sposed ter gits and Marser Newman thought he got about all outten dem dey could do (S1. 4. 3:1126–1127 [TX]).

Following spinning, the weft fibres were measured into hanks (or "cuts") and wound around a wooden bat and the warp threads were attached to the loom.

Callie Williams (b. 1861): *when [a reel] had spun 300 yards it popped, and then the spinner tied it, that was a 'cut'. A full days work was 4 cuts* (S1. 2:452 [AL]).

Weaving

Aunt Martha, enslaved in Virginia: *At the loom, Mammy stand an' put the shuttle back an' forth in the warp, an' 'bloomp – bloomp' press the thread firm to make the cloth. Mammy was right expert at it. She'd go up to the mansion right frequent to see Missus Custis 'bout the cloth* (Armstrong, 193).

Rachel Cruze (b. 1856): *I can still hear the lam-lam-lamlam, lam-lam-lamlam of the big loom* (S1. 5. 2 [TN/OH]).

Sina Banks (86): *Weaving was hard work. The whole body was in constant motion as there was five pedals to be operated and in throwing the shuttle through you had to use both feet and hands* (S1. 12:17 [MO/OK]).

William Harris: *Talk 'bout good weavin': Mammy could weave cloth so you could pour a teacup o' water on it, an' it wouldn' run t'rough* (Armstrong, 1931:193).

The commentary on the times of day and work related to cloth production seems to contradict the largely accepted belief that the enslaved worked for the master "from sunup to sundown" but that the enslaved had the evenings to themselves. The other adage, "from can to can't" seems more apt for Black women, especially those involved in textile manufacture.

Bill Collins: *We always wore home spun pants and shirts. They were spun by the older slave women. They did most of this at night. Some of them had to work in the fields all day and spin at night* (S. 2. 3. 2:880 [TX]).

George Caulton (92 years): *Every night each slave was given ten pounds of cotton to seed. Then it was turned over to the women who spun it and finally passed on to the seamstress* (S1. 3. 1:172 [GA]).

Again, we find that some boys assisted the weaving women.

Henry Chestam (b. 1850): *De li'l niggers at night went to de big house to spin an' weave. I'se spun a many roll an' carded a many bat of cotton* (6. 1:68 [AL]).

Allen Thomas (97 years): *Me and mammy work in de spinnin' wheel many a night – sometime' up to one or two 'clock. I uster card de bats* (S2. 9. 8:3779 [TX]).

Spaces

A separate room or a separate building might serve as the cloth production site. In the Upper South, a one-and-a-half story, log loom house stood in the back yard of the 1806 Sherman-Fisher-Shellman House in Westminster, Maryland (Figure 13).[18] In the 1850s, Frederick Law Olmstead saw such a building in the Deep South in Mississippi and makes an interesting observation about those working there:

On reaching the nearest "quarters," we stopped at a house, a little larger than the ordinary cabins, which was called the loom house, in which a dozen negroes were at work making shoes, manufacturing coarse cotton stuff for negro clothing. One of the hands so employed was insane, and most of the others were cripples, invalids with chronic complaints, or unfitted by age, or some infirmity, for field work (1959:268).

Aunt Martha, enslaved in Virginia: *Loom house was near the quarters. Mammy had a big spinin'-wheel in our house, too, so she could spin when she was restin'. Big wheel whirrin'round, with the thread bein' pulled out an' wound up* (Armstrong, 193).

George Jackson (b. 1858): *I was born in de storeroom close to masa's home. It was called de weavin' room – place where dey weaved cotton and yarn* (16. 4:45 [VA/OH]).

Frank Hughes (78 years): *Dere was a regular loom house and two women who worked in dere. All de hanks that had been prepared in de quarters was brought to dis house to be weaved into cloth* (S1. 8. 3:1061 [AL/MS]).

Milton Lackey (77 years): *There wuz a loom room an some of the slaves would weave in there by light of a pine knot at night . . .. I saw lots of sojiers marchin by the road in front of the big house but didn't none of 'em come in. Yes'um we*

Figure 13. Enslaved women worked in this one-and-a-half story loom house located behind the 1806 Sherman-Fisher-Shellman House, Westminster, Maryland. The loom house was demolished between 1904 and 1908. Undated photograph, Historical Society of Carroll County, Maryland, J. Leland Collection, gift of the Commissioners of Carroll County, 1995.

wuz all scarred alright. I remember how some of them would chunk rocks at the loom house an try to make the darkies come out an' go wid' them (S1. 8. 3:1290 [MS]).

Silvia King (b. Morocco, 1804): *De cobbler had he log cabin an' cobbler's bench jes' lak dar wuz cabins wid de spining wheels an' looms in 'em. Dey wuz big long cabins wid er chimbly in each end* (S2. 6. 5:2228 [TX]).

Linley Hadley (77 years): *I can recollect old Master Collins calling up all the niggers to his home. He told them they was free . . .. Most of the niggers took what all they have on their heads and walked off. He told mama to move up in the loom house, if she would go off he would kill her. We moved to the loom house till in 1866* (9. 3:197 [MS/AR]).

At other plantations, a room in the owner's house served as the production site.

Tom Wilson (84 years): *My mammy worked in de loom room at night by light of a pine knot. In de Big House dey had taller can'les 'cause I'member mammy moulded 'em. N'm, de spinnin' wheels was kep' in de kitchen of de Big House. Hit had a dirt flo'* (7. 2:166 [MS]).

J. C. Alexander (b. 1850): *De loom-room, which had a loom, spinnin' wheel and cardin' rack, was up in de big house* (S2. 2. 1:40 [TX]).

On some plantations, the tasks associated with cloth-making depended on the weather and the seasons:

Andrew Goodman (97 years): *He didn't put the niggers out in bad weather. He give us something to do, in out of the weather, like shellin' corn and the women could spin and knit* (4. 2:75 [TX]).

Amanda Jackson: *All of de hard work on de plantation wuz done in de summertime. The rainy weather an' other bad weather all dat dey had to do wuz to shell corn an' help to make cloth* (12. 2:290 [GA]).

George Austin (75 years): *De thread dat am used in de clothes makin' loom am made in de winter months by de women folks. De Marster have de spinnin' room built fo' de spinnin' wheels to wo'k in. We'n de weather am too bad fo' to work in de fields in de winter de Marster have de womens do de spinnin'. Dey am two kinds of thread made an' 'twas cotton and wool. De wool comes f'om de sheep de Marster keep on de place* (S2. 2. 1:110 [TX]).

Age or physical condition might be the deciding factor concerning who would produce cloth and clothing.

> The interviewer paraphrased Richard Orford (b. 1842) who was on a plantation of about 250 enslaved people: "All of the clothing worn on this plantation was made there. Some of the women who were too old to work in the fields did the spinning and the weaving as well as the sewing of the garments" (13. 3:150 [GA]).

> Cato Carter (b. 1836 or 1837): *I used to tend to the nursling thread. When the slave women were confined with the babies having to suck and they were too little to take to the fields, the mammies had to spin. I would take them the thread and bring it back to the house when it was spun. If they didn't spin seven or eight cuts a day they would get a whuppin. It was considerable hard on a woman when had a fretting baby* (S. 2. 3. 2:642–643 [AL/TX]).

Whatever the particular place where clothing was made or whatever the particular reasons for certain people to be there, it was predominantly a women's space.

Sometimes white women were responsible for making all the clothing used by Blacks and whites.[19]

> Lidia Jones (94 years): *Miss Fannie . . . she had a loom half as big as this house. Lord a mercy, a many a time I went dancin' from that old spinnin' wheel. They made all the clothes for the colored folks. They'd be sewin' for weeks and months. Miss Fannie and Miss Frances – that was her daughter – they wove such pretty cloth for the colored. You know, they went and made themselves dresses and the white and colored had the same kind of dresses* (9. 4:151 [MS/AR]).

In several instances, Black women appear to be in charge of cloth and clothing production. William S. Pettigrew's overseer, Moses, wrote to him in 1857, telling of the progress being made to train enslaved women to be weavers on the North Carolina plantation:

> *. . . somptin on the subject of these weavers I have enquired of gilly an lizzy an tha think that tha canot give the instruction. thinking if thera be any person to hire I have understood that miss White is a veary good weaver undeed an can give good instructions an master can inform me as he wishes* (reprinted in Starobin, 21–22).

> Sam Kilgore (92 years): *Aunt Darkins am de culled overseer dat bosses de spinnin', weavin' an' de makin' of de clothes. Aunt Lou am de one dat tuks de measure an' see what clothes am needed. She gives de measure an' orders to Aunt Darkins* (S2. 6. 5:2197 [TN/TX]).

Julia Bunch (85 years): *My ma was head weaver. It tuk two or three days to set up de loom 'cause dere was so many little bitty threads to be threaded up* (12. 1:156–157 [GA]).

In 1842, Elizabeth Sherman of the Sherman-Fisher-Shellman House, Westminster, Maryland, (cited above) died. Lucy Behoe, a free Black living in the Sherman household, "received a large bequest including livestock, household furnishings and a 'Weaver's Loom' all appraised at $241. 55. The latter item suggests that Lucy had been trained as a weaver" (Graybeal, 1991:4). It also suggests that Lucy Behoe alone had been the sole weaver in the Sherman loom house. More often, Black and white women shared this particular space. The space in which they made cloth may be seen as a microcosm for the myriad ways and innumerable times when enslaved African American women and white women interacted and worked closely together.[20]

The *Narratives* testimony illustrates that in this space each group of women possessed the specialized knowledge that went into producing woven fabrics. Here women produced a vast array of items that they knew would be distributed by social class.

Sarah Felder (b. ca. 1853): *Old Mistis work hard all de time. She had a big room whar sum of de women wus busy wide de cards, an' spinnin' an' de looms. Miss Vickey never lowed de women ter rest. She med 'em wurk at night an' when it wus rainin' she wus rite dar ter see dey wus wurkin'. She kep' de looms goin' an' made all kind uf pretty cloth, an' dey made 'coverlets' jes as pritty as dey make 'em now. She made sum uf de wimin git bark out uf de woods an' dye sum uf dat thread, an' it sho' made pritty coverlets. An' den she hed ter dye her thread ter make pants an' coats. She made de pants an' coats outern blue jeans. She kep' sum uf de wimin sewin an' dey made mity fine things fur old Mistis an' her chilluns, an' dey made sum things fer us, but what we got wus made frum cloth spun dar at home, an' it niver wore out* (S1. 7. 2:716–717 [MS]).

Robert Shepherd: *Us had a great long loom house whar some of de slaves didn't do nothin' but weave cloth. Some cyarded bats, some done de spinnin', and dere was more of 'em to do de sewin'. Miss Ellen, she looked atter all dat, and she cut out most of de clothes . . .. Sometimes Marster would go to de sewin' house, and Mist'ess would tell him to git on 'way from der and look after his own wuk, dat her and Aunt Julia could run dat loom house. Marster, he jus' laughed den and told us chillun what was hangin' round de door to jus' listen to dem 'omans cackle* (13. 3:253–254 [GA]).

The places where cloth was produced were not always associated with harmonious relationships between the enslaved people and the whites for whom they labored.

> Lou Smith (female, b. 1854): *Once he [master] whipped a woman for stealing. She and mother had to spin and weave. She couldn't or didn't work as fast as Ma and wouldn't have as much to show for her day's work. She'd steal hanks of ma's thread so she couldn't do more work than she did . . .. He caught up with her and whipped her* (7:304 [TX/OK]).

> Louis Hughes (b. 1843, enslaved in Mississippi and Virginia):*One woman did all the weaving and it was her task to weave from nine to ten yards a day. Aunt Liza was our weaver and she was taught the work by the madam. At first she did not get on so well with it . . . [but] Liza finally became equal to her task and accomplished it each day. But the trouble and the worry to me was when I had to assist the madam in warping – getting the work ready for the weaver* (40–41) . . .. *I was young and consequently not very strong . . .. I had to help the madam warping the cloth. I dreaded this work, for I always got my ears boxed if I did not or could not do the work to suit her. She always made the warp herself and put it in, and I had to hand her the thread as she put it through the harness. I would get very tired at this work, and like any child, wanted to be at play, but I could not remember that the madam ever gave me that privilege*(18).

Colors and Patterns

The Black people living in the antebellum South descended from Africans with long traditions of processing fibres into threads to be woven into cloth for clothing and other purposes. As well, Africans had long traditions of ornamenting their cloth and clothing with color and pattern, and their descendants in the Southern United States often explicitly noted colored and patterned fabrics.

Dying

Comments about colored cloth formed the largest body of statements concerning clothing ornamentation found in the *Narratives*. Most often, the cloth was dyed at home, and men as well as women show an expanded knowledge about dye sources and the procedures for coloring thread and fabrics [see Appendix III]. Obviously the Black people and the whites appreciated this diversity in a stock of clothing lacking in much color.

Della Mun Bibles (b. ca 1856): *All the dresses was made a lot alike and most all of them buttoned up behind. If a person, white or black, had a calico dress in them days, they was dressed up. The homespun cloth was, some of it, checked, and some striped. Most of the clothes were dyed dark blue or brown. All the girls, young girls, bout fourteen and over, wore blue; the children on the yard, white and colored, wore brown most of the time* (S2. 2. 1:292 [TX]).

Charlie Meadow (83 years): *For our summer clothes we plaited de hanks to make a mixtry of colors. De winter clothes was heavy, drab and plain* (3. 3:180 [SC]).

James W. Smith (77 years): *De clothes am not as purtty as sich dat can be bought now, wid all de diffen't colors all mixed up, but deys am wahm an' lastin'. Deys am cullud, too. Deys am dyed brown, an' black. De dyes am made f'om Black Oak, Cherry, an' tudder tree bark* (S2. 9. 8:3631 [TX]).

Color was added either before or after weaving.

Bob Mobley (ca. 90 years): *[The] wool . . . had been dyed before the cloth was cut* (13. 3:137 [GA]).

Rachel Cruze (b. 1856): *Dye stuffs would be gotten from the barks and roots of different trees, and with these we would be able to make red, brown and black dyes. We would then weave it into jeans, a heavy cotton for men's coats and pants, or lighter linsey for women's clothing* (S1. 5. 2:297 [TN/OH]).

Julia Woodberry (70–80 years, born after slavery): Dey would get dis here indigo en all kind of old bark out de woods en boil it in de pot wid de yarn en make de prettiest kind of colors. Den dey would take dat colored yarn en weave all kind of pretty streaks in de cloth (3. 4:240 [SC]).

Sarah Waggoner (93 years): *You want to know what kind of clothes did we wear in them days? I'm gwine to tell yer. I jes' had two dresses. De best one was made out of plain, white muslin. I went out in de woods and got walnut bark to color it brown* (11. 7:359–360 [KY and MO/MO]).

Sometimes commercial dying products were procured.

Charlie Meadow (83 years): *Our dyes was made from bark skinned from de maple tree. Dis was mixed with copperas for a pretty yellow. Green dye was bought from a store in Union . . .* (3. 3:180 [SC]).

The interviewer paraphrased John Harrison (b. 1847): "The thread was usually dyed before it was woven. The dye was made with sumac, and copperas which would make a very good tan. Indigo was purchased at trading posts and all shades of blue could be made. Sycamore and Red Oak bark would make a pink or red" (S1. 12:146–147 [OK]).

Marie Askin Simpson (b. ca. 1858): *Indigo made blues and purples. Just according to how long or how strong the dye was used. The indigo was bought at the drugstore* (S1. 2:232 [MO]).

More usually, the contributors told of gathering cultivated or wild plants to make natural dyes.

Emma Tidwell: *Ah'll tell yuh how tuh dye. Er little beech bark dyes slate color set wid copper. Hickory bark an bay leaves dyes yellow set wid chamber lye; bamboo dyes turkey red, set color wid copper. Pine straw an sweet gum dyes purple, set color wid chamber lye. Ifa yuh don' bleave hit try um all* (10. 6:331 [AR]).

Louis Fowler (84 years): *How dey dye de cloth am dis away: de dyes am made f'om de bahk ob walnut, cherry an' red oak trees while some am made f'om berries dat am found in de woods. Now, de bahk am out in watuhan' boiled 'til it am an ooze, de diffe'nt bahk makes de diffe'nt colors. Also, if weuns want clay red, weuns bury de cloth in red clay fo'a week an' de cloth would took on de red clay color. To make de dye fast color, weuns soak de cloth in cold salt wautah aftah it am dyed* (S1. 4. 3:1389 [GA/TX]).

In order to insure that the color will hold, the fabric must be immersed in a mordant (setting agent).

Queen Elizabeth Bunts (73 years): *The clothes were simple and conservation due to the fact that . . . they had very little dye and most all of the clothes were of ecru as the dye used was not fast colors and was not practical for wash dressed [sic], shirts . . .* (S1. 3. 1:127 [GA]).

A number of comments from the formerly enslaved people show very close parallels with the African dying techniques, including knowledge of mordants.[21] This suggests that "acculturation" is a two-way process; that is, the Africans not only learned from the European Americans, but they also made valuable contributions to American know-how.

Joseph Holmes (81 years): *I doesn't 'member whut dey used fer dye, but I knows dey used copperas as sizin' tuh hol' de colors. Sum ob de cloth wuzed dyed, red blue an' black. I jes' can't 'member about de dye, but dey use copperas, 'dat wuz de qualifications ob de intelligence ob de primitive age* (S2. 1:10 [AL]).

Bascom writes that among the modern Yoruba of southwestern Nigeria:

> The most popular dye is indigo, which produces varying shades ranging from a light sky blue to a purplish blue-black, depending upon the number of batches of dye used. Imported indigo has long been available, but it is considered inferior to that produced locally (101).

> Emma Tidwell: *We planted indigo an hit growed jes like wheat. When hit got ripe we gathered hit an we would put hit in a barrel an let hit soak bout er week den we would take de indigo stems out an squeeze de juice outn dem, put de juice back in de barrel an let hit stay dere bout nother week, den we jes stirred an stirred one whole day. We let hit set three or four days den drained de water offn hit an dat left de settlings an de settlings wuz blueing jes like we have dese days. We cut ours in little blocks. Den we dyed clothes wid hit. We had purty blue cloth. De way we set de color we put alum in hit. Dat make de color stay right dere* (10. 6:331 [AR]).

Sieber says that in Africa, "[a]lthough there are [early-traveler] reports of other colors – black, yellow, and red in particular – indigo seems to have been the most common and popular" (201).

> Lidia Jones (94 years): *I helped weave cloth. Dyed it? I wish you'd hush! My missie went to the woods and got it. All I know is, she said it was indigo. She had a great big kettle and she put her thread in that.* No *Lord, she never bought her indigo – she raised it* (9. 4:151 [MS/AR]).

But, with the exception of indigo, the Africans in the American South, like their white counterparts of European descent, had to learn which of the unfamiliar plants and minerals would produce cloth dyes.

> Nicey Kinney (86 years): *. . . but dere didn't nobody have no better or prettier dresses den ours, 'cause Mistress knowed more'n anybody 'bout dyin cloth. When time come to make up a batch of clothes Mistress would say, 'Ca'line help me git up my things for dyein'.' and us would fetch dogwood bark, sumach, poison ivy, and sweet gum bark. That poison ivy made the best black of anything us ever tried, and Mistress could dye the prettiest sort of purple wid sweet gum bark. Cop'ras was used to keep the colors from fadin', and she knowed so well how to handle it dat you could wash what she had dyed all day long and it wouldn't fade a speck* (13. 3:26–27 [GA]).

Woven and Applied Ornamentation

Cloth was ordinarily dyed in solid colors.

Lou Austin (female, b. 1850): *Us wimmins had blue, brown er white dresses* (S. 2. 2. 1:126 [TX]).

But multi-hued cloth could be attained by combining threads of different colors during weaving. In this way, patterns appeared in the clothing.

Hagar Lewis (b. 1855): *She'd make our Sunday Dresses. My mother put colored thread in woven material and they was pretty* (S2. 6. 4:2334 [TX]).

Stripes and then checks were the woven patterns usually mentioned.

Mandy Jones (80 years): *We had good loom made close, checks an' stripes* (S1. 8. 3:1229 [MS]).

Victoria Taylor Thompson (80 years): *Mother took me with her to the weaving room, and the mistress learn me how to weave in the stripes and colors so's I could make up one hundred kind of colors and shades. She ask me the color and I never miss telling her. That's one thing my sister Patsy can't learn when she was a little girl* (S1. 2:322 [OK]).

Henry Clay (100 years?): *Old negroes make our clothes from homespun cotton, and some mixed wool in cold weather. I had one long shirt that had five different colors in the stripes* (S1. 12:110 [SC/OK]).

Patterned ornamentation might also be applied after the cloth was woven. Stripes, again, were most often mentioned.

Tildy Moody ("six years old when freedom came"): *If we want' t'color d' hanks we tie dem wid strings t' mak checks. If we want' plain color dey jus' dip in d' big boil dye pot* (S2. 7. 6:2727–2728 [TX]).

Morris Sheppard (b. 1852): *Everything was stripedy 'cause old Mammy liked to make it fancy. She dye wid copperas and walnut and wild indigo and things like dat and make pretty cloth* (7:287 [OK]).

Sally Dixon: *Some of the cloth was dyed in colored stripes. It sure was beautiful, but most of it was left white* (S1. 9. 4:626–627 [MS]).

Catherine Slim (87 years): *I wore a little calico dress in de summer, white, red, and blue. Some had flowers and some had stripes* (16. 4:79 [VA/OH]).

Stripes, checks, and calico (usually figured and commercially produced) are the dominant types of patterns noted by the contributors. There is little evidence for any other decoration in the fabric itself. One noteworthy account, however, comes from the Rev. James W. Washington, whose paternal grandmother was born in Madagascar and enslaved by the French. His maternal great-grandmother was from the "Congo Free States." Rev. Washington's description of the pattern of his mother's dress fabric seems more African-inspired than American. This suggests that one of the older African-born relatives decorated it, or that it had been decorated by his mother who had passed on the family stories to her son.

> The Rev. James W. Washington (b. 1854): *Yessum, I has a good memory. I ken remember a dress my mammy wore. It was blue en had pictures uf gourds in it en mammy sed I wus 3 years old when she had dat dress* (S1. 10. 5:2198 [MS]).

A final way in which clothing might be enhanced was by attaching objects to it, but the formerly enslaved gave little evidence for these additions.

> Henry Lewis (b. 1835): *[W]e make buttons for us clothes out'n li'l round pieces of gourds and kiver them with cloth* (5. 3:13 [TX]).

> Frances Willingham (78 years): *Summertime us wore homespun dresses, made wid full skirts sewed on to tight fittin' waisties what was fastened down de bak wid buttons made out of cows and rams horns* (13. 4. 155 [GA]).

> Mary James: *The men had wool clothes with brass buttons that had shanks on em. They looked good when they were new* (16. 3:42 [VA/MD]).

Clothing Manufacture

Sewing

> "Do you know how to sew?" said Miss Ophelia . . ..
> "No, Missis," [replied Topsy].
> "What can you do?" (Harriet Beecher Stowe [1852] 1984:357)

Once the cloth was woven, it was ready for tailoring. Of the "contraband" girls whom Elizabeth Botume taught in 1863, she wrote: "Sewing had a great fascination for them all. They learned readily, and soon developed much skill and ingenuity. They had never had the free use of sewing materials before . . ." (64–65). And, of the "contraband" boys, Botume wrote: "The boys begged to be allowed to sew too . . .. So in time, when our stock of goods increased, we had a class of boys in sewing, some of whom did most credible work" (68–69). Botume's first-hand account of boys who sewed is unusual according to the people recorded in the *Narratives*; sewing as they knew it during the period of enslavement was, with few exceptions, a woman's craft.

Elias Howe received the first patent for a sewing machine in 1846, but few of the formerly enslaved people indicated that they had experience with sewing machines during the antebellum period.[22]

> Lucy A. Delaney (enslaved in Missouri): *Those were the days in which sewing machines were unknown, and no stitching or sewing of any description was allowed to pass muster, unless each stitch looked as if it were a part of the cloth. The art of sewing was lost when sewing machines were invented, and though doubtless they have given women more leisure, they have destroyed that extreme neatness in the craft* (reproduced in Andrews, 54–56).

> Aunt Sally: *We had no sewin' machine – had to sew by hand* (12. 1:144) [GA]).

> Marie Askin Simpson (b. ca, 1858): *Dresses in those days were tight fitting waists and full skirts. The dresses and petticoats had yards of lace and tucks. There were no sewing machines. All the women learned to sew by hand. I never learned to sew very young because I had to nurse the children, so the older ones could be free to sew* (S1. 2:232 [MO]).

It is interesting to note that in the few instances when sewing machines were employed, men often spoke of them. The early mechanisms were cumbersome and took physical strength to operate which may account for the male involvement in sewing with them. The narration by Louis Hughes (b. 1843, enslaved in Mississippi and Virginia) is a good example. Hughes relates his own experiences in making clothing on a sewing machine when his "owner's" family went on an extended visit and left him in charge of their house.

> *[I] . . . was expected to keep everything in order, and also to make the winter clothes for the farm hands. The madam and I had cut out these clothes before she left, and it was my principal duty to run the sewing machine in their manufacture. Many whole days I spent at this work. My wife made the button holes and sewed on the buttons. I made hundreds of sacks for use in picking cotton. This work was always done in summer. When the garments were all finished they were shipped to the farm at Bolivar, to be ready for the fall and winter wear. In like manner the clothes for summer use were made in winter* (107).

Hughes was later taken to work at his "owner's" farm, and there:

> *I had to look after the house at the farm, attend the dining room, and, between meals, sew every day, making clothes for the hands. I could run on the machine eighteen to twenty pairs of pants a day, but two women made the button holes and did the basting for me, getting the goods all ready for the machine* (122).

In spite of the division of labor according to sex implied in Hughes' account, women occasionally were credited with operating the machine.

> William Branch (b. 1850): *How'd us slaves git de clothes? We carded de cotton, den de women spin it on a spinnin' wheel. After dat dey sew de gahment togeddah on a sewin' machine. Yahsur, we's got sewin' machine, wid a big wheel and a handle. One women tu'n de handle and de yuther woman do de sewin'* (4. 1:143 [TX]).

In the decades just following the Civil War, sewing machines apparently were among the material status symbols acquired by some. Booker T. Washington, however, condemned the poor, rural Blacks of Alabama for spending their earnings on what he felt were follies, considering their adverse economic circumstances. Washington apparently did not wish to delve into the psychological underpinnings which prompted these people to want to own "showy clocks," "organs" or "*sewing-machines which had been bought or were being bought, on installments, frequently at a cost of as much as sixty dollars . . .. In most cases the sewing-machine was not used . . .*" ([1901] 1986:113).

During the period of enslavement, according to the contributors to the *Narratives*, almost all clothing was stitched by hand.

> Tildy Moody ("six years old when freedom came): *Eb'ry feller big 'nuf mek dey own dress. I mek my own since I big 'nuf t' tell* (S7. 6:2728 [TX]).

Moody's statement that she and others she knew were responsible for making their own clothes is unusual for, more often, narrators mention that clothing was produced either by specially trained Black women or their white "mistresses" or by professional seamstresses who were hired for that purpose. Arthur Colson (ca. 86 years) said that African American women wove all the cloth on the cotton plantation where he was enslaved, but that poor, white widows who lived nearby sewed the enslaved people's clothing (S1. 3. 1:221 [GA].

Georgina Gibbs: *All de cloth during slavery time was made on de loom. My mastah had three slaves who worked in de loom house. After de cloth was made, mastah sent hit over town to a white woman who made hit in clothes* (16. 5:15 [VA]).

Lulu Scott: *A dressmaker come twicet uh year 'm' make clo'es fuh us, she'd come down the pike to meet 'er, a-swegin' on 'er, pesterin' 'er, ca'yin' bunnels fuh ih. All th' soots fuh th' little boys uz made fum the same cloth, all they soots look jes alike* (S1. 5. 1:188 [KY/IN]).

Enslaved men might also be employed as tailors. The Historical Society of Carroll County, Maryland, owns a wooden doll made by a Black enslaved tailor in about 1830 (Figure 14). According to Ruth Woodyard, a Black

Figure 14. A male tailor, enslaved to the Woodyard family of Carroll County, Maryland, made and dressed this wooden doll for his daughter or granddaughter, ca. 1830. The wool trousers are original. Collection of the Historical Society of Carroll County, Maryland; Woodyard Doll: gift of Mr. Charles M. Clark, 1963.

Carroll Countian and a descendent of the tailor, he made the doll for his daughter or granddaughter. The doll remained in the Woodyard family for about 120 years. The eyes of the hand-carved doll are made of flattened buckshot. The doll is dressed in male clothing: wool trousers are original, the under jacket is a copy of the original pattern, while the jacket was the idea of a later seamstress.

Upon greeting the interviewer, one contributor made known that men might sometimes be responsible for mending their apparel. At the same time, he also alluded to a folk belief related to sewing tasks:

> Charlie Robinson (87 years): *Glad you come out here but sorry of de day, 'cause it is a Friday and all de jay-birds go to see de devil dat day of de week. It's a bad day to begin a garment . . .. Does I believe all dat? I believe it 'nough not to patch dese old breeches 'til tomorrow* (3. 4:35 [SC]).

In some cases, white women were responsible for clothing the Blacks. For example, a South Carolina judicial case (Bogan v. White, Dudley 87, December 1837) records: "the negro woman . . . was sick, and he wished the mother of defendant's wife to stay . . . and take care of the negro . . .. The mother made clothes for these negroes . . .." On the other hand, another South Carolina juridical case (Lyles v. Lyles, I Hill Eq. 76, January 1833) reads: "In the middle and upcountry, the usual habit is to clothe the negroes by the labor of the females, at times when they can be conveniently dispensed with in the field . . ." (ibid. , 351). Figure 15 is a photograph of an enslaved boys' outfit made by enslaved women in Louisiana. Harriet Jacobs (b. 1813, North Carolina) notes that one of her chores as a servant for the Flints was sewing (20).

> Louis Hughes (b. 1832, enslaved in Mississippi and Virginia): *Bright mulatto girls, well versed in sewing and knitting, would sometimes bring as high as $1,800, especially if a Virginian or a Kentuckian* (12).

> Harriet Lee (b. 1861): *Mah mammy wuz a seamstress. She nevuh work in de feel', an' she don' know nothin' 'bout cookin', but she do fine sewin'. When dey put her in de block dey has some o' her work dar tuh show what fine sewin' she kin do. Yuh know all de sewin war done by han' and mah mammy'd sew sometimes till huh finguhs nearly drop off. She sew de fines' tuckes an' she make all dem fine tuck bosom shurts fo' de men* (11. 7. 8:222 [MO].

> Hannah Hancock (past 80 years): *My mistress didn't do much. Miss Becky Hancock wove cloth for people . . .. She made checked dresses and mingledy*

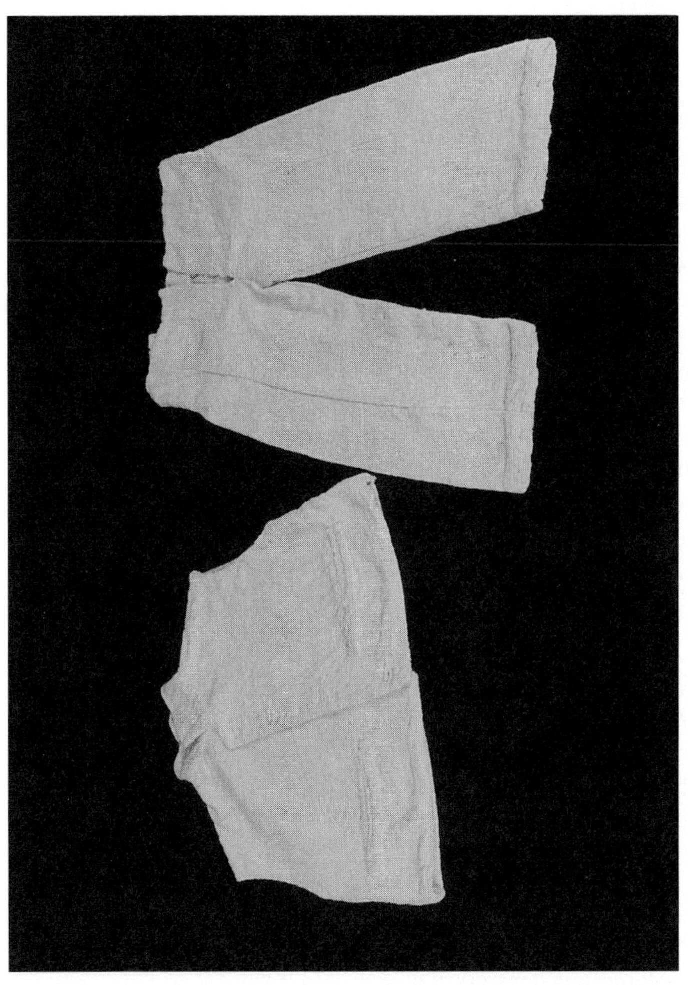

Figure 15. Enslaved boy's sleeveless jacket and trousers, slave-made, ca. 1850s. Rough, homespun, natural cotton; undyed. Boys who wore this type of outfit probably worked as domestics, but the clothing is similar to that worn by older male field and mill hands. Collection of Shadows-on-the-Teche, a museum property of the National Trust for Historic Preservation, New Iberia, Louisiana.

> *looking cloth. Mrs. Sellers got a bolt of cloth and have it all made up into dresses for the children. Sometimes all our family would have a dress alike . . .. Granny made de dresses on her fingers . . .. Granny didn't have no patterns. She jess made our dresses lack come in her haid* (9. 3:142, 143 [SC/AR]).

The *Narratives* provide examples of both Black and white women, sometimes working together, sewing the clothes.

> Vina Moore (b. 1845): *We had plenty gingham dresses of all kinds. Dey had women dat jest done de weavin and dey made our clothes. Mah missus sometimes made me dresses. Dey was shore nice too* (S2. 7. 6:2757 [MS, TX/TX]).

> Betty Cofer (b. 1856): *I was trained to cook an' clean an' sew. I learned to make mens' pants an' coats. First coat I made, Miss Julia told me to rip the collar off, an' by the time I picked out all the teensy stitches an' sewed it together again I could set a collar right!* (14. 1 [NC]).

> Sarah Anne Green (78 years): *Hannah, my mammy, wuz de head seamstress [for a plantation of about 300 enslaved people]. She had to 'ten' to de makin' of all de slaves clothes. De niggers had good clothes. De cloth wuz home woven in de weavin' room. Ten niggers didn' do nothin' but weave, but every slave had one Sunday dress a year made out of store bought cloth* (14. 1 [NC]).

> Queen Elizabeth Bunts (73 years): *My mother, Angeline Smith, made all the clothes worn by the Norris family. She could card, spin, weave, and dye. She never used a pattern to cut by, but would take your measure and every dress had to fit snug and tight. The clothes worn by the slaves were made by young negro women who were taught to sew. The clothes were simple and conservative due to the fact that they had no patterns* (S1. 3. 1:126–127 [GA]).

Polly Colbert (83 years) was enslaved to a couple who were both half Choctaw. The following may indicate that "Miss Betsy" had attended a mission or government school for Native Americans:

> *De women done all de spinning and de weaving but Miss Betsy cut out all de clothes and helped wid de sewing. She learned to sew when she was away to school and she learnt all her women to sew* (7:36 [OK]).

Margaret Davis Cate gives brief biographical portraits of the African Americans she knew on St. Simons Island. She began recording their histories and customs in 1936, but Cate's narrative implies that she is actually recounting antebellum occurrences.

> Tyrah Wilson was the matua maker of Mrs. George C. Dent . . . of Hofwyl Plantation. Trained as a seamstress, Tyrah was in charge of the sewing room and of a group of women who worked under her direction and whose task it was to make the clothes for the Negroes of the plantation. Measuring and cutting the cloth under the direction of the mistress of the plantation, the sewing room workers were a busy group (185).

Free Black women in the North had the advantage of becoming independent workers at earlier dates than their enslaved Southern counterparts, yet often the northern women's occupations also related to clothing production. Mrs. Sarah Johnson of New York advertised in the *Freedman's Journal*, 29 April 1829, "that she had commenced Bleaching, Pressing and Refitting Leghorn and Straw-Hats, in the best manner. Ladies Dresses made, and plain Sewing done at the most reasonable terms" (Sterling, 98).[23]

Because she published her autobiography (1868), Elizabeth Keckley (1818–1907)is perhaps the best-known African American seamstress of her day. Enslaved in Virginia, Keckley bought her own freedom and moved to Washington before the end of the Civil War. There she opened a dress-making establishment, employing twenty girls. She made clothes for the wives of several cabinet ministers and senators. Her most famous customer was Mary Todd Lincoln, with whom she became a close friend.

After emancipation, many Southern African American women continued in occupations related to making cloth and clothing. An 1880 series of articles in *Harper's Weekly* found that after the Civil War, Black women continued to carry an exceptional work load, including making cloth and clothing (Sterling, 325). The newspaper noted that in South Carolina:

> Generally, the woman is the provider of the whole family and even when the man works, the wife takes in washing or sewing, or goes out to day's work, it being an understood thing that she is to provide clothing, while he undertakes for the rent and food. In most cases, however, the woman takes care of the whole family (326).

Knitting

Techniques used in the manufacture of cloth and clothing, such as spinning and weaving, were known to Africans. Knitting, however, was a European craft. Nonetheless, many African Americans picked up this skill.

> Hagar Lewis (82 years): *When I was turned loose Miss Mary was teaching me and mister to do hand work, knitting and such. She'd teach us our lesson in the evening in the big house* (S2. 6. 5:2334 [TX]).

The refugees whom Botume lived among in South Carolina came from the surrounding tidewater region as well as from the islands off the coast. Botume noted that

> . . . [the Combahee River] women knew how to do many things of which the island people were quite ignorant. Before spring I saw many pairs of shapely gloves and stout stockings made of the coarse yarn spun in a tin basin and knitted on reeds, cut in swamps. These were sent to husbands, sons, and lovers, off duty as soldiers . . ..
>
> It was not an unusual thing to meet a woman coming from the field where she had been hoeing cotton, with a small bucket or cup on her head, a hoe over her shoulder, contentedly smoking a pipe and briskly knitting as she strode along. I have seen, added to these, a baby strapped to her back (53).

African American women produced a variety of knitted articles of clothing.

> Sarah Graves (b. 1850): *I have gathered the wool off the fences where it had been caught off the sheep, an' washed it, an' used it to make mittens* (11. 7. 8:131 [MO]).

> Mary Johnson: *My mother mek lotser knit sweaters and sox for mens, and mek lotser money for herse'f dat way. She git dat sheep wool w'at has been ruin' wid cockle burrs. Den she mek us chillen set by de hour and pick out de cockle burrs so she could mek de thread* (S2. 6. 5:2026 [MS/TX]).

> Lulu Scott: *All th' scarfs, mittin's, stockin's, socks, caps 'n' sich like muther's knit. She knit ever'theng; wuddent no sto' to be a-runnin to ever minnit* (S1. 5:188 [KY/IN]).

The contributors noted particularly hand-knit socks and stockings.

> Tildy Moody ("six years old when freedom came"): *I was fas' I could knit a real good pair 'r' sox in two weeks* (S2. 7. 6:2727 [TX]).

> Hattie Thompson (b. 1867): *I have seen big balls [of thread] this big (2 ft. in diameter) down on the floor and mama knitting off of it right on. When the feet wore out on socks and stockings, they would unravel them, save the good thread, and reknit the foot or toe or heel* (10. 6:315 [AR]).

> Unidentified: *[Y]ou'd knit your own stockings. They would shear the sheep and sell the best wool and then the second wool you would take and knit your stockings and hang them up for Christmas* (18. 5 [TN or KY]).

Often, contributors mention that white women taught them the skill.

Mariah Robinson (ca. 81 years): *I knitted my stockin's but Missus Joe had to drop de stitch foh me to turn my heels an toes* (S2. 8. 7:3353 [GA, TX/TX]).

Patsy Hyde: *Mah Missis nit all de white chilluns stockin' en she made me sum, I had ter hold de yarn on mah hans w'en she wuz nittin'* (16. 6:33 [TN]).

Interestingly, a few men related that they also knit.

Harrison Beckett: *I used to could knit socks and I was jes' a li'l boy then* (4. 1:55 [TX]).

But James L Smith (enslaved in Virginia) recalled his lack of success with knitting as a boy:

At last, night came and I was relieved from working so steady. When I was not Carding I was obliged to knit; I disliked it very much; I was very slow; it used to take me two or three weeks to knit one stocking, and when I had finished it you could not tell what the color was (reprinted in Bontemps, 152).

Caring for Clothes

Janey Landrum (b. 1851): *Don' sew or wash or iron on New Year's Day, or dar will be some member ob the family die befo' the year git gone* (S2. 6. 5:2268 [TX]).

Enslaved people, usually women, were responsible for keeping their own families' clothes clean, as well as washing the white peoples' clothes.

Hattie Sugg: *My Ma would make soap fo' Missus Nancy an steal a gourd full of it an' bury it some place to wash our Sunday clothes with. She had to do all our washin on Sunday* (S1. 10. 5:2076 [MS]).

Many plantation owners insisted that the Blacks wear clean clothes on Sundays and at the beginning of the work week. Most often the enslaved people cared for their clothing during free-time on weekends.

Amanda Jackson: *You had to do yo' own work on Saturdays an' Sundays – I 'members seeing my po' mother wash her clothes on Sundays many times* (12. 1:290 [GA]).

Adline Marshall: *We works every day 'cept Sundays, and we had to do our washing den* (S2. 7. 6:2578 [SC, TX/TX]).

Mary Reynolds (over 100 years): *Once in a while they would give us a little piece of Saturday evenin's to wash our cloths in the branch. We hung them on the groun' in the woods to dry. There was a place to wash clothes from the well but they was so many Niggers that all couldn't get 'round to it on Sundays* (S2. 8. 7:3289 [LA/TX]).

C. B. McRay (Male, b. 1861): *Master's niggers all got Sunday clothes and shoes. Every one of dem have to dress and come to the parlor so he could look dem over 'fore dey go to church* (5. 3:41 [TX]).

Washing clothes must be typical of all societies, but recipes for soap are not. In the 1810s, Osifekunde reported on the manufacture of soap among the Ijebu:

I have already shown that making cloth is the usual task of women. Each household also makes a black soap, or rather a detergent made of ashes without the use of oil, for washing clothes and other domestic uses (Lloyd, ed., 169).

In the United States, soap was also homemade. Ashes, to form lye, were ingredients in American soap as well as African; but, unlike the African soap described by Osifekunde, American soap also contained oil or grease.

Margrett Nickerson: *My pa made soap from ashes when cleaning new ground – he took a hopper to put de ashes in, made a little stool side de house put de ashes in and po'red water on it to drip; at night after gittin' off frum work he'd put in de grease and make de soap – I made it sometime and I make it now, myself* (17. 1:251 [FL]).

Salena Taswell (b. 1844): *The lye was very strong. They had to be careful not to get any of it on their hands or it would take the skin off. As they would stir the grease and lye it would form and cook like a jelly and when it cooled we had soft soap. It would sure chase the dirt, but It was hard on the hands* (17. 1:306 [FL]).

In the United States, certain articles of clothing received the addition of stiffening agents. Like soap, the starch was homemade. The contributors noted a number of glutenous substances that made suitable cloth starch. Making and applying starch and then ironing the starched fabric were labor–intensive chores that we might expect in the maintenance of nineteenth-century white peoples' clothing. More surprising is the fact that several Blacks also noted that their own clothes were starched.

> Callie Elder (78 years): *Us wore de same on Sunday as evvy day, 'cept dat our clothes was clean, and stiff wid meal starch when us got into 'em on Sunday mornins'* (12. 1:309 [GA]).

The interviewer paraphrased Della Briscoe: "The crudely made garments were starched with a solution of flour or [?] and water which was strained and then boiled" (12. 1:129 [GA]).

A few men told of helping with the clothes washing.

> George Earle (b. 1850): *I had to help wash [the whites' clothes]. I used a battlin' stick lots of days till my hands blistered for a week. Dat was de times we washed de rugs and de quilts though. De clothes wasn't washed dat way. Dey was jist flapped against de rubbin' board till dey was clean, and den dey was washed through some clean water and hung on wires and bushes till dey was dry. It allus took all day to do de washin'* (S1. 4. 3:1246–1247 [TX]).

But most remembered that washing almost always fell to the women. The earliest-known published autobiographical narrative from a formerly enslaved Black woman is that of Mary Prince(b. ca. 1788) who describes the amount of exertion it took to wash her "owners'" clothes. Nonetheless, the industrious Prince noted: "*When my master and mistress went from home . . . I took in washing . . . for I wanted to earn money to buy my freedom*" (15–16).

Lucy A. Delaney (enslaved in Missouri) described her first attempts to do her "mistress's" washing: "*I had no more idea how it was to be done than Mrs. Mitchell herself*" (reproduced in Andrews, 24). In despair, "*in the morning, before the white people had arisen, a friend of my mother came to the house and washed out the clothing*"(25).

> Julia Stubbs (b. ca. 1852): *When I growed big enough to Wuk I wuz put at mos' enything dat come handy, jis' doing fust one thing den another. Mos'o' my Wuk wuz 'round de house. I learnt to spin, knit an' weave. I helped wid de washing an' dey wuz some washing to do, wid loads o' water to be drawed an' toted to de long wash troughs made by hueing out big logs, dey wuz put on racks. We had to rub de clo'se by hand, so we beat 'em on blocks wid hickory battling sticks. It took 'bout all day to do dem washings* (S1. 10. 5:2069 [MS]).

> James Jackson (b. 1850): *Whin de darkies wazn't wokkin' in de fiel', de women, dey wosh an' patch de clothes. De men, dey would build de fire an' carry de*

water fur de woshin', den some of dem would wokke in de gardens (S. 2. 5. 4:1897 [LA/TX]).

Jacob Branch (ca. 86 years): *My pore mama! Every washday old missy give her a beatin' She couldn't keep de flies from speckin' de clothes overnight. Ole missy . . . snort and say, 'Renee, I's gwine ter teach you how to wash. 'Den she beat mama with de cowhide* (4. 1:139 [TX]).

Olivier Blanchard (95 years): *The Bayou Teche, it run close by and the women do all the clothes with a big paddle with holes in it to clean them in the bayou. They paddle them clean on the rocks and then wash them in the water* (4. 1:90 [LA/TX]).

Minus Biddie (b. 1833): *Washing was done in home made wooden tubs, and boiling in iron pots similar to those of today* (17. 1:34 [FL]).

Fannie McCullough Driver (b. 1857): *[M]ammy was washin' clothes on de bank ob de Guadalupe River. Tubs had been hauled to de bank ob de river, fires was made and de washin' was done right dere. De washed clothes was den brought back to de big house and hung up to dry . . .. While de wimmen was washin' de clothes dey would sing songs. Some ob 'em made up songs while dey washed* (S1. 4. 3:1233 [TX]).

If a "master" denied the enslaved people the opportunity to hold spiritual meetings, they found another use for wash tubs. This entailed speaking and singing the service into an overturned tub in the belief that it would "catch" their voices, and that the master would be no more the wiser.

Charlotte Brooks (enslaved in Virginia and Louisiana): *Sometimes when we met to hold our meeting we would put a big wash-tub full of water in the middle of the floor to catch the sound of our voices when we sung . . .* (Alberts, 12).

Henry Chestam (b. 1850): *He [overseer] wouldn't 'low no meetin' on de place. Sometimes us would slip down the hill an' turn de wash pot bottom up'ards so de soun' of our voices would go under de pot, an' us'd have a singin' an' prayin' right dere* (6. 1:68 [AL]).

Oliver Bell: *When de had de prayer meetin's dey shut de do' so won't let de voice out, en day turn de wash pot down at de do' – some say ter keep it in* (S1. 1:55 [AL]).

Dorothy Scarborough collected a "rubbing song" in Louisiana:

A very little Negress down on the bayou
Washing shirts, oh, Mama,
Oh, lady, the washer woman
(*On the Trail*, 212; cited in Jackson-Brown, 390).

Making soap, hauling wash tubs, or taking bundles of clothes to a natural water source, scrubbing and rinsing without the advantage of piped water, and making and applying starch for members of two families – all were physically draining, arduous weekly tasks. And then, the clothing had to be ironed. The final laborious task associated with caring for clothes meant using a heavy tool actually cast from iron and warmed by direct contact with a heated stove or fireplace.

Ellen Claibourn (b. 1852): *Yes, ma'am, everybody did they own work. De cook cooked, and the washer, she didn't iron no clothes. De ironer did that* (12. 1:187 [GA]).

Julia Woodberry (70–80 years, born after slavery): Den de people never wore none of dese kind of clothes like de people wear dese days neither. When a person got a dress den, dey made it deselves en dey made dey own underskirts den, too. You see, all dese underskirts en bloomers like de people dose buy dese days, dey didn' have nothin like dat den. Used to put 10 yards in a dress en 10 yards in a underskirt en would tuck em clean up to dey waist. En, child, when dey would iron dat dress, it would stand up in de floor just like dere been somebody in it. When I say iron, I talkin bout de people would iron den, too. Yes, mam, when I come along, de people been take time to iron dey garments right. Oh, day clothes would be just as slick as glass. Won' a wrinkle nowhe' bout dem (3. 4:235 [SC]).

One woman offered folk beliefs about ironing boards.

Janey Landrum (b. 1851): *Don'd nebber leabe the i'ronin' bo'd up ober night. Effen' you set on a ironin' bo'd, you'll sho' fail to git a husban'* (S2. 6. 5:2267 [TX]).

William Hayden (b. 1785, enslaved in Virginia and Kentucky) was allowed to hire out on his own time and "*I commenced cleaning clothes, boots, shoes, &c. , for such gentlemen as gave me employment . . .*" (1846:43). Paralleling Hayden's experience are those "free" Blacks to whom Robert Roberts addresses his instructions in *The House Servant's Directory*. Appearing in 1827, it was "the first book by a black American published by a commercial publisher [and] also has the distinction of being the first directory of its kind(white and black) in the performance of the innumerable duties as the detailed title page of the book proclaims . . ." (Maxwell Whiteman, reprint n. d. , p. i). A number of entries detail such items as: "Brushing and folding gentlemen's clothes," "Brushing and cleaning gentlemen's hats," "A secret against all kind of spots on silk or cotton," "To take spots of any sort, from any kind of cloth," "To revive the color of cloth," "To preserve furs or woollen clothes from moths," and so on. Though women might take advantage of his advise, Roberts' manual was clearly written for male servants. Julia Blanks (b. 1862) remembered: "*My grandfather bought my grandmother's time and they run a laundry house*" (4. 1:93 [TX]).

In spite of the evidence that some Black men became "washerwomen," out of slave times emerged the more persistent image of the Black woman as "washerwoman." For instance, in a sketch written about Harriet Tubman, William Still's notes that when Tubman arrived in the Sea islands in 1862, shortly after their capture by Union forces, "To help the freed-women become self-supporting she taught them how to do the soldiers' washing and built a washhouse, which she paid for out of her earnings" (quoted in Sterling, 258). After the Civil War, as many of the newly freed people began migrating from rural areas to the cities, it was the women who often found a ready source of income by doing other people's laundry. Dorothy Sterling asserts that "Washerwomen were so indispensable to city life that they ventured to get together to ask for higher wages;" and recounts newspaper articles about these attempts in Jackson, Mississippi; Texas, and Atlanta during the decades between 1866 and 1881 (355–359).

> Phillis Hicks (71 years): *I washed and ironed in Memphis till washing went out of style* (9. 3:236 [SC/AR]).

Even after migrating to the North, washing other peoples' clothes remained one of the only independent occupations open to Black women. Louis Hughes (b. 1843, enslaved in Mississippi and Virginia) and his wife settled in Milwaukee in 1868. Hughes relates that in his job at a hotel, he "*was allowed to take washing from any of the guests who desired their work done privately.*" Hughes continues, "*In this way I worked up quite a business. I still continued my coat room duties, as my wife managed the laundry work*" (200). By 1874, he says, "*The laundry business had increased to such an extent that my wife could not manage it alone. I, therefore, gave up my position at the hotel, and went into the laundry business on a somewhat larger scale . . .*" (205).

Washerwomen figured in one of Booker T. Washington's lessons for his people:

> *In Washington I saw girls whose mothers were earning their living by laundrying. These girls were taught by their mothers . . . the industry of laundrying. Later, these girls entered the public schools and remained there perhaps six or eight years. When the public-school course was finally finished, they wanted more costly dresses, more costly hats and shoes . . . their six or eight years of book education had weaned them away from the occupation of their mothers. The result of this was in too many cases that the girls went to the bad. I often thought how much wiser it would have been to give these girls the same amount of mental training . . . but at the same time to give them the most thorough training in the latest and best methods of laundrying and other kindred occupations* (90–91).

As an educator, Washington practice what he preached. In the early days of the founding of Hampton Institute, Washington directed the night-school students and oversaw the tasks they performed for their keep and education. Of this period, he wrote: "*During the day the greater part of the young men worked in the school's sawmill, and the young women worked in the laundry*" (104).

Notes

1. Norris W. Preyer (1961) follows the development of the textile industry in the antebellum South, noting especially the reasons for the decline in using African Americans in cloth-manufacturing factories in the late 1830s and 1840s. Preyer also makes the point that, in spite of Southern attempts to foster industrial textile manufacture in their own territory, "Northern textile products even after being shipped South still sold for less than did the local goods" (79; also see Beatty, 1987).

2. Michael Mullin demonstrates that some enslaved people in the Virginia piedmont were able to buy from a local store, often paying in kind with items they had produced. Mullin says that the 1801–1804 account books for a factor's store show that " [t]he slaves bought mostly cloth, an item cited more than any other as stolen goods in slave trials"(152).

3. I include the following accounts because we do not generally recognize that the enslaved sometimes purchased their own cloth and clothing. When we consider how very little disposable income they had, these statements become even more significant because they point up the importance which the enslaved placed on dressing themselves.

Phillip Evans (85 years): *Yes, sir, Marster general give me small coins. Whar I do wid de money? I buy a pretty cap one time* (2. 2:36 [SC]).

Pauline Johnson: *Us daddy he work de ground he own on Sunday and sold the things to buy us shoes to put on us feet and clothes. The white folks didn't give us clothes but they let him have all the money he made in his own plot to get them* (4. 2:225 [LA/TX]).

Hannah Allen (107 years): *Den dey would get paid for working for others and deh buy clothes. Dey had de finest boots* (11. 8:9 [MO]).

Millie Ann Smith (b. 1850): *Master would take the cotton they [enslaved people] raised to Shreveport to sell it and bring us back calico, plaid and nice cloth for clothes and everything else we wanted* (S. 2. 9. 8:3654 [TX]).

Cato Carter (b. 1836 or 1837): *My marster used to give me a little money along to buy me what I wanted. I always bought fine clothes* (S2. 3. 2:642 [AL/TX]).

Benjamin Russell (88 years): *Yes, sometimes white folks and visitors would give me coppers, 3-cent pieces, and once or twice dimes. Used them to buy extra clothing for Sundays . . .* (3. 4:51 [SC]).

Annie Coley (80 years): *We bought Sunday close with our cotton money. Boss giv us plenty good work close* (S1. 7. 2:440 [MS]).

Hattie Sugg: *De few Sunday clothes me Ma had we got from Pa splittin' rails on Sunday fo' another fellow* (S1. 10. 5:2076 [MS]).

Henry Ryan: *Judge Butler used to give us a little money, too, before freedom come, for our work. We bought clothes and things we had to have* (3. 4:71 [SC]).

Genia Woodberry (89 years): *[H]e 'low eve'y family to hab uh acre uv land uv dey own to plant. Hadder work dat crop in de night . . . dat crop who' dey buy dey Sunday clothes wid. Ne'er hadder hunt no clothes but dey Sunday clothes cause dey hab seamstress right dere on de plantation to make aw us udder clothes* (3. 4:219 [SC]).

Mr. Reed: *[M]y father give us three boys a patch to make us a tobacco patch. We would take the money and buy us clothes. I remember the first shirt I bought was a pleated bosom shirt. I bought me some shoes and a hat* (18. 50 [TN or KY]).

4. However William Dosite Postell asserts that "On the whole, the cloth from which the clothes were made for slaves was manufactured in the North and East" (40).

5. Fox-Genovese writes: "Northern women also spent much of their lives needle in hand, but their households had, by the antebellum period, effectively shed most substantive textile production . . ." (121).

6. Patricia Mainardi writes about the work of white women during that time:

"For most of the Colonial period, and in rural areas up to and even after the Civil War, women were responsible for an amount of work hardly to be believed: besides the cooking and cleaning and raising and educating the children, they spun, wove and dyed cloth, made the clothing and bedding, curtains and rugs for the entire family, canned the food, milked cows, tended garden and chickens and made soap and candles" (1973:18).

Concerning textile production, specifically, Warren Roberts notes:

The folklife researcher must be interested in textiles because such a tremendous amount of people's time was spent on textiles in earlier days. I suppose that if we could know how people – especially women – spent their time in the small, self-sufficient communities, we

> would find that day-in day-out, year-round most time was devoted to raising, preserving and preparing food . . .. Second in importance, however, would probably be the time spent on textiles (1988:22).

For an earlier account of the agricultural and cloth-making tasks which two women, enslaved in Virginia in the mid-eighteenth century, were expected to undertake, see Gundersen, 1986:369.

7. William Kauffman Scarborough quotes from Thomas Affleck's *Cotton Plantation Record and Account Book* (1855) in demonstrating "the ideal criteria by which the planter judged the performance of his overseer" (70). Among his duties, the overseer was to insure that "both summer and winter clothing [were] made at home; also, leather tanned, and shoes and harness made when practicable."

8. Fox-Genovese suggests that the delegation of jobs by sex was due to male bias, but leaves open whether it was due to Black or white men's bias (319). On the other hand, Jacqueline Jones argues: "Within well-defined limits, the slaves created – or preserved – an explicit sexual division of labor based on their own preferences" (41; see also Patricia Morton, 140–141).

9. In a survey of "Skilled Blacks in Antebellum St. Mary's County, Maryland," Bayly E. Marks lists the nonagricultural occupations held by Black women, but notes that "between 1790 and 1864 only eighty-four black women could be found with known occupations outside farming, seventy of whom were free . . .." Marks also states, "In general it is difficult to uncover women's occupations" (1987:542).

10. The shift in pronoun gender is correct African American dialect in some parts of the United States.

11. For properties and production methods of wool, see Hollen, et al., 1988:44–56.

12. For brief historical background, production and properties of silk, see Hollen, et al., 1988:60–63.

13. For bast fibres, and properties and production methods of flax and hemp, see Hollen, et al., 1988:36–39, 40.

14. Kroll notes that flax "resembles long golden hair" when it is prepared for spinning; thus derive the terms "flaxen locks" and "tow-head" (36).

15. For a brief historical overview of the importance of cotton as a clothing fabric, see Hollen, et al., 1988:24; for production methods and properties of cotton, see ibid., 25–34.

16. In his autobiography, Louis Hughes (b. 1843, enslaved in Mississippi and Virginia) gives a detailed account of raising cotton in the antebellum period, from preparing the ground, to planting and harvesting, and finally for ginning in preparation for market (26–32).

17. *Weevils* contains the lyrics to three spinning songs, pp. 70, 88–89 and 309.

18. Jay Graybeal, "Visitor's Guide: The Sherman-Fisher-Shellman House," 1991:11–12. John Michael Vlach includes descriptions of separate buildings for textile manufacturing as part of "the architecture of plantation slavery" (1993:83–

84) and illustrates with photos of a loom house, a weaving house (100), and a spinning house (101).

19. See, for example, Catherine Clinton, *The Plantation Mistress*, who quotes from nineteenth-century Southern, white women's letters and diaries on the tasks associated with producing clothing (1982:26–28).

20. Elizabeth Fox-Genovese has explored the roles played by enslaved African American women and the Southern white women for whom they labored (1988). Hortense Spillers comments on the interrelationship of American Black and white women during the period of enslavement:

> . . . we could say that African-American women's community and Anglo-American women's community, under certain shared conditions, were the twin actants on a common psychic landscape . . .. In fact, from one point of view, we cannot unravel one female's narrative from the other's, cannot decipher one without tripping over the other (77).

21. Concerning modern West African techniques, Eicher writes that at present: "Some Yoruba women use caustic soda to make their dye solution alkaline. The use of the caustic soda in place of the pot-ash solution reduces the time required to prepare the dye . . ." (1976:79).

22. Postell contends that "Sewing machines were employed on a number of plantations," but gives only one documented example (40).

23. Based on her research, Dorothy Sterling estimates that " [p]erhaps 15 percent of [New York's Black] female work force were dressmakers and hairdressers" (216).

3

Wearing Antebellum Clothing

Vain trifles as they seem, clothes have, they say, more important offices than merely to keep us warm. They change our view of the world and the world's view of us.

Thus, there is much to support the view that it is clothes that wear us and not we them; we may make them take the mould of arm or breast, but they mould our heart, our brains, our tongues to their liking.

Clothes are but a symbol of something hid deep within (Virginia Woolf [1928] 1981:117).

Is fashion such a trifling thing? Or is it, as I prefer to think, rather an indication of deeper phenomenon – of the energies, possibilities, demands and *joie de vivre* of a given society, economy civilization? . . .

I have always thought that fashion resulted to a large extent from the desire of the privileged to distinguish themselves, whatever the cost, from the masses who followed them; to set up a barrier (Fernand Braudel 1979:323, 324).

The narrators' remarks about clothing usually combine two forms of insight: 1) itemization and description of specific articles of dress which very often include 2) additional critiques that illustrate attitudes held about clothing.

Clothes as Status Symbols

Black Perspectives on Whites' Clothing

Among the "slave codes" devised by Southern governments during the eighteenth century were those relating to dress. These legalities functioned to maintain white supremacy in a society based economically and socially on racial slavery. In effect, whites used these dress codes to outwardly distinguish those without power from those who held it. The earliest, South Carolina's Negro Act of 1735, "specifically set a standard of dress for the enslaved and free African Americans"(Wares, 1983:131–136). A. Leon

Higginbotham notes of the 1735 code: "when a slave managed to obtain clothing that might accord him some dignity or prestige, the act declared that when such clothing was 'above' that which a slave should wear, it could be taken from the slave by 'all and every constable and other persons' to be used for his or her own benefit" (1980:173). In 1740 amendments, South Carolina's slave code further elaborated the dress regulations (Genovese, 1974:359). Another early example of legalization of dress standards by class comes from Louisiana which was a Spanish colony in 1786, when the governor enacted a dress code.

Southern codes, used to demarcate status by regulating appropriate types of clothing according to the skin color of the wearer, were in place in the colonial era. As demonstrated in the *Narratives*, these ideas continued in common circulation through the antebellum period, entrenched, by then, more by custom than by law. Nowhere is this more striking than in the observations the narrators made about the clothing of whites. Although not asked, this often became a topic of their testimonies.

In general, during the antebellum period, just as now, age, sex and class determined who would wear what, and when specific articles of clothing would be worn. These factors determined not only the African American dress of the period, but that of white Americans as well. Simply put, children and adults wore different clothing; women and men wore different clothing; and poor people wore different clothing from middle-class people, and each of these groups wore different clothing from the wealthiest segment of society.

Relative poverty meant that some whites wore the same type of clothing as did enslaved African Americans.[1] In certain cases, the clothes of some whites might even be of lesser grade than the clothes of the enslaved. African Americans certainly made comparative judgments about "quality" and "not-quality" whites, and clothing often served as a metaphor for those whites judged to be of inferior status.

> Kisey McKimm (b. 1853): *Our Master was what white folks call a 'miser' . . .. He used to go to de stock auction, every Monday, 'n he didn't weah no stockings. He had a high silk hat, but it was tore so bad, dat he held de top n' bottom together wid a silk handkerchief . . .. [A]h heard some of de men wid kid gloves, call him a 'hill-billy' 'n make fun of his clothes. But he said, 'Don't look at my clothes, but look at de man'* (16. 4:65 [KY/OH]).

> Ellen Claibourn (b. 1852): *Sometime the po' white folks in the neighborhood would come an' ask to make they cloth on mistis' loom, and she always let 'em* (12. 1:187 [GA]).

James Bolton (85 years): *The overseers warn't no quality white folkses like our marsters and mistess but we never heard nuffin' 'bout no poor white trash in them days . . .* (12. 1:95 [GA]).

In her autobiography, Harriet Jacobs twice describes lower-class whites, marking them by their dress. Both descriptions concern the events that followed Nat Turner's rebellion in 1831. The first episode focuses on the formation of a local militia. Jacobs writes, "*The poor whites took their places in the ranks in every-day dress, some without shoes, some without hats*" (63). In the second account, she says that these "*country bullies and the poor whites*" searched the homes of Black people and, among other objects, robbed the Blacks of their clothing (64).

Sometimes, merely being the servant of a less well-to-do white caused derision from within the Black community.

Louis Hughes (b. 1843, enslaved in Mississippi and Virginia): *A servant owned by a man in moderate circumstances was hooted at by rich men's slaves. It was common for them to say: 'Oh, don't mind that darkey, he belongs to po'r white trash'* (63).

Clothing served as a standard whereby African Americans differentiated between "poor whites" and those whom they considered "better quality." Clearly, they observed and understood quite well the importance of clothing in denoting status. It may come as a shock to some readers that, in describing certain whites, very often African Americans appear to regard upper-class whites – often the very people to whom they were enslaved – with a sense of respect and admiration because of the clothes they wore. Yet if we consider that in nearly all societies, including those of West Africa, clothing serves to define the prestige of the more powerful, then this apparent anomaly in the enslaved peoples' descriptions is not so difficult to comprehend after all.

Rebecca Jane Grant: *And the little [white] babes had long dresses. Come down to your feet when you hold the baby in your lap. And embroidered from the bottom of the skirt all the way up. Oh, they embroidered up in the finest sort of embroidery* (2. 2:184 [SC]).

Hamp Kennedy (b. ca. 1857): *De white folks though, dey wear linen an 'fine silk clo'es fer de big times* (7. 2:87 [MS]).

Josh Miles (b. 1859): *De ole Martser wear de big stove-pipe hat an' de long skirt coat, an' his big boots, an' in de winter a big muffler roun' his neck* (S2. 7. 6:2655 [VA/TX]).

African Americans perceptively noted what white gentlemen wore, what they expected their servants to wear, and they appreciated the appropriate functions of dress at specific events.

Jim Polk Hightower ("over twenty years old when . . . set free"): *And when the old time Southern gentleman and Lady would fix to go to some intertanement we would see the gentlemen with his frock tail brodcloth coat on and his white lining busom shirt, they did not think themselves dress up if they did not have on a frock tail coat. Such a thing a white gentlemen going to church or to a wedden with a short coat on was not known with the old time archtercrats . . . and the carriage driver would be dressed up and jest as proud as his old master, and that was the way they wanted him to be . . ..*

[N]ever . . . did I see a young gentlemen walking with a Young Lady in his shirt sleeves . . .. And when a young gentlemen came calling on the Young Lady he entered the house with his hat off (S1. 8. 3:1008 [MS]).

Both male and female African Americans demonstrated a particular interest in white women's clothes.

Addie Vinson (86 years): *White ladies wore hoop skirts wid deir dresses, and dey looked lak fairy queens* (13. 4:102 [GA]).

Robert Shepherd: *De white ladies had nice silk dresses to wear to church. Slave 'omans had new calico dresses what dey wore wid hoop skirts dey made out of grapevines. Day wore poke bonnets wid ruffles on 'em and, if de weather was sort of cool, dey wore shawls. Marster allus wore his linen duster. Dat was his white coat, made cutaway style wid long tails. De cloth for most all de clothes was made at home* (13. 3:253 [GA]).

Bob Maynard (79 years): *Old Mistress was a fine lady and she always went dressed up. She wore long trains on her skirts and I'd walk behind her and held her train up when she made de rounds* (7:225 [TX/OK]).

Harriet Jones (b. 1844): *What did [white women] wear dem days? Dey wore de hoop skirts, w'en dey goes ter church an sits down dey has ter pull dem up in de back so dey hang down in de front. After freedom de styles change, dey wear de dresses long wid a train an leave off de hoop skirts, dey has ter hol' up de trains wen dey goes in de church lessen dey has a nigger ter go 'long and hol' dem up fer dem* (S2. 6. 5:2098–2099 [TX]).[2]

House Servants, Carriage Drivers, and People Drivers

Mattie Stenston (76 years): *You know, der was 'field niggers', 'house niggers', 'cooks' 'Maids, ' 'servers' spinners and weavers'. Every nigger had his or her own job* (S1. 10. 5:2037 [MS]).

Very often dress marked the status of these jobs; for some enslaved African Americans, their clothing coded an improved social standing from others. Although it defined them in relation to the tasks they performed for white people, many enslaved people clearly enjoyed the fancier clothes and appreciated the standing that these items of dress denoted. Domestic servants, in particular, dressed differently from Blacks working at other tasks (Figure 16).

> Frederick Douglass (b. ca. 1817, enslaved in Maryland): *These [house] servants constituted a sort of aristocracy on Col. Lloyd's plantation. They resembled the field hands in nothing, except in color .... The delicate colored maid rustled in the scarcely worn silk of her young mistress, while the servant men were equally well attired from the overflowing wardrobe of their young masters; so that, in dress, as well as in form and feature, in manner and speech, in tastes and habits, the distance between these favored few, and the sorrow and hunger-smitten multitudes of the quarter and the field, was immense . . .* ([1855] 1969:109–110).

Figure 16. *Portrait of a Black Woman Holding a White Child*, ca. 1850. Unknown daguerrotypist, American, hand-colored, 2 7/16″ × 1 7/8″. Collection of the J. Paul Getty Museum, Malibu, California.

William Wells Brown (b. ca. 1819, enslaved in Missouri): *I was a house servant – a situation preferable to that of a field hand, as I was better fed, better clothed* (reprinted in Katz, 15).

Alfred Robinson (enslaved in Kentucky): *Listen whilst I tell you what de valet do: He dress nice an' stan' roun' 'mongst de white folks* (Armstrong, 112).

Melinda Pollard: *I nebber libed in de slave quarters 'cause I wuz nussmaid for my mistiss two chillun . . .. Dat caused me to lib in de big house wid de w'ite folks. Yes'um I felt big w'en I got 'roun' de uther niggers, 'cause I allus wore nice close an' wuz allus clean an' had my haid com'ed. My close wuz nuthin' fine but dey didn't have no holes in dem, dey wuz jes' spun close but I wuz 'bout de bes' lookin' slave on de plantation* (S2. 8. 7:3113 [MS, GA, AR/TX]).

Mariah Robinson (ca. 81 years): *They loved to dress me to make me look to be de best lookin' an' neatest slave. I had such as, pretty starched dresses, neat shoes and dey helped me fix my hair nice* (S2. 8. 7:3354 [GA, TX/TX]).

Jim Johnson (87 years): *I had store-bought clothes give to me, too. 'Course dey is what young Marse Eddie or George have wore, but dey is better'n what most slave folk wear* (S2. 6. 5:2016 [SC, TX/TX]).

Ellen Claibourn (b. 1852): *The house servants was better dressed than the fiel'-hands – and marster uster buy us cloth from the 'Gusta Fact'ry in checks and plaids for our dresses, but all the fiel'-hands clothes was made out of cloth what was wove on mistis' own loom* (12. 1:186–187 [GA]).

Louis Hughes (b. 1843, enslaved in Mississippi and Virginia) was a house servant and reported

. . . my clothes were somewhat different. I wore pants made of Bosse's old ones, and all his old coats were utilized for me. They rounded them off at the tail just a little and called them jackets. My shoes were not brogans, but made of lighter leather, and made suitable for the house. I only worked in the farm in the busy seasons, and did not have the regular wear of the farm hands (42).

From many of the comments, it becomes evident that the formerly enslaved were fully aware that domestic servants' clothes were meant to serve the purposes of their white "owners."[3] For example, Hughes recalled that when the family moved to the city, as a house servant, "*My outfit was a new cloth suit, and my aprons for wearing when waiting table were of snowy white linen, the style being copied from that of the New York waiters*" (63). And although Hughes relates that "*I felt big, for I never knew what a white bosom shirt was before . . .,*" he realized that his personal appearance "*was merely for the gratification of my master's pride*" (63–64).

Aware of the same message, by which "owners" tried to convey their own importance with the appearance of their house servants, William Wells Brown wrote: "*Mrs. Price was very proud of her servants, always keeping them well dressed*" (reprinted in Katz, 85).

> Lucinda Vann: *Marster Jim and Missus Jennie wouldn't let his house slaves go with no common dress out. They never sent us anywhere with a cotton dress. They wanted everybody know we was Marster Vann's slaves. He wanted people to know he was able to dress his slaves in fine clothes. We had fine satin dresses . . . we never wore cotton except when we worked* (S1. 12:344–345 [OK]).

An important aspect about domestic servants' clothes is that they were regulated from the white outlook on the "correct" way in which servants should dress (Figure 17). For example, from a Southern aristocratic perspective, Margaret Davis Cate gives a cogent description of the clothing worn by Tyrah Wilson in an undated photograph. Rather than an actual

Figure 17. *Southern Man with Daughters and their Mammy*, 1848. Thomas Easterly, daguerreotypist; hand-colored. Collection of the J. Paul Getty Museum, Malibu, California.

"slave" costume, the clothing may post-date the Civil War. Nevertheless, the photo and Cate's description represent Cate's appraisal of the appropriate attire of a Georgia house servant during and after the period of enslavement:

> This old picture shows the correct dress of a house servant of the plantation. The gingham dress consists of a shirt waist with long sleeves and a high neck finished with a collar, while the skirt is ankle-length and made of several widths of cloth gathered to the waistband.
>
> The white apron, with two big pockets, covers the front and reaches almost to the bottom of the skirt.
>
> The kerchief at the neck and the cap on her head complete this perfect picture of an old-time servant (185; photo on facing page).

Black males employed as carriage drivers also received better clothing in which they expressed pride (Figure 18).

> Lewis Jones (86 years): *Massa have de fine coach and de seat fer de driver am up high in front and I's de coachman and he dresses me nice and . . . 'twarnt anyone bigger dan dis nigger* (4. 2:238 [TX]).

> Benjamin Johnson: *You wuz so proud whenever dey give you a pair o' shoes or a ol' straw hat dat dey wuz through wid at de house you went back an' showed it to everybody an' you wus mighty proud too. I used to drive my martser's hoss an' buggy for 'im an' so I used to git a lots a stuff like dat* (12. 2:324–325 [GA]).

Just as female domestic servants often dressed in what may be termed "uniforms," in many instances, carriage drivers actually used this term to describe their outfits.

> Josh Miles (b. 1859): *An' my pappy, (de coachman) wear de tall hat [like de ole Marster] wid de blue uniform an' de brass buttons an' de black shiny boots* (S2. 7. 6:2655 [VA/TX]).

> Willis Woodsen: *De most fun I guess I ever had was wehen Massa let me be a footman for his carriage. He got me a uniform, mos like a soldier's uniform, ceptin mine was red, wid black stripes down de sides. I member it jist like it was yestidy, de first time I puts it on* (S2. 10. 9:4279 [TX]).

William Grimes (b. 1784, enslaved in Virginia and Georgia) remembered that a "new master" bought Grimes to drive his carriage and Grimes received "a new coachman's dress" (reprinted in Bontemps, 83). Grimes

Figure 18. Uniformed Drivers standing with a *Group of People and Carriages in Front of a Southern Home*, 1851–1860. Unknown ambrotypist, American, 4″ × 5 1/4″. Collection of the J. Paul Getty Museum, Malibu, California.

also related how, partly because of his better clothing, he was able to walk around Savannah in the evenings even though guards were posted to prevent Blacks on the streets at such times.

> *I have frequently walked the streets of Savannah in an evening, and being pretty well dressed, (generally having on a good decent suit of clothes,) and having a light complexion . . . I would walk as bold as I knew how, and as much like a gentleman . . .* (95).

Once, when a freed Black man, who lodged at a local tavern, was late getting home, Grimes reports, "*I put on my best suit, took a rattan in my hand, he walked behind me and continued on until we reached the tavern, where we found about fifteen or twenty of the guard seated on the steps of the door.*" Grimes walked right through the guard and entered the tavern with the other man walking behind, pretending to be Grimes' servant (96).

Clearly, Grimes' adroit ability at playing the role of a white man, aided by the better clothing he wore as a domestic servant to a wealthy planter, allowed him to undertake these bold adventures on the Georgia city's streets. On the other hand, the enslaved people of smaller landowners might not fare well as far as clothing was concerned, probably due to the fact that they worked in the house as well as in the fields. Trollope visited the house of a small landed proprietor in Maryland in the late 1820s. The family "consisted of a young man, his wife, two children, a female slave, and two very young lads, slaves also" (204). Trollope noted, "The slaves, particularly the lads, were considerably more than half naked . . ." (205) .

As well as domestic servants and carriage drivers, field hands who had been given positions of power over other enslaved people might receive better clothing. In an unusual circumstance, Henry and Moses were placed as overseers by William S. Pettigrew on his two North Carolina holdings, "Magnolia" and "Belgrade," during the 1850s. Apparently unable to read or write, their reports to the plantation owner were dictated to a white neighbor in the form of letters. One letter shows that Henry and Moses were responsible for the other enslaved people's clothing, as well as the fact that they received better clothing than did the other Blacks. In this letter they asked for "18 hats . . . for men at magnolia. 13 hats . . . for the womens. 9hats . . . for Boys and girles"; as well, they included long list of shoes for the enslaved at Magnolia and Belgrade with such specifications as how many pairs in what sizes and in single- or double-soles. The two overseers added their own foot sizes in a request for boots (reprinted in Starobin, 26). Robert S. Starobin notes that " [a]s accoutrements to their considerable responsibility, Pettigrew invested his overseers with special privileges, provided them with boots, greatcoats, and whips (all symbols of power on the plantation)" (22).

Another plantation owner employed enslaved Blacks as drivers in Georgia. In the following, we again see that an owner's particular concern for the well-being of Blacks who were placed in positions of power often took the form of more adequate clothing than was generally distributed to other field workers.

> But I am sorry – & very much troubled to hear how sick you have been . . .. Have you plenty of flannel? I wish you to get Mr. Shepard to get you some good flannel & have your *shirts made of it, coming down well over the hips, with long sleeves & two or three pairs of Drawers of the same*: & so keep yourself warmly clad. Let Phoebe cut them out & make then at once & nicely for you, and whatever *outer* clothing you want, Mr. Sheperd will get for you.
>
> . . . Carry your cloak & umbrella, and have you good fires . . .. Keep your feet dry with thick heavy shoes or Boots (reprinted in Starobin, 44).

From these accounts, it becomes clear that besides the differences in clothing between that worn by wealthy whites and enslaved Blacks, and differences in clothing between that worn by field workers and those who worked in domestic situations, wearing apparel also denoted class differences *within* the groups. In addition, there appear to be distinctions between the clothing worn by enslaved peoples in the rural areas and those who lived in cities.[4]

Strong evidence from both Blacks and whites who observed the peculiar system supports the usual assumption that house servants and carriage drivers dressed better than field hands.[5] But two additional patterns stand out concerning the division between the types of clothing worn by the former and those worn by agricultural workers. First, the dress codes of those Blacks who worked in close contact with a white family, often in the "owner's" house, were strictly enforced; and, second, these codes were designed by the whites. That is, whites controlled what domestic servants wore, and there was no latitude given. Fanny Kemble offers a first-hand illustration of this when she describes the clothing worn by "Old House Molly," who was in domestic service to Kemble's husband.[6]

> Her dress, like that of her daughter, and all the servants who have at any time been employed about the family, bore witness to a far improved tastes than the half-savage adornment of the other poor blacks, and upon my observing to her

how agreeable her neat and cleanly appearance was to me, she replied that her old master . . . was extremely particular in this respect, and that in his time all the house servants were obliged to be very nice and careful about their persons (94).

Note Kemble's specific inference that the house servants "improved their tastes" in dress and in their "neatness and cleanliness" because of their close proximity to the whites. In a later passage, Kemble drives her point home:

[O]n St. Simons, owing I suppose, to the influence of the resident lady proprietors of the various plantations, and the propensity to imitate in their black dependents, the people that I see all seem to me much tidier, cleaner, and less fantastically dressed than those on the rice plantation, where no such influences reach them (220).

From a white perspective, "tidier and cleaner" might seem more important; but from a Black perspective, "fantastically dressed" may have been more in tune to the African Americans' own aesthetic sensibilities. Thus, although Blacks who worked at jobs away from the big house apparently received less clothing and of poorer quality than that worn by domestic servants, this inequality may have been offset by the fact that they had more freedom of choice in what they would wear than did the seemingly more privileged domestic servants and carriage drivers.

Work and Weekday Clothing

The largest segment of the enslaved population in the antebellum South were employed as field hands (i.e., agricultural laborers). Their comments form the bulk of the testimony in this section.

Seasonal Wear

George Jones (b. 1853): *We dressed to meet the weather condition* (16. 3:45 [MD]).

Peter Randolph (b. 1820, enslaved in Virginia): *As for clothing, Edloe would give us a coarse suit once in three years; mother sometimes would beg cast-off garments from the neighbors, to cover our nakedness . . .* (1855:20).

Thomas H. Jones (b. 1806, enslaved in North Carolina): *Once a year [the master] distributed clothing to his slaves . . .. The slaves were obliged to make up their*

> *own clothes, after the severe labor of the plantation had been performed. Any other clothing, beyond this yearly supply, which they might need, the slaves were compelled to get by extra work, or do without* (1857:6–7).

Another example of an annual distribution of clothing is noted for a Virginia plantation which Frederick Law Olmstead visited in the 1850s: "As to the clothing of the slaves on the plantation, they are said to be usually furnished by their owners or masters, every year" (1959:92). Rather than doling out clothing just once a year as Jones and Olmstead recalled, or every three years as Randolph remembered, the more ordinary procedure on many plantations was a seasonal distribution of specific types of clothing. In this regard, the formerly enslaved again express divergent experiences as to whether or not the clothing was adequate. Many told of receiving clothing twice a year: a lighter set suitable for warmer months, a heavier set for colder months.

> Jerry Eubanks (91 years): *You know we'd change stripes and it wouldn't be as thick in summer as winter* (S1. 9. 4:689 [MS]).

> James W. C. Pennington (b. ca. 1816, enslaved in Maryland): *At the beginning of winter, each slave had one pair of coarse shoes and stockings, one pair of pantaloons, and a jacket.*
>
> *At the beginning of summer, he had two pair of coarse linen pantaloons and two shirts* (reprinted in Katz, 66).

> Susan Castle (b. 1860): *In summer time us wore checkedy dresses made wid low waistes and gathered skirts, but in winter de dresses was made out of linsey-woolsey cloth* (12. 1. 179 [GA]).

> Addie Vinson (86 years): *Boys wore plain shirts in summer, but in winter dey had warmer shirts and quilted pants. Dey would put two pair of britches to gadder and quilt 'em up so you couldn't tell what sort of cloth dey was made out of. Dem pants was called suggins* (13. 4:103 [GA]).

> Sarah Wilson (b. 1850, enslaved to a Cherokee in the Indian Territory): *[I]n winter we had a sheep skin jacket with the wool left on the inside. Sometimes sheep skin shoes with the wool on the inside and sometimes real cow leather shoes with wood peggings for winter* (7. 349 [OK]).

Slaveholders had an economic investment in Blacks; as such, it was to the slaveholders' advantage to keep the enslaved people healthy. Adequate clothing was part of that responsibility. Although some slaveholders distributed clothing "to meet the weather condition," it appears that many did not overly concern themselves with what the enslaved wore during the warmer months when their physical health was less likely to be impaired because of insufficient clothing.

Alice Green (76 years): *Us jus' wore what we could ketch in summer* (12. 2:41 [GA]).

Anderson Furr (87 years): *Boys wore long blue striped shirts in summer and nothin' else a t'all. Dem shirts was made jus' lak mother hubbards. Us wore de same thing in winter only dem shirts was made new for winter. By summer dey had done worn thin* (12. 1:317 [GA]).

Cornelia Robinson: *[D]idn't wear no clothes hardly in hot weather* (S1. 1:352 [AL]).

Contributors sometimes noted that, whatever the season, their clothing allotments were never adequate.

Gill Ruffin (b. 1837): *They give us one garment at a time and that had to be slap wore out 'fore we got another* (5. 3:263 [TX]).

Richard Carruthers (100 years): *Come a norther and it blow with snow and sleet and I didn't have 'nough clothes to keep me warm* (4. 1:200 [TN. TX/TX]).

Clay Bobbit (b. 1837, 100 years old): *[A]n' we wucked on short rations an' went high naked* (14. 1:118 [NC]).

Undergarments

Many items of underwear and all items of outerwear appear to have been worn by most enslaved people only during the winter, if they received such clothing at all. Regardless of the season, some of the formerly enslaved said they never wore underwear.

Robert Burns (b. 1856): *I never seed any under-wear until I wuz bout 12 years of age* (S1. 12:79 [MS/OK]).

Fleming Clark (74 years): *We wore geans and shirts of yellow cotton, we wore no shoes up til Christmas. I wore just the same during de summer except a little coat. We had no under shirt like we have now* (16. 4:23 [VA/OH]).

M. Fowler (female): *I never had a undershirt until just befo' my first child was born. I never had nothin but a shimmy an' a slip fer a dress, an' it made outen the cheapes' cloth that could be bought. Unbleached ausenburg cloth, coarse, but made to las'* (S1. 1:151 [VA, GA, LA/AL]).

Others noted that underwear was worn only during the colder months.

Reuben Fox: *When winter came they made heavy wool underwear for us to put on under the shirts. They kept us good and warm* (S1. 7. 2:776 [MI]).

Most comments concerned womens' more elaborate undergarments.

Georgia Baker (87 years): *Winter clothes was good and warm; dresses made of yarn cloth made up jes' lak dem summertime clothes, and petticoats and draw's made of osneburg* (12. 1:41 [GA]).

Precilla Gray (107 years): *We wore yarn hoods, sha'ls, en pantletts which wuz 'nit things dat kum fum yo tops ter 'bove yo knees* (16. 6:25 [TN]).

Addie Vinson (86 years): *[D]e winter clothes was good and warm. Under our heavy winter dresses us wore quilted underskirts dat was sho nice and warm* (13. 4:102 [GA]).

Lina Hunter (ca. 90 years): *Honey, dem old balmoral petticoats was some sight, but dey was sho warm as hell. I seed a piece of one of mine not long ago whar I done used it to patch up a old quilt* (12. 2:258 [GA]).

In noteworthy instances, Black women, and not the whites, provided these extra female garments for themselves and for others.

Eda Raines (b. 1853): *In the winter we wore woolen clothes. If we didn't have a woolen petticoat we quilted the cotton one from the knee down cause that made it warmer* (S2. 8. 7:3224 [AR, TX/TX]).

Martha Colquitt (85 years): *In winter grandma made us yarn underskirts and yarn drawers buttoned down over our knees* (12. 1:241 [GA]).

Louis Hughes (b. 1843, enslaved in Mississippi and Virginia): *The women who could utilize old clothes made for themselves what they called pantalets. They had no stockings or undergarments to protect their limbs – these were never given them. The pantalets were made like a pant-leg, came just above the knee, and were caught and tied. Sometimes they looked well and comfortable. The men's old pant-legs were sometimes used* (42).

A fortunate few apparently wore undergarments year round. Two men noted their underwear.

William Henry Towns (b. 1854): *In der summer we would wear underwear that was made uv cotton, in der win'er our underwear was made uv flannel* (S1. 1:411 [AL]).

Will Parker (b. 1842, 95 years): *We wore dyed lowels – cotton dyed with red oak and slippery elm. We wore underwear of the same goods. In winter we wore 'ball' woolen underwear and outer garments* (S2. 8. 7:3018 [GA/TX]).

But again, most comments on year-round underclothing concerned what females wore.

Frances Willingham (78 years): *Slave gals' pantelettes warn' t ruffled and tucked and trimmed up lace and 'broidery lak Miss Polly's chilluns' was. Ours was just made plain. Our white petticoats and pantelettes was made on bodices* (13. 4:155 [GA]).

Virginia Sims (93 years): *My master put good clothes on me. I'd say, 'Master, I want a dress like so and so . . ..' Yes, ma'am, and he got em for me. I was forty-three and married to a nigger fore I knowed what twas to cry for underwear* (10. 6:164 [AR]).

Outerwear

Few contributors noted special outerwear; in any case, it was described only as a item of winter clothing. Outer garments took a variety of forms which derived from current fashion or just plain making do with anything available in order to gain added warmth.

Unidentified man (b. 1842): *You see they used to make our coats then – all our overcoats too. I never seen but one overcoat until after the War. Even the white people didn't wear them. But these would keep us just as warm as if they were overcoats. We just called them that anyway. They didn't wear overcoats, just wore dress coats* (18:149 [TN or KY]).

Susan McIntosh (b. 1851): *In winter . . . the men [wore] winter coats what come down to their knees, and the women wore warm wraps what they called sacks* (13. 3:81 [GA]).

Lina Hunter (ca. 90 years): *Look at dis old black shawl. See how big it is? Dat's what I used to wear for a wrap on church days 'fore I ever had a coat* (12. 2:271 [GA]).

In a song, a coat is used to express humorously the disparity between the clothing of the "master" and the enslaved. William Mayfield:

> *Ole Massa take dat new brown coat,*
> *And hang it on de wall;*
> *Dat darkey take dat same old coat,*
> *An' wear it to de ball,*
> *Oh, don't you hear my tru lub sing!*
> (16. 2. 2:102 [KY]).

The following belief narrative includes an overcoat-wearing "haint."

> Caroline Wright (ca. 90 years): *On de trip to Texas, one evenin' a big storm come up and Mr. Bob he axed a man to let us use a big empty house. Dey put me by de do'r to sleep 'cause I was de lightest sleeper. Sometime in de night, I woked up an' dere stood de biggest haint I ebber seed. He was ten feet high an' had on a big beaver coat. I hollers . . .. Ebbery body woked up, an' de haint looks at us all an' went tromping all ober de house, breakin' dishes and tearin' our clos. Nex mornin' we got up and' dey ain't nothin' out of place* (S2. 10. 9:4282 [LA, TX/TX]).

And one woman recalled a frightening episode which concerned her relative's coat.

> Clarinda Grobe: *Becky Ford am my auntie too. Her hab but one arm; t'other one groun' off in de rice-mill. Massa mad one day, an' say him didn't feed de mill fas' 'nuff, an' him beat her, an' w'en him raise de arm to fend off de blow him jacket sleeve ketch in de wheel, an' 'fore dey could stop de wheel she arm groun' off clear up to de shoulder* (Botume, 137).[7]

Age and Sex

> James L. Smith (enslaved in Virginia): *Our dress was made of tow cloth; for the children, nothing was furnished them but a shirt; for the older ones, a pair of pantaloons or a gown, in addition, according to the sex. Besides these, in the winter season an overcoat, or a round jacket; a wool hat once in two or three years for the men, and a pair of coarse brogan shoes once a year* (reprinted in Bontemps, 151).

The recitation by the formerly enslaved people of their recollections of clothing often includes a break-down of specific items by age and by sex.

Children

> Frederick Douglass (b. ca. 1818): *The children unable to work in the fields had neither shoes, stockings, jackets, nor trousers, given to them; their clothing consisted of two coarse linen shirts a year. When these failed them, they went naked until the next allowance-day. Children from seven to ten years old, of both sexes, almost naked, could be seen all seasons of the year* ([1845] 1968:28).

Several historians have used Douglass' well-known description to "prove" one more act of violation on the part of whites against enslaved African Americans. Scholars have apparently overlooked what Douglass wrote about the clothing of African Americans enslaved in urban areas.

> *I had resided but a short time in Baltimore before I observed a marked difference, in the treatment of slaves, from that which I had witnessed in the country. A city slave . . . is much better fed and clothed* (50).

Douglass understood the self-serving reason for the urban whites' better treatment of the enslaved:

> *There is a vestige of decency, a sense of shame, that does much to curb and check those outbreaks of atrocious cruelty so commonly enacted upon the plantation. He is a desperate slaveholder who will shock the humanity of his non-slave holding neighbors . . .* (ibid.).

Secluded away from other whites, the slaveholder in the country obviously had less cause to worry about what his neighbors thought. I found two interviewees, both women, who remembered going naked as children. In each instance, the ordeal was caused by the whim of a cruel "mistress." The unfortunate children's dilemmas, however, were resolved.

> Mrs. Lancy Harris (84 years): *So many chillen didn't wear clothes. But the missus owned the loom and de servants weave. When de chillen are big enough to work dey gib 'em cloth from the loom. When I got my issue and my clothes wus good I wud make my cloth into dresses and gib to de chillen* (S2. 1:256 [NC/DC]).

> Lou Smith (female, b. 1854): *Miss Jo wasn't no good Mistress . . .. She was what we called 'low-brow.' . . . She said us kids didn't need to wear any clothes and*

one day she told us we could jest tak'em off it cost too much to clothe us. I was jest a little child but I knowed I oughten to go without my clothes. We wore little enough as it was . . .. Well, anyway she made me take off my clothes and I just crept off and cried. Purty soon young Master come home. He wanted to know what on earth I was doing without my dress on. I told him, and my goodness, but he raised the roof (7. 1:301 [TX/OK]).

And yet, contrary to these appalling experiences and contrary to Douglass' statement about the lack of clothing for rural Black children as he remembered it, in the *Narratives*, few people described themselves as without clothing during their childhoods. According to the *Narratives*, enslaved African American children in the United States, whether in rural or urban servitude, normally wore some form of body covering.

Della Mun Bibles (b. ca. 1856): *Us children . . . had more space to grow up in and less work to do and did not pay much attention to clothes, just so us was covered up* (S2. 2. 1:291 [TX]).

Boys. They do agree, however, with Douglass' statement about the most usual form of clothing for rural Black boys: a shirt.

Smith Simmons: *The clothes we had wasn't nothing to brag on. The children wore shirt tails the year round. When the weather was cold, they put one on over the other. They didn't wear shoes neither winter or summer. Their foots would crack open from the cold if they went outside in bad weather. The grown folks had good shoes cause they had to go out side to work* (S1. 10. 5:1936 [MS]).

George Washington Miller (b. 1856): *I never did wear any short pants. Ours were long like the men* (S1. 9. 4:1486 [MS]).

Lina Hunter (ca. 90 years): *Most of de other places jus' put long shirts on little boys, but dat warn't de way dey done on our place, 'cause us didn't belong to no pore folks . . .. Course in de summertime none of de chillun didn't wear nothin' but little slips, so they could keep cool* (12. 2:258 [GA]).

Miller's and Hunter's statements are exceptional for, overwhelmingly, other contributors remembered that boys wore only a shirt in all seasons.

Elisha Doc Garey (age 76): *All dat us chillun wore in summer was jus' one little shirt. It was long time 'fore us knowed dere was folks anywhar dat put more dan one piece of clothes on chillun in summer* (12. 2. 4:4 [GA]).

James Lucas (b. 1833): *When I was a little chap I used to wear coarse lowell-cloth shirts on de week-a-days. Dey was long an' had big collars* (7. 2:91 [MS]).

Mark Discus (b. 1845): *We just wore a one-piece garment called a shift. It was a hol' lot like a long night shirt. It was the coarsest of cotton stuff an' had no collar. . .. In the winter we had ol' clothes of the master's family* (S1. 2. 4:174 [MO]).

The singleton shirt was so ubiquitous an article of boys' clothing that it accounted for a popular nickname given their age-group.

Winn Willis (b. 1822): *I'se knowed my birthday since I was a shirt-tail boy, but can't tells how ole I is by figures* (S2. 10. 9:4249 [LA/TX]).

George Rutherford (b. 1854): *Us wus called shirt-tail fellows and dey wus made at home and below our knees, outer orsanburg* (S1. 1:357 [AL]).

In the following description, an elderly man recounts his childhood clothes with ironic humor.

A. C. Pruitt (b. ca. 1861): *Dem was sho' fancy shu't tails dey mek us wo' in dem days. Dey mek em on de loom, jes' in two pieces, wid a hole to put de head through, and a nudder hole at de bottom to put de legs through. Den dey split dem up de sides so's us could run and play widout dem tyin' us 'roun' de knees and throw' us down. Even at dat, dey sho' wasn' no good to do no tree-climbin' less'n you pull dem mos' over yo' head* (S2. 8. 7:3201–3202 [LA, TX/TX]).

Although wearing only a shirt was the norm, young boys might wear pants if they went off the plantation to a more public place.

Isaac Stier (99 years): *As a little tike I wore long slip-lak shirts. When dey sont me to town I put on britches an' stuffed de tail o' my slip in 'em so's it pass' for a shirt* (7. 2:144 [MS]).

Albert Henderson (95 years): *On Sunday when I got to drive master, I'se have white pair loyal breeches to ware on* (S2. 5. 4:1697 [KY/TX]).

Gus Pearson (ca. 97 years): *I's gwine along wid her [his mother] and so I had to wear some pants to go to de [trading] post as dat was big doings fer a lil' darky boy to git to go to de trading center. So aunt Abbie fotched me a pair of new pants dat was dat stiff, dat dey made me feel like I was all closed up in a jacket, atter being only used to a shirt-tail!* (2. 2:69 [SC]).

In many societies, puberty marks a change in dress (Figure 19). Sieber notes that in Africa: "The achievement of adulthood is in part celebrated by the assumption of adult dress. Coming-of-age ceremonies may include the change, symbolically, from nudity to dress" (19). Osifekunde, born in Ijebu, between Oyo and Benin, said that in his country "*Children of both sexes remain absolutely nude to the age of fifteen years, which is that of puberty*" (Lloyd, ed., 255). In the antebellum South, the specific age at which the enslaved male was thought to change from boy to man varied from age 10 to 15 and even as late as 21 years; nevertheless, the addition of pants to his wardrobe very often clearly coded this rite of passage.

> George Austin (75 years): *When him git so much older him gits reg'lation men's clothes* (S2. 2. 1:110 [TX]).

> James Lucas (b. 1833): *I weared course 'lowell cloth' shirts when I wuz little . . .. When I got big enough to wait 'bout de 'big house' an go to town I wore rough*

Figure 19. *Young Black Male Standing, or, Giving Tribute*, ca. 1855. Unknown daguerreotypist, American; hand-colored, 2 5/8″ × 2 1/8″. Collection of the J. Paul Getty Museum, Malibu, California.

clean clothes. My pants wuz white 'linsey woolsey' en my shirts wuz rough white cotton what wuz wove at de plantation (S1. 8. 3:1344 [MS]).

Steve Weathersby: *I dressed den in long shirts an' on 'till I wuz a big boy. I wuz plump proud ob de fust pants I wore. Dey made me feel growed up an' wuz proud de days of just shirts wuz gone* (S1. 10. 5:2246 [MS]).

Filmore Ramsey (b. 1851): *I always wore long tail shirts, made of home spun cloth. That was good cloth, it never wore out. My pants* [received at age 10] *was made of homespun cloth too* (S1. 9. 4:1792 [MS]).

Willis Cofer (b. 1860): *Boys jes' wore shirts what looked lak dresses 'til dey wuz 12 years ole and big enough to wuk in de fields. Den dey put 'em in pants made open in de back. Dem britches would look awful funny now, but dey wuz all us had den, and all de boys wuz mighty proud when dey got big enough to wear pants and go to wuk in de fields wid grown folkses. When a boy got to be a man enough to wear pants, he drawed rations and quit eatin' out de trough* (12. 1:203 [GA]).

Alice Hutcheson (b. 1862): *[B]oys didn't wear nothin' 'cep' long shirts widout no britches 'till dey was 'bout twelve or fo'teen* (12. 2:285 [GA]).

Lewis Jefferson (84 years): *I neber had a pair uf pants till I wus bout eighteen years old* (S1. 8. 3:1141 [MS]).

J. W. Whitfield (ca. 60): *The women spun the thread and wove the cloth. For the boys from five to fifteen years old, they would make long shirts out of this cloth . . .. No young fellow ever wore pants until he began to court* (11. 7:139 [AR]).

Mary Johnson: *My brudder Robert he was a pow'ful big boy. He wasn't 'lowed to hab no pants 'till he was 21 year' ol', but dat didn 'scourage him from co'tin' on de gals. I try tease him 'bout go see de gals wid dat split shu't . . .* (S2. 6. 5:2024 [MS/TX]).

For some, the recollection of wearing pants for the first time continued to be an important memory even after emancipation.

A. C. Pruitt (b. ca. 1861): *Wid all de talk I couldn't hardly wait 'till I's 21 so's I could go vote. Dat was my ideer of sump'n'. Dat was mos's good as de fus' time dey 'low me to wear pants. I muster been mos' 12 year' ol' when dey do dat* (S2. 8. 7:3205 [LA, TX/TX]).

Girls.
Elisha Doc Garey, 76 years:

> *Whose been here*
> *Since I been gone?*
> *A pretty little gal*
> *Wid a blue dress on.*
> (12. 2. 4 [GA])

Many contributors remembered that girls and boys dressed alike in the singleton shirt.

> Mary Reynolds (over 100 years): *In them days I wore shirts like all the young girls and boys. They was made with collars like boys have today and they come below the knees and were split up the sides. Thats all we wore in hot weather* (S2. 8. 7:3291 [LA/TX]).

> Joe Rawls (past 90 years): *Us dresses 'n' shu'ts all look 'like. You couldn't tell d' boys from d' gals from d' way dey dress, cause dey all dress jis' di same, d' boys 'n' d' gals, all dey clo's mek outn' d'sam stuff 'n' d' same color 'n' d' same way* (S2. 8. 7:3250 [TX]).

> Rosa L. Pollard (b. 1842): *My wedding dress was white royal clothes trimmed in red. That was the first dress that I ever put on, all the rest was called shirts* (S2. 8. 7:3119 [GA/TX]).

> Jasper Battle (80 years): *All de nigger babies wore dresses made jus' alak for boys and gals. I was sho'ly mighty glad when dey 'lowed me to git rid of dem dresses and wear shirts. I was 'bout 5 years old den, but dat boys' shirt made me feel powerful mannish* (12. 1:65 [GA]).

> Henry Lewis (b. 1835): *Us . . . didn't pay much 'tention to clothes. Boys and gals all dress jes' alike, one long shirt or dress. They call it a shirt iffen a boy wear it and call it a dress iffen the gal wear it. There wasn't no difference, 'cause they's white when all made out'a somethin' like duck and all white. That is, they white when you fus' put them on, but after you wears them a while they git kind of pig-culled, kind of grey, but still they's all the same color* (5. 3 [TX]).

Although children often dressed in an asexual manner, the clothing, nevertheless, was gendered if only by calling the one-piece item "a shirt iffen a boy wear it and call [ing] it a dress iffen the gal wear it." One woman reported how girls attempted to feminize the generic shift.

Mary Johnson: *[Mistress] say us jes' chillen and kep' us in short dress so us won't t'ink we growed up. We pull out de stitchen' inde hem so us dress drag, but she sho' wo' us out for dat* (S2. 6. 5:2024 [MS/TX]).

Unlike the way in which extremes in forms of clothing highlighted the sexual differences between white men and women, asexual forms of clothing perhaps were meant to downplay the sexuality and physical appeal of Black girls and women. With their explicit recollections about the inadequacies of much female clothing, the contributors display a deep sensitivity to this chilling attempt by some whites to dehumanize African American females.

Harriet A. Jacobs (b. ca. 1813, enslaved in North Carolina): *I have a vivid recollection of the linsey-woolsey dress given me every winter by Mrs. Flint. How I hated it! It was one of the badges of slavery* ([1861] 1987:11).

Julius Jones: *Children didn't have nothing to wear no how but shirts, and the women folks wore things that looked like shirts only longer* (S1. 8. 3:1216 [MS]).

Charlotte Willus (63 years): *We never had but 'bout two dresses at the same time. When I come on, dresses was scarce. If we tore our dresses, we wore patches. We was sorter 'shamed to have our dresses patched up* (11. 7:199 [AR]).

Rosa L. Pollard (b. 1842): *In hot weather we had royal clothes, long shirt opened all the way down the front pinned together with thorns* (S2. 8. 7:3119 [GA/TX]).

Two women recalled the influence of female relatives on the better clothing they received as young girls:

Lillie Williams (age 69): *Grandma was old-timey. She made our dresses to pick cotton in every summer. They was hot and stubby. They looked pretty. We was proud of them. Mama washed and ironed. She kept us clean, too. Grandma made us card and spin. I never could learn to spin but I was a good knitter. I could reel. I did love to hear it crack. That was a cut. We had a winding blade. We would fill the quills for our grandma to weave. Grandma was mighty quiet and particular. She came from Kentucky* (11. 7:177–178 [AR]).

Kate Dudley Baumont: *Grandmother en my aunt wuz very fine seamstresses, en dey would go to town to de Preston house [town house of the master], en sew foh weeks at a time makin' close foh de whole fam'ly. Us chidrun's close wuz well made en we had much more den some slaves, cause my grandmother en aunt sees to it dat we had t'ings, en dey made some of de t'ings dey made foh de Preston girls* (S1. 5. 2. 277 [KY/OH]).

A significant body of evidence indicates that males received trousers at the onset of puberty, but I found only one explicit mention in the *Narratives* that clothing marked this rite of passage for adolescent females.

> Mattie Curtis (98 years): *I went as naked as Yo' han' till I was fourteen years old. I was naked like that when my nature come to me. Marse Whitfield arn't carin', but atter dat mammy tol' him dat I had ter have clothes* (14. 1:218 [NC]).

An important addition to our present knowledge about clothing as markers for rites of passage comes from Lydia Parrish who writes that Katie Brown, one of her contributors on St. Simon's island, told her.

> . . . that the record book of the Spalding Plantation has her age as ten years when the War Between the States began, but she believes she was two years older, for she wore a shift at the time her family left Sapelo . . . (131).

Parrish goes on to note:

> The slaves count their age by some such event, Katie seemed to be proud of the fact she was old enough to wear a shift. Shad Hall must be younger, for he still wore a "binyan" (apparently an African word), which was the kind of shirt worn by young boys before they wore pants. With a grin, he told me their first pants had no pockets so that it would be less easy for them to steal eggs (ibid.).

Status Among Children. As with adults, children of both sexes who worked as house servants often wore better quality clothes than did those who were occupied elsewhere on the plantation (Figures 15 and 19).

> Georgia Flourney (90 years): *I was raised a house girl and slept in Miss Georgia's room and wore good clean clothes all de time, cause I was a nurse made [sic] and did not associate wid de common niggers* (S1. 1:141–142 [AL]).

> Cato Carter, (b. 1836 or 1837): *I was trained as a houseboy. . . . I did have plenty of fine clothes; good woolen suits they would spin on the place and doeskins and fine linens. I drove in the carriage with the white-folks and I was about the most dudish Nigger in those parts* (S2. 3. 2:642 [AL/TX]).

Very often, the enslaved children who worked as house servants were given hand-me-downs. Passing along previously worn clothing still in serviceable condition is not a custom isolated to the antebellum period nor to enslaved people. Although hand-me-downs are not limited to a slave-master relationship, it is relevant that Blacks who were given "used" clothing rarely, if ever, were able to choose other clothes for themselves.

Candis Goodwin: *Missus Scott gimme good clothes; cose sh [e] didn't git 'em mone twice a year, but day's good when ah gits 'em. She gimmie Sis' dresses. Sis' one ob Missus' lil'le girls* (16. 5:18 [VA]).

Gabe Emanuel (85 years): *Course all de time us gits han'-me-downs from de white folkes' in de Big House. Us what was a-servin in de Big House wore de Marsters' old dress suits. Now dat was sumpin. Mos' o' de time dey didn' fit so good, mebby de' pants hang a little loose an' de tails of de' coat hang a little long, but me bein' de house boy I use to look mighty sprucy when I put on my frocktail* (S1. 9. 4:682 [MS]).

Finally, it is important to note that several informants testified that white children dressed in clothing of the same style and quality as did enslaved children.

Hannah Mullins (81 years): *De Johnson kids could have made it hard gwine fo' me but deys good to me an' we all plays togedder lak Ise white as dey is. Ise fed de same victuals an' wears de same clothes as dey does* (S2. 7. 6:2876 [TX]).

Joe Hawkins (83 years): *We always had to pick seeds out of so much cotton befo' going to bed at night. This cloth then wuz made into a one piece garment. This garment reached the knees and this wuz all the clothes we had on. White children wore this kind of garment too* (S1. 8. 3:957–958 [MS]).

Adults

Men. Evidence shows that as far as clothing, some enslaved Blacks fared better than poor whites. One formerly enslaved man noted that during the period when indentures were still the norm, a person's skin color was not a concern as far as adult male clothing allotments went.

The Rev. G. W. Offley (b. 1808, enslaved in Maryland): *[O]ne pair of shoes, one pair stockings, one pair woolen pants, one coat, two pairs coarse tow linen pants, two shirts, and board, is the law of the State of Maryland allows a man, free or slave, black or white, who hires for one year* (reprinted in Bontemps, 133).

As illustrated, African American girls and boys often dressed in identical "shirts" during their younger years. While many of the narrators related this in a matter-of-fact way, as they grew older, clothing became, as it does for all human beings, an important material manifestation of presenting the sexual self. The period of slavery was not without confrontations between adult Black and white Americans concerning clothing. In noteworthy instances these confrontations appear to have sexual overtones. The following items point up the certainty that both Black males and white males attached great importance to the ways in which clothing might be used to devalue or maintain maleness. Clothing and sexuality figure in certain forms of punishment inflicted upon the enslaved. In a society which professed to embrace Christianity, the first incident below surely tested the Old Testament admonition: "The woman shall not wear that which pertaineth to a man, neither shall a man put on a woman's garment" (Deuteronomy 25:5).

Scarborough related that "a more sophisticated punishment was devised by another Louisiana planter, Bennet H. Barrow, who made one habitual troublemaker 'ware womens cloths for running away & without the least cause'" (93). But soon after the Civil War, a legend appeared in African American folklore that turned the tables.

> Everett Ingram: *Ah nevvah will fawgit der capshure uv Mistah Jefferson Davis, Confedrit Presi-den', ah wuz right dah an' see'd hit wid mah own vay eyes. Dey says hit weren't so 'bout dat dress affaih but hit sho Gwad wuz! He done had er gals dress awn right evvah his man's britches, an' hit wuz his foots in man's shoes whut gint 'im er way jiss en he done liff his feet tew han am' der skirt tail cotchawn his shoe strap!* (S1. 1:202 [AL]).

Although the third incident occurred 300 years earlier in West Africa, in noteworthy respects, it demonstrates that clothes offer potent signs of a man's masculinity across cultures. But in an ironic twist, In the Benin story, it is lack of clothes which proves the point.

> [About 1606] Prince Odogbo, the only son of Ehengbuda, was placed on the throne of Benin with the title Ohuan, after his father's death.
>
> While his father was alive Odogbo was very handsome and girlish in appearance so that people thought he was a girl. When his father heard of this he told his son to walk naked from Uselu to Benin City. The prince and his attendants, who were also naked, had their hair well cut and dressed before they began their unusual procession. Thus Odogbo was shown publicly to be a young man, and he and his naked servants were termed *Ofieto* (Hair curlers) which term exist [*sic*] to this day (Egharevba, 33–34).

White disregard for the femininity or masculinity of the enslaved took many forms and happened under a variety of circumstances. One noticeably apparent time for the abuse of white power in this regard occurred during the sale of enslaved people. As noted in Chapter 1, in the slave-holding pens on the West African coast, captured Africans often were groomed for sale before the Middle Passage. In the Southern United States, the concern for the appearance of people on the auction block continued, and American Black men and women were often groomed and dressed in better clothing than usual in order to improve the prospects of their sale (Figure 20).[8] One cannot imagine the discomfort felt by the recipients of this contemptuous behavior.

William Wells Brown (b. ca. 1819, enslaved in Missouri) commented on the practice of getting the enslaved bodies ready for sale, as he knew from first-hand experience:

> *I had to prepare the old slaves for market. I was ordered to have the old men's whiskers shaved off, and the grey hairs plucked out, where they were not too numerous, in which case he had a preparation of blacking to color it, and with a blacking-brush we would put it on . . . after going through the blacking-process, they looked ten or fifteen years younger* (reprinted in Katz, 43).

Moses Roper (enslaved in North Carolina) described his duties during the time that he worked for a slave drover:

> *I had to grease the faces of the blacks every morning with sweet oil, to make them shine before they are put up to sell . . .. I traveled with him for a year, and had to look over the slaves, and see that they were dressed well, had plenty to eat, and to oil their faces* (n. d. :54–55).

Louis Hughes (b. 1843, enslaved in Mississippi and Virginia) described a Richmond auction:

> *It was expected that all the slaves in the yard for sale would be neatly dressed and clean before being brought into the show-room. It was the foreman's business to see that each man was presentable* (8).

> Lizzie Grant (1847): *They way they did when they were going to sell a slave was to make that slave clean up real good, then he would grease their face, hands and feet real good so they would look fat and slick. If you went to buy a yearling you would want that yearling to be real fat and his hide to look slick and good, or you would not want the yearling. That was just the way with the slave when*

Figure 20. Enslaved people groomed for sale. Frontispiece, *The White Slave: A Story of Life in Virginia*, R. Hildreth, ed., 1852.

you went to buy one, you would want that slave to look like he been taken good care of and in the best of shape or you would not want him or her (S2. 5. 4:1558–1559 [WV/TX]).

For both male and female enslaved people, the times of their sale precipitated humiliating experiences. The very fact that such a procedure was possible was debasing enough, but there were often additions to the depraved practice. Just as Africans were sometimes stripped nude for the Middle Passage, so too were enslaved people in the antebellum South sometimes shorn of clothing for the auction block.

> Charles Anderson (ca. 78 years): *I seen a woman sold. They had on her a short dress, no sleeves, so they could see her muscles, I reckon* (8. 1 [AR]).

> Sarah Benjamin (82 years): *Once when I's little, marse stripped me stark naked and puts me on de block, but he wouldn't sell me, 'cause he was bid only $350.00 and he say no, 'cause I was good and fat* (4. 1:70 [LA/TX]).

That Blacks carried tales that turned the tables becomes evident in the following narrative:

> Anna Williamson (between 75 and 80 years): *Mama muster been a pretty big sorter woman when she young. A ridin' boss went to whoopin' her once and she tore every rag clothes he had on offen him. I heard em say he went home strip stark naked* (11. 7:193 [TN/AR]).

The next episodes concern this procedure as it affected enslaved men. James Redpath noted the dress of a male during a slave auction, also in Richmond, in 1854. Redpath's description is one of many which shows that, as well as having the power to cover the enslaved person's body, whites had the power to uncover it.

> The slave was dressed in his pantaloons, shirt and vest. His vest was removed and his breast and neck exposed. His shoes and stockings were next taken off and his legs beneath the knees examined. His other garment was then loosened, and his naked body, from the upper part of the abdomen to the knees, was shamelessly exhibited to the view of the spectators.
>
> "Turn around!" said the body-seller. The negro obeyed, and his uncovered body from the shoulders to the calves of his legs was laid bare to criticism (1854:9–10).

The following scene provides a description of a man's dress for the sale and the demeaning aftermath:

> Stopping opposite Tom, who had been attired for sale in his best broadcloth suit, with well-starched linen and shining boots, he briefly expressed himself as follows:
>
> "Stand up."
>
> Tom stood up.

> "Take off that stock!" and, as Tom encumbered by his fetters, proceeded to do it, he assisted him, by pulling it, with no gentle hand, from his neck, and putting it in his pocket.
>
> Legree now turned to Tom's trunk, which, previous to this, he had been ransacking, and, taking from it a pair of old pantaloons and dilapidated coat, which Tom had been wont to put on about his stable-work, he said, liberating Tom's hands from the handcuffs, and pointing to a recess in among the boxes,
>
> "You go in there, and put these on."
>
> Tom obeyed, and in a few moments returned.
>
> "Take off your boots," said Mr. Legree.
>
> Tom did so.
>
> "There," said the former, throwing him a pair of coarse, stout shoes, such as were common among the slaves, "put these on."
>
> "Now, Tom, I've relieved you of any extra baggage, you see. Take mighty good care of them clothes. It'll be long enough 'fore you get more. I go in for making niggers careful; one suit has to do for one-year on my place" (Stowe, 481–483).

Literary fiction and eye-witness testimony direct attention to the fact that sometimes enslaved Black women and men were the victims of degrading acts that very often concerned their clothing or lack of clothing. These kinds of episodes occurred during punishments, during times of sale, and they might also happen on a more daily basis.

> Louis Thomas (b. 1844): *When I was a slave, I had to plow bar-footed, hooked to a double horse plow. For 8 or 10 years of dat time we had a white overseer in de summer. I did not only plow barefooted but naked as well* (11. 7. 8:349 [AL/MO]).

In cases specifically involving the demeaning of Black men by depriving them of adequate clothing, the evidence suggests that white men, but not white women, inflicted the humiliation. In particular, two narrators showed that some white women insisted upon Black males wearing suitable clothing at puberty.

> Morris Sheppard (b. 1852): *I wore a stripedy shirt till I was about eleven years old, and den one day while we was down in Choctaw Country old Mistress see me and nearly fall off'n her horse! She holler, 'Easter [Sheppard's mother], you go right now and make dat big buck of a boy some britches!'* (7:287 [OK]).

> Jerry Boykins (92 years): *All the boys in my time jest wore a home-made shirt hanging loose summer and winter. One day when I was 'bout fo'teen, ol' missie say to Marster when he fix that day to go to town, 'See here, I can't stan' the*

sight of this black boy runnin' 'round in this house without 'nuf clothes to hide his nakedness. You bring him back from town a pair of long pants,' and that's how I got my first pants (S2. 2. 1:372 [TX]).

The power held by whites to intimidate the enslaved is evident; nevertheless, in the matter of clothing, it is clear that the hegemony of whites was never absolute. Numerous other factors were at play which help account for a wide variety of Black male dress than has just been outlined. A good starting point is, again, West Africa.

Mungo Park noted the attire of West African men in the 1790s: "The [Mandingo] dress of both sexes is composed of cotton cloth, of their own manufacture; that of the men is a loose frock, not unlike a surplice, with drawers which reach half-way down the leg" (14). Apparently, this type of costume was widespread, for Park continues: "This account of their clothing is indeed nearly applicable to the natives of all the different countries in this part of Africa . . ." (15).

As described by Park, the simple, loose cotton clothing worn by West African men in the late eighteenth century compares in significant respects to the ordinary clothing of enslaved African American men during the antebellum period in the American South.

Celia Henderson (b. 1849): *De men's jes have a kinda clothes like – well, like a chemise, den some pantaloons wid a string run through at de knees* (16. 4:44 [KY/OH]).

In particular, the ubiquitous shirt, worn by so many enslaved Blacks, may well be an adaptation of a West African article of clothing, and not merely something thrust upon them by white overlords. In addition to Park's description, there is linguistic evidence that the shirt is a carry-over from West Africa. Two contributors referred to the shirt as a "banyan" or "binyan" which is a Hindu term for a loose shirt, gown, or jacket (*Webster's Third New International*). The word was used by Shad Hall of Georgia (above in Parrish, 131), and by:

Amy Perry (82 years): *Dey mek banyans for de chillen. Sleebe bin cut in de cloth, and dey draw it up at de neck, and call um bayan* (3. 3:252 [SC]).

One conclusion is that the word came into West Africa with Arab or European merchants who dealt in Indian trade cloth and clothing, and the word, as well as the shirt itself, was then transported to the United States by the enslaved Blacks, some of whose descendants retained both. "Bayan," however, was also the term applied by Europeans to a highly fashionable, loose outer garment worn in the late eighteenth century. From the slave owners' viewpoint, a comment by Elizabeth Barber probably serves to account for the ubiquitous shirts worn by most young enslaved children. Barber writes, "Because an outfit required a huge expenditure of time, effort, and materials, older folk costumes are usually constructed so that the person could grow in the usual directions – taller or fatter – without making the garment useless" (1994;140).

Many contributors named the shirt as an item of clothing worn by nearly all enslaved children. On the other hand, although a number of male informants said that their only article of clothing was a shirt, they made these statements without clarifying at what age this was true. This may mean that they had not reached maturity during the time of enslavement or that, in some cases, pants were not always an addition to an adult man's clothing.

Clothing invariably figures in the folklore of the enslaved. Integrating articles of dress into the most deeply entrenched of all communal beliefs and expressive habits serves as another example of the ways in which African Americans defined their independence regarding dress.

One genre of prose narrative folklore is the trickster tale, and several formerly enslaved people narrated such tales in which themes develop around articles of male clothing. Two of these concern the omnipresent "shirt" and were told by Joseph Stroyer (b. 1849, enslaved in South Carolina). John Roberts analyzes the dual-nature of the trickster in the tales told within African American communities during the period of enslavement (1989:17–64). Perhaps it is significant that Stroyer's father was born in Sierra Leone, because Roberts also demonstrates that, although these tales obviously have African antecedents, as told in the United States, they were firmly grounded in an American reality (ibid.). One character In particular, the "slave trickster," emanated directly out of African American communities.

Stroyer first tells the tale of a slave trickster named Joe who was cooking a stolen turkey in a pot. The turkey's knees stuck out, so he covered them with his shirt. When his "mistress" inquired what he was doing, he replied that he was washing his shirt. When the woman found the turkey under the shirt, "*[s]he asked him how the turkey had got into the pot; he said he did not know but reckoned the turkey got in himself, as fowls were very fond of going into the kitchen.*" Joe's trick backfired, however, when he "*was whipped because he allowed the turkey to get into the pot*" (reprinted in Katz, 44). But the denouement also suggests a double-meaning because it points out the white woman's stupidity at believing Joe's fabricated excuse.

Stroyer related another slave-trickster tale concerning a shirt and its owner. Josh was roasting some stolen corn when the overseer approached. "*Josh took the ears out with some live coals stuck to them and put them in his shirt bosom. In running away his clothes took fire and Josh jumped into the creek to put it out.*" Josh explained when the overseer asked why he was in the creek, that "*it was a warm day and he was cooling off.*" Again, the ending may be interpreted in two ways: although Josh was not punished by the overseer, who never discovered the stolen corn, Josh nevertheless got burned(reprinted in Katz, 59–60).

Yet another African American riff on the theme of clothing is humor. Throughout the *Narratives* the reader often encounters delightful passages wherein a contributor expresses memories and feelings about long-ago clothing with a touch of whimsy. The following involves yet another man and yet another shirt:

> Felix Haywood (93 years): *I tell my chillen we didn't know no more about pants than a hawg knows about heaven; but I tells 'em that to make 'em laugh. We had all the clothes we wanted and if you wanted shoes bad enough you get 'em . . .. And shirts! Mister, there was shirts that was shirts! If someone gets caught by his shirt on a limb of a tree, he had to die there if he weren't cut down. Them shirts wouldn't rip no more'n buckskins* (4. 2:132 [TX]).

For all the remarks about shirts, most adult men also wore other articles of clothing. The total antebellum outfit worn by the enslaved African American male was a syncretism which included African-style loose shirts and European-style items of dress adaptable to the conditions of the American South. A strictly American addition to the wearing attire of many enslaved men was jeans. Ever since their invention in the nineteenth century, blue jeans have been worn by American agricultural workers of all ethnic groups.

> Mary Reynolds (over 100 years): *The older men wore jeans and the women wore ginghams* (S2. 9. 8:3291 [LA/TX]).

> John William Mathews (77 years): *I wore jeans and they got so stiff when they were wet that they would stand up* (16. 4:72 [WV/OH]).

Sometimes the jeans were attached to another piece of fabric and called by special names; today, we call them "overalls."

> Anna Peek: *The men wore pants known as apron pants. The cloth was known as jeans . . .* (S1. 4. 2:478 [GA]).

> The interviewer paraphrased George Womble (b. 1843): "the men were given a garment that was made into one piece by sewing the pants and shirts together. This was known as a 'roundabout'" (1. 4:184 [GA]).

> Sabe Rutledge (b. 1861): *First time I big enough to realect (recollect) him [grandfather] he have on no pants but something built kinder like overall and have a apron. Apron button up here where my overall buckle and can be let down. All been dye with indigo* (3. 4:65 [SC]).

As we know, much of the cloth and clothing for both Blacks and whites was manufactured domestically, and formerly enslaved women outlined their roles in supplying African American men with clothing.

> Sina Banks (86 years): *When the women had plenty of cloth woven they would go to work and make it up into clothes. The men were looked after first* (S1. 12:17 [MO/OK]).

> Mary Johnson: *Mammy make fasten-back dresses and fasten-back drawers and knit sweaters and socks for the mens* (4. 2:221 [TX]).

The clothing that human beings wear depends on both physical environmental conditions as well as local custom. The clothing of the enslaved reflects this duality. For example, male informants from Texas and the Indian Territory (Oklahoma)sometimes wore what may be popularly described as typical "frontier" clothing:

> William Byrd (b. 1840): *In cold weather we had sheepskin clothes, made with the fur part turned in side . . . we wrapped our feet in fur hides* (S. 2. 3:574 [TX]).

> Tucker Smith (b. 1851): *Well son, I'se wore buckskin clothes the most of the time when I'se on them wild horses but then when I'se not riding horses I had in warm weather what they called royal shirts to wear made from cotton and put together with hand work . . .. On Sunday we just had plain white royal shirts to wear, boss them old shirts they opened all the way down the front and came clear down to our ankles* (S2. 9. 8:3673 [TX]).

Tom Windham (87 years): *I had an Indian wife and wore Indian dress and when I went to . . . Tenn. , I had to send the outfit home to Okla.* (11. 7:214 [TN, OK/AR]).

Certain articles of male clothing were not worn until after emancipation. For some informants, these items became emblems of one difference between enslavement and freedom.

Della Mun Bibles (b. ca. 1856): *I never saw a man wear a store-bought shirt until I was grown and married* (S. 2. 1. 1:292 [TX]).

Bill Simms (b. 1839): *[Long after emancipation] my oldest daughter bought me my first suit of clothes I ever had* (16:13 [KS]).

Women. Mungo Park's description provides evidence for some similarities between the clothing of West African and African American men. He also provides references to African women's clothing (see Chapter 1).

According to Parks' description, African women's clothing does not show a specific correspondence to African American women's dress except in the noteworthy detail that both groups usually wore a type of skirt, rather than pants as men did. Concerning their clothing, enslaved women had a wide range of experiences to relate. A few women remembered ample and suitable attire.

Mary Overton (117 years): *I wore cotton dresses in summer and linsey dresses and a shawl in de winter . . .. My white folks was pretty good to keep me in clothe* (5. 3:163 [TX]).

Julia Cole (78 years): *Our dresses was well sewed and made wid belts to 'em. Nobody went 'bout half naked on our plantation lak some of de old folks f'um other farms talks 'bout. Us had good well-made clothes, even if dey was made out of common cloth* (12. 1:234 [GA]).

Abundant evidence shows that white women usually oversaw the manufacture of the enslaved people's clothing. It is less certain whether they or white men were responsible for the distribution of that clothing. But it is clear that white women had a strong influence on some Black women's sense of decorum and of suitable female dress. It was, after all, the Victorian era, and white American women still took their own cues about proper attire and fashion from Europeans, most notably English women.

Melea Malone: *My mistress wouldn't let me wear short dresses and I don't like a short dress yet* (S2. 7. 6:2566 [TX]).

Rosa Maddox (b. ca, 1849): *[Miss Fannie] used to buy me good calico dresses and make them up for me. Shucks, I had good clothes as any body. Maybe that was why I had lots of beaus* (S2. 7. 6:2529 [MS, LA/TX]).

Rivana Boynton (b. 1850): *My missus, she made me a pair of hoops, or I guess she bought it, but some of the slaves took thin limbs from trees and made their hoops. Others made them out of stiff paper and others would starch their skirts stiff with rice starch to make their skirts stand way out. We thought those hoops were just the thing for style* (17. 1:44 [FL]).

Although some Black women enjoyed adequate and even fashionable attire, other women remarked on the poor quality or inadequacies of their clothing.

Charity McAllister: *(I wuz 'bout grown when [the Yankees] come through): Our clothes were poor. One-piece dress made o' carpet stuff, part of de time* (15. 2 [NC]).

Annie Osborne (81 years): *[Master gave only] half 'nough clothes. I had one dress the year round, two lengths of cloth sewed together(5. 3:157 [TX]).*

James Lucas (b. 1833): De colored wimmins wore lin'sey woolsey dresses an' leggins wrop 'round dey laigs lak sojers wear. Dis was a long wool cloth an' it woun' 'round an' 'round day laigs an' fastened at de top wid a string (S1. 8. 3:1345 [MS]).

The inadequacies of clothing which some women remembered illustrate a form of humiliation and are comparable to certain forms of debasement to which their male counterparts were subjected. But deficiencies were only one manner of the degradations inflicted on African American women through their clothing. In this regard, the experiences of Black women differed significantly from that of Black men. Charlotte Brooks, enslaved in Virginia and Louisiana, related an example of a Black woman who, among grotesque forms of punishment, was forced to wear male clothing.

Nellie was sold to a mighty bad man. She tried to run away to her Virginia home, but the white man caught her and brought her back . . .. When they got her back they made her wear men's pants for one year. They made her work in the field in that way. She said they put deer-horns on her head to punish her, with bells on them. Aunt Jane said once while she was passing on the levee she saw Nellie working with the men on the Mississippi River, and she had men's clothes on then (Albert, 1890:64).

In two accounts, Black women donned men's clothing by choice. An Auburn [New York] resident, who recounted Harriet Tubman's exploits during the Civil War, noted: "She was proud of the fact that she had worn 'pants' ["bloomers"] and carried a musket, canteen and haversack, accoutrements which she retained after the war" (quoted in Sterling, 260).

For quite a different reason, Harriet Jacobs also donned men's clothes. The disguise given to Jacobs to wear for her escape from enslavement was "*a suit of sailor's clothes, – jacket, trowsers, and tarpaulin hat*" (111). In order to pull off the masquerade, Jacobs' friend advised her to " *[p]ut your hands in your pockets, and walk rickety, like de sailors*" (112). Jacobs succeeded.

One narrator recalled the practicality of wearing pants while performing agrarian tasks.

Adeline Hedge: *De women had pantelettes made an' tied to dere knees, to wear in de fields to keep dew off dere legs* (S1. 1:185 [MS/AL]).[9]

If Black women could not be degraded by being forced to wear men's clothing, many African Americans testified that the clothing which Black women received from slaveholders was purposefully unfeminine. And there were other ways of humiliating them.

Claude C. Robin noted in Louisiana in the early 1800's: *the women worked in the fields in rags, their breasts exposed* (quoted in Crété, 267).

Sojourner Truth (b. ca. 1770s): *[D]ey used to weave what dey called nigger cloth, an' each one of us got jes' sech a strip, an' had to wear it width-wise. Them that was short got along pretty well, but as for me . . .* [Truth was nearly 6 feet tall](*Narrative* of Sojourner Truth, 1873:165–166).

One part of African American women's attire seemed to be particular to their sex and to their class – a large pocket attached to the waist of a dress or skirt.

Hattie Jefferson (81 years): *My Mammy always wore dresses made uf lowels, made plain frum de neck all de way down, wid a band at de waist an' a pocket in de side; dat pocket wus long an' she kept her 'backer an' pipe in dat pocket, an' one time her dress was sot on fire frum de pipe, an' my grandpappy had to wrap mammy up in a quilt to put out de fire* (S1. 8. 3:1133 [MS]).

Lina Hunter (ca, 90 years): *See here, Chile . . . here's a sho 'nough pocket. Jus' let me turn it wrong-side-out to show you how big it is. Why, I used a whole 25 pound flour sack to make it 'cause I don't lak none of dese newfangled little pockets. I lak things de way I was raised. Dis pocket hangs down inside and nobody don't see it. De chilluns fusses 'bout my big pocket, but it ain't in none of dem dresses, and I's sho gwine to wear 'em 'till de is wore out to a gnat's heel* (12. 2:259 [GA]).

In Cate's description of Tyrah Wilson's attire as a "house-servant," given earlier, she refers to "The white apron, with two big pockets, covers the front and reaches almost to the bottom of the skirt." Cate goes on to speculate about the reason for the oversized pockets:

In these pockets, no doubt, Tyrah carries the keys to her workrooms since she would be responsible for the materials kept there. [Wilson was head seamstress on the Hofwyl plantation.] Keys were considered a badge of authority and the person who carried them was a trusted servant (185; photograph on facing page).

But two other women, both from Kentucky, gave folk beliefs as their reasons for wearing the large pockets:

Cora Torian (71 years): *My Mammy always wore and* [sic] *ole petticoat full gather at de waist band wid long pockets in dem and den to keep peace in de house she would turn de pocket wrong side out jes as she would go to somebody elses house* (16. 2:105 [KY]).

The interviewer describes her interview with Mary Woolridge (ca. 103 years): "[S]he dresses as the older slave women dressed in the past days. She wears an old lace bodice with a very full skirt that comes to her ankles and this skirt has very long deep pockets and when I asked her why she had such pockets in her skirt her answer was: '*Wal you sees honey I jes am used to dis dress and thar is no way foh youse to had me git shud of it, dese pockets is powerful venient foh wen I goes inter some ones house why I turns dese pockets wrong side out and dat always brings me good luck*'" (16. 2:107 [KY]).

Beads and Such

Another possible source of evidence for this study might have been the growing body of archaeological data which is helping to fill in the picture of the material life of enslaved communities in the South. As Teresa Singleton points out, however, archaeology probably will not be of much use in helping us understand what enslaved people wore, since the cloth, textiles, and animal skins rarely survive.[10] But African Americans adorned themselves with more than clothing, and it is these more permanent articles of adornment, such as metal buckles, stone and shell beads, and bone buttons, that have been recovered archaeologically.[11] Early evidence for jewelry comes from the "Negro's Burial Ground" in New York City where 20,000 enslaved and free Blacks were buried between 1712 and 1792 (Fitzgerald, 1992:19).

Pictorial representation is an added source for examining the African American's use of jewelry at the time. An important photograph taken between 1855 and 1860 shows an African American woman wearing a necklace fashioned from African trade beads (Figure 21). In the *Narratives*, people who referred to jewelry most often described it as objects threaded on strings.

Figure 21. *Portrait of a Seated Black Woman* wearing trade beads, 1855–1860. Unknown daguerreotypist, American, ambrotype, hand-colored, 1 11/16″ × 2 3/16″. Collection of the J. Paul Getty Museum, Malibu, California.

Eda Raines (b. 1853): *[At Christmas master] generally gave us fo-bits to spend as we wanted to. Maybe we'd buy a string of beads or some notion* (S2. 8. 7. 3223 [AR/TX]).

Alice Hutcheson (b. 1862): *Us used to string chinquapins [chestnuts] and hang 'em 'round our necks* (12. 2:285 [GA]).

All cultures view "beads and notions" as a way of beautifying the wearer, and an aesthetic sense about decorating the body is one obvious purpose for wearing such items. The contributors, however, spoke far more often about another reason for wearing these kinds of objects on their bodies: the belief in the objects' protective powers.

Victoria Taylor Thompson (80 years): *[Daddy] was a herb doctor, that's how come he have the name 'Doc.' He made us wear charms. Made out of shiny buttons and Indian rock beads. They cured lots of things and the misery too* (S1. 12:322 [OK]).

Two women gave nearly identical statements about wearing china berry beads as children for just such a purpose:

Rosa Washington (90 years): *My mammy give me beads fo my neck. China-berry beads, to keep me well* (S2. 10. 9:3981 [LA/TX]).

Martha Patton (91 years): *My mammy give me beads for my neck, china berry beads to keep me well. They'd pretty. I never had no other kind* (4. 1:137 [TX]).

A man reckoned these beads had other powers as well.

Gus Feaster: *In dem days dey [de gals] dried cheney berries (chinaberries) and painted dem and wo' dem on a string around dere necks to charm us* (2. 2:52 [SC]).

Another woman, who wore a "bronze medal of Our Lady of Mount Carmel," explained the other objects on the string:

Pauline Johnson ("6 yers old when freedom come"): *W'at dese other t'ings on de string? O, dem's nutmeg. Dey's wo'n for de food of de heart. Bofe us [she and her sister] hab bad heart. Dey's 'spose to be two of dem togedder* (S2. 6. 5:2038 [TX]).

The interviewer paraphrased Amanda McCray who was "a grownup during the Civil War," reporting that "children wore moles feet and pearl buttons around their necks to insure easy teething" (17. 213 [FL]). Several other people, including men, told about the protective power of wearing a coin:

> Elisha Doc Garey (age 76): *Slaves wore a nickel or a copper on strings 'round dair necks to keep off sickness. Some few of 'em wore a dime; but dimes was hard to git* (12. 2:7 [GA]).

> Silvia Witherspoon (ca. 90 years): *Sometimes I wears dis dime wid de hole in it aroun' my ankle to keep off de conjure, but since Monroe King tuk an' died us ain't had much conjerin' 'roun' here* (6. 1:431 [AL]).

The belief that certain inanimate objects worn on the body have powers to ward off harm is not limited to Southern Blacks. To point out just one example, many Christians wear a cross or saint's medal for the same reason. In the case of enslaved Blacks, however, a closer link to Africa may be hypothesized, such as the artifacts found at the slave quarters at Thomas Jefferson's Monticello. William Kelso, the excavator at the site, remarks: "an African cowry shell, 'mojo' magic ring (?), and pierced silver eighteenth-century Spanish coins show that African tradition was very much alive within the Monticello community" (1986:30).

A number of scholars have shown the remarkable degree of African retentions among the Gullah people living on the Sea Islands off the Georgia coast. Robert Pickney of Wilmington Island recalled the enslaved Africans he had known:

> *Doze Africans alluz call one anudduh 'countrymen' . . .. [Some] weah eahring in duh eah. Some weahs it in duh lef eah an doze from anudduh tribe weahs it in duh right eah* (*Drums and Shadows*, 100).

The narrative collected from a formerly enslaved man living on St. Catherine's demonstrates that the earrings were yet another survival of an African belief in wearing jewelry for protection. In 1939, London Grayson was interviewed by a member of the Georgia Writers Project. Grayson wore a gold earring in his left ear and reported to the interviewer that the earring "tended to improve his eyesight" (ibid., 73). On St. Simon's, Ben Sullivan said that an old African woman on the Couper plantation where he had been enslaved "*weah one ring in he eah fuh he eyes*"(ibid., 171).[12]

Special Events

No matter when or how the agricultural laborers received the clothing used for daily work, these items were often inadequate, rather uniform, and had little, if any, added ornamentation. Special events, however, often offered the opportunity for wearing unusual clothing. African American people acquired this additional and more expansive clothing in a variety of ways. As has been noted, certain enslaved people, usually domestic servants or those in positions of authority over other Blacks, received non-ordinary clothes as hand-me-downs from whites. Many enslaved people actually purchased items when extra money came their way. Still others were able to gain special items of dress by trading them for either garden crops that they had raised or with craft objects they had made. Enslaved women who worked as weavers or seamstresses had access to homemade cloth or clothing that they might give to relatives and friends. On certain occasions, the "master" might dole out special clothes. These occasions were usually special events in themselves.

> Mary Kincheon Edwards (b. 1810): *I didn't mind pickin' cotton, 'cause I never did have de backache. I pick two and three hunnert pounds a day and one day I picked 400. Sometime de prize give by masa to de slave what pick de most. De prize am a big cake or some clothes . . .. I gits a dress one day and a pair shoes* (4. 2:16 [LA, TX/TX]; cf. S1. 4. 3:1280 [TX]).

Fanny Kemble noted that on her husband's Georgia plantation: "On the birth of a child certain additions of clothing and an additional weekly ration are bestowed on the family . . ." (95). Several hundred enslaved people worked on another Georgia plantation where Dink Walton Young (a woman) was enslaved.

> The interviewer paraphrased Young: " [E]very time a Negro baby was born on one of his plantations, Major Walton gave the mother a calico dress and a 'bright, shiny silver dollar'" (S1. 4. 2:667 [GA]).

A number of interviewees remembered Christmas as a particular occasion when whites distributed articles of clothing to the enslaved. For some, Christmas only marked the distribution of the workers' winter clothes.

> Sam Polite (93 years): *Ebery year in Christmas month you gits four or eider fibe yaa'd cloth 'cording to how you is. Out ob dat, you haffa mek your clote* (3. 3:272 [SC]).

Bert Mayfield (b. 1852): *On Christmas each of us stood in line to get our clothes; we were measured with a string which was made by a cobbler. The material had been woben by the slaves in a plantation shop* (16. 2:13 [KY]).

The interviewer paraphrased Rosaline Rogers (b. 1827; 110 years): "The slaves were given a pair of shoes at Christmas time and if they wore out before summer, they were forced to go barefoot" (6. 2:165 [SC, TN/IN]).

But sometimes, Christmas meant receiving special clothes.

Mary Reynolds (over 100 years): *Christmas was the best time of the year . . .. The highest cotton picker gets a new suit of clothes and all the womens that has twins that year gets a outfittin of clothes for the twins* (S2. 8. 7:3294–3295 [LA/TX]).

Lee Pierce (b. 1850): *Spencer just had my mothers family on his place and allus give us new clothes and the old ones money for Christmas* (S2. 8. 7:3094 [TX]).

Jacob Stroyer (b. 1849, enslaved in South Carolina): *[At Christmas] some of the masters would buy presents for the slaves; sich as hats and tobacco for the men, handkerchiefs and little things for the women; these things were given after they had been pleased with them; after either dancing or something for their amusement* (reprinted in Katz, 45).

Henry Johnson (b. 1842): *Christmas was a good time. Den de white folks give me clothes an' candy an' things, an' dere wasn't no work to do* (S2. 6. 5:2007 [MS/TX]).

Bert Strong (b. 1864): *Christmas was the big time . . .. [Massa] give the big folks somethin' to wear* (5. 3:71 [TX]).

Mary James: *We all got shoes for Christmas, a dress and $2.00 or suits of clothes* (16. 3:38 [VA/MD]).

Secular Socials

More important than the special times when clothing was distributed to the enslaved were the times when African Americans dressed up for special events. As they described these times, they give us a better understanding of their personal style and of their attitudes regarding how they wanted to appear.

Ida Rigley (82 years): *I don't think everyday frocks was stiffened but our dress up clothes was. It was made out of flour – boiled flour starch. We had striped dresses and stockings too. We had checked dresses* (10. 6:44 [AR]).

The narrators portray themselves as people who relished dressing up for non-ordinary occasions, be they secular or sacred. Although born after the Civil War, the following narrator's story exemplifies the passion which many African Americans displayed for items of finery.

Ophelia Jamison (b. 1868): De holy Scripture say: 'Lub thy neighbor as thyself,' but ef you had a neighbor lak dat colored gal what lib two do (door) next to me but one house, it defame you bery soul to look in dat slack eye she hab an' say 'I lub you honey.' One day I come home unexpected an' dere she be in me house. She aint oughter be een dere, but dat fedder boarer (boa) in me bureau drawer ontice dat gal to come dere, an' I axe you was it lub dat crawl up me back bone an' mek me hand rech (reach) out an' grab dat gal by de hair befo' 'e foot git her nowhere? I hab time dat night to t'ink 'bout what I done, an' down on me knee I bend. I tell de Lord de whole t'ing, how I wuk had (hard) to buy dem neck fedder, an' I aint wanna gib dem up widout a fight. An' I say to de Lord, 'O Lord! ef somebody come 'long an' snatch de wing off one ob you angel, what dey go do 'bout dem? Tell me Lord, cause I sorry I done trifle wid dat poor gal sperrit. She aint mean to do nuttin' but borrow dem fedder, an' I go lend em too, when we too git out ob dis jail house' (S1. 11:224 [SC]).

The formerly enslaved described dances as the secular event wherein they most often had occasion to dress differently. Clearly, for many in the enslaved communities, dancing was one form of entertainment they savored when they had the chance, and they often include comments about the clothing worn to dances.

Nellie Boyd: *Niggers had lots of dancing and frolics. Dey danced de 'flat-foot'. Dat was when a nigger would slam his foot flat down on de floor. De wooden bottom shoes sho would make a loud noise* (11. 1:64 [NC]).

Calvin Moye (b. 1842): *Saturday nights all de slaves on de plantation would either has a dance or go to a dance on another plantation and dey would dance til daylight on Sunday mornings sometimes . . .. When we started to a dance I first remembers, we would puts on our cotton or wool clothes and a cotton wool hat and knitted socks all made on de plantation and wears knitted gloves if it was cold and puts on our ole rawhide moccasins* (S2. 7. 6:2841–2842 [GA, TX/TX]).

Pick Gladdeny (b. 1856): *Used to rather dance than to eat . . .. Pats our feets and knocks tin pans was the music dat us niggers danced to all night long. Put on my clean clothes dat was made right on the plantation and wear them to the dance. Gals wore their homespun stockings. Wore the dresses so long dat they kivered their shoes. My britches were copperas colored and I had on a home wove shirt with a pleated bosom. It was dyed red and had wristbands. I wore that shirt for five years* (2. 2:127–128 [SC]).

Richard Carruthers (100 years): *I used to dance . . .. Was them womenfolks knock kneed? You sho' couldn't tell, even when you swung 'em 'round, 'cause they dresses was so long* (4. 1:200 [TN, TX/TX]).

In stark contrast to Gladdeny's and Carruthers' complaints, Isaac D. Williams (enslaved in Virginia) told of seeing

. . . some [dancing] colored women grasp their dresses on each side, holding them so you could see their feet take every step known to the art, and do it as well as the most talented professional, all done easily and gracefully with no apparent effort (61).

Two people told of secretly "borrowing" the finery of whites in order to make good appearances at dances:

Mary Wyatt (b. 1839): *Ole Missis had one dress dat she wore only in de spring time. Lawdy, I used to take dat dress when she warn't nowhere roun' an' hole it up against me an' 'magine myself wearin' it. One Christmas de debbil got in me good. Got dat gown out de house 'neath my petticoat tied round me an' wore it to de dance. Was scared to death dat Missus gonna come in, but she didn't. Marsa come, but I knowed he warn't able to tell one dress from 'nother. Sho' was glad when I slipped dat dress back in de place nex' day. Never did dat no mo'* (*Weevils*, 333).

Jerry Boykins (92 years): *Marster had a cousin libbin with him. He have good clothes and he just my size. So on nights when I begs a pass to go over to a social to some of the othah plantations then I slip in to his room and sneaks out some clothes of hissen and sneak off, all dress up – then I sneaks back and puts his clothes back 'fore he gets up. He never cotch me* (S2. 2. 1:372 [TX]).

Two women related family folklore that revolved around their mothers and dances. The stories, however, express completely divergent experiences:

Anna Wallace: *You know they used to wear petticoats starched with hominy water . . .. They were starched so stiff that every time you stopped they would pop real loud. Well, she [mother] would go out at night to a party some of the colored folks was havin' and she would tell us kids to stay in the house and open the door in a hurry when we heard her a comin'. And when we heared them petticoats a poppin' as she run down the path, we'd open the door wide and she would get away from the patteroll* (*Weevils*, 294).

Jane Sutton's father tricked her mother into drinking some "hoodoo" liquid which drove her insane. In her tale, Sutton explained how clothing worn to a dance played a part in causing her father to take such drastic action:

Jane Sutton (84 years): *You mean hoo doo? Dat's whut my pappy done to my mammy. You see, dey was allus fussin' 'bout fust one thing, den 'nother, an' mammy got mad 'caus'n pappy slipped her clo'es out'n her ches' an' taken over to de other gals for to dance in, an' when he brung 'em back mammy would see finger prints on 'em whar he been turnin' 'em'roun' un' she sho' be mad an' fight him. She could lick him too caus'n she was bigger* (S2. 7:162 [MS]).

Candis Goodwin sang a song in which the lyrics mention clothing worn to a dance:

Gwine to de ball
Feet de de diddle
. . . .
Gwine wear a raid gown
Feet de de diddle
. . . .
Gwine wear a velvet coat.
(*Weevils*, 106)

Items of clothing figured especially in the lyrics of dance tunes such as this ring-game song:

Millie Ann Smith (b. 1850): *On Saturday nights Master made us gang up and sing and dance and play ring plays. Our favorites was 'Eleven Stars, Eleven Stars Gwine to Fall' [and] 'Gwine Up North, Newbound wearing broadcloth'* (S2. 9. 8:3655 [TX].

The last verse of a song sung for a reel dance contains an item of clothing in the lyrics. Mollie Williams (b. 1854):

Run nigger run, de patterrollers ketch you
Run nigger run, fer hits almos' day,
De nigger run; de nigger flew; de nigger los' his big ol' shoe.
(7. 9:162 [MS]; full text, S1. 10. 5:2348 [MS])

After much coaxing, Green Harris (b. ca. 1854), a fiddler, sang and played "old-fashioned dance tunes which had been favorites south of the Mason-Dixon Line in ante-bellum days" for Lydia Parrish in about 1932. One of Harris' song lyrics includes a refrain about shoes:

Tune my fiddle, tune it good
The little neighbor in the neighborhood.
I do I do I tries to do
Put on de silver slippers.
An' I do I do an' I do no mor'
Put on de silver slippers (118).

Parrish notes the lyrics to a "promenading piece" titled "It's a Cold Frosty Morning":

O the lady – she wear a pretty green shawl
pretty green shawl
pretty green shawl
O the lady – she wear a pretty green shawl
So early in the mornin' (104).

In this "shout song," Parrish notes the use of an article of dress:

Oh, Eve – where is Ad-u-m?
Oh, Eve – Adam in the garden
Pickin' up leaves.

Parrish then thoroughly describes the dance that accompanied the song:

[This] is a good example of the combination of dancing and pantomime. After swinging deliberately around the circle, singing the slower part of the chant, the dancers, when the time quickens, go through the motion of picking up leaves. With aprons gathered up and bodies bent, the women add greatly to the interest of the dance. All are amusingly industrious, but the men, without the assistance of the aprons, are not quite so convincing in following the action indicated by the text (85).

A close comparison to the shout song and dance that Parrish observed is Mary Johnson's description of another shout song, although the latter one was delivered in a sacred context. Johnson said, *"dat chu'ch was jes' a rollin' and rockin' during the shouting of songs."*

Shoo de debil out de corner,
Shoo, members, shoo
Shoo de debil out de corner,
Shoo, members, shoo.

Johnson remembered that accompanying this song "*all de wimmen folks would 'shoo' wid dey aprons*" (S2. 6. 5:2026 [MS/TX]).

Sacred Times

In 1850s, Frederick Law Olmstead noted this about enslaved Virginians: "On Sundays and holidays they usually look very smart, but when at work, very ragged and slovenly" (1959:92). In South Carolina, Olmstead remarked to an elderly enslaved man that Blacks "did not look so well here as they did in North Carolina and Virginia." To which the man replied: "*Well, massa, Sundays dey is mighty well clothed, dis country; 'pears like dere an't nobody looks better Sundays dan dey do. But Lord! workin' days, seems like dey haden no close dey could keep on 'um at all, master*" (1959:112–113).

Olmstead's observation and that of the old man's are born out in the testimony of most narrators. It appears that on the days during which they labored for whites, the enslaved gave little regard for their clothing. But on the days granted to themselves – Sundays and holidays – the enslaved put great care and thought into what they wore.

Earlier, we saw how European travelers often overlooked or misunderstood deeper aspects of West African life. And yet, because many of the commentators considered the clothing outlandish or comical when compared to their own styles, their descriptions give us excellent pictures of what Africans actually wore during special events. Several Europeans took particular notice of the unusual clothing that Africans wore during sacred events, providing us with evidence of one important way in which West Africans marked religious ceremonies.

Catholic and Protestant Europeans and white Americans often wear unusual clothing for such occasions also; and, in several other important respects, West Africans held views about customs associated with religion that are similar to those of Christians. William Leo Hansberry, for instance, emphasizes that all Africans believe in one god and that religion, itself, permeates African society (99). It should come as no surprise, then, that sacred events and deeply held notions about proper attire for those events, played such an important part in the lives of African Americans who lived among another group of people who also believed in one god, and who also professed that religion permeated their own way of life, and whose clothing also often marked those convictions.

Sundays and Camp Meetings.

Millie Randall (*"jes' 'bout six year' ol' w'en peace was 'clared"): Dey didn't give us no Sunday dress cause dey didn' 'low is to go to chu'ch or nuthin' like dat* (S2. 8. 7:3239 [MS, LA/TX]).

Washington Dozier (90 years): *Jos wear who'e'er white folks gi'e us. Didn't take no foot tall 'bout Sunday clothes* (2. 1:331 [SC]).

Countering the comments about a lack of special Sunday dress, other people belie the sour memories of the above narrators. In fact, no other occasion generated as much information from the formerly enslaved about distinctive clothing as did descriptions of getting dressed-up on Sunday.[13]

Caroline Wright (90 years): *On Sunday us had lawn dresses and us sho' did come out looking choice some* (5. 3:221 [TX]).

Gabe Emanuel (85 years): *Yas 'im Missey dress up right smart some Sundays. Us dyke out in spic' an' span clean clo'es* (S1. 7. 2:682 [MS]).

Jane Sutton (84 years): *When us dress' up in Sunday clo'es us had caliker [calico] dresses. Day sho' was pretty. I 'members a dress dat Old Master bought for my granny. It was white an' yeller, an' it was de prettiest thing I ever seen* (7. 2:152 [MS]).

Gus Pearson (ca. age 97): *Sunday clothes was dyed red for de gals, boys wore de same. We made de gals' hoops out'n grape vines. Dey give us a dime, if dey had one, fer a set of hoops* (2. 2:47 [SC]).

Kitty Reese (83 years): *On Sunday 'n' w'em us go t' camp-meetin' on d' uder plantation us wear some 'r' young mistus shoe' 'n' dress'. W'en us come back us hafter tek 'em off 'n' put 'em up in d' big house careful f'r unudder time* (S2. 8. 7:3281 [MO, TX/TX]).

Squire Irvin (b. 1849): *On Sunday our clothes were made of the same material but the color was different. The old woman would go to the woods and gather indego [*sic*] and sumac to make the dye to color the cloth, what they had woven, a pretty color* (S1. 8. 3:1080 [TN/MS]).

Mary James: *On Sunday we wore the clothes given to us at Christmas time and the shoes likewise* (16. 3:38 [VA/MD]).

Silvia Witherspoon (ca. 90 years): *Mistus gave me a dress dat de white chilluns done out-growed an' on Sunday I was de dressed-upest nigger in de quarter* (6. 1:430 [AL]).

Lizzie Atkins (b. 1859): *Sunday white dress was trimmed with poke-berries* (S2. 1. 1:94 [TX]).

Gus Pearson (ca. 97 years): *During the preaching . . . [u]s wore de best clo'es dat us had. De Marse give us a coat and a hat and his sons give all de old hats an coats 'round. Us wore shirts and pants made from de loom. Us kept dem clean't and ironed jes' like de Marster and de young marsters done their'n. Den us wore a string tie, dat de white folks done let us have, to church. Dat 'bout de onliest time dat a darky was seed wid a tie. Some de oldest men even wore a cravat, dat dey had done get from de old marster . . .* (2. 2:62 [SC]).

Robert Weathersby (b. ca. 1847): *When us [boys] got 'bout fourteen years old us wuz give a pair o' pants to wear on Sundays. We'd put 'em on an' wear 'em to Church, an' when we got home we had to take 'em off an' put 'em up till de next Sunday* (S1. 10. 5:2240–2241 [MS]).

Addie Vinson (86 years): *Dey made up our summertime Sunday dresses out of a thin cloth called Sunday-parade. Dey was made spenser fashion, wid ruffles 'round de neck and waist. Our ruffled petticoats was all starched and ironed stiff and slick, and us jus' knowed our long pantelettes, wid deir scalloped ruffles, was mighty fine. Some of the 'omans would wuk fancy eyelets what dey punched in de scallops wid locust thorns. Dem pantalettes was buttoned on to our drawers. Our Sunday dresses for winter was made out of linsey-woolsey cloth* (13. 4:103 [GA]).

Although many people spoke of special clothes for church, the term "Sunday clothes" could also denote best clothes worn for any distinctive occasion.

Vina Moore (b. 1845): *We had wintah clothes and summer clothes, Sunday clothes, and everyday clothes. I never did jest wear mah Sunday clothes jes any time* (S2. 7. 6:2757 [MS, TX/TX]).

Liza Jones (81 years): *Us allus have de white tarelton Swiss dress for dances and Sunday. Dem purty good clothes, too and dey make at home* (4. 2:244 [TX]).

Scott Bond (84 years): *My mother had a large chest . . .. She would take out her calico dresses, which we people called 'Sunday Clothes'* (S2. 1:32 [AR/AZ]).

Many Blacks wore special shoes only for special occasions, and often this meant that the shoes were saved for going to church on Sunday.

Calvin Moye (b. 1842): *We always had a special made pants and hat to wears on Sunday and to things to do. We had buckskin shoes to wear ever day and we had a pair of shoes made by de shoe maker fer us to wear to church and other places* (S2. 7. 6:2831–2832 [GA, TX/TX]).

Lucy Lewis: *We uster go barefoot an' only when I go to church an' dances I wo' mah shoes* (S2. 6. 5:2363 [TX]).

Sophia Ward (b. 1837): *We had high topped shoes fer Sunday* (16. 2:68 [KY]).

Benjamin Johnson: *On Sunday we would take soot out of de chimney an' wet it an' den go an' borrow de marster's shoe brush an' go an' brush our shoes. We was gittin' ready to go to church* (12. 2:325 [GA]).

Concerning Sunday shoes, African Americans developed their own particular custom.

Nicey Kinney (86 years): *Dey was dressed in deir Sunday go-to-meetin' clothes and deir shoes, all shined up, was tied together and hung over deir shoulders to keep 'em from gittin' dust on 'em . . . Dey went barfoots wid der shoes hung over deir shoulders, jus' la' de mens . . .* (13. 3:41 [GA]).

Hannah Mullins (81 years): *We uns nevah puts de shoes on gwine to chu'ch 'til weins am sev'al hundred feet away; 'twas done dat way to save de shoes* (S2. 7. 6:2877 [TX]).

Elisha Doc Garey (76 years): *Us toted our shoes 'long in our hands goin' to church. Us puts 'em on jus' 'fore us got dar and tuk 'em off again soon as us got out of sight of de meetin' house on de way back home* (12. 2:4 [GA]).

Myra Jones (b. 1849): *All through the week we wore plain solid colored dresses an' barefooted but on Sunday us felt dressed up fer our dresses wuz striped an' plaid. We put on our shoes too on Sunday. Mos' an' generally dey felt too heavy an' on comfo'table so's we didn't usually keep 'em on long* (S1. 8. 3:1248 [MS]).

In many instances, the formerly enslaved people again make obvious that they knew that the slaveholders' underlying motivation for presenting well-groomed servants in public, particularly at church, was for the whites' own self-aggrandizment.

Georgia Baker (87 years): *Us had pretty white dresses for Sunday. Marse also wanted everybody on his place dressed up day day. He sent his houseboy, Uncle Harris, down to de cabins evvy Sunday mornin' to tell evvy slave to clean hisself up. Dere was a big old room sot aside for a wash-room* (12. 1:42 [GA]).

Lizzie Grant (b. 1847): *On Sunday we had clean white royal shirts to wear but we must keep them clean as Maser would tear us up for wearing dirty clothes on Sunday than for anything else* (S2. 5. 4:1555 [WV/TX]).

Lawrence Hampton (77 years): *We all had preaching clothes to wear. He had his slaves be somebody when they got out of the field. They went in washing at the fish pond, duck pond too . . .. They was black but they didn't stink sweaty. They wore starched clean ironed clothes* (9. 3:139 [SC/AR]).

Unidentified female: *On Sunday they would get us ready to go to church. They would dress us up after we ask them if we could go and they would have me walk off from them and they would look at me, and I'd hear them saying, "She's got a fine shape; she'll make a good breeder," but I didn't know what they were talking about* (18:1 [TN or KY]).

Moses Grandy, who was born in 1786 in North Carolina, offers another report on the importance that enslaved people held for dressing properly for religious services; but, according to Grandy, this sometimes provoked dire consequences:

If a negro has given offense to the patrol, even by so innocent a matter as dressing tidily to go to a place of worship, he will be seized by one of them, and another will tear up his pass; while one is flogging him, the others will look another way . . . (reprinted in Katz, 38).

Seasonal religious gatherings, or camp meetings, were also sacred occasions which the Blacks emphasized by wearing special clothes.

> Gus Pearson (ca. 97 years): *De gals come out in de starch dresses for de camp meeting . . .. [The mammies] wore de best aprons wid long streamers ironed and starched hanging down dey backs . . .. De [other] nigger gals and winches did all de dressing up dat dey could fer de meeting and fer de barbecue* (2. 2:62 [SC]).

Outsiders, as well, often noted the dress donned by Blacks for religious events. As early as 1806 in Louisiana, Claude C. Robin remarked that on Sundays, the Black female field hands: "decked themselves out like ladies" (quoted in Crété, 268).

Frances Kemble wrote at length on the enslaved South Carolinians' Sunday attire:

> You cannot conceive anything more grotesque than the Sunday trim of the poor people . . .. Their Sabbath toilet really presents the most ludicrous combination of incongruities that you can conceive – frills, flounces, ribbons; combs stuck in their wooly heads, as if they held up any portion of the stiff and ungovernable hair; filthy finery, every color in the rainbow, and the deepest possible shades blended in fierce companionship round one dusky visage; head handkerchiefs, that put one's very eye's out from a mile off; chintzes with sprawling patterns, that might be seen if the clouds were printed with them; beads, bugles, flaring sashes, and above all, little fanciful aprons, which finish these incongruous toilets with a sort of airy grace . . .. One young man . . . came to pay his respects to me in a magnificent black satin waistcoat, shirt gills which absolutely engulfed his black visage, and neither shoes nor stockings on his feet (1865:93).

John Dixon Long, meanwhile, commented on how clothing was used during a Maryland prayer meeting:

> At a given signal of the leader, the men will take off their jackets, hang up their hats, and tie up their heads with handkerchiefs; the women will tighten their turbans, and the company will then form a circle around the singer, and jump and bawl to their heart's content (Long, *Pictures of Slavery in Church and State* . . . , 1857:383, quoted in Epstein, 387).

At an Indiana camp meeting, Frances Trollope recorded this scene:[14]

> One tent [at the Indiana camp-meeting] was occupied exclusively by negroes. They were all full-dressed, and looked exactly as if they were performing a scene on the stage. One woman wore a dress of pink gauze trimmed with silver lace;

another was dressed in pale yellow silk; one or two had splendid turbans; and all wore white pantaloons, with gay coloured linen jackets (1832:140).

On another occasion, Trollope related that in Baltimore:

Another slave in the house told us, that she "liked religion right well, but that she never took fits in it, 'cause she was always fixed in her best when she went to chapel, and she did not like to have all her best clothes broke up" (1832:177).

Trollope offers a particularly detailed account of urban Black dress on Sundays:

I have often, particularly on a Sunday, met groups of negroes elegantly dressed; and have been sometimes amused by observing the very superior air of gallantry assumed by the men, when in attendance of their *belles*, to that of whites in similar circumstances. On one occasion we met in Broadway a young negress in the extreme of fashion, and accompanied by a black *beau*, whose toilet was equally studied; eye-glass, guard-chain, nothing was omitted; he walked beside his sable goddess uncovered, and with an air of the most tender devotion (310).

Trollope's concise, but detailed description of the Black people whom she observed, together with comments made by the formerly enslaved, give information about Black women's special affinity for dressy clothing. This we expect. Somewhat more unusual from a white perspective, perhaps, is the portrayal of so many Black men's concern for personal dress style. The West African documentation about important male leaders offers us one clue about this particular cultural phenomenon. The social critic, bell hooks, finds a more immediate reason for the continued emphasis that Black men place on individual style, and she grounds it firmly in American reality:

Black males in the United States have shared in the cultural history where fashion has been a site for confrontation and resistance . . .. Living and working in a racially segregated environment where domination of black folks via dramas of humiliation and disregard were the norm, dressing up, expressing one's style, was a declaration of independence (27).

As Trollope's description of New York "free" Black Christians in the late 1820s attests, the impetus to dress up in finery for religious functions was not limited to Southern Blacks; nor was it limited to African Americans, as West African evidence shows. The formerly enslaved people who talked about Sunday clothing are therefore linked temporally and spatially to previous generations of Africans and to Northern African Americans by each groups' firmly held, deeply embedded concepts about the proper attire for public worship. Recently, Ernest J. Gaines described how a Louisiana community presented itself for church in the mid-twentieth century, thereby offering us another link through time and space, no matter what the material circumstances of the people happened to be.

> Reverend Ambrose . . . parked his car along the highway and walked to the church. As usual, he was dressed in a dark suit, white shirt, and dark tie, but tonight he also wore a yellow slicker. Most of the other people wore their "going-to-town" clothes. Going-to-town clothes were old clothes, but without visible patches. The shirts and the dresses may have been faded, but they were clean and they were neat (1993:143).

Joining the Church. The narrators demonstrate that all religious ceremonies in which Blacks were involved featured special clothing. The religious ceremonies that they described relate to Christian events. Two contributors particularized what they wore when they "joined the church" (Figure 2):

> Jane Sutton (84 years): *I 'members when I joined de church . . .. I was dressed up in a white lowell slip* (7. 2. :152 [MS]).

> Eva Martin (82 years): *My fus' communion was mek in de big house. I sho' be dress' up for dat day. Dey dress me up all in white. Nan-nan, dat my godmother, she a white woman, she give me all I hab on dat time to mek my fus' communion. But we pay for all dat favor. Our po' back hafter pay for it. Dey was mo' wuk to do 'till it git pay for and if we ain't git de work done dey tek a rope and lay it on our back* (S2. 7. 6:2585 [LA/TX]).

Jane Sutton and Eva Martin (who was probably a Roman Catholic) were among the few informants who reported on the dress associated with formally joining the church. Lydia Parrish, however, witnessed a Black baptism earlier in this century which, from her description, was most likely a Baptist ceremony and may compare to antebellum customs.

> On a frosty morning many years ago, I happened to be on the bank of the Frederica River . . .. The girls were dressed in white, but the boys wore ordinary overalls and work shirts . . ..
>
> While those on the river bank sang, 'Wade in the Water,' the candidates, each escorted by a church member, followed to the water's edge. There the girls' skirts were tied above their knees to prevent undignified billowing, and the assisting

deacon led each candidate to the spot where the minister stood in about two-and-a-half feet of water (1933:168–169).

Elsie Clews Parsons adorns another article about Sea-Island baptisms with quotations (in dialect) from some of her informants. She writes that thirteen or fourteen was the age for "*join' de church*" in the Sea Islands. She says that during the two or three weeks previous to the baptizing, "'Around the head [of the candidate] is tied a little white cloth or a string *'jus' to mark deirse'f diffun' f'om de res*'" (1923:204–205). The actual baptism takes place by immersion in the river, the girls in "*Long white gown wid cotton in de ear, head done up*" (205).

Each of the four preceding informants note that white-colored clothing was worn when formally joining the church. While the tradition of girls wearing white clothing for first communion and baptism is Christian, it may also be another instance of syncretism of West African practice with Christian practice; for instance, in the use of white during the Mende female initiation rites described by Boone (see Chapter 1).[15]

Weddings.

Mattie Gilmore: *Weddins didn't mount ter much in de slavery times so we didn't have no extry clothes* (S2. 5. 4:1487 [AL/TX]).

Gus Pearson (ca. 97 years): *Wan't no dressing up fer marrying in slavery times; just say, 'Gwine to be married tonight' and you see 'bout 40 or 50 folks dar to see it* (2. 1:47 [SC]).

In spite of Gilmore's and Pearson's assertion, numerous contributors experienced weddings wherein clothing helped marked this sacred event as a special occasion. For some enslaved women, marriage was the only female rite of passage recognized by special clothing. In at least one instance, the "master" provided an enslaved woman's bridal clothes, although apparently as a cruel joke.

Unidentified woman: *When I was quite a girl I went to a colored person's wedding. She was as black as that thing there (card table top) but she was her young marster's woman and he let her marry because he could get her anyhow if he wanted her. He dressed her up all in red – red dress, red band and rosette around her head, and a red sash with a big red bow* (18:8 [TN or KY]).

That story of the "young marster" who dressed the enslaved woman in red for her wedding was an exception. Overwhelmingly, most people noted that the "mistress," the acknowledged upholder of nineteenth-century, white Christianity, was responsible for any bridal clothing worn by Black women. Thomas Nelson Page notes in his memoirs of Virginia before the Civil War:

> There was almost sure to be a negro wedding during holidays. The ceremony might be performed in the dining room or in the hall by the master, or in one of the quarters by a colored preacher; but it was a festive occasion, and the dusky bride's trousseau had been arranged by her young mistress . . . ([1892] 1994:62).[16]

> Mandy Jones (80 years): *My mammy often told me how she was married right in the white folkses house, they dressed her up for it. Her mistis made her a suit of close on her loom. They was white and she said her dress was low necked an' short-sleeved* (S1. 8. 3:1230 [MS]).

> Matilda Pugh (96 years): *De dress I married in was one of her [mistress'] party dresses, hit sho was fine, made out ob white tarelton, wid a pink ribbon tied round my head* . . . (S1. 1:109 [AL]).

> Nancy King (93 years): *I was married durin' the war . . .. Old Missie give me the cloth and dye for my weddin' dress and my mother spun and dyed the cloth, and I made it. It was homespun but nothin' cheap 'bout it for them days* (4. 2:288 [TX]).

> Richard Kimmons: *We had what dey all had when we married. I had a dark homespun suit, good 'nuff, an' my wife wore white. De fust wife had her veil what de w'ite folks fixed* . . . (S2. 6. 5:2197 [MO/TX]).

> Charley Johnson (b. ca. 1850): *I gits married in a black suit an' Mary wuz all dressed up in w'ite by de w'ite folks* (S. 2. 6. 5:1977{TX]).

There is an ironic twist in the concern that white women showed for the enslaved women's wedding attire: white woman symbolically perpetuated a Eurocentric view of the sanctity of marriage and home when, in fact, this sanctity could be legally torn asunder by the enslaver when Black couples were involved.

In addition to descriptions of the bridal clothing, contributors noted the groom's clothing.

> Richard Carruthers (100 years): *When a nigger marry, he slick up his lowers and put on his brass-toed shoes* (4. 1:200 [TN, TX/TX]).

Lee McGillery (b. 1832): *We wore loyal clothes as our wedding clothes, and I'se have great red tie on, boss. I'se sure dress then and I have on black shoes* (S2. 7. 6:2493 [NC, TX/TX]).

Charlotte Beverly (ca. 90 years): *Me and my husban' was married by a Yankee sojer. I was dress in white Tarleytown weddin' dress and I didn' wear no hoopskirt. I had a pretty wreath .... My husban' dress in suit of white linen. He sho' look handsome* (4. 1:85–86 [TX]).

Those who married after the Civil War described in detail their wedding costumes and often those of their partner. In some instances, white women continued to help the Black women mark this event by giving them special clothing. African American men, on the other hand, appear to have relied solely on their own personal, stylistic resources. In either case, the descriptions usually offer very precise details and exhibit a pronounced *joie de vivre.*

Lina Hunter (ca. 90 years): *Well, me and Jeff Hunter got married up whilst I was still stayin' on Marster Jack's place .... My dress was mighty pretty; it was white lawn, and made long waisted lak dey wore dresses den. Mrs. Lizzie Johnson made it, and it had long sleeves, and a long full skirt wid lots of ruffles. De two petticoats she gimme to wear wid my weddin' dress was ruffled to beat de band and had trimmin' on evvy ruffle. My weddin' drawers even had ruffles on 'em; I was really dressed up* (12. 2:270 [GA]).

Sarah Allen: *My [wedding] dress was [w]hite and trimmed with blue ribbon. My second day dress was white with red dots. I had a beautiful veil and a wreath* (4. 1:13 [VA/TX]).

Hannah Crasson (84 years): *I wuz not married till after de surrender. I did not dress de finest in the world; but I had nice clothes. My wedding dress wuz made of cream silk, made princess with pink and cream bows. I wore a pair of morocco store bought shoes. My husband was dressed in a store bought suit of clothes, the coat wuz made pigeon tail. He had on a velvet vest and a white collar and tie* (14. 1:189 [NC]).

John Barker (84 years): *I was 'bout 20 when I marries de fust time [after emancipation] .... I had on a black, alpaca suit with frock coat and, if I ain't mistaken, a right white shirt .... I wore de loudest shoes we could find, what you call patent leather* (4. 1:43 [OH, MO, TX/TX]).

This final description is an outstanding tribute to the positive outlook which the formerly enslaved salvaged from all the years of pain.

> Eliza Hasty (85 years), probably married after the war: *When us marry, him have on a long-tail coat, salt and pepper trousers, box-toed shoes, and a red lead pencil over his ear, just as long as de one I 'spects you is writtin' wid, tho' I can't see it.*
>
> *How I dressed? I 'members 'zactly. I wore a blue worsted shirt, over a red underskirt, over a white linen petticoat wid tuckers at de hem, just a little long, to show good and white 'long wid de blue of de skirt and de red of de underskirt. Dese all come up to my waist and was held together with string dat held my bustle in place. All dis and my corset was hid by de snowy white pleated piqué bodice, dat drapped [sic] gracefully from my shoulders. 'Round my neck was a string of green jade beads. I wore red stockin's and my foots was stuck in soft, black, cloth, gaiter shoes* (2. 2:255 [SC]).

Clothing figured in the folklore about marriage. It is of interest that beliefs concerning weddings and marriage centered solely around certain articles of women's clothing, but not men's.

> Nannie Bradfield (85 years): *I stayed on de plantation 'till I mah'ied. My old Miss gave me a brown dress and hat. Well dat dress put me in de country, if you mahie in brown you'll live in the country* (6. 1:45 [AL]).

> Liza Jones (81 years): *At de weddin' . . . I had a white tarelton dress with de white tarelton wig. Dat de hat part what fo over de head and drops on de shoulder. Dat de sign you ain't never don no wrong sin and gwinter keep bein' good* (4. 2:244 [TX]).

Contributors offered stories about the marriages of whites. Serena Mulberry Anders (b. ca. 1852) related a story about an old maid, rather a Blanche du Bois type of character. Anders delineated the woman especially by the woman's choice of clothing, just as clothing characterized Tennessee Williams' more famous creation. Because Anders' caricature of "Mis' Henrietta" is stereotypical from an African American viewpoint, it does justice as the flip-side of the white-perpetuated "Aunt Jemima" stereotype.

> *Mis' Henrietta was ole an' she walked wid a cane. But you better not say she was ole . . ..*
>
> *Mis' Henrietta wuz dressy too. She try to dress like she was sixteen 'stead of sixty, an' when she got all dem curls hangin' down side her face, de blue taffeta dress on wid de white lace ruffles at de wris' an' neck, an' de white lace mits on her hands, she dare anybody to say she wusn' young an' pretty as Mis' Lovey. Sometime Mis' Lovey would look at her an' say 'Aunt Hennie, you look jus' like you is waitin' for your fus' beau. 'Den she would wink at Mammy and Mis'*

> *Henrietta would puff up like a pigeon an' open her little fan an' wave it 'cross her face an' say: 'Love, my dear, dat ain't been so might long, an' de man still swarm 'roun' me like bees 'roun' a blossom.' . . .*
>
> *Mammy say Mis' Henrietta like dat kaze she ain't never married no man . . .. She done got her weddin' dress made an' ready. It done been made so long it done turned yellow as a symlin [squash] (S1. 1. 11:43–44 [NC]).*

Three men offered three widly different personal experiences with white weddings.

> Bob Mobley (ca. 90 years) who served as a house servant remembered the clothing worn for his master's wedding: *Before the war started, I took my young master to get married, and we were certainly dressed up. You have never seen a Nigger and a white man dressed up as we were on that occasion* (13. 3:137 [GA]).

> Bill Homer (b. 1850): *In de year ob 1860, Missy Mary gits mai'ied to Marster Bill Johnson an' at de weddin', Marster Homer gives me an' 49 udder niggers to her fo' de weddin' present . . ..*
>
> *Aftah de weddin' was over, deys give de couple de infare. Dere's whar dis nigger comes in. I's wid de udder niggers was lin' up, all wid de clean clothes on, an' new suits. Den de Marster says, 'Fo' to give my lovin' daughter de staht, I's give you dese 50 niggers'* (S. 5. 4:1785 [LA/TX]).

> Ben Johnson (85 years): *I don't know nothin' 'bout my mammy an' daddy, but I had a brother Jim who wuz sold ter dress young missus fer her weddin'. De tree am still standin' whar I set under an' watch 'em sell Jim, I set dar an' cry an' cry . . . an' I ain't never felt as lonesome in my whole life. I ain't neber hyar from Jim since* (15. 2:9 [NC]).

Funerals. African Americans place great importance on funerary displays, just as their West African ancestors did. Cloth and clothing, again, are among the tangible goods which helped them to define the passing of one person's life. Richard C. Wade draws attention to the strong meaning that appropriate clothing for the deceased held for African Americans in the antebellum period. He relates two contemporary newspaper reports of the preparations made by two slaves before they committed suicide in 1850's New Orleans:

> In one, Sampson had saved up $1200 to buy his freedom in an arrangement with his owner. After succeeding "by long years of patient toil," he discovered that the man who was banking his money had in fact spent it all. "This turned the mind of the poor wretch . . . and caused him to commit the desperate deed."

"Before killing himself," the story continued, "he had dressed himself in his best clothes and left a request on a slate that he should be buried in them." In the other case, an elderly woman hanged herself. But before "committing the fatal act, . . . the old woman had dressed herself in her best clothes, and was perfectly neat and clean, with the exception of the bottom of the stockings which were soiled while walking in the yard in quest of a cord" (128).

Norrece T. Jones, Jr. , offers grisly evidence that whites knew the significance that African Americans placed in special funerary attire. He reports that during the period of enslavement

> . . . black Carolinians by the thousands were on occasion forced to witness an execution, usually by hanging. To make sure that one did not miss the point of these exhibitions, slaves were often sentenced to die at the scene of their crimes. Condemned blacks were sometimes dressed in "grave clothes," then carried through the community upon the coffins that were shortly to be their final home (92).

Coding certain colors as appropriate for both the deceased and for the mourners is almost a universal tradition, but the specific colors chosen by societies are not universal. Parsons wrote in 1923 of the funerary customs of the Sea Islanders of South Carolina.

> At Beaufort and throughout the Sea Islands black is worn by everybody in mourning; but the period seems variable. For a parent it might be five or six months, or it may be much longer. A widow may dress in black for years – "*never hardly see dem come out widout dey goin' to marry again*" (216).

From that description, we are given to understand that black was the customary color of mourning among Sea Islanders. But in Parsons' more detailed notes on how members of various social organizations attired themselves for a deceased member's funeral, we find the African Americans giving different attributions to certain colors:

> When the deceased is a Mason or an Odd-Fellow or a Good Samaritan (the women's society), there is the elaboration characteristic of these secret benefit societies, whose members '*fo' respec' tu'n out*.' They turn out in black coat and trousers, over which hangs a white satin embroidered apron suspended from the neck, and they wear white gloves . . .. As for the women, '*diffun' lo'ges dress diffun', – some all in black; some wear white waist, black skirt*.' And the women wear badges. '*Badge on right, ain't no fune'al; badge on lef', fo' fune'al*.' The badge is blue on the upper side, and black on the under (215).

Quite contrary to black as the traditional European (and white American) mourning color, touches of white appear in the African American mourners' clothing just described by Parsons: white aprons, white gloves, white shirt waists. Although white and Black Masons wore white aprons, much earlier documentation for the use of this color by African Americans during funerals comes from Benjamin Latrobe's descriptions of two funeral processions in New Orleans in the later eighteenth century. The first procession was for a "freed Black."

> At some distance came the coffin. It was carried by four well-dressed black men and to it were attached six white ribbons about two yards in length, the ends of which were held by six colored girls, very well dressed in white, with long veils (quoted in Crété, 178).

The second funeral witnessed by La Trobe was for an old slave, and for it "everyone was dressed in white" (ibid.).

In the lyrics to a spiritual, white clothing again appears as emblematic of death:

> Dere's a long white robe in the hebben for me
> I won't die no mo
> Dere's golden slippers in the hebben for me
> I won't die no mo' (Crété, 179).[17]

In many societies, the deceased is dressed in special clothes or is wrapped in special cloth.

> Yesterday evening the burial of the poor man, Shadrach, took place. I had been applied to for a sufficient quantity of cotton cloth to make a winding-sheet for him . . . (Kemble, 1839, quoted in Parrish, 76).

If we assume that the cotton cloth which Kemble gave for the winding sheet was not dyed, then the African American association of the color white with funerals may support another West African connection. Osifekunde (born in Ijebu, between Oyo and Benin)gave the following information concerning burial customs in his homeland:

> *The body is first washed in a solution of olosun leaves from a kind of coconut tree .... Afterward, it is wrapped in white cloth rolled like bandages wound around Egyptian mummies .... Cloth after cloth is wound around the body until it takes on a size proportionate to the wealth and power of the individual* (in Lloyd, ed., 262).

In a manner similar to the Ijebu custom, in the American South, funerals continued to highlight the importance of the deceased, and cloth and clothing served as significant material aspects of the elaboration. In the United States, however, a blending of customs often transpired. Lulu Coleman related a fascinating account of her grandfather who was reputed to be an African king: "*He acted proud-like, like he hadn' never done work, was used ter havin' other folks do fer him. He didn't talk like we did an' white folks couldn' understan' what he say, but we could understan' him*" (S1. 7. 2:428 [MS]). Coleman's grandfather owned a large wooden box in which he kept his personal belongings which no one dared to go near until the man died.

> *Then his son, the one he had ter set at de head of de table, he opened hit an' they was some clothes an' some – some breas'-pins-like – they wasn't breas'-pins but leetle fancy things – like, you know. His clothes was made out of white 'lowell' cloth. An' dat day he lef' his son settin' at de head of de table an' say, 'Come see me befo' you go, 'an' he put him on pants an' socks – sompin' he aint never wo' befo' – an' . . . he was stiff dead when they found him* (ibid., 430).

Another instance of the mingling of customs occurs in a passage from Parrish, wherein black cloth replaced the West African white. "Old residents" of St. Simon's island reported to Parrish that "before the days of automobiles . . . a Negro' buryin' was an impressive thing." They told her that " [t]he home-made coffin, lined with 'paper cambric' and covered with black calico or darkened with lampblack, was placed in the 'rough box' and carried on a one-horse wagon." Parrish continues, "The Negroes . . . spare no expense in making them [funerals] elaborate affairs." Parrish also notes that she was once asked for a black hat by a St. Simon's woman to wear to her husband's funeral (192). But in the quote of another of Parrish's informants, white clothing again appears:

> One that took place on St. Simon's years ago will be long remembered: '. . . *it cost four hundred dollars. They sent to Savannah for flowers, and she was buried in new white slippers that cost six dollars . . .!*' (ibid.).

A similar tradition comes from one contributor to the *Narratives*:

> Joseph James (b. 1845): *When anybody die dey bury 'em in a home-made coffin. It line with black cloth. Dey put nice clothes an' white gloves on 'em* (S2. 6. 5:1929 [LA/TX]).

One final link between African American and West African funerary custom may be the important roles that women play at these times. Margaret Strobel traces religious beliefs in contemporary tropical African communities, noting especially the ways in which Christianity and Islam meshed with indigenous religions. In addition, she examines the various roles which are open to African women (87ff.). Irene V. Jackson-Brown also gives specific examples concerning women's valuable place during modern African funerals and writes:

> The authority of women over life and death is also evident in the degree to which women are involved in funeral rites. The participation of women in matters surrounding death insures the 'rebirth' of the deceased (386).

> Cindy Kinsey (86 years): *My ma, she boss all de funerals ob de niggahs on de plantation an she got a long white veil for wearin, lawzy me, chile, she suah look bootiful, jes lak a bride she did when she boss dem funerals in dat veil. She not much skeered nether for dat veil hit suah keep de hants away. Whisht I had me dat veil right now, mout hep cure dis romutizics in me knee what ailin me so bad. I disrememba, but I sposen she got buried in dat veil* (17. 1. 191 [FL]).

In the *Narratives*, funerals and dead people gave rise to personal experiences concerning clothing.

> Harriet Casey (75 years): *When my mother died I did not know what a coffin was or what death was. So I went to my dead mother where she was on de cooling board and brushed my dress and said, 'Look at my pretty dress'* (11. 7. 8:74 [MO]).

> Sophia Ward (b. 1837): *Sho dar is ghosts. One night I war going home from work de tallest man I eber seed followed me wid de prettiest white shirt . . .. I seed him plain as day en de did not speaken jes disappeared right fore my eyes* (16. 2:93 [KY]).

Beliefs included avoiding the clothing of the dead. (See Chapter 4 for beliefs on this order relating to shoes.)

> Annie L. Burton (b. 1850, enslaved in Alabama): *I remember at the beginning of the war, two colored men were hung in Clayton . . .. The clothes of the two victims were hung on two pine trees, and no colored person would touch them* (reproduced in Andrews, 5).

Belief might even be centered on umbrellas, items used to protect the person and clothing.

> Janey Landrum (b. 1851): *Don't ever put your umbrella on the bed 'cause hit is sho' to bring bad luck and if you put hit on the bed of a friend then you all is sho' gwine fall out . . .. When an umbrella is raised in the house, dat am sho' sign dat a coffin am gwine to be brought in for some ob the fambly* (S2. 6. 5:2267 [TX]).

Concerning the choices which enslaved African Americans made when they dressed for special events, outwardly it often appears that they copied white fashion. But clothing must be seen as a specific sign to be read as a marker of a specific social group. Clothing is a system, structured by the society itself which, alone, is capable of comprehending its meanings and nuances. Eugene Genovese writes that dressing like whites has "only limited significance if it had been confined to an urge to imitate or rival white dress"(560). Instead, he argues that "there was something impudent, and therefore subversive, about the slaves' finery."

> Its more important meaning emerges from the slaves' insistence on dressing up for church and for plantation parties. In those instances they demonstrated respect for their brothers and sisters and therefore that self-respect without which respect for others is impossible (ibid.).

Punishments and Escape

> Sarah Ford (*I's been here for a long time): My . . . papa he part Indian [and] he runs off. One time he gone a whole year . . .. Papa was mighty good to mama and me and dat de only reason he ever come back from runnin' away . . .. While he hides . . . lots of mornin's when us open de cabin door on a shelf jus' 'bove is food for mama and me, and sometime store clothes. No one ain'ts see papa, but dere it is. One time he brung us dresses . . .* (94. 2:44–45 [TX]).

African Americans had recollections wherein their clothing became entangled with memories of physical abuse and escape. None of them remembered those situations with the happiness by which Sarah Ford recalled her father's deeds.

At age 17, Hilley Chavious (b. 1833) of Virginia, a free born, began "to steal slaves away from plantations and work them over the border." He told of his deeds to his grandson, Arthur Shaffer, who paraphrased:

> "In most instances the master would rally his overseer and his bloodhounds and give a determined chase to save his property. On missing the slave or slaves, the

first thing to be done was to procure a garment or a shoe that bore their body scent, call up the dogs and allow them to familiarize themselves with the smell. This was the dog's identification of the person he was to trail" (S1. 5. 19 [VA/IN]).

Julius Jones: *I had an uncle named Abe Jones he [overseer Bryant] whipped him till his shirt stuck to his back and my mother had to put grease on him to get the shirt off. What he was getting punished for was telling the slaves they was going to be set free* (S1. 8. 3:1217 [MS]).

In at least one instance, a bitter injustice was caused by the "marse" taking off his clothes.

Mary Wood: *[My Grandma's sister] would get stubborn sometimes. Her old mistress would tell her to do something and if she didn't feel like hit, she didn't do hit. Ole misus got mad dis time wid her and tole marse Ben dat he jes had to whip Fannie. So he told her, 'You come on down to de barn dis evening, Fannie. I'm going to whip you.' She knowed better. Ole misus thought hit strange to take Fannie to barn all de time when others were kept away whenever Fannie is to be whipped. Betty, his wife, thinks something curious; watches his moves; and follows him 'cause Fannie has three white chillun .... So marse Ben makes hit comfortable fer Fannie on de flo' in dis barn, takes his coat off, next his pants. Ole missus standing outside barn peeping through a crack. Ole devil starts on his knees. Says to Fannie, 'Dis is de way I like to whip you.' Ole miss speaks, 'Yes, I jes knowed you and Fannie been doing that all the time!' .... Ole lady reared and charged so the next week they sold Fannie and the new marster carried her somewhere down South* (*Weevils*, p. 332).

As it had on the Atlantic coast of West Africa, stripping the body of clothing and marking the skin continued to figure in many of the African's experiences of punishment in the American South. Pronounced are the memories of the Black woman's body in these circumstances. From a judicial case in Tennessee:

Britain v. State, July 1842: indictment charged that. . 1840, . . 'Britain. . did. . commit. . notorious lewdness by. . causing and permitting his. . slaves to go about . . so naked and destitute of clothing, that their organs of generation and other parts . . . which should have been clothed and concealed, were publicly exposed' . . Proof. . that the slave was seen on various occasions. . almost entirely destitute of clothing, with some tattered rags hanging upon her, and her body exposed indecently . . . verdict of guilty . . . judgment. . against the defendant, that he pay a fine of $25 and cost (Catterall, 1929:515).

William Grimes (b. 1784, enslaved in Virginia and Georgia): *I have seen women brought there and tied hand and foot, and their clothes turned up and tied there, up to their shoulders, leaving their bodies perfectly naked, then whipped with a keen raw-hide (or cow-skin sometimes called) until the blood ran down to their heels* (reprinted in Bontemps, 90).

Hattie Sugg: *Dey whipped Aunt Jane. I 'member they made her pull her clothes down to her waist* (S1. 10. 5:2076–2077 [MS]).

Ellen Betts (84 years): *[Old Marse] don't 'low no overseer to throw he gals down and pull up dere dress and whup on dere bottoms like I hear tell some of 'em do* (4. 1:75 [LA/TX]).

Louis Hughes (b. 1832, enslaved in Virginia and Mississippi): *Men were stripped of their shirts in preparation for the whipping, and women had to take off their dresses from the shoulders to the waist* (9).

In the *Narratives*, however, people continually confound our usual notions about the ways in which clothing and lack of clothing were used as a means of humiliating Blacks:

Jerry Boykins (92 years): *When the old missie try to whip me I jest wrop up in her big skirts and she neber could hurt me much* (S2. 2. 1:372 [TX]).

Elizabeth Sparks: *Old Masa done so much wrongness I couldn't tell yer all of it. Slave girl Betty Lilly had good clothes an' all the privileges. She wuz a favorite of his'n. But cain't tell all! God's got all!* (*Weevils*, 277).

Clothing also played an important part in triumphant escapes from enslavement. Harriet Jacobs' successful sailor's disguise was already noted, but even after she made it to Philadelphia, so great was Jacobs' fear that Dr. Flint would catch up with her, she bought "double veils" to hide her face and gloves to hide her hands (159).

In numerous ex-slave autobiographies, people relate that securing clothing became their utmost concern during the flight from bondage (Figure 22). Planning his escape, Venture (b. ca. 1729) noted that along with food, he and his fellow escapees "*gathered all our own clothing and some more* . . ." (13). They were much distressed when, having come ashore at Long Island, they discovered that one of their comrades had absconded with all their clothing (13–14). Louis Hughes (b. 1843, enslaved in Mississippi and Virginia) wrote that when he had made up his mind to try

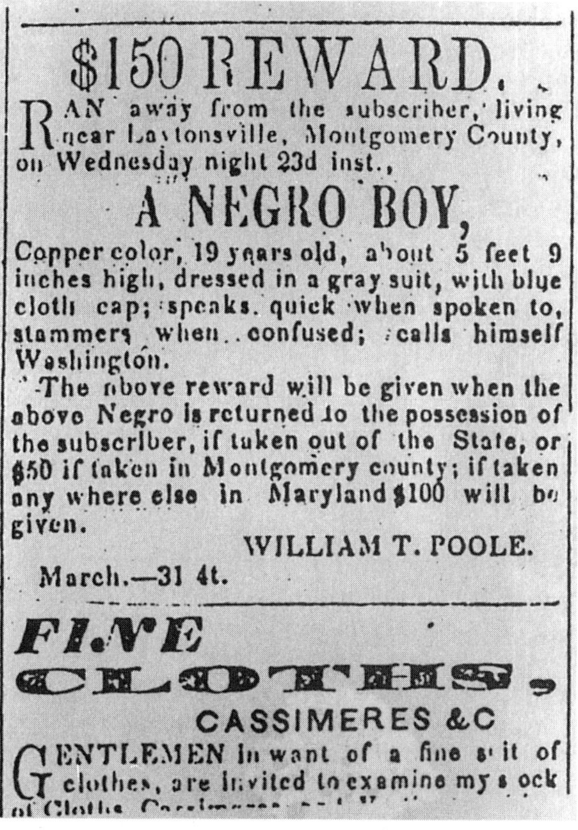

$150 REWARD.

RAN away from the subscriber, living near Laytonsville, Montgomery County, on Wednesday night 23d inst.,

A NEGRO BOY,

Copper color, 19 years old, about 5 feet 9 inches high, dressed in a gray suit, with blue cloth cap; speaks quick when spoken to, stammers when confused; calls himself Washington.

The above reward will be given when the above Negro is returned to the possession of the subscriber, if taken out of the State, or $50 if taken in Montgomery county; if taken any where else in Maryland $100 will be given.

WILLIAM T. POOLE.

March.—31 4t.

FINE CLOTHS, CASSIMERES &C

GENTLEMEN in want of a fine suit of clothes, are invited to examine my stock

Figure 22. "Runaway" advertisements included descriptions of the escapee's clothing. [Carroll County, Maryland] *Democratic Advocate*, 14 April 1859. Collection of the Historical Society of Carroll County, Maryland.

to run away, "*I got my clothes, and put them in an old pair of saddlebags*" (127).

Andrew Jackson (b. 1814, enslaved in Kentucky) revealed the clever way in which he used his clothing for his escape attempt:

> *On Saturday night, early in August, I gathered my clothes together, and after selecting the best, which were not very good, I started off in the direction of a piece of woods, and there tore up those I desired least, and threw them down, besmeared with blood which I obtained to give them the appearance of having been torn from me by a wild beast, in order that I might prevent any one from pursuing me until I could escape beyond their reach* (1847:9).

In quite another but equally clever way, William Hayden also used clothing to ensure his movement to freedom. Hayden dressed in an "*old ragged suit*", complete with "*patched and repatched pantaloons*" and an old hat which he pinched into "*a three cornered cock*" and decorated with leaves in each corner. His ploy was to be taken as a beggar and, by his account, he succeeded (1846:132–133).

James W. C. Pennington (b. ca. 1826) ran from enslavement in Virginia. He escaped recapture and made his way to Pennsylvania by which time, he recalled, "*I had but four pieces of clothing about my person, having left all the rest in the hands of my captors*" (reprinted in Katz, 41). William Wells Brown (b. ca. 1819, enslaved in Missouri) was about 21 years old when he escaped. Making his way to the North, he remembered, "*It being winter, I suffered intensely from the cold; being without an overcoat, and my other clothes rather thin for the season*" (reprinted in Katz, 96). "*On the fifth or six day, it rained very fast, and it froze about as fast as it fell, so that my clothes were one glare of ice*"(ibid. , 99).

John Atkinson, who escaped to the North in 1854, wrote two letters to a benefactor in an attempt to regain the clothes he had lost during his flight. In the first, he writes:

> *I hope you will intercede for my clothes and as soon as they come please to send them to me, and if you have not time, get Dr. Lundy to look out for them, and when they come be very careful in sending them* (reprinted in Woodson, 606).

In the second letter, dated a month later, the urgency for his clothes becomes more pronounced and Atkinson is more explicit in his request:

> *I have learned from my friend, Richard Bohm, that my clothes were in Philadelphia. Will you have the kindness to see Dr. Lundy and if he has my clothes in charge, or knows about them, for him to send them on to me immediately, as I am in great need of them. I would like to have them put in a small box, and the overcoat I left at your house to be put in a box with them, to be sent care of my friend, Hiram Wilson* (ibid.).

Along the escape route to Philadelphia, an acquaintance advised James Williams (b. 1805, enslaved in Virginia and Alabama) that he would recognize "friends" by their dress.

> *In parting he cautioned me against conversing with any man on the road, unless he wore a plain, straight collar on a round coat, and said 'thee' and 'thou'* (n. d.: 98).

Lorendo Goodway, who had been enslaved in Louisiana, told a runaway tale in which clothing again became part of the tragic narrative:

> *Hattie – she used to run away and live in the woods for three or four weeks at a time. I remember I was out in the field hoeing cane . . . and I heard somebody over the fence in the woods calling me, and at first I did not know what to do; but as I looked up through the fence I saw it was Hattie . . .. Hattie was almost naked that day! . . . Hattie said, 'Lorendo, I had my child here in the woods; it is dead and I buried it in a piece of my frock shirt'* (Albert, 1890:71).

Clothing During the War

Southern Blacks' memories of the Civil War included recollections about their clothing.

> Randolph Johnson (84 years): *Den de War came, and all de good clothes dat we made on de loom turned to tatters* (6. 1:231 [AL]).

> Lawrence Hampton (78 years): *When the War come on their [slaves'] clothes was ironed and clean but the wheat was scarce and the clothes got flimsy* (9. 3:139 [SC/AR]).

Louis Hughes (b. 1843, enslaved in Mississippi and Virginia) remembered this scene when he and fellow slaves left their "owners" as the Union Army approached near the end of the War:

> *[N]ine other slaves followed our wagon, as it moved off. They had no hats on; some were bare-footed, – they had not stopped to get anything; but, as soon as they saw a chance to get away, they went just as they were at the moment (184). [Likewise] my wife and sister were shoeless, and the latter had no hat on – she had hurried out of the house in such excitement that she thought of nothing but getting away* (186).

Remarkably, many comments made by the formerly enslaved do not concern their own clothes; instead, they detail the reduced circumstances of the white population as symbolized by their dress. This telling absorption implies that many Blacks were cognizant that a retributory form of social justice had been carried out on their behalf.

> William Henry Towns: *Dem Yankees . . . took der white fo'kes clos' and did away wid dem; sometimes dey would tear dem up or give dem ter der slaves ter wear* (S1. 1:414–415 [AL]).

Maria Sutton Clements (85–90 years): *Rich folks had fine silk dresses – jes' rattle when they walked . . . but folks didn't have fine clothes when it ended like when the war started* (8. 2:26 [AR]).

Rebecca Jane Grant: *Times got so hard during de war dat de white folks had to use de cloth woven by hand, themselves. De ladies wear bustles, and whoops made out of oak* (2. 2:184 [SC]).

Julia Williams (ca. 100 years): *After de Yankees come even de house people, de white people didn get shoes. But I hab some, I save. I have some othah shoes I didn dare go in de house with* (1. 4:103 [VA/OH]).

Whether willingly or not, during the War, the enslaved continued to help bolster the Confederate cause. Louis Hughes (b. 1843, enslaved in Mississippi and Virginia) recalled that his "owners"

. . . put away their valuables, to keep them from the Union soldiers . . .. Great packages of the finest clothing I had to make up, and these were given in charge of certain servants whose duty it was to run into the big house and get them, whenever they heard that the Yankees were coming, and take them to their cabins. This was a shrewd arrangement, for the Yankees never went into the cabins to get anything (153).

Benjamin Johnson: *When de war broke out ol' marster enlisted an' he took me 'long to wait on him an' to keep his clothes clean* (12. 2:325 [GA]).

Weavers and seamstresses, in particular, continued to be productive assets as they provided cloth and clothing for domestic use.

Frances Cobb: *When de war was on dey was wearing dat stuff [osnaburg, cotton sacking cloth]. Long towards de last my ma was spinning as many cuts a day* (S1. 9. 4:417 [MS]).

Mary Divine (85 years): *I 'member during de war years, my old miss use to boast 'bout her littlest darkey, don spun enough thread to clothe her whole family for de next three years to come* (11. 7. 8:104 [MO]).

Sarah Waggoner (93 years): *Durin' de war, old Miss keep tellin' me I had to help her put new cloth in de loom and when little Jane, that's her little girl, wanted me to play, her mother would say, 'Sarey has to work fast now, 'cause she goin' to be free'* (11. 7. 8:360–361 [KY, MO/MO]).

Black women also were responsible for making clothing that was used at the battle fronts by Confederate soldiers.

Charlotte Beverly (ca. 90 years): *I see sojers and knits socks for 'em by moonshine* (1. 4:85 [TX]).

Charlie Trotty: *Member maw stayin up lots of nights, nearly all de night, spinnin and weavin for de soldiers, makin socks and shirts. Marster sent lots of cow hides to a man what made lots of shoes for defightin men* (S2. 9. 8:3888 [TX]).

Elsie Reece (90 years): *Ise 'membahs de wah time good. Sho do, 'cause young Marster Jim, an' Marster Sam, jines de army. Ise he'p make de cloth an' de clothes dey wears to de army. Ise 14 years old den. Missie Mary sho am pa'ticular 'bout how de suits am made. She helps me wid de wo'k, an' we uns all sho proud w'en de two young Marsters am dressed in de suits* (S2. 8. 7:3274–3275 [TX]).

Maria White (b. 1853): *They had a big loom that the cloth was made on. Besides making the cloth for uses clothes, they made it for the soldiers too. They used dye to color the soldier's clothes, but ours was just left natural. The hardest thing to get was shoes. They would buy them for the work hands in winter, but us children had to go barefooted* (S1. 10. 5:2278 [MS]).

Lucy Lewis: *We make clo'es fo' de so'jers, too. Miss Nancy cut de parts out and I sew dem up befo' dey sent away. We uster make bandages and light jackets too. Den dey wah heavy jackets – leaded jackets wif shirts. Dey wo' unifawn coats wif lead in de skirts of de coat to hold dem down. De lead wah put up in de shape of a marble an' den we cut it out in long strips and hammer it down and put it in de bottom of de coat* (S2. 6. 5:2367 [TX]).

The interviewer paraphrased Cora Shepherd (82 years): *My old Miss sent de little ones in de field, 'we got wheat and oat straw to make hats for de soldiers in de army. My old Miss have clothes made and send to de army for soldiers, too. Dere was two seamsters in de house cuttin' and sewin' every day for de hands and de soldiers'*. ... The interviewer added: "When de army was disbanded, according to Cora, the worn army men, returning to their homes, repaid Mrs. Walden [the mistress] with poor courtesy. ... *'Dey was wuss'n de Yankees. Some had de 'decity to go to de house and search for clothes!*" (S1. 4. 4:556–557 [GA]).

Cull Taylor (b. 1859): *'Bout de war, I does 'member how mah maw was a-weavin' cloth when de Yankees come through. An' atter de niggers was freed ol' Marse Tom gib mah maw de loom* (61:363 [AL]).

Often, during the War, Black womens' work was doubled. In the absence of men, Black women took on tasks traditionally done by Black males even as they carried on with their usual assignments.

Annie L. Burton (b. 1859, enslaved in Alabama): *The time had come when our good times were over . . .. These were all gone. The boys had to leave school and take the runaway slaves' places to finish the planting and pick the cotton. I myself have worked in the cotton field, picking great baskets full, too heavy for me to carry. All was over!* (reproduced in Andrews, 38).

Alice Sewell (b. 1851): *[D]e war had started, so we had to pack all de cotton up in bales, and in sun face houses and sun face cribs to be out of the weather. The seed cotton was kept in de gin house, 'cause dey didn't had no time to fool wid dat. Den dey up and bought spinning wheels and cards, so us women could spin it to make cloth, and make clothes at home, and would not have to go to de factory to buy clothes.*

Dey stopped raising cotton after de war, and just raised food stuff cause dey had to send food to de battlefield for de soldiers. De poor white folks what lived up in de hilly country, too poor to own slaves, while de war was going on, had to come down to have food for dem and der children. Der men folks was taken away from dem to war. . .. Dey use to say dey had to go and fight a rich man's war but dey couldn't help demselves no better'n us slaves could (11. 7. 8:301–302 [MO]).

The formerly enslaved people remembered the Union and Confederate soldiers by their clothing.

Eva Martin (82 years): *De sojers? Sho', I see lots of sojers . . .. Dey was Yankees. I never see no other kind. I 'member dey had pretty caps on wid pretty yaller t'ing on 'em, a bird like a eagle. It was pretty shiny yaller like dat shiny t'ing on de en of your pensil . . .. Dem sojers had big yaller buttons on dey clo'se too* (S2. 7. 6:2585 [LA/TX]).

Cato Carter (b. 1836): *The young men in grey uniforms used to pass so gay and singin', in the big road. Their clothes was good* (4. 1:207 [AL/TX]).

Anna Williamson (75–80 years): *I seen the Yankees, they camped at the fair grounds. I thought they wore the prettiest clothes and the brass buttons so pretty on the blue suits . . .. My old mistress slapped me till my eyes was red cause one day I says, 'Ain't them men pretty?'* (11. 4:194 [AR]).

John Day (81 years): *Master was in de Confederate army . . . after he done come out dat war he sho' hated anythin' what was blue color. I got hold a old Yankee cap and coat and is wearin' dem and master yanks dem off and burns dem* (4. 1:303 [TN/TX]).

The Union Army soldiers, in particular, received nicknames because of their uniforms.

Rosina Hoard (b. 1859?): *One day de blue bellies come to de fields. Dey yankee sojers . . ..* (4. 2:142 [TX]).

Betty Brown: *Yes'm I seed sojers, an' we seed lot's o' 'em. Dah wuz de' blue-coats* (11. 7. 8:53 [MO]).

Orelia Alexie Franks (ca. 90 years): *Dey Yankees. Dey call 'em blue jackets* (4. 2:61 [LA/TX]).

A final item about clothing during the War concerns something worn by a brave woman:

Madison Bruin (age 82): *My mother wore de Yankee flag under her dress like a petticoat when de 'federates come raidin'. Other times she wore it top de dress* (4. 1:3 [KY/TX]).

Emancipation and Clothing During Reconstruction

The formerly enslaved related a variety of personal impressions about clothing following the War. The account of Olaudah Equiano (b. 1745, Benin) is markedly different from the experiences of so many Southern Blacks just after their emancipation. Equiano's long road was no less arduous, but he gained his freedom a century earlier in 1766 and in England. Yet, as with those who would be freed later, clothing was an emblem of Equiano's sense of self-worth.

In short, as well the black people immediately styled me by a new appellation, to me the most desirable in the world, which was freeman; and at the dances I gave, my Georgia superfine blue clothes made no indifferent appearance, as I thought (163).

Like Equiano, a few Southern Blacks connected happy memories of clothing with the end of the War.

The interviewer paraphrased Joseph Mosley: "On Christmas morning Joseph was told he could go see his mother; he did not know he was free and he couldn't understand why he was given the first suit of clothes he had ever owned, and a pair of shoes. He dressed in his new finery and was started out on his six mile journey to his mother. He was so proud of his new shoes; after he had gotten out of sight, he stopped and took his shoes off as he did not want them dirty before his mother had seen them, and he walked the rest of the way in his barefeet" (6. 2:148–149 [KY/IN]).

Maggie Westmorland (85 years) related that after the War, Mr. Cargo, her mean master, had been shamed into sending her to visit her sister. In order to stop rumours that he was mistreating Westmorland, the man had clothing made for her:

He told Miss Betty they would fix me up and let me go stay a week at my sister's Christmas. He went back to town, brought me the first shoes I had had since they took me. They was brogan shoes. They put a pair of his socks on me. Miss Betty made the calico dress for me and a body out of some of his pants and quilted the skirt part, bound it at the bottom with red flannel. She made my things nice – put my underskirt in a little frame and quilted it so it would be warm. Christmas day was a bright warm day. In the morning when Miss Betty dressed me up I was so proud (11. 7:100–101 [AR]).

Hannah Travis (b. 1864): *My grandmother belonged to another slaveholder and they would allow her to go to see my mother. She was allowed to work and do things for which she was given old clothes and other little things. She would take em and bring em to my mother. As soon as she had gone, they would take them things away from my mother, and put em up in the attic and not allow her to wear them. They would let the clothes rot and mildew before they'd let my mother wear them .... Then [after the war] she got out among the colored people and got to working and got some clothes for herself and me* (10. 6:317–318 [AR]).

Amanda McCray (a house servant and "*a grownup during the Civil War"): After de war Negroes blossomed out with fine phaeton buggies and ceiled houses, and clothes – oh my!* (17. 1:215 [FL]).

Contrary to McCray's enthusiastic memory, most contributors remembered their post-War clothing in terms of complete destitution and intertwined with memories of their continued ill-treatment by whites.

Lou Austin (female, b. 1850): *On de day Marse Henry Masters tell de servants dey free, he jes' call 'em togedder an' he tell dem dey wuz free. Nebber gibed 'em*

> *noddin'. Dey didn't git what de Children of Isre'l got – dey wuz sont fo'th to make dere way barefoot an' almos' nakkid* (S. 2. 2. 1 [TX]).

> Eli Davison (b. 1844): *He kept tellin' us a black nigger never would be free. When it come, he said to us, 'Well, you black – you are just as free as I am. 'He turnt us loose with nothin' to eat and no clothes* (4. 1:296 [WV, TX/TX]).

> Elvira Boles (94 years): *When we started from Mississippi [running to Texas "from de Yankees"], dey tol' us . . .. 'You ain't got no time to take nothin' to wher you goin'. Take your little bundle and leave all you has in your house.' So when wė got to Texas I jus' had one dress, what I had on. Dat's de way all de cullud people was fer freedom, never had nothin' but what dey had on de back . . . they was skeered and dey lef' everything* (4. 1:108 [MS/TX]).

> Sylvia Watkins (91 years): *I wuz tole 'fore freedom dat de slave would git a mule, land an a new suit, but our missis didn't gib us a thing* (16. 6:77 [TN]).

> Julia Brown (13 years old at surrender): *My mama died the year of surrender. Ah didn't fare well after her death . . .. Ah was give to the Mitchell fambly and they done every cruel thing they could to me. Ah slept on the flo' nine years, winter and summer, sick or well. Ah never wore anything but a dress, a shimmy and draw's* (12. 1:142 [GA]).

> Ann Ulrich Evans (b. 1843): *I kept company with a nigger who worked for a man he didn't like. I was barefooted, so I asked Moses Evans to please buy me some shoes, my feet was so sore and I didn't have no money nor no home neither. So he said for me to wait till Saturday night and he'd buy me some shoes. Sure 'nough when Saturday night come, he buyed me some shoes, and handkerchiefs and a pretty string of beads . . .. Den in a few weeks me and him got married* (11. 7. 8:115 [MO]).

In 1865, Jourdon Anderson wrote to the man he had been enslaved to for thirty-two years. The letter was a reply to his former "owner's" request that Anderson and his family return to the old plantation and work for him again. Anderson argued in his biting, ironical refusal that the man owed him for thirty-two years back wages. Anderson suggested that the man "*[a]dd to this the interest for the time our wages have been kept back, and deduct what you paid for our clothing . . . and the balance will show what we are in justice entitled to*" (reprinted in Woodson, 538).

A few people even remarked on the clothing of whites after the War. Certain white Southerners were remembered negatively, and it was their clothing that marked them:

Alice Hutcheson (b. 1862): *'Twarn't long 'fore dere was plenty of Ku Kluxers 'round 'bout. Dey had on dough face and long white robes what come down over de hosses der was a-ridin'* (12. 2:288 [GA]).

Cato Carter (b. 1836): *The paddyrollers was bad . . .. They wore black caps and put black rags over their faces* (4. 1:207 [AL/TX]).

Comments make it evident that the narrators realized that the War had caused major disruptions and changes for whites as well as for Blacks. Articles of clothing, once considered part of proper outfits for the whites, were gone.

Liza Jones (81 years): *[A]fter de war . . . times was hard. De white boys, dey go out in de field and work den . . .. I used to see de purty, young white ladies, all dress up, comin' to de front door. I slips out and tell de white boys, and dey workin' in de field, half-naked and dirty, and dey sneak in de back door and clean up to spark dem gals* (4. 2:244 [TX]).

Another example of the changed circumstances of some whites was noted by James L. Smith while he was on a post-War visit back to the home of his former "mistress" in Virginia. Smith was astounded to find:

. . . her in the garden, in the hot sun, hoeing. Said I, 'is it possible that you can work out in the hot sun?' She replied, 'Lindsey, we can do a great many things when we are obliged to, that we thought we could not do.' I saw the changes that freedom had wrought, and I thought, 'how people can accommodate themselves to circumstances.' When we were on the plantation together she would not allow herself even to walk out doors in the hottest part of the day, without a servant to hold an umbrella over her (reprinted in Bontemps, 208–209).

But it was the newly freed African Americans, in particular, who felt the changes. In the *Narratives*, very few remembered any beneficial changes in their clothing just after the War.[18] Smith portrays the destitute conditions of Virginia freed Blacks at this time. Lack of adequate clothing proved to be an urgent concern. Smith tells of the freedman's horrendous lot in Washington, D.C., again driving his message with a depiction of their lack of clothing:

A host of miserable women with children, besides old, crippled and sick persons who were driven out of Maryland and sought refuge here . . .. Hundreds of old persons and children were without shoes and stockings, and were badly frost-

bitten. Infants, only a few days old, without a garment, perished with cold. Very few of the older persons had any under-garments, for they came from Maryland and Virginia clothed in rags . . . (reprinted in Bontemps, 236).

On the other hand, when he returned to his former home in Virginia after the War, Smith noted:

During my repeated visits to Heathsville I have carried clothing and a large trunk closely packed, for the benefit of the freedman and their families. The little sacks and other children's clothes were presented to mothers whose children stood in great need of them, and were very thankfully received. 'God bless the friends of the North,' was the hearty exclamation of many (reprinted in Bontemps, 211).

The people whom Smith encountered recognized that the clothing had been donated by Northerners. Smith specifically recalled the deeds of Elizabeth Osgood, a Connecticut white woman, and her charitable group, whom he had encountered after his escape to that state:

[T]hrough her instrumentality many poor children were clothed so as to be presentable for the Sabbath School. She went out into the highways and hedges and gathered them in with their tattered garments, with the promise of a new suit of clothes . . . Miss Osgood was then a member of the Washington Society. The object of this society was for the benefit of the poor. Useful articles of all kinds of wearing apparel were made for the needy (183).

Smith further pointed out that it was not only white women who promoted these charities:

At this time the colored ladies of the Chapel [in Connecticut] resolved to organize a Sewing Society . . .. There is also a committee of ladies who went around to solicit funds to carry out their plans. They had no regular sewing room, but went around from house to house.

After accumulating thirty or forty dollars' worth of sewing, they opened a fair in Masonic Hall; the proceeds were used towards building a more commodious Church for worship . . .. There were fancy articles of all descriptions, and the needle-work was finely executed (185).

A decade earlier, however, William Grimes (b. 1784), who had escaped from Virginia recalled Connecticut charities in a different light. Here again, clothing serves to mark the point.

They have kind of societies to make clothes for those who, they say, go naked in their own countries. The ladies sometimes do this at one end of a town, while

> *their fathers, who may happen to be selectmen, may be warning a poor family out at the other end, for fear they may have to be buried at the town expense. It sounds rather strange upon a man's ear who feels he is friendless and abused in society, to hear so many speeches about charity*. . . (reprinted in Bontemps, 120).

Changes in their clothing, whether good or bad, were but outward marks of emancipation. Legalities also accompanied freedom, such as the Black male's right to vote. Freedom from bondage also meant that, for the first time in the Southern United States, African Americans could legally learn to read and write. Most wanted this type of education, but for Southern Blacks, the first concern had to be feeding and clothing themselves and their kin. Thus, many remained chained to a life of raising crops on the land that they did not own.

In the South, the most valuable crop continued to be cotton. The great nineteenth-century champion of Black education, Booker T. Washington, seems to have missed this point when he castigated the Blacks he found in rural Alabama at the end of the last century. Describing their living conditions, he wrote: "*Their one object seemed to be to plant nothing but cotton; and in many cases cotton was planted up to the very door of the cabin*" (113).

In addition to his comments about raising this most important staple crop, Washington also wrote about training the freed people who came under his tutelage. As director of Tuskegee Institute in the early 1880s, Washington's foremost concern was that his students learn to present a proper appearance; this training involved body grooming and care of clothing. He wrote:

> . . . *absolute cleanliness of the body has been insisted upon from the first (175)* . . .. *For a long time one of the most difficult tasks was to teach the students that all the buttons were to be kept on their clothes, and that there must be no torn places and no grease-spots* (176).

Then and Now

> Frank Hughes (78 years): *Times do change. Don't see nuffin like dat now* (S. 1. 8. 3:1060 [AL/TX]).

The contributors to the *Narratives* proved adept at evaluating their past experiences during the antebellum period by comparing them with what they were currently experiencing during the Depression. For instance, two elderly men looked back with particular fondness on the fashions of girls in their youth:

> Gus Feaster: *Den de gals charmed us wid honeysuckle and rose petals hid in dere bosoms. Now de gals goes to de ten cents sto' and buys cheap perfume* (2. 2:52 [SC]).

> Jasper Battle (80 years): *What would gals say now if dey had to wear dem kind of clothes? Dey would raise de roof plumb offen de house. But jus' let me tell you, a purty young gal dressed in dem sort of clothes would look mighty sweet to me right now* (12. 1:65 [GA]).

In a more profound way, by the 1930s, very often clothes served as a metaphor for the changes that the people had seen in their lifetimes; and very often, the people perceived the changes as neither beneficial nor as virtuous additions to American social customs. While this happenstance occurs in many societies as one generation's customs give way to those of a younger generation, the comments made by this group of older people must be viewed as unique to their own particular situations as African Americans.

> Mariah Barnes (age 83): *But I ain't got nothin' fittin' to wear to church now. I washed my old dress till it done faded out: jes' any rag won't do for church. I ask the Welfare for a dress to wear last first Sunday; my old shoes I could hide under my skirt, if I could jes' git a print dress or somethin' decent. The Welfare said dey didn't have no dresses. I told her other folks got 'em and said dey was jes' piled up yonder in Jackson. Den she promised she'd try to git me a dress 'fore next preachin' Sunday. It's harder on us some ways den 'twas 'fore de county help us, 'cause white folks use to gin us old clothes and somethin' t'eat on and off. Now if I goes and asks for anything from my white folks like I always done, dey say: 'Here she come beggin', and de county a-helpin' her.' Dis was de fust Christmas I 'member dat Miss Mitt didn't gin me a dress for a present, but I ain't faultin' her; it was a hard year on everybody*. . . (S1. 11. 1:2 [NC]).

> Elsie Reece (90 years): *Thar an tudder thing dat changed a heap. 'Tis de buyin' all weuns wear an' eat now. Gosh fo' mighty Ise a gal on de Marster's place, 'twas awful little dat am bought. What weuns eat an' wears, am raised an' fixed by de cullud fo'ks* (S2. 8. 7:3273 [TX]).

> Lillie Williams (69 years): *There is something wrong about the way we are doing somehow. It is hand to mouth . . .. They say work is hard to get. One thing now*

didn't used to be, you have to show the money before you can buy a thing. Seem like we all gone money crazy. Automobiles and silk stockings done ruined us all (11/7:178 [AR]).

An unidentified contributor: *Us made everythin' us wore. Us knitted our socks and stockin's. Things was much better then than they are now. Shoes lasted two and three years, and clothes didn't tear or wear out as easy as they do now. Us made all our cloth at night or mos' times durin' the winter time when us didn't have so much other work to do* (13. 4:363 [GA]).

Calvin Moye (b. 1842): *We wore cotton clothes in summer and wool clothes in de winter and plenty to keeps us warm too, but now we wears summer clothes in winter with plenty of patches on dem to make dem last six or eight years and den we can't live like human folks* (S2. 7. 6:2831 [GA, TX/TX]).

Louella Williams: *De race of people now ain't like dey used to be, neither black nor white. You take de way dey dress now, why my white folks wouldn't a thought a puttin' on dese tight dresses like dey wear* (S. 1. :456 [AL]).

Georgia Telfair (6 months old when freedom came): *Our dresses wuz made long to keep our legs warm. I don't see, for to save me, how dey keeps dese young-uns from freezin' now since dey let 'em go 'roun' mos' naked* (13. 4:4 [GA]).

Hattie Thompson (b. 1867): *When I was a child . . . [f]olks had better made clothes and had to take care of them. Clothes don't last no time now* (10. 6:316 [AR]).

In the litany about nineteenth-century clothing, two pronounced positive elements stand out: first, its durability and, second, it was modest attire (i.e., it adequately covered body parts). The corresponding negative attitudes about modern clothing was that it quickly wore out and that it was immodest. Three contributors, however, viewed modernity as positive, again using clothing as the criteria.

Sarah Graves (b. 1850): *Nowadays, when you all want a nice wool dress, all you got to do is go to the store an get it . . .. When I was growin' up an' wanted a nice wool dress, we would sheer the sheep, wash the wool, card it, spin it and weave it* (11. 7. 8:130{MO]).

Hardy Miller (85 years): *I think they is doin' a whole lot better. Got better clothes. Almost look as well as the white folks. I just say the niggers dressin' better than the white folks used to* (10. 5:77 [AR]).

In the final statement concerning then and now, clothing becomes the actual symbol used to demonstrate the difference between enslavement and freedom.

> Eliza Overton (b. 1849): *I hear a woman stan' up an' say we would be bettah off today in slavery. I say, "Why?" She say: "You would hab ta look aftah nothin' of your welfare." "If that's what she wuz talkin' 'bout," I said, "us fauthuh wuz ten years ole' fore he put on a pair of pants. He had ta wear wooden shoes an' a tow-shirt." I wud not liv' twenty-four hours, bein' a slave now* (11. 8:268 [MO]).

Styling the Refusal

> Clothing, right from our first direct evidence twenty thousand years ago, has been the handiest solution to conveying social messages visually, silently, continuously (Elizabeth Barber 1994:148).

> I thought about another border, the one existing between two cultures in the same country . . . it was invisible, . . . places in the heart and mind (Ted Conover 1987:246).

> We have not had the same past, you and ourselves, but we shall have, strictly, the same future. The era of separate destinies has run its course (Cheikh Hamidou Kane, Senegal, 1985:79).

> [C]ulture consists of connections, not of separations: to specialize is to isolate . . ..
> [T]he I, the You, and the We were only separate and dried up because of a lack of imagination (Carlos Fuentes 1988:103, 109).

> An absolute and immense democracy is not all that we find in America; the inhabitants of the New World may be considered from more than one point of view (Alexis de Tocqueville [1835] 1954:343).

> "Folks what can look at things in more than one way is done got rare," says Grange Copeland (Alice Walker 1970:129).

Because this chapter forms the core of my book, I present a summary before proceeding with the following chapters on more detailed aspects of antebellum clothing. My unanticipated conclusions evolved as I pursued my research. As have others, I found it difficult to formulate neat answers as I wrestled with various assumptions about American social boundaries. Where do the boundaries start? Where do they stop? The test was in trying to examine the evidence from "more than one point of view," to "look at things in more than one way." The results were unexpected.

Within the *Narratives*, binary poles of perception about the abuses and generosities of Southern whites glaringly confront the reader, as do all those reported white behaviors that fall somewhere in between. But the fact is that self-empowering stances were taken not only by the whites, but by the seemingly less powerful Blacks as well; thus, the least powerful also offered their own multilayered modes of behavior. The *Narratives* demonstrate that the enslaved acquired clothing by means other than just what the "master" or "mistress" doled out. The clothing served multiple purposes for the enslaved during periods of work, during leisure time, and during special occasions. Specific forms of dress varied from one plantation, geographical region, and state to another. Although often a necessity for physical survival during the period of enslavement, in the end, perhaps clothing took a second place to food as the most important material concern:

> Joe Rawls (past 90 years; 21 siblings): *Us didn' bodder 'r' t'ink near so much 'bout dem clo's den's people does now, cause dey wasn' no flappers 'n' dudes den. People all lib 'like 'n' dress 'like 'n' lib at home, but dey was so many 'r' us in dat fambly dat it sho' kep' us a-scrimmagin' fo' sump'n' t' eat. Dat was d' bigges' question* (S2. 8. 7:3250 [TX]).

Nevertheless, clothing was a "big question," for it often served as a potent means towards other kinds of survival: the survival of self and of community values.

With one exception, by the antebellum period, enslaved African Americans wore types of clothing that were of European American derivation (Figure 23).[19] The assimilation of European American fashion reflects the universal human regard we all have for outward signs of stability; more to the immediate point, it reflects arability on the part of the displaced Africans to improvise and to creatively adopt new materials. The enslaved peoples' capacity for improvisation and adaptability in the clothing they wore was due to deeply ingrained West-African cultural habits. Therefore, in appraising the dress of the enslaved, the most important consideration does not concern any particular article of dress nor whether the clothing was adequate or inadequate. Nor does it concern who wore

Figure 23. *Portrait of a Black Man Wearing a Bow Tie and Top Hat*, ca. 1856. Unknown daguerreotypist, American; 2 1/2″ × 2 1/16″. Collection of the J. Paul Getty Museum, Malibu, California.

what, when, and where. Instead, the most important consideration concerns the behavior displayed by the enslaved as they made conscious choices and decisions in terms of styling their adopted attire. That is, rather than examining the items of clothing, themselves, we must look at *how* the articles were used. This is the point at which the material objects become cultural material. Sterling Stuckey has written:

> That is the argument that one must make for slave culture . . . when African values were drawn upon, there was no necessary opposition between being African and having command of or responding to the values of another people (1987:48).

Stuckey's succinct statement helps explain the contradictions, the anomalies, the discrepancies, the novelties, the antitheses, the paradoxes, the diversities, the vagaries which confront us as we listen to the narrators' testimonies. The paramount contradiction, of course, is that very often,

African Americans expressively adopted European American artifacts – musical instruments, art and craft media, food, and yes, even clothing – in ways that contrast markedly to the ways in which other Americans used these materials. As Stuckey astutely maintains, the reasons for the differences may be accounted for if we acknowledge that "African values" are innate to African American worldview. After all, we have always accepted the fact that white Americans behave as they do because they possess "European values": ideals of property ownership, the nuclear family, and Christian ethics, for example.

The African values inherent to African American culture are most easily discerned as a particular style. And by "style" I mean a studied way of presenting the self – an idea of how one ought to appear before others. Clothing is one of the most public symbols of personal style, and if the viewer is sometimes confused or disturbed by the style of dress, perhaps this in itself signifies an important purpose. Cornel West's style of dress serves as a contemporary example of a phenomenon that stretches far back in time and over vast spaces:

> West . . . wore a navy-blue three-piece suit, with a brown-and-black striped tie and a white shirt. A silver watch chain dangled across the front of his vest, and a pair of jewelled cufflinks sparkled at the end of his shirtsleeves. This, I gathered is West's usual form of dress (Jervis Anderson, *The New Yorker*, 17 January 1994:39).

> . . . Antonio Gramsci's idea of the "organic intellectual" . . . can explain details as perplexing as Cornel West's dress and mannerisms (Michael Bledsoe, "In the Mail," *The New Yorker*, 21 February 1994:8).

> [A]sk him how he's dealing with all the fuss being made over his vestment or highbrow tenor of his arguments . . ..
>
> "Well it messes with me, you know? It's not as bad as talkin' about my mama or nothin', but yeah, especially when it comes to clothes. If the clothes gets in the way, then maybe I need to just be in my jockstrap or somethin' . . .. I mean I don't want that to get in the way of the message and so forth. Because I'm much more concerned with deeds than I am just clothes" (Cornel West, Interview with Rosalind Bentley, *[Minneapolis] Star Tribune* 27 Sept 1993).

John Szwed warns how differences in style may inflate into racism: "It is possible to see from this way of looking at the world that throughout history we have been confusing cultural style with race" (1975:25). Mintz and Price place great emphasis on African American style when they write:

> [T]his acceptance of cultural differences combined with the stress on personal style to produce in early African-American cultures a fundamental dynamism, an expectation of cultural change as an integral feature of these systems . . .. African Americans learned to put a premium on innovation and individual creativity; there was always a place for fads and fashions; "something new" (within certain aesthetic limits, of course) became something to be celebrated, copied, and elaborated (51).

On the necessity for recognizing the deeper meanings that individual style may express, Barbara Kirschenblatt-Gimblett suggests:

> . . . it is not precisely because so many people do not have the power to control the image-making machinery that it is so important to examine what they do control, namely the expressive shaping of their immediate and everyday lives. For them, style can be a form of refusal (1983:221).

All human groups are dynamic – they do not stay suspended in timeless tradition. Adjustments are constantly being made. Fixed social boundaries are illusions; they are always being crossed because acculturation is what human existence is about. This phenomenon is most evident when one group has close social intercourse with another group. In American society, assuming we could lump all the customs of Africans into one "culture" and those of all Europeans into another single "culture", we would still have a difficult time sorting out just what is West African in European American culture and just what is European in African American culture. In the United States, the experiences of African Americans and European Americans have always been different, but on the way to becoming Americans each group's experiences have been tempered by the customs of the others. Or, as Cornel West puts it: "These [black] styles and modes are diverse – yet they do stand apart from those of other groups (even as they are shaped by and shape those of other groups)" (1993:28).

West Africans appear to have been particularly adept at acculturating to American society, with ties to the homeland becoming attenuated over the centuries, but never being completely severed. The distinctive ways in which the enslaved wore their clothing and the special manner in which they viewed clothing were important demonstrations of their refusal to accept cultural annihilation by the European community in the United States. The African Americans set their cultural boundaries with demarcations of style, and in refusing to give up their style, they freed themselves and preserved their heritage.

Notes

1. Rhys Isaac writes that the Reverend Devereux Jarratt of Virginia noted in 1806 that: "Slaves 'had Course Shirts and . . . Drawers given [to] them' – two pairs per annum. The material was osnaburg [. . .] of which the young Jarratt's clothing had also been made. As in the case of the common planter's son, shoes were only given as winter wear" (1982:44).

2. Bill McCarthy uses the term "folk" to mean "imagined," and emphasizes that the stereotypical, Southern white woman's costume, as envisioned after-the-fact, was not the usual reality: "The 'southern belle' outfit may also qualify as a folk costume, since it represents not a historical picture of antebellum women's clothing, but a folk sense of the period" (467). Jeanette C. Lauer and Robert H. Lauer analyze the role that white women, themselves, had in projecting this image even in the post-bellum period: "The southern woman, viewed as inferior by nature and thus subject to the domination of her husband, was nonetheless idealized as the possessor of higher morals and purity. As she kept her place and her purity, she played an important role in a threatened society" (613). Fox-Genovese, however, uses the image of the "southern belle" to argue that the white, Southern woman had neither "a life of ease and privilege" nor did she live "a life of ceaseless responsibility and toil" (46–47ff.).

3. For a particularly cogent description of this phenomenon from the white viewpoint, see Fanny Kemble's account of her husband's expectation for his house servants' dress (94).

4. Richard C. Wade has drawn a strong case for this (125–142), but it should be noted that these differences between rural and urban clothing are not confined only to the types of clothing that were worn during the period of enslavement. Such contrasts between the clothing worn in rural areas and urban areas are still often evident in the United States (and elsewhere) today, and are not conditioned, and probably were not in the antebellum period, solely because of one's skin color.

5. Norrece T. Jones, Jr. sees this as one more instance of the "divide-and-conquer" technique used by whites during the period of enslavement: "Whatever the source of slave ideas about style and proper attire, there is no doubt that masters and other controllers pursued a deliberately divisive clothing scheme" (110). In his argument, Jones cites specific examples of the differences in clothing allotted to field hands and house servants, noting also the propensity of dress codes affecting all enslaved people no matter what their place in the hierarchy of the labor force (109–111).

6. Fanny (Frances Anne) Kemble (1809–1893) was a British actress who made her American acting debut in New York City. Although she was an ardent abolitionist, Kemble married Pierce Butler, slave-holder and co-owner of a large plantation off the Georgia coast. Butler, an absentee landowner, resided in Philadelphia, but in 1838–1839 he brought his wife for a visit to the Georgia plantation. The letters she wrote of her impressions and experiences during the

visit were published as a journal in 1863, by which time she had divorced Butler. Kemble is a complex character. She fully believed in the immorality of the system of slavery and her writings exhibit her strong sympathy for individual enslaved people, particularly women. Interwoven with these assets, however, Kemble's writings also show that she judged the African Americans with whom she came in contact on the Georgia plantation from a Eurocentric viewpoint. That is, Kemble's underlying theme is her conviction that the Blacks needed to be "civilized." Her European values are particularly evident when Kemble describes the clothing of Blacks and compares this attire to that of whites.

7. The shift in pronoun gender is correct in some African American communities.

8. Russell William, an Irish journalist, however, found an enslaved man on the auction block in Montgomery, Alabama, in 1861: "badly dressed and ill-shod" ([1863], Gunther, ed., 1978:41).

9. Ina Corrine Brown comments:

> Almost all over the world, clothing is used as sex symbol, and taboos against wearing the garments appropriate to the other are found in many societies. In our own society, women may wear men's clothing but there is the strongest kind of feeling directed against men who wear feminine attire (10).

10. Singleton, 1991:55, Tables, pp. 149, 154, and 295.

11. Singleton, 1991:155 and *passim*; Ascher and Fairbanks, 1971:8, 13.

12. The enslaved Africans of whom Sullivan spoke are discussed by Allan D. Austin who edits the letter of James Hamilton Couper in *African Muslims in Antebellum America*, 1984.

13. One of the characteristics that Ibn Battuta admired most about fourteenth-century, Black African Muslims was "their putting on of good white clothes on Friday. If a man among them has nothing except a tattered shirt, he washes and cleans it and attends the Friday prayer in it" (Hamdun and King, 1994:58).

14. Frances Trollope (1780–1863), an English woman, visited and traveled in the United States from 1827–1830. Trollope's observations about the people whom she encountered on the visit were published as *Domestic Manners of the Americans* in 1832. Like Frances Kemble, Trollope was an abolitionist, and, like Kemble, Trollope's writings show that she paid particular attention to the lifestyles of American women. Unlike Kemble, however, Trollope does not negate African American styles of dress even as she views them as quite different from the fashions of white Americans.

15. Also see Sterling Stuckey on similarities in the ceremonial use and meaning of the color white between West African religions and African American Christian baptizing (34–35).

16. Gladys-Marie Fry illustrates with a photograph the wedding dress made by a white woman for her enslaved servant (1990). For a brief historical and global examination of the distinctive dress worn by the bride over time and space, see Ernest Crawley, 53–56.

17. A "robe" also figures in the lyrics of a song collected by Parrish, but in this case, its color is not given. Parrish attributed the tune to African Americans improvising on one they had borrowed from Irish ditch-diggers who were hired in 1838–1839 to dig a canal and "employed in repairing the banks enclosing the rice fields of Glynn County," [Georgia].

O de robe de robe my Lord
De robe all ready now.
. . . .
My mother gone an' she lef' me heah
De robe all ready now. (180).

18. Jacqueline Jones, in her documentary history of African American women, includes a brief essay, "New Dresses, Defiant Words, and Their Price," wherein she outlines how "clothes served to announce a woman's awareness of her new status" after the War (69). Jones explores the toll exacted from Black women as they were criticized and punished by some in the white communities as well as from Black men for their "abandonment of deference and old clothes" (68–72).

19. The exception was the headwrap to be discussed in the final chapter.

4

Having Footwear

Malinda Murphy (b. ca, 1857): *We had no shoes and made tracks of blood in de snow* (11. 8:261 [MO]).

Booker T. Washington (1856–1915): *The first pair of shoes I recall wearing were wooden ones. They had rough leather on the top, but the bottoms, which were about an inch think, were of wood. When I walked they made a fearful noise, and besides this they were very inconvenient, since their was no yielding to the natural pressure of the foot. In wearing them one presented an exceedingly awkward appearance* (11).

On Footwear

The amount of comments on footwear demonstrates that these items of clothing were a particular obsession of the contributors. The formerly enslaved especially made mention of shoes or lack of shoes, however the narrators offered little about socks and stockings.

Lewis Favor (b. 1855): *We all wrapped our feet in bagging sacks to help them to keep warm* (12. 1:320 [GA]).

Anderson Furr (87 years): *Our shoes was rough old brogans what was hard as rocks, and us had to put rags inside 'em to keep 'em from rubbin' de skin off our foots. Us didn't know what socks and stockin's was den* (12. 1:317 [GA]).

As noted in Chapter 2, stockings, when they existed for enslaved people, were most often hand-knit.

Martha Colquitt (85 years): *Ma made our home-knit stockings* (12. 1:241 [GA]).

Jasper Battle (80 years): *Dey knitted all de socks and stockin's for winter* (12. 1:65 [GA]).

Compared to the dearth of statements about stockings and socks, the people were very preoccupied with the subject of shoes. As for shoes, some people might fare worse than others.

Emma Hurley (more than 80 years): *I never had no shoes 'til after freedom come. I've walked on snow many a time barefooted with my feet so cold my toes was stickin' straight up with no feelin' in 'em* (12. 2:275 [GA]).

Georgia Baker (87 years): *Us went bar'foots in summer, but bless your sweet life us had good shoes in winter and wore good stockin's too. It tuk three shoemakers for our plantation. Dey was Uncle Isom, Uncle Jim, and Uncle Stafford. Dey made up holestock* [sic] *shoes fer de 'omens and gals and brass-toed brogans for de mens and boys* (12. 1:42 [GA]).

Moses Grandy (b. 1786, enslaved in North Carolina): *In severe frosts, I was compelled to go into the fields and woods to work, with my naked feet cracked and bleeding from extreme cold: to warm them, I used to rouse an ox or hog, and stand on the place where it had lain* (reprinted in Katz, 7).

Julius Jones: *I recollect hunting once with my young master and I had to cover my feet with old carpet* (S1. 8. 3:1217 [MS]).

Esther Green (b. 1855): *Us chillun' had shoes, same as de grown folks* (S1. 1:173 [MS/AL]).

William Mathews (b. 1848): *Winter time dey give you shoes wit' heels on 'em as big as biscuits* (S2. 7. 6:2612 [LA/TX]).

At times, foot coverings or lack of them denoted age and status.

Annie Stephenson (80 years): *Chilluns wus not given shoes at our place till dey wus big enough to work* (15. 2:313 [NC]).

Phyllis Fox (101 years): *I worked 'round de house mostly . . .. Dey give me plenty to eat an plenty clothes to wear. De workin hands would get new shoes but we wore second hand ones* (S1. 9. 4:763 [MS]).

Jennie Simms (over 80 years): *We wore toe-shirts which were ankle-length, and no shoes. Of course, some of the master's favorites had some kind of shoes* (16. 4:81 [VA/KY]).

Harriet Jacobs recalled that shoes caused the first punishment she received from Mrs. Flint, her "mistress":

It was in the month of February. My grandmother [a free woman] had taken my old shoes, and replaced them with a new pair. I needed them; for several inches of snow had fallen, and it still continued to fall. When I walked through

> Mrs. Flint's room, their creaking grated harshly on her refined nerves. She called me to her, and asked what I had about me that made such a horrid noise. I told her it was my new shoes. "Take them off," said she; "and if you put them on again, I'll throw them in the fire."
>
> *I took them off, and my stockings also. She then sent me a long distance on an errand. As I went through the snow, my bare feet tingled. That night I was very hoarse . . .* (19).

In the South, shoes were not necessary during the warmer months; many contributors, in fact, seemed to prefer going barefooted.

> Susan Castle (b. 1860): *Us wore coarse, heavy shoes in winter, but in summer us went splatter bar feets* (12. 1:179 [GA]).

> Sarah Ford ("seven years old first year of emancipation"): *We has shoes too . . . all 'cept Uncle Tom what would't wear no shoes no time. He say 'de Lawd didn't put shoes on me an' I ain't gwineter wear none* (S1/4/3:1363 [TX]).

> Marion Johnson: *My feets was tough. Didn't wear shoes much till I was grown. Went Barefooted. My feets was so tough I could step on stickers and not feel em. Just to show how tough I was I used to take a blackberry limb and take my toes and skin the briers off and it wouldn't hurt my feets* (9. 4:116–117 [LA/AR]).

> Robert Franklin Smith (ca. 80 years): *We sho' didn' wear no shoes in de' summertime 'cause us couldn' carry d' shoes fas' 'nough t' git 'bout' n' wuk* (S2. 9. 8:3658 [TX]).

> Chris Franklin (82 years): *De white folks 'low dem to have de frolic with de fiddle or banjo or windjammer. Dey dances out on de grass, forty or fifty niggers, and dem big gals nineteen year old git out dere barefoot as de goose. It jes' habit of de times, 'cause dey all have shoes* (4. 2:58 [LA/TX]).

Nevertheless, slave owners apparently realized that shoes were an important investment towards physically protecting the enslaved people and their valuable labor.

> Lee McGillery (b. 1832): *We wore brogan shoes nearly all the year, cause master say he no want cripple negro* (S2. 7. 6:2493 [NC, TX/TX]).

> Phoebe Henderson (105 years): *We didn't wear shoes in Georgia but in this place [Texas] the land was rough and strong, so we couldn't go barefooted* (4. 2:135 [GA, TX/TX]).

George Jones (b. 1853): *[W]e . . . wore shoes to suit rough travelling through woods and up and down the hills of the country* (16. 3:45 [MD]).

Soul Williams (96 years): *Yessir, we have shoes, old brogans, that were heavy, we never were allowed to become lame* (S2. 10. 9:4132 [MS/TX]).

Constructing Shoes

Commercially manufactured shoes, like textiles, were available.[1]

Lulu Scott: *The chillun go barefooted in th' summer, but' gin' fall'd come we'd git shoes. They'd sin off in th' fall fuh shoes fuh us, fuh win'er shoes. Muh daddy's git a fine pair uh boots fuh nin-ey-eight cints, 'n' reck'n muh mother pay roun' bout the same fuh her'n* (S1. 5:188 [KY/IN]).

Richard Macks (b. 1844): *[F]or shoes our measure were taken of each slave with a stick, they were brought to Baltimore by the old mistress at the beginning of each season, if she or the one who did the measuring for the shoe too short or too small you had to wear it or go barefooted* (16. 3:54 [MD]).

The entry for a judicial case from Kentucky (Hughes v. Waring, October 1821) states: "For the hire of five negro men . . . not exceeding the sum of eighty dollars in each month, . . . I am to return the said negroes to the said Waring, well shod, with new, strong, double-soled shoes, and in the meantime I am to keep them well shod . . ." (Catterall, ed., 1926:298). It is unclear whether the men hired out to Hughes received store-bought shoes or shoes made on his plantation; but according to the people interviewed for the *Narratives*, store-bought shoes were a rarity. Instead, they provided overwhelming evidence that, at least from their experiences, most often enslaved people's shoes were produced on the spot, either by a local or itinerant cobbler.

Julia Bunch (85 years): *Us bought some shoes from de market but dere was a travelin' shoemaker dat wukked by days for all de folks. He was a slave and didn't git no money; it was paid to his Marster* (12. 1:157 [GA]).

Bert Luster (b. 1853): *And whenever we killed beef we tanned the hide and dere was a white man who made shoes for de white folks and us darkies* (7:203 [TN/OK]).

Tap Hawkins (94 years): *Onct a year de cobbler comes ter de plantation en mak one pair of shoes fer all de slaves. Our shoes were home made, with brass toes and bradded soles to keep the flint rocks from cutting through the leather* (S1. 5. 2:358 [NC/OH]).

On a plantation of about 100 enslaved people, Addie Vinson (86 years) related this astonishing fact:

Old Miss had a shoe shop in de cellar under de big house, and when dem two white 'omans dat she hired to make our shoes come, us knowed wintertime was nigh. Dem 'omans would stay 'til dey had made up shoes enough to last us all winter long, den dey would go onto de next place what dey 'spected to make shoes (13. 4:103 [GA]).

Evidence supports that most shoes were handmade and that, except for Addie Vinson's noteworthy statement, men were the shoemakers. Betty Brown said that the master's sons made the shoes: "*Two o' the Nutt boys made shoes too, heavy, big ones dey wuz . . .*" (11. 8:52 [MO]). All other contributors, however, said that African American men were the cobblers.

When Mungo Park emphasized the importance of leather workers in West Africa in the late 1790s, he did not say whether the shoemakers were men or women. If women had held such occupations, no doubt Park would have remarked on this. Presumably, then, the West African leather workers were men. Strong evidence shows that African men and their descendants continued to hold onto this craft in the American South. Historians of early American industrial craftsmen, for example, present documentation for African Americans as tanners and cobblers by the 1750s (Stavisky, 427; Jernegan, 230, 234). In a much earlier account, *A Perfect Description of Virginia*, 1649, the author notes that "an old Planter . . . hath . . . a Tan-house, causes leather to be dressed, hath eight [Negro] Shoemakers employed in their trade . . ." (quoted in Jernegan, 227–228). Further evidence suggesting a gender-specific link to West Africa is supplied in the *Narratives* where, although a few narrators recalled Black women making simple types of shoes, overwhelmingly they name Black men as the official shoemakers.

Phillis Hicks (71 years): *My father was a shoemaker at old age. He said he learned his trade in slavery times* (9. 3:235 [SC/AR]).

Nicey Pugh (b. 1852): *Marse Jim had plenty ob hides an' he had George tuh make de shoes. Det wuz plain heavy red tanned shoes* (S1. 1:302 [AL]).

Margrett Nickerson: *My step-pa useter make shoes from cowhides fur de farm han's on de plantation and fur eve'body on de plantation 'cept ole Marse and his fambly; dey's wuz diffunt, fine* (17. 1:251 [FL]).

Lizzie Williams (88 years): *De ole shoe maker on de place made every nigger one pair shoes a year an' if he wore 'em out he didn't get no more. I's been to de field many a frosty mornin' with rags tied 'round my feet* (S1. 10. 5:2335–2336 [MS]).

Bill Heard (75 years): *Most evby plantation had its own shoemaker man dat tanned all de leather and made up all de shoes* (12. 2:141 [GA]).

As concerns the leather-curing process and the manufacturing of shoes, women contributed only cursory information:

Esther Green (b. 1855): *Massa had one man who tanned de leather. He would take it and put it into a long trough for a long time and den whatever was done dat was supposed to be done to it, he would take it out and made shoes* (6. 1:166 [AL]).

With men dominating this craft, it is not surprising that in the *Narratives*, men explained the production methods far more knowledgeably and more explicitly than did women.

William Curtis (93 years): *We made our own brogan shoes too. We'd kill a beef and skin it and spread the skin out and let it dry a while. We'd put the hide in lime water to get the hair off, then we'd oil it and work it 'till it was soft. Next we'd take it to the bench and scrape and 'plesh it with knives. It was then put in a tight cabinet and smoked with oak wood about 24 hours. Smoking loosened the skin. We'd then take it out and rub it to soften it. It was blacked and oiled and it was ready to be made into shoes. It took nearly a year to get a green hide made into shoes. That's no wonder we had to go barefooted* (7:49–50 [GA/OK]).

The first machinery "capable of sewing soles of shoes to the uppers" was patented in 1858, and these "were widly adopted by 1876" (Morris, 537). That is, until the eve of the Civil War, shoe manufacturing was basically a handcraft. Obviously, many of the Southern Black shoemakers were master craftsmen. As such, an overseer could write to Sarah Childress Polk:

. . . he is a right smarte blacksmith and A good shu maker and a good huar [hewer] . . . he wants to sell his boy which I have bargende for him at $600 and I thinke he is a verry cheape boy I bought him for you and if you are afriade to

I am not. By him be shore he is such a handy boy (letter to Polk, 1834, in Bassett, 80–81).

While enslaved in Virginia, young Noah Davis was put to work in a boot and shoe-making shop (14) and found:

The shoemakers, at that time, in Fredericksburg, were considered the most intemperate of any class of men in the place; and as the apprentice-boys had always to be very obliging to the journeymen, in order to get along pleasantly with them, it was my duty to be runner for the shop; and I was soon trained how to bring liquor among the men with such secresy as to prevent the boss, who had forbidden it to come on the premises, from knowing it (15).

The bravado shown by the shoemakers with whom Davis came into contact perhaps demonstrates their self-esteem in this occupation. Many people contributing to the *Narratives*, likewise, make evident that they, too, were keenly aware of the prestige associated with this particular craft.

The interviewer paraphrased Stephen Varner: "My father was one of the slaves who made the shoes for the slaves to wear. When there was time to make them after he had finished the shoes his master wanted he was allowed to make some for sale. The money that he made in this way was used to buy the things that was needed by the family" (S. 1. 1:427 [AL]).

James L. Smith (enslaved in Virginia): *During this time my mother died; then I was bound out to his uncle, John Langsdon [a white man], to learn the shoemaker's trade .... I took hold of shoe-making very readily; I had not been there a great while when I could make a shoe, or a boot – this I acquired by untiring industry .... I remained with him four years* (reprinted in Bontemps, 134).

Cicely Cawthon (78 years): *Uncle Jeff Hames, the shoemaker, he made all of the shoes that all of 'em wore on the place. He was about the first slave Marster had. He come from Virginny. They paid big money for him cause he was a valuable darkey. He was 'bout as valuable as the blacksmith. I don't remember how much they paid for him, but it was big money* (S1. 3. 1:181 [GA]).

George Austin: *De shoes an' things made f'om leather am all made right on de place. De leather am took fo'm de cattle an' a nigger dat am bought fo' de special pu'pose 'cause him am trained in tannin' hides tans an' make de special things* (S2. 2. 1:110 [TX]).

Lawrence Holt (b. 1858; 79 years): *[D]addy, he de shoemaker. Dat consider'a fine job on de plantation, 'cause he make all de shoes de white folks uses fer everyday and all de cullud people shoes* (4. 2:151 [TX]; cf. S2. 5. 4:1780 [TX]).

People often took special note of the responsibilities of the cobbler:

Henry Lewis (101 years): *I was marry in slav'ry times. I was growed up and 'bout 21 or 22 year' ol' . . .. Us had a big weddin'. She was dress all in w'ite. I had a nice hat and a nice suit of black clo'se. My father was a shoemaker and he mek me a good pair of shoes for me to git marry in* (S2. 6. 5:2345 [LA/TX]).

Madison Frederick Ross (90 years): *Mah fathuh was the shoemaker, made all the shoes – for the white folks an' us too. We bought the leathah from the tan-yard at the edge of town an we'd sell them tan-bark* (11. 8:299 [MO]).

Other items were also made at the plantation tan-yard:

Cato Carter (b. 1836 or 1837): *They wupped the womens and they wupped the mens. I used to work some in the tannery on the place and we made their whips* (S2. 3. 2:642 [AL/TX]).

Brogans

"I often felt more like a shoe," he said; "a pair of farted-over brogans, just for feets to stand on" (Alice Walker 1970:166).

Jefferson . . . had on a pair of faded denims and brogans with no laces (Ernest J. Gaines 1993:188).

Patsy Perryman (80 years) was enslaved to Cherokees in the Indian Territory (Oklahoma): "*There was nobody around the place but Indians and negroes; I was a full grown girl before I ever saw a white man*" (S1. 12:251). Nevertheless, Perryman described wearing the same types of shoes as did other formerly enslaved people throughout the South. The most common footwear consisted of shoes made with wooden or thick leather soles pegged to a sturdy leather upper and often studded at the toe with brass tacks. This type of footwear was known as "brogans" (Figure 24).

Sarah Waggoner (93 years): *[W]e had brogan shoes. Didn't you never see any brogan shoes? . . .. Don't you know what dey looked like? Huh. Dey was neither lined nor bound, and we used a peggin' awl to make holes in the laces. Some of 'em had copper toes . . .. [I]f dey hurt, we had to wear 'em anyway. Dem old brogans; I'm sure glad they're gone* (11. 8:360 [KY, MO/MO]).

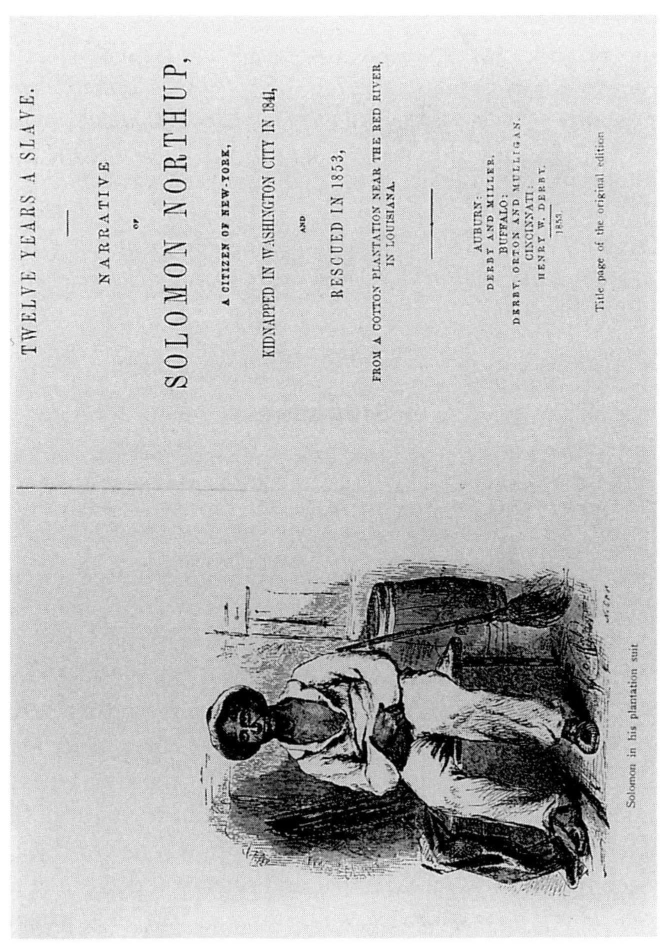

TWELVE YEARS A SLAVE.

NARRATIVE

OF

SOLOMON NORTHUP,

A CITIZEN OF NEW-YORK,

KIDNAPPED IN WASHINGTON CITY IN 1841,

AND

RESCUED IN 1853,

FROM A COTTON PLANTATION NEAR THE RED RIVER,
IN LOUISIANA.

AUBURN:
DERBY AND MILLER.
BUFFALO:
DERBY, ORTON AND MULLIGAN.
CINCINNATI:
HENRY W. DERBY.
1853.

Title page of the original edition

Figure 24. Solomon Northup shown in the clothes he wore during his enslavement, including brogans. Frontispiece, *Twelve Years a Slave: Narrative of Solomon Northup*, 1853.

> Charlie Davenport: *In winter we had . . . heavy cowhide shoes. Dey wuz made in three size, big, little en mejum. Dey wuzn't no right or left, but sorta club shaped so us could wear 'em on either foot* (S1. 9. 4:561 [MS]).

Demsey Pitts (b. 1830) said the shoes had a wooden bottom and a leather upper, and " *[w]hen the tops wore out, new tops were screwed on*" (S1. 9. 4 [NC/MS]).

The contributors made constant complaints about brogans:

> John Ellis (b. 1852): *[W]e makes our shoes out of rawhide, and Lawdy! Dey was so hard we would have to warm dem by de fire and grease dem wid tallow to ever wear dem 'tall* (4. 2:22 [TX]).

> Carrie Davis: *[O]ur shoes wus made at er tan yard and dey wus brogans and hard as rocks* (S1. 1:118 [prob. GA/AL]).

> Julia Williams (ca. 100 years): *Da had wood shoes. Oh Lamie how da hurt ugh feet. One day I come down stair too fas and slip an fall. Right den I tile de Mrs. I couldn wear dem big heavy shoes and besides dey makes mah feet so sore* (16. 4:103 [VA/OH]).

> Ann Hawthorne (b. 1851 or 1853): *Dat ledder was hard and lots of times it mek blister on us feet. I uster be glad when summer time come so's I could go barefoot* (4. 2:121 [TX]).

> Callie Washington (b. 1859): *The shoes were made in the place too. Everybody wore shoes, when it was cold. They was made pretty good, and would have been comfortable if the tacks, what held the soles on, hadn't always been coming through and sticking in your foots* (S1. 10. 5:2186 [MS]).

> Mary Reynolds (over 100 years): *Shoes was the worstest trouble. We wore rough russels when it got cold and it seems powerful strange that they never could get them to fit. Once when I was a young gal they got me a new pair and they was all brass studded in the toes and in the heels and ankles. They was too little for me but I had to wear them. The brass cut into my ankles and the places got miserable bad. I rubbed tallow into the sore places and wropped rags around my ankles and worked in the fields and my sores got worser and worser. The scars are there to this day. I thought my feet would rot off of me* (S2. 8. 7:3291 [LA/TX]).

The narrators often tempered bad memories of the uncomfortable brogans with humor:

Tom Hunley "Hambone" Greenwood (b. 1855): *Us chillens shoes had brass toes and dey was red rust leather. We couldn't wear 'em out. We could have worn our foots out sooner dan dem shoes. All we did was outgrow 'em* (S1. 8. 3:1069 [MS]).

Mary Johnson: *I call mine 'Gol' toes' and 'Lawd' dem boys to dem country dance dey better not step on my Gol' toe' shoe. I kick dem a mile. Dem shoe' was hard 'nuff to knock a mule out* (S2. 6. 5:2024 [MS/TX]).

Mollie Dawson (b. 1852): *Dey sho' was ugly lookin' things . . . and when dey gits wet dey was like tryin' ter hold a eel, sho' did feel messy and look messy too* (S1. 4. 3:1127 [TX]).

John McCoy (b. 1838): *Dey was hard and heavy and hurt de feet, but dey wear jes' like you has iron shoes* (S2. 7. 6:2483 [TX]).

Alec Pope (84 years): *Our shoes wuz jes' common brogans, no diff'unt on Sunday, 'ceppin' de Nigger boys what wuz shinnin' up to de gals cleaned up dair shoes dat day* (13. 3:173–174 [GA]).

Henry Probasco (79 years): *A [wooden] mouldboard would last 'bout a yeah. Deys am not lak de iron one dat last fo' several yeahs. Now, wid de shoes, dat am diffe'nt. Dem last mo' dan twice de time as de tore shoes. Gosh fo' mighty! Weuns can't weahs dem out* (S2. 8. 7:3185 [TX]).

Julia White (b. 1858): *We were going across Third Street, and there was a Union woman told mama to bring us over there, because the soldiers were about to attack the town and they were going to have a battle. I had on a pair of these brogans with brass plates on them, and they were flapping open and I tripped up just as the rebel soldiers were running by* (11. 7:122 [AR]).

Nevertheless, the brogans could also be a source of pride. People who owned shoes cared for them by applying various home-made polishes and lotions.

The interviewer paraphrased Mariah Halloway (prob. b. 1852): " [E]veryone was given a pair of Sunday shoes which they kept shined with a mixture of egg white and soot" (12. 1:174 [GA]).

Mollie Dawson (b. 1852): *When de slaves was gittin' ready ter goes ter a dance er church you could see dem all gittin' soot outten de chimney and mixin' it wid water der shoe polish, and dis is what dey all polish der shoes wid. It didn't look nice and slick like it does now, but it made dem ole buckskin shoes looks a lot bettah though* (S1. 4. 3:1127 [TX]).

Eda Raines (b. 1853): *Most time [the shoes] were red and I'd allus paint mine black. I'se one nigger that didn't like red. I'd skim grease offen the dishwater, mix it with soot from the chimney and paint my shoes* (S2. 8. 7:3223–3224 [AR, TX/TX]).

Henry Probasco (79 years): *It am real oak tanned [leather], an' as strong as steel. Weuns grease de shoes wid mutton tallow, an' den yous sho have wautah proof shoe* (S2. 8. 7:3185 [TX]).

One of the tasks born by enslaved people was the care of white people's shoes (Figure 25), and Black men living in the urban North also took up

Figure 25. Enslaved man polishing boots. Illustration from David Hunter Strother, *Virginia Illustrated*, [1857] 1871:238.

this occupation. William Hayden reports that after his escape from enslavement, "*Whilst I was in Lexington, I had learned to make a good article of blacking, and also a polish for morocco shoes of every color, so that I soon got more work of this kind, than my leisure hours would allow me to perform, from the good citizens of Georgetown*" (38). African American Robert Roberts of Boston offers a number of directions associated with the care of boots and shoes in his *House Servant's Directory* of 1827. He includes, for instance, instructions for "cleaning boots and shoes" (17), for making "the best liquid blacking for boots and shoes" (80), and for making "boots and shoes water proof" (80).

The formerly enslaved often remembered fondly their first pair of shoes:

> George Rutherford (b. 1854): *Fust [shoes] I ever had wus jest as fuller tacks and pegs as could be but I had ter have dem shoes, I wus so sceered somebody ud show git um ef you left dem out so I slept wid dem* (S1. 1:357 [AL]).
>
> Lina Hunter (ca. 90 years): *Chillun's shoes was finished off wid brass knobs on de toes, and us shoe mighty dressed up Niggers when us got on dem shoes wid deir shiny knobs* (12. 2:257 [GA]).
>
> Sabe Rutledge (b. 1861): *First shoe I have, Pa get a cowhide and tan it. And a man name Stavley make my first pair of shoes. I was way nearbout grown. Make the sole out the thickness of the cow hide. Short quarter. No eye – just the hole. Last! Yes man! .... Keep 'em grease! Them shoes never wear out!* (3. 4:65 [SC]).
>
> Sylvia Watkins (91 years): *We got one pair ob shoes a ye'r, dey had brass on de toes. I uster git out en shine de toes ob mine, we called hit gol' on our shoes* (16. 6:77 [TN]).

More special than the first pair of brogans, however, were the first pair of store-bought shoes or boots.

> Larence Holt (79 years): *I 'member de fus' pair of shoe' I git from a sto'. I thought dey was Gol'. My daddy bought dem. Dey was a Crissmus gif' 'bout de las' one befo' freedom, I t'ink. Dey hab a brace in de toe an' dey was natural black* (S2. 5. 4:1780 [TX]).
>
> Reuben Fox: *Our shoes was bought. I felt like I was the finest thing in the land when I got a pair of them boots with brass tips on the toes* (S1. 9. 4:771 [MS]).
>
> Fil Hancock (86 years): *I 'member once, my missus bought me a pair of high top red boots. My! I was proud. In dem days, we went bare-foot most all year*

round. But my missus tried to make us happy on Christmas. I put dem boots on and I pranced round and round jes' to hear dem squeak. I done thought day was the purtiest noise I ever heard. I asked old missus, could I go to old Massy's house. He were our neighbor, bout half mile – but its were dark. Old missus said, 'Hain't you scared to go?' I said, 'no'. I went up de road, my boots squeaking and squeaking. Didn't have time to be scared – listenin' to dem boots.

Aunt Rachel, my own aunt, lived at Massy's house . . .. I wanted my old aunt to see my new boots. When I got dere I called my aunt to come see my boots. She come and say, 'Hain't you scared coming here all 'lone'. I say, 'no'. I twisted and turn, round and round so she could hear 'em squeak. But when it come time to go home, I got plum' scared. Aunt Rachel had to take me (11. 8:158 [MO]).

George Morrison: *Mr. Ray . . . he gave me a pair of boots with brass toes. I shined them up every day, til you could see your face in them* (6. 2:145 [KY/IN]).

Brogans also figured in the lyrics of a dance tune:

Rina Brown (84 years): *Yassum, de white folks an' de colored folks uster have big dances an' old Joe wud play de fiddle while dey stepped lightly all de fancy steps, an' jes' fore dey wud break up in morning dey wud dance de Old Virginia Reel an' den sing*

> *Run Nigger, Run, de patroller'll git yo'*
> *Run Nigger, run, it's almost day.*
> *Dat nigger run, dat nigger flew*
> *Dat nigger lost his brogan shoe*
> *Run nigger run, Its almost day*
> (S1. 6. 1:279–280 [MS]).[2]

Other Types of Shoes

Besides brogans, the narrators described several other types of footwear. Interestingly, men most often made these statements.

George Fleming (b. 1854): *Lawd, I wore many pair of Marse Luntt's boots, I means sho 'nuff good boots. Marse had his own shoe-makers, sot wan't no use us gwine without* (S1. 11:134 [SC]).

Ada Davis (b. 1851): *[D]e shoes was made out ob cloth with pieces of thin board in each side ob de shoe to sho' which foot it belonged on, an' also had brass toes* (S1. 4. 3:1418 [MS/TX]).

Charlie Sandles (b. 1857): *No we did not have shoes, but when it got cold Maser would have lots of cowhides tanned in ashes with the fur left on them and we wrapped our feet and legs in them. Believe me, our feet would keep warm* (S2. 9. 8:3443 [TN, TX/TX].

Andrew Goodman (97 years): *My paw was a shoemaker. He'd take a calf hide and make shoes with the hairy side turned in, and they was warm and kept your feet dry* (4. 2:75 [TX]).

William Henry Towns (b. 1854): *Slippers wasn't worn then. Der fust pair uv slippers I ever 'member havin' was de ones I bought fer my weddin'. Dey didn't cos' but er dollar and sebenty-five cent* (S1. 1:411 [AL]).

Susan Snow (b. 1850): *I never had a pair o' shoes o' my own. Old Mis' let me wear her'n sometimes* (7. 2:138 [AL/MS]).

Pirrie [?] Kelly ("growed up when set free"): *We didn't have no clothes like we do now, jes' cotton lowers and rubber shoes* (4. 2:254 [TX]).

A number of narrators mentioned "moccasins":

Sarah Benjamin (b. 1855): *[D]e older ones had what we calls moccasins, one seam kims up de foot* (S2. 1. 1:254 [TX]).

Abram Sells (well into his 80's): *They tan the leather at home and make the shoe at home, allus some old nigger that kin make shoe. They was more like moc'sin, with lace made of deerskin. The soles was peg on with wood pegs out'n maple and sharpen down with a shoe knife* (5. 4:4 [TX]).

An unexplored aspect of African American clothing during the period of slavery is its connection to Native American dress. Items of American Indian attire that may have been adopted include forms of hats woven from indigenous plant material. However, this is more likely another instance of an African holdover where American Blacks made use of different plants while retaining the African hat styles. As indicated in this text, a few contributors to the *Narratives* were enslaved to Native Americans; servitude to Indians offers an obvious happenstance in which Blacks would adopt the former's clothing.

Although we have little evidence that African Americans actually adopted items of Native American dress (other than those they picked up during times of servitude to Indians), it is certain that a Native American term for footwear entered the African Americans' vocabulary, just as it became part of the vocabulary of white Americans. Several contributors used the Native American word "moccasin." Perhaps it is important to note that usually the narrators specifically reported that women made the moccasins. The importance lies in the fact that in many Native American cultural groups, women produced the leather clothing.

Betty Brown: *An' mammy wuz a shoe-maker, she'd make moccasins for allo' us* (11. 8:52 [MO]).

Emma Knight (b. ca. 1853): *Our feet would crack open from the cold and bleed . . .. Mother made us moccasins for our feet from old pants* (S1. 2. 4:202 [MO]).

Maggie Westmorland (85 years): *When I was at Cargo's he wouldn't buy me shoes. Miss Betty would have but in them days the man was head of the house. Miss Betty made me moccasins to wear out in the snow – made them out of old rags and pieces of his pants. I had risings on my feet and my feet frostbite till they was solid sores* (11. 7:102 [AR]).

The narrators mention various types of shoes for which I was unable to locate meanings; these obsolete terms obviously indicate the vagaries of fashion. Anna Peek, for instance, used the term "*gator shoes*" (S1. 4. 2:478 [GA]); and Hanna Fambro (94 years) said, "*Yes, we had shoes – in wintah – oh, jes' 'bout de kin' I wear now.*" The interviewer then wrote: "And up came a little soft-soled black shoe of the type worn by grandmothers half a century ago" (S1. 5. 2:337 [GA/OH]).

From most descriptions, however, the peculiar names seem to be just colloquial terms for brogans.

Preely Coleman (b. 1852): *Master Tom made us wear shoes all the time for there were so many stumps an' snags we would keep our feet sore and lost too much time from the field, so he decided he'd gain more to keep us in shoes, old red russets* (S2. 3. 2:859 [TX]).

Milton Lackey (77 years): *We woe' . . . red russets, guess you didn't never hear of russets did you? They were shoes made out'n hide. My mama made 'em for us out'n the hide with the hairy side turned out. My, but they wuz stiff an' would rub blisters on our feet when we walked much* (S1. 8. 3:1289 [MS]).

Stearling Arnwine (b. 1853): *My mother made the first shoes I had, we called 'em red rippers* (S. 2. 1. 1:85 [TX]).

Cato Carter told about his "*red russels shoes*" (S2. 3. 2:642 [AL/TX]). Perhaps "red russells" and "red rippers" are corruptions of "russet," the natural color of brogans.

Bill Heard (75 years): *Leather for slaves' shoes warn't allus tanned and shoes made out of untanned leather looked lak dey had been done dyed red* (12. 2:141 [GA]).

From one narrator, we know that white's also might wear this type of shoe:

Will Parker (b. 1842): *I never was whupped but once. My ole missus tied me to a mahogany bed and she whupped me with her old russet shoe. She whupped me on my bare meat* (S2. 8. 7:3019 [GA/TX]).

Two Texans mentioned "bachelor shoes" which again seems to have been a local expression for brogans:

Bert Strong (b. 1864): *[We wore] 'bachelor' brogan shoes with brass tacks* (S2. 9. 8:3756 [TX]).

Allen Thomas (97 years): *[We wore] batchler shoes and boots wid brass tacks in 'em* (S2. 9. 8:3779 [TX]).

The interviewer paraphrased Annie Price (b. 1855): "After the leather had been cured it was taken to the Tannery where crude shoes called 'Twenty Grands' were made"(13. 3:179 [GA]).

The next three contributors spoke of "Jackson" shoes which perhaps refers to either shoes made in Jackson or a style popular in Jackson. Again, the term apparently is just another name for brogans.

Sol Webb: *Our shoes wus Jackson ties, brogans, and no Sunday shoes, all alike . . . but us thought us wus so dressed up* (S1. 1:440 [AL]).

Frances Willingham (78 years): *I wore de shoes what Miss Polly's chilluns had done out growed. Dey called 'em Jackson shoes, 'cause dey was made wid a extra wid piece of leather sewed on de outside so as when you knocked your ankles 'gainst one another, it wouldn't wear no holes in your shoes* (13. 4:155 [GA]).

Anne Maddox (113 years): *Us had home-made shoes, hard brogans, called 'Jackson ties.' Dey had brass caps on de toe an' would rub blisters on de feet* (6. 1:273 [AL]).

But if the terms "Jackson ties," "Twenty Grands," and "bachelor shoes" have passed out of the vocabulary, the brogan, itself, lasted as an article of dress in some parts of the South until quite recently. As Dr. John Roberts and I discussed this project, I mentioned "brogans," which I pronounced *bro'* gans, to which Dr. Roberts, who grew up in South Carolina, responded, "Oh, you mean bro *gans'*, we all wore them when I was growing up in the 1950s." Dr. Roberts described a heavy leather shoe with brass tacks, that "never wore out."[3]

Thus, 100 years after the period about which the formerly enslaved people talked, the sturdy pre-Civil War shoe continued to be worn in certain Southern areas. Dr. Roberts said that in his youth both African American and white children wore brogans. A white informant, who grew up in North Carolina, also said "brogan" was the common term for shoes worn by children during his youth in the 1930s. The retention of the word in the vocabulary of both Black and white Southerners suggests that this type of footwear was not worn exclusively by Blacks in antebellum times.

> Mary Johnson: *Us wo' li'l brass toe shoes, bofe de w'ite chillen and us* (S2. 6. 5:2024 [MS/TX]).

One final note on continuities associated with brogans: although a century had passed since the antebellum period, the tradition of the male as leather-worker continued – at least within the African American community which Dr. Roberts knew as a boy in the 1950s – because he also noted that his grandfather repaired the family's brogans.

Shoe Folklore

As they did with other items of clothing, narrators also included shoes in their folklore. An elderly man turned this well-known cliché about shoes into a tribute to his wife:

> Will Parker (b. 1842, 95 years): *My wife's been dead fifty-two years, I'se never found no other woman whats foot could fit my dead wife's shoe* (S2. 8. 7:3018 [GA/TX]).

Folklore about day-to-day happenstance featured shoes:

> Janey Landrum (b. 1851): *Gran'ma uset to tell us 'bout cuttin' our nails an' what would happen effen' us cut finger nails on certain weekdays . . .. Cut your nails on . . . Tuesday, for a pair ob new shoes . . .* (S2. 6. 5:2268 [TX]).

> Georgia Gibbs: *Ef a girl walks around with one shoe off and one on, she'll stay single as many years as de number of steps she taken* (16:15 [VA]).

Folk beliefs sometimes centered on shoes. The statements of two men from Maryland, who called their shoes by yet another name, allude to one such belief:

> Dennis Simms (b. 1841): *We wore ox-hide shoes, much too large. In winter time the shoes were stuffed with paper to keep out the cold. We called them 'Program' shoes* (16. 3:62 [MD]).

> The interviewer paraphrased Rezin Williams (116 years, who, in 1928, was said to be the oldest "freeman" in the U. S. [16. 3:68, MD]): "In winter oxhide shoes were worn, much too large, and the shoes contained several layers of paper. He called them 'program' shoes, because the paper used for stuffing, consisted of discarded programs" (ibid., 76 [MD]).

Besides serving to line shoes as added protection from the cold, or as a way of making large shoes fit more comfortably, the printed paper may have served as a charm that safeguarded the wearers of "program shoes" against bad spirits. Maude Southwell Wahlman connects the protective symbolism of "African religious writing" to African American culture "even when the writing was in English." She mentions:

> In the United States newsprint was placed on the walls in Southern homes, and into shoes as well, to protect against the elements or evil enslaving spirits, in the believe that 'evil spirits would have to stop and read the words of each chopped up column' before they could do any harm (3).

Shoes also figured in premonitions about death and about the supernatural. For some African Americans, as well as for some Native Americans, the hooting of an owl signalled that a death was imminent. Counteracting this belief was the conviction that the death could be avoided if the hooting could be stopped.

> Mr. Huddleston: *If a screech owl get to hollerin' they would take a poker and stick it in the fire, and stop him from hollerin'.*
>
> Mrs. Moore: *I don't know about a poker, but if you take your left foot shoe, and turn it over under the bed, it would stop. They said there would be death around the neighbourhood. I don't know whether that stopped him or not, but they would stop* (18:38 [TN or KY]).

Cate reports that on St. Simons Island, Georgia, in the 1930s, "Neither would they [the Negroes] wear clothes that had belonged to a dead person, for that person might come back in search of his apparel" (211). A woman formerly enslaved in Louisiana held the same belief:

> Eva Martin (82 years): *De fus' time I put on shoes I like to break my neck. My sister die in N-Yawlins and dey sen' me her shoes. I put my foot 'gainst de bench when I tryin' to put 'em on and when I push and pull, de bench and de box and eb'ryt'ing fall down right on me* (S2. 7. 6:2584 [LA/TX]).

In a different, but related, context, archaeologists found six instances wherein "a single shoe had been placed on the coffin lids" in a Philadelphia Black church cemetery in use from 1824 to 1842 (1986:60). Michael Paddington and Janet Widman, the principal excavators, propose several symbolic connotations stemming from African American folk beliefs which might explain the presence of these shoes in a burial context: 1) as items required for the return of the spirit back to the African homeland, 2) as a symbol of power in "the belief that the burial of a shoe will keep the devil away," 3) as a good luck symbol, or 4) "as a symbolic attempt to hobble the dead and prevent their return to the land of the living" (61).

Why Footwear?

The information that the narrators offered about this subject separates into a variety of subtopics ranging from practical know-how to individual feelings to metaphysical beliefs. Contributors expressed technical skill in knowing how to make shoes, boots, and stockings, as well as in knowing how to care for them. Personal memories could be warm as when they had recollections about special shoes, such as the first pair or those worn to dances and at church. And although some people wore no shoes by personal choice, others held bitter memories because of the physical pain caused by having no foot coverings.

How are we to unravel all this information about shoes in order to be able to understand their prominence in the narratives about clothing? I hypothesize that the observations about shoes are influenced by the different associations that men and women had concerning footwear. Boys and men expressed pride in footwear in two important ways: first, with their knowledge that shoemaking was an important craft, overwhelmingly carried out as a masculine trade; and, second, with their concern for wearing some form of foot covering, most notably boots, a type of footwear that often denoted the status of powerful men.[4]

Girls and women, on the other hand, most often talked about their lack of shoes, rather than demonstrating pride in any that they might have had. But, again, this does not reflect every woman's opinion. It was mostly women, after all, who incorporated shoe imagery into their metaphysical concepts – those most deeply embedded expressions of belief.

Notes

1. For contemporary shoe advertisements in Alabama newspapers, see Sellers, pp. 99–101. Postell writes that the enslaved peoples' "Shoes were usually bought, but there were exceptions" (41).

2. Mollie Williams (b. 1854) contributed similar lyrics:

> *Run nigger run, de patterrollers ketch you*
> *Run nigger run, fer hits almos' day,*
> *De nigger run; de nigger flew; de nigger los'*
> *his big ol' shoe.* (7. 9:162 [MS]; full text, S1. 10. 5:2348 [MS])

3. Conversation, 23 March 1992. Ella Williams Clarke, age 70, who grew up in North Carolina said that brogans were "heavy, leather work shoes" (conversation, 10 Sept 1992).

4. A mid-twentieth-century phenomenon suggests a continuation of this preoccupation with footwear among African American men. Jack Schwartz sampled copies of *Ebony* magazine for men's clothing advertisements, comparing them to those in *Life* magazine for a period covering 1947–1956. He concluded that "Hats and shoes were found to be the two items exhibited most frequently to *Negroes*, and in proportions significantly exceeding that shown to whites . . ." (173). A more recent example may be the preoccupation of many young Black American men for wearing very specific types of expensive athletic shoes.

5

Embellishing the Head

I commented on her chic new hairstyle, and she told me she loved to experiment with her hair (Cathleen Rountree in an interview with Charlayne Hunter-Gault, 1993:44).

Fannie Mae to Bukka Doopeyduk: "And speakin' of good-lookin' mens, why don't you get yo hair konkalined? Yo hair looks nappy. Why don't you slick it down with some lye?" (Ishmael Reed, 1967:24).

Hair

Musings on Conks

In *400 Years Without a Comb* (1973, revised 1984), Willie L. Morrow sets forth a history of African American hair grooming that begins with hair care in Africa. As a professional African American barber, Morrow's hands-on knowledge is vast. The book, however, has a bias: Morrow views the African American as the victim of both white racist concepts of beauty and ugliness and as the victim of the Black mother who, according to Morrow, internalized the white viewpoint and then tortured her children as she attempted to make their hair "more white."

In a similar manner, E. Adamson Hoebel observed in 1965:

> In Africa, the various patterns [of children's hairstyles] indicate different social affiliations. In America, some of the [African] styles can frequently be seen on small children among American Negroes, who have long since lost all vestiges of clan organization; the practice apparently expresses no more than a style convention that is but a survival of the old practice. A definitely New World symbolism has arisen among American Negroes in the matter of hair form. The passion for hair-straightening and kink-removing compounds among American Negroes reflects an identification of non kinky hair with the social status of Caucasoids (23).

One of the most meticulously detailed passages in Malcolm X's autobiography is his description of his transformation in 1941 from Nebraska country boy and small-town Michigan teenager (Malcolm Little) to Boston "home boy." The passage concerns the changes in his outward appearance. He first gives a contrast between his old set of clothes and the new: "My green suit's coat sleeves stopped above my wrists, the pants showed three inches of socks. Justa shade lighter green than the suit was my narrow-collared, three-quarter length Lansing department store topcoat" (39). These, Malcolm X exchanges for "a zoot suit that was just wild: sky-blue pants thirty inches in the knee and angle-narrowed down to twelve inches at the bottom, and a long coat that pinched my waist and flared below my knees" (52). Completing this ensemble were "a narrow leather belt with my initial 'L' on it . . . a hat . . . blue, with a feather in the four-inch brim . . . [and] a long, thick-linked, gold-plated chain that swung down lower than my coat hem"(ibid.).

Next, Malcolm X demonstrates that urban "home boy" was not complete without a change of hairstyle: "My kinky, reddish hair was cut hick style, and I didn't even use grease on it" (39). The remedy includes straightening with lye, potatoes and eggs, then combing with a big comb and then a fine-tooth one, then a shave around the back of the neck and shaping the sideburns (52–55). As a result of these manipulations, Malcolm X had received his first conk – "as straight as any white man's" (54) and a nickname, "Red."

In his second transformation, from street hustler to Muslim minister, besides abandoning his former name and nickname, Malcolm X abandons the flashy clothes and the conk and he exhorts his followers to also banish "from their lives forever that phony, lye-conked, metallic-looking hair . . ." (258–259). Malcolm X brands this hairstyle a "symbol of ignorance and self-hate" and says the wearer is really stating "'I'm ashamed to be a Negro'" (259).

Kobena Mercer, in his article "Black Hair/Style Politics" (1987), puts forth a more self-empowering argument than do Morrow or Hoebelor even Malcolm X by stressing that African American hair grooming can not be understood as only a submissive and self-degrading act. Rather, he says that we can not "exclude the whole life-style of which . . . [hairstyle] is a part" (46). In discussing hair-straightening versus the conk, for instance, Mercer astutely maintains:

> . . . the element of straightening suggested resemblance to white people's hair, but the nuances, inflections and accentuations introduced by artificial means of stylization emphasized difference . . . its ambiguity, the way it "played" with the

given outline shape of convention only to "disturb" the norm and hence invite a "double take" demanding that you look twice (47).

Mercer's "both/and" dialectical approach allows for multilevelled meanings for hairstyling and provides a better alternative to interpreting the choices that African Americans made and continue to make concerning their physical appearance. The African American accentuation of the hair and the head encompasses *both* African concepts *and* concepts derived from the American experiences, and this adornment of the head and adornment of the rest of the body cannot be separated (Figure 26).

An essay written forty-five years before Mercer's provides a humorous parallel to his more "political" arguments and a positive counterpoint to Malcolm X's later regrets. The piece was published in 1942, just two years after Malcolm X's make-over in Boston. In this classic article, "Story in Harlem Slang," Zora Neale Hurston captures the same cultural milieu into which Malcolm X emerged himself for a time in Boston. Hurston appends to the "story" a "Glossary of Harlem Slang" that includes thirteen entries which denote both contemporary dress as well as characterizations of hair types. These items in Hurston's record correspond to Malcolm X's obvious concern for the interrelationship between particular kinds of hair styles and fashionable clothing. Malcolm X's and Hurston's works each also demonstrate that African Americans of the time (at least within North-eastern urban communities) shared a common sensibility regarding current fashion trends:

Bad hair – Negro type hair
Conk buster – cheap liquor; also an intellectual Negro
Draped down – dressed in the height of Harlem fashion; also *togged down.*
Good hair – Caucasian-type hair
Handkerchief head – sycophant type of Negro; also an *Uncle Tom*
Made hair – hair that has been straightened
Naps – kinky hair
Nearer my God to Thee – good hair
Nothing to the bear but his curly hair – "I called your bluff," or "Don't be afraid of him; he won't fight."
Righteous mass or *grass* – good hair
Righteous rags – the components of a Harlem-style suit
Young suit – ill-fitting, too small. Observers pretend to believe you're breaking in your little brother's suit for him.
Zoot suit with the reet pleat – Harlem style suit, padded shoulders, 43-inch trousers at the knee with cuff so small it needs a zipper to get into, high waist line, fancy lapels, bushels of buttons, etc. (1942:94–96).

Figure 26. Celebrating heritage includes West African hair styles. Street advertisement, Philadelphia, 1992. Collection of the author.

Hair and Gender

In spite of the fact that modern sociological analyses of African American hairstyles often target the male conk as the subject, the people who contributed to the *Narratives* discussed women's hair grooming and hair styling far more extensively than they did that of men.[1] African American men were "conking" or straightening their hair by the 1930s when the

Narratives were being collected, but none of the narrators mention this. The assumption then must be that, at the time, African Americans were either purposely avoiding discussing the subject, or they simply were not reading political messages or psychotic behaviour into this form of male hair grooming. On the other hand, two women made comparative comments about hair styling in the time of slavery and as it was practiced in the 1930s; both concern hair straightening as it was practiced by women:

> Mary Williams (82 years): *I don't think nothin' of this here younger generation. They ain't nothin' to 'em. They say to me 'Why don't you have your hair straightened' but I say 'I've got along this far without painted jaws or straight hair'* (11. 7:185 [AR]).

> Jane Mickens Toombs (b. 1854): *[A]n' in dem times ef a nigger wanted to git de kinks out'n dey hair, dey combed hit wid de cards. Now dey puts all kinds ov grease on hit, an' buy straightenin' combs. Sumpin' dat costs money, dat's all dey is, old fashion cards'll straighten hair jess as well as all dis high smellin' stuff dey sells now* (13. 4:36 [GA]).

Certain cultural forms of bodily appearance – be they physical or material additions – certainly help to define the sexual self. But almost universally, hair exemplifies the sexual self far more for women than it does for men. Perhaps this plays a part in the contributors' substantial consideration of female hair, and not men's. But the formerly enslaved were not the only Southerners who showed an interest in Black women's hair. At times, white Southerners also displayed an inordinate interest in the subject, which certainly explains particular forms of punishment that aimed to debase the feminine sexual self.

Whites sometimes shaved or cut enslaved people's hair as a punitive measure (cf. White, 1989:38, for a case in New York State). In the known cases in the southern United States, this form of punishment was inflicted only on Black women. The instances of shaving an enslaved woman's hair may be likened to forcing enslaved men to don women's clothes.

> James Brittian (b. 1852): *My grandma ... said she was a Molly Gasca negro [HBF: Madagascar?]. That was the race she belonged to. She sure did look different from any the rest of us. Her hair it was fine as silk and hung down below her waist. The folks said Old Miss was jealous of her and Old Master .... Old Miss she was mighty fractious. One day she whipped my grandma and then had her hair cut off. From that [time?] on my grandma had to wear her hair shaved to the scalp* (S1. 6. 1:217–218 [MS]).[2]

Harriet Jacobs also had "a fine head of hair," but when Jacobs became pregnant by a Black man, she received the following punishment at the hands of her jealous "master."

> *When Dr. Flint learned that I was again to be a mother, he was exasperated beyond measure. He rushed from the house and returned with a pair of shears. I had a fine head of hair; and he often railed about my pride of arranging it nicely. He cut every hair close to my head, storming and swearing all the time* (77).[3]

The humiliation that Jacobs suffered by this act was probably among those remembered wrongs that prompted her to write: "*Slavery is terrible for men; but it is far more terrible for women. Superadded to the burden, common to all, they have wrongs, and sufferings, and mortifications peculiarly their own*"(ibid.).

On the other hand, Moses Roper, who had very fair skin color, shaved his own head in an attempt to disguise himself after his escape from slavery in North Carolina.

> *At Boston . . . I did not consider myself safe . . .. I shaved my head and bought a wig . . .. Some of the family discovered that I wore a wig, and said that I was a runaway slave, but the neighbours all round thought that I was a white . . .* (1838:81).

Caring for the Hair

> Gus Pearson (ca. 97 years): *Us combed our hair on Sunday fer church. But us never bothered much wid it no other time. During slavery some o' de old men had short plaits o' hair* (2. 2. :62 [SC]).

Several terms used by the contributors need to be explained. These have to do with either the tools used or with particular ways of styling the hair. As mentioned, for the most part the *Narratives* supply comments that concern day-to-day hair care by Black women. Enslaved women made do with a variety of objects for untangling their hair.

> Ebenezer Brown (80 years): *De wimen had no combs, an' seed my mammy comb her hed with a cob . . .* (S1. 6. 1:249 [MS]).

The interviewees mentioned combs, brushes, or cards as the basic tools. Combs were apparently often handmade. Sieber (115) illustrates two West African combs, one fashioned from wood, the other from bone, perhaps similar to those mentioned by:

Charley Williams (b. 1843): *We made purty, long back-combs out'n cow horn* (7:336 [LA/OK]).

Guinea-born Venture, after escaping to freedom in the northern United States and acquiring land, hired two Black workmen: "*One, being a comb-maker by trade, . . . requested me to set him up, and promised to reward me well with his labor. Accordingly I bought him a set of tools for making combs, and procured him stock*" (23).

Besides using combs for hair grooming, Botume offers an interesting example wherein combs might also be worn as decoration in the hair. Botume noted that after combs were distributed to the formerly enslaved children whom she taught in South Carolina, "Each child wore the wooden comb stuck on the top of the head like a top-knot, for ornament . . ." (111).

Frederick Law Olmstead observed mutual hair grooming in South Carolina in the 1850s and described: "an old Negro man, sitting with this head bowed down over a meal sack, while a negro boy was combing his wool with a common horse-card" (1959:111). Contributors also spoke of women using "cards" for combing their hair, but in these instances, the cards were the metal-toothed combs used to disentangle animal and plant fibres in preparation for spinning.

Unidentified woman: *In them days they make me comb my hair with an old kyard (card) what we used for spinning* (18. 110 [TN or KY]).

Two contributors enslaved in Mississippi described a similar device. One said it was used for combing, the other referred to it as a hairbrush, but each called the tool a "Jim Crow":

Robert Franklin (b. 1851): *[De women] combed dey hair wid a "Jim Crow card"* (S1. 4. 3:1418 [MS/TX]).

Lucy Key (70 plus years): *I recollect what we called after the War a "Jim Crow." It was a hairbrush that had brass or steel teeth like pins 'ceptin' it was blunt. It was that long, handle and all (about a foot long). They'd wash us and grease my legs with lard, keep them from looking ashy and rusty. Then they'd come after me with them old brushes and brush my hair. It mostly took skin, hair, and all* (9. 4:198–199 [MS/AR]).

It is interesting to speculate on the contributors' use of the term "Jim Crow" because, during Reconstruction and well into the present century, "Jim Crow" meant racial segregation. Charles Reagan Wilson says the term "probably originated in nineteenth-century minstrelsy" from "a song-and-dance routine called 'Jump Jim Crow'" (213).[4] An unanswered question remains however: what was the connection between segregation laws and the name given to the steel-toothed cards used to untangle both weaving fibres and African American hair?

Interviewees used the term "wrapping" when referring to the way in which women most commonly kept their hair during the work week. Usually the hair was wrapped with bits of string, but one man remembered:

> Olivier Blanchard (95 years): *I think it eel fish they strip the skin off and wrap round the hair and make it curly* (4. 1:90 [LA/TX]).

In the early part of the twentieth century, Elsie Clews Parsons glossed the remarks of a woman from the South Carolina Sea Islands. In the passage we learn how and when the hair was wrapped, and why it was wrapped:

> Underneath [a kerchief], the hair is likely to be "wrapped." you "wrap um" (ie., wrap strings around wisps of hair), beginning at the roots of the hair, and winding to the ends, "to make um grow." Thereby the hair is supposed to grow long and straight. "Ef I keep it plat, it don' stretch." Thus wrapped, the hair is "due to comb out ev'y day," but often it will not be combed out until a person is "going somewhere" (204).

An elderly man's memories predate Parson's by half a century, yet both speak of women wrapping their hair in strings. Amos Lincoln used his memories to proclaim that former times were "moral times," providing his lesson in the form of a description of how women styled their hair during the antebellum period compared to contemporary methods.

> Amos Lincoln (85 years): *I 'member how d' gals uster dress up some Sunday. All week dey wear dey hair all roll up wid cotton dat dey unfol' off d' cotton boll. Sunday come dey comb dey hair out fine. Dey didn' put all dat grease on it. Dey want it nice an' nat'ral curly. Monday dey put d' cotton string back so it hab all week t' git curly ag'in* (S2. 6. 5:2371 [LA/TX]).

Both statements show that women wrapped their hair during ordinary days, but that the strings were taken out if "a person is going somewhere" or when she "dressed up for Sundays." On the other hand, Parsons reports that wrapping was supposed to help the hair grow "long and straight," while Lincoln said the strings made the hair "curly." Perhaps these conflicting statements indicate a change in fashion between the "nat'ral curly" style of the antebellum period and the desire for "long and straight" hair by the 1920s when Parsons was collecting.

Hair grooming equates with leisure time; that is, the more leisure one has, the more time one has to care for the hair. For most of the enslaved, their only free time to attend to personal chores was during some part of the weekend. This was when women had the chance to do something with their hair beyond merely wrapping it in strings.

Clearly the lack of time that the enslaved had for personal grooming is attributable to whites. Whites might also be held accountable for unleashing divisions in the African American communities when they caused the hair of the enslaved to function as a status symbol. Three women who served their time of enslavement as house servants remembered that well-groomed hair constituted an important outward form of status just as did the better types of clothing they possessed in relation to field hands:

> Josie Brown (b. 1859): *I didn' do nothin' 'cep' eat and sleep and folloer ole mistus 'round . . .. I hab to keep de head comb and grease with lard* (4. 1:164 [TX]).

> Melinda Pollard: *I nebber libed in de slave quarters 'cause I wuz nuss maid for my mistiss two chillun . . .. I allus wore nice close an' wuz allus clean an' had my haid com'ed* (S2. 8. 7:3113 [MS, GA, AR/TX]).

> Mariah Robinson (ca. 81 years): *They loved to dress me to make me look to be de best lookin' an' neatest slave. I had such as, pretty starched dresses, neat shoes an dey helped me fix my hair nice* (S2. 8. 7:3354 [GA, TX/TX]).

In a similar manner, one woman's obvious jealousy helps to explain another way in which whites might contribute to community divisiveness. Mary Reynolds' recollections centered on instances when white people singled out a Black woman to receive special favours and, in this case, compliments on her hair:

> Mary Reynolds (over 100 years): *My sister Charity, which was by my maw's first husband was made plenty over by the white folks. Every time she has twins. And she thinks she is something special. They tell her that she wrops her hair in a nice style and every now and then she goes down to the big house* (S2. 8. 7:3295 [LA]).

These statements illustrate that because their positions put them in closer proximity to white people, house servants apparently were given more time to see to their hair. Conversely, taking away this privilege may also be viewed as another form of sexual degradation for women.

Lou Smith, female (b. 1854): *My mother was a house woman and she could keep herself looking nice. My, she went around with her hair and clothes all Jenny-Lynned-up* [see Appendix II] *all the time until we went to live with Miss Jo. She took all the spirit out of poor mother and me too* (7:303 [TX/OK]).

Although several of the comments strongly suggest that white women helped African American house servants to care for their hair, and even praised them for the way they kept it, most Africans displaced in Europe and in the Americas continued personal or communal hair-styling. Mintz and Price cite an entry from John Gabriel Stedman's 1790 journal:

Stedman tells us how, at the end of the nightmare Middle Passage, off the shores of Suriname: 'All the slaves are led upon deck . . . their hair shaved in different figures of Stars, half-moons, &c, /which they generally do the one to the other (having no Razors) by the help of a broken bottle and without Soap/' ([1796] 1971:11).[5]

Africans even became barbers to white men. For example, after gaining his freedom in 1766, and settling in London, Olaudah Equiano (b. 1745, Benin) took up the profession of hairdressing. His wages, however, did not defray the cost of being trained; nevertheless, within a short time Equiano was hired to be hair-dresser to a merchant aboard the man's vessel (199–201). Barbering was one of the occupations that William Hayden practiced after his escape from enslavement. He relates that he quickly learned the techniques of the trade and earned a good salary shaving guests who lodged at a local inn (1846:44–45). Langston Hughes and Milton Meltzer offer the interesting story of Pierre Toussaint, an enslaved hairdresser who was brought by his master from Santo Domingo to New York during the time of the Haitian Revolution. The master died, so "Toussaint assumed the family burden and, earning a living as a hairdresser, supported his mistress" who later freed him (1963:22). Whether Toussaint dressed men's or women's hair, and whether he coifed the hair of Blacks or whites, is not known.

A final note: included among the many recipes for the care of household and personal articles offered by Robert Roberts in his *House Servant's Directory* is one for "a safe liquid to turn red hair black" (1827:17).

Hair Lore

People narrated personal and communal lore about hair, all centered around females. A woman offered her personal experience during the Civil War:

Laura Redmoun (b. ca. 1855): *Bouten' that time the Federals came into Memphis and scared the daylights out of folks. Miss Gusta called me and wropped my hair in the front and put her jewelry in under the plaits and pulled them back and pinned them down on my head where you couldn't see nothing* (S2. 8. 7:3267–3268 [TN/TX]).

Hair also generated folk beliefs:

Janey Landrum (b. 1851): *To lose a hair pin am the sign dat you gwine lose a frien. Never comb your hair at night, kase dat will make you forgitful* (S2. 6. 5:2268 [TX]).[6]

Hats, Caps and Bonnets

Nomenclature

When the contributors to the *Narratives* spoke of embellishing the head, their discussions generally centered around two aspects: hair care and the head coverings they wore. The contributors mentioned four types of head coverings: headrags, hats, caps and bonnets. The final chapter is devoted to headrags.[7]

As used by the narrators, "hat" was the generic term meaning any type of head covering that was not a head cloth. "Caps" apparently were brimless or had a visor. For men, the term seems to denote either a stocking cap or a visored hat with ear flaps. For women, a cap meant a circular cloth drawn together with string to cover the hair. Known as "mop caps," these were worn in the home by most women during the colonial period through much of the nineteenth century. In the engraved frontispiece to the 1773 edition of Phillis Wheatley's *Poems on Various Subjects, Religious and Moral*, the poet wears a mop cap. Houston A. Baker, Jr., includes a photograph of a woman wearing a mop cap in the early twentieth century (1991:5).

The "bonnets" mentioned or described in the *Narratives* were of two kinds. The first were simple work hats with large brims, usually woven from plant fibres and most commonly known as "straw hats." If women wore them, they might be called "sun bonnets." If men wore them they were called "sunhats." The Black woman standing in the bow of a row boat in William Sidney Mount's *Eel Spearing at Setauket*, 1845, wears a straw bonnet over a headscarf. James Goodwyn Glonney's painting, *In the Cornfield*, 1844, portrays a Black man wearing a straw hat while seated on a mule; the white boy kneeling beside the mule, attaching trace lines to a plow, wears an identical hat. Women's sun bonnets could also be made of cloth, in which case, they might be held on with ribbons tied under the chin. Pictorial examples of the ribbonless type are the two young women illustrated by Winslow Homer in his 1876 painting, *The Cotton Pickers*, and the cover photograph (first-half of the twentieth century) of Houston Baker's book cited above. An earlier work, David Claypoole Johnston's, *Bee Catching*, 1818, shows a woman in a white bonnet that is tied under her chin.[8]

The second type of bonnet was worn when dressing up for special occasions. These types changed with the fashions; during the antebellum period, the most fashionable bonnet appears to have been the "poke" bonnet. Like the women's cloth sun bonnet, the poke bonnet fit over the entire top and back of the head and was held on by tying ribbon under the chin. But the poke bonnet differed from the work bonnet in several ways: it was often made of better fabrics, ruffles often trimmed the front around the wearer's face, and it was stiffened by inserting wooden slats into seams sewn through the double-layered cloth construction of the main part of the bonnet.

In some instances, because they interchanged various terms, it is difficult to discern exactly what type of head covering the contributors we redescribing and which types were more highly prized. The words "bonnet" and "hat" serve as good illustrations of this. Some women, for instance, considered a "bonnet" less stylish than a "hat" and vice versa.

> Cicely Cawthron (78 years): *Honey, you didn't see any of 'em with a hat in those days. Our white folks didn't buy no hats for us. When we went to preaching, we had to go clean. I had a pretty white piqué bonnet with buttons. I thought bonnets looked mighty pretty when they done 'em up with flour starch. People don't make flour starch now* (S1. 3. 1:181–182 [GA]).

> Gus Pearson (ca. 97 years): *All de other darky wimmens wore black dresses and dey got hats from some dey white folks; jes' as us mens got hats from our'n. De wimmens couldn't git no hats, mostly wore black bonnets* (2. 2:62 [SC]).

But contrary to those statements,

> Mary Donatto (b. 1850, told by her daughter): "De li'l children ain' never had no hats but de growed wimmen have dem lov'ly white bonnets for Sunday. Dem was sho' fine bonnets. Dey save all de maney what dey could git and buy de bes' white clo'f dey could git fo' de money. Dem bonnets was huge, and dey was

mek wid slats runnin' all 'roun' de front, and wid ruffles" (S2. 4. 3:1222–1223 [LA/TX]).

Acquiring Head Gear

The enslaved people in the American South acquired their caps, hats, and bonnets by various means, but it is not always clear how they did so. Contributors indicate that hand-me-downs from whites served as one source for head wear.

Jasper Battles (80 years): *Dem [slave] gals wore shawls, and dere poke bonnets had ruffles 'round 'em* (12. 1:65 [GA]).

Georgia Telfair ("6 months old when freedom came"): *Us wore homespun dresses wid bonnets to match. De bonnets wuz all made in one piece an' had drawstrings on de back to make 'em fit, an' slats in de brims to make 'em stiff an' straight* (13. 4:4 [GA]).

Ellen Claibourne (b. 1852): *[G]ranpa came to see us of'en. He wore a long tail coat and a big beaver hat. In that hat granma had always pack a pile of ginger cakes for us chilrun . . . an' we all stood 'round to watch him take off his hat* (12. 1:186 [GA]).

The bonnets and the beaver hat just described were types of head coverings worn by whites and, therefore, were probably more fashionable than day-to-day hats. More practical head coverings, used by all agricultural laborers, were usually included as part of the seasonal or annual clothing allotment distributed to the enslaved. These were meant to be used for protection from the sun in hot weather and from the cold in winter.

Hanna Fambro (94 years): *[D]e sunbonnets dey was made of Oldenburg too, wid long tales [sic] that come ovah de shouldahs like a cape. Dey tied undah de chin, an' 'bout noonday dose sunbonnets ud make us so hot and keep off so much air dat we'd open de strings an' tie 'em on de top of our heads. Then us ud take de tail a little bit from 'round our neck. But ef we see de ole man comin' we'd drop 'em in a hurry 'cause he'd whip us ef he ketch dose tales up. You see, he 'fraid to have us get brain fever* (S1. 5. 2:336 [GA/OH]).

Joseph Holmes (81 years): *Dey not only made our clos but also made our hats. Ob course de warn't very hatty, but wuz more cappy. Dey made dem wid tabs ober de ears, an' tuh tie under de chin, an' wuz dey warm, I'll say!* (S2. 1 [AL]).

House servants in particular make it evident that the special head coverings they received had more to do with the white peoples' self-esteem than with that of the enslaved.

> Maria Sutton Clements: (85–90 years): *When she [Old Mistress] want the cook to go wid her she dress her up in some her fine dresses – big white cap like missus slep in an' white apron tied round her waist* (8. 2:25 [AR]).

In some cases, however, we sense that whatever the "master's" ulterior motive, the gift of a hat may have been a genuine expression of kindness. At least this was the perception held by the following narrators:

> Mandy Hadnot: *One Easter he [ol' Marster] brung me d' purties' little hat I eber did see. It was straw wid little bitty flowers 'n' a big ribbon down d' back. I sho' was proud 'r' dat little hat specially w'en d' ol' mistus tuk me t' Sunday school wid her 'n' I spruce up in dat hat* (S2. 5. 4:1627 [TX]).

> Jeff Hamilton (b. 1840): *I was sold to General Sam Houston . . .. I hated to leave my mother and sisters. The separation from them caused me to weep. General Sam Houston went in a store and bought me a new straw hat with a feather on the side, which I was very proud of* (S2. 5. 4:1633 [KY/TX]).

A few people remembered purchasing millinery supplies (e.g., Mary Donatto, above) or hats.

> Gus Pearson (ca. 97 years): *Us allus traded at de post ["While de Yankees had everything closed up down in Charleston"] . . . during this period Marse Tom let my Mammy go up to de post to fetch her a bonnet.*
>
> *Up dar dey took cotton and corn and anything like dat in trade . . .. So Mammy took a lot of cotton wid her to de post. She knowd dat it was gwine to take lots to git dat bonnet . . ..*
>
> *Well, it wasn't fur and we arriv' . . ..*
>
> *Den she talk about de bonnets. Finally she git one fer ten dollars worth o' cotton . . .* (2. 2:69–70 [SC]).

Making Hats

The most common way to acquire a hat was to make it.

> A. M. "Mount" Moore (b. 1846): *I've known some owners that let their slaves that were industrious enough to work make hats, shoes and other things and sell them to the neighbours to get a little money with* (S2. 7. 6:2731 [TX]).

Certain African craft forms did not survive under slavery in the United States for want of materials or the necessary time to produce the objects. The crafts that did survive appear to be those for which materials could be substituted for the ones known in Africa, and those crafts that produced utilitarian objects. In this way, for instance, communities of the enslaved maintained their tradition of textile manufacture even though the clothing styles they produced in the United States were altered from those that had been made on the native continent.

Another form of weaving is basketry – the patterned twisting of pliable plant parts to form a serviceable article. The FWP interviewees provided ample evidence that basketry, particularly as it was used to construct hats, was obviously another African craft form maintained in America (Figure 27).[9] As well, the formerly enslaved proved once again the African

Figure 27. David Anaba, master basketweaver, Tamale, Northern Region, Ghana, 1995. Photograph by the author.

American capacity for creatively adapting to change as they continued the craft of basketry by substituting the plant materials available in the American South for those formerly used in Africa.

Louis Hughes (b. 1843, enslaved in Mississippi and Virginia): *Every season at least 200 cotton baskets were made. One man usually worked at this all the year round, but in the spring he had three assistants. The baskets were made from oak timber, grown in the home forests and prepared by the slaves* (35).

Rev. G. W. Offley (b. 1808, enslaved in Maryland): *When I was ten years old I sat down and taking an old basket to pieces, learned myself to make baskets. After that I learned to make foot mats and horse collars, not of leather but of corn husks . . .. These articles I used to make at nights and sell to get money for myself* (republished in Bontemps, 132).

Along with making items that had probably not be made in Africa (such as oak cotton baskets and corn-husk horse collars), many of the formerly enslaved noted that they constructed hats out of various indigenous American plants.

Josh Hadnot (in his 80s): *Dey hab folks on de place dat could plait a hat jes' like dat one you got on now* (S. 2. 5. 4:1622–1623 [TX]).

W. S. Miles (b. 1854): *The little boys wore . . . 'Wahoo' hats made from the bark of trees* (Cade, 298).

Sylvia Connon (85 years): *Don get oak leaves en make a hat what to wear to church* (2. 1:190 [SC]).

Louise Collier (78 years): *Aw de colored peoples wear wh' dey call shuck hats den cause dey been make outer shuck. Dat aw de kinder hat we is hab* (2. 1:221 [SC]).

Mary Frances Webb ("I've heard my grandmother tell a lot about her experiences during slavery"): *[I]n the spring one of the jobs for the women was to weave hats for the men. They used oat-straw, grass, and cane which had been split and dried and soaked in hot water until it was pliant, and they wove it into hats* (7. 314 [MI/OK]).

Sina Banks (86 years): *Another job the women had was to make hats for the men. They would plait wheat and rye straw and weave it into hats. They would line the hats with green material so it would shade their eyes* (S1. 12:17 [MO/OK]).

Abram Sells (well into his 80's): *Us have hats make out'n pine straw, long leaf pine straw, tied together in li'l bunches and platted round and round till it make a kinder hat* (5. 4:4 [TX]).

Elisha Doc Garey (76 years): *Summer us went bar headed, but Unker Ned made bullrush hats for us to wear in winter* (12. 2:4 [GA]).

James W. C. Pennington (b. ca, 1816, enslaved in Maryland)explains how an expanding commercial marketing system changed hand-crafting, including weaving hats, as he knew it:

I used to assist my father at night making straw-hats and willow-baskets, by which means we supplied our family with little articles of food, clothing and luxury, which slaves in the mildest form never get from the master. . . (reprinted in Katz, 8).

The men had no hats, waistcoats or handkerchiefs given them, or the women any bonnets. These they had to contrive for themselves. Each laboring man had a small "patch" of ground allowed him; from these he was expected to furnish himself and his boys hats, &c . . .. Years ago the slaves were in the habit of raising broom-corn, and making brooms to supply the market in the towns; but now [1849] of later years great quantities of these and other articles, such as scrubbing-brushes, wooden trays, mats, baskets, and straw hats which the slaves made, are furnished by Shakers and other small manufacturers, from the free states of the north (ibid., 66).

In each of the above narrations, each contributor refer to the head coverings made of plant materials as "hats," but one contributor called them "bonnets":

Georgina Gibbs: *We'd plait blades of wheat to make us bonnets*(16. 5:15 [VA]).

Patsy Perryman noted another use for indigenous plant material on her "bonnet":

Patsy Perryman (80 years, enslaved to Cherokees): *[O]ur bonnets was trimmed up with corn stalks* (S1. 12:251 [OK]).

Perryman's description leads to currently unanswered questions concerning cultural exchanges between Native Americans and African Americans. Did Blacks borrow the corn stalk decoration from the Indians? Or was there a similarity between the Native American form of adornment and that of West Africans?

Head Coverings for Sacred Events

Head coverings serve three functions: protective, ornamental, and ceremonial. The majority of the hats described in the previous sections are of the first type, but just as African Americans marked their special events by donning other forms of clothing, they also wore noteworthy head coverings at these times. In these instances, the ornamental aspect often combines with the ceremonial when, in particular, religious events meant wearing unusual headgear. In the 1930s, Zora Neale Hurston says she was given "a high headpiece – the crown" made from a coiled snake skin to wear during her three-day initiation into a "hoodoo" sect ([1935] 1963:208). Hurston notes, however, that other hoodoo doctors had crowned her "with flowers, with ornamental paper, with cloth, with sycamore bark, with egg-shells" (207). She astutely recognizes that the head piece, itself, had no symbolism outside its ceremonial context: "It is the meaning, not the material that counts. The crown without the preparation means no more than a college diploma without the four years' work" (207–208).

Most people spoke of special head coverings for more tradition Christian events:

> Adele Frost (93 years): *On Sunday I wear a ole time bonnet* (2. 2:88 [SC]).[10]

> Unidentified woman: *My mistress would buy a handkerchief and tie around my head . . .. [On Sunday] sometimes they would straighten out my hair with a wooden comb and take a rag and tie it up* (18. 110. 111 [TN orKY]).

Solomon Northup (b. 1808) wrote that at Christmas:

> *As a general thing, the women wear handkerchiefs tied about their heads, but if chance has thrown in their way a fiery ribbon, or a cast-off bonnet of their mistress' grandmother, it is sure to be worn on such occasions* ([1853] 1968:164).

Chapter 3 offers more extensive examples of the headgear worn on Sundays and for baptisms, weddings, and funerals, but the following comments made by Gus Pearson best describe the full range of hair care and head coverings that might have been available to the enslaved people. In this passage, note that Pearson gives the distinct differentiations in hairstyles and items of headgear as worn by men and women of various ages, and for work and for celebratory occasions. His words especially add emphasis to the important belief that particular grooming of the hair and the wearing of specific head attire were linked with spiritual ceremonies, and that the styles clearly were meant to denote both sex and age:

> Gus Pearson (ca. 97 years): *Us [men] combed our hair on Sunday for church. During slavery some o' de old men had short plaits o' hair.*
>
> *De gals . . . dey took dey hair down out'n de strings fer de [camp] meeting. In dem days all de darky wimmens wore dey hair in string 'cep' when dey 'tended church or a wedding. At de camp meetings de wimmens pulled off de headrags, 'cept de mammies. On dis occasion de mammies wore linen headrags fresh laundered . . .* (2. 2:62 [SC]).

Hat Folklore

Hats appear as elements of folk belief. One narrator noted that soot and cobwebs were common folk remedies for staunching and closing a bleeding cut, but in an emergency, the felt from a hat could serve the same purpose:

> Marion Johnson: *And I was always cutting myself too when I was a chap . . .. One time we wasn't close to neither [soot nor cobwebs] and one man scraped some felt off from a old black hat and put it on to stop the bleedin'* (9. 4:116 [LA/AR]).

Two people related trickster anecdotes about hats. In the first, the trickster is duped:

> Mattie Stenston (76 years): *My pappy said he stole some sugar one day and his mistress saw him. She axed him, "Robert what have you in your hat?" – "Not a thing, Miss, not a thing" – With that he pressed on the top of his hat, and the sugar ran all down his face* (S1. 10. 5:2036–2037 [MS]).

The Rev. G. W. Offley (enslaved in Maryland) recalled another incident wherein a Black man used his hat to conceal an object; this time, the trickster succeeds:

> *At this time there was an old colored man working for my father [a freeman] . . .. He would give me lessons nights and Sabbath mornings. He said when he used to take his master's children to school, he would carry his book in his hat and get the children to give him a lesson in the interval of the school* (reprinted in Bontemps, 133).

One custom for random selection is carried out by placing names into a container and then drawing them out. In stark contrast to the humorous trickster tales told about the hats of the enslaved, one woman related how the age-old method of drawing names caused the disintegration of her childhood community. In her case, the names were drawn from a hat.

> Lou Smith (b. 1854): *None of our family could be sold and that was why old Master just loaned us to young Master. When old Master died, dey put all our names in a hat and all the chilluns drew out a name. This was done to 'vide us niggers satisfactory* (7:301 [TX/OK]).

Returning to West Africa

> "Where is Ojiugo?" he asked his second wife, who came out of her hut to draw water from a gigantic pot in the shade of a small tree in the middle of the compound.
>
> "She has gone to plait her hair" (Chinua Achebe, Nigeria, [1958]1988:21).

I return to Africa to point out the continuities and discontinuities concerning hair grooming and head coverings that occurred after the diaspora. A comparison between West African and antebellum customs in the American South shows that although many outward transformations transpired, many more deeply ingrained beliefs held their place.

Although Black African works of art are as diverse as the many social groups which compose the tropical region, all are united by the dominance of the human head in figurative representations. This distinctive feature is temporal as well as spatial. From the massive Nok (Nigeria) terra-cotta heads dating to ca. 500 B. C. to 200 A. D., to a more recent but undated Songye (Congo) mixed-media mask, Black African craftsmanship shows the human head to be the bodily part most obviously held to be of paramount importance. Frank Willett notes that in much West African figural sculpture:

> ... the head was greatly exaggerated in size in relation to the rest of the body, equalling about a quarter of the estimated over-all height of the figure. In the Greek and European tradition, the head would occupy only one-seventh or less of the overall height (1968:357; also see Willett, 1993:161–164).

Beyond their art, Africans have shown a heightened regard for the human head in several other ways. Elaborations on the head include elegant and ornate hairstyles and added ornamentation.[11]

West African Hair Styling

Hair grooming and ornamentation in Africa is a highly developed art form possessing a lengthy historical past. In one of the earliest European textual accounts, the traveler Cado Mosto wrote in 1456: "Both sexes . . . weave their hair into beautiful tresses, which they tie in various knots, though it be very short" (Sieber, 94). Roy Sieber quotes from:

> Other accounts [which] refer to a fantastic range of hair treatment: "platted or twisted, and adorn'd with some few trinkets of gold, coral, or glass;" a "coif, standing five or six inches above the head, which they think a fine fashion"; "They are very proud of their Hair; some wear it in Tufts and Bunches, and others cut it in Crosses quite over their Heads . . ." (ibid.).

The next account shows how a powerful man, in this instance the king of the Yorubas, controlled the ways in which ordinary people adorned their bodies, including their hairstyles:

> When Oyoyo became pregnant the Oba [Ewuare the Great, ca. 1440] sent her to the Ihama at Idumwihogbe for proper care and there she gave birth to a daughter and both she and the child were healthy and strong. In token of his gratitude the Oba awarded the Ihama *odigbokofo* (a large collar made entirely of red beads) and gave the Ihama's wives the right to dress their hair in the *ukpokhokho* style, like the Oba's own wives (Egharevba, 19).

Salih Balali (b. ca. 1765, 200 miles southwest of Timbuktu) noted that the hair of the people of his region was "curled and woolly; and both men and women wear it in long plaits, extending down the sides of their heads" (Couper letter, 1830s, in Austin, 324).

Comparable to the interest in African American women's hairstyles shown by the formerly enslaved, the hairstyles of modern African women continue to be a feature noted by modern commentators. In his 1969 ethnography of the Yoruba of southwestern Nigeria, for instance, William Bascom writes:

> Hair dress is an important form of decoration for women. The hair of men and elderly women is often shaved close, but younger women's hair is dressed in various ways. The most easily described forms are composed of parallel, tightly braided stripes running from the forehead to the back of the head where they end in a row of tiny queues, from the back of the head to the forehead, from the top of the head downward and ending in a circle of tiny queues, and from the hairline to the top of the head ending in a small topknot (101).

Just as African American women's hairstyles change over time, modern African women's hairstyles are not to be thought of as static. Eve de Negri details the Nigerian women's hairstyles that were popular in 1960, and Boone illustrates the variety and functions of women's Mende hairstyles in Sierra Leone in the 1970s. Chinua Achebe demonstrates the dynamic quality of West African women's hairstyles in his description of a modern Nigerian bride's coiffure in his novel, *Arrow of God*([1967] 1989):

> [The bride] wore a different coiffure befitting her imminent transition to full womanhood – a plait rather than the regular patterns made with a razor . . ..
>
> Her hair was done in the new *otimili* fashion. There were eight closely woven ridges of hair running in perfect lines from the nape to the front of the head and ending in short upright tufts like a garland of thick bristles worn on the hairline from ear to ear(116).

From the beginning of contact, Europeans showed a curiosity in the ways in which African peoples groomed and styled their hair. Often, they closely examined and then made qualitative comparisons about the differences between their own hair and that of the people from tropical Africa. Counteracting this broader interest, they sometimes shaved an enslaved person's hair, perhaps as a symbolic act to show their dominance over the other. This perverse practice began on the West African coast.

> In the first place, the factor takes great care in selecting the slaves for shipment . . .. A few days before the embarkation takes place the head of every male and female are shaven (Captain Theophilus Conneau *A Slaver's Log Book* [1854] 1977:96).

Conneau does not explain why this was done. Two possible reasons may account for the practice: either it was a hygienic measure taken because of the problem of lice in the cramped ships' quarters or it was another deliberate attempt to subdue the Africans by insulting their bodies, or both. For whatever reasons, the desecration must have had a particularly devastating effect on the Africans bound for the Americas. Nevertheless, in the long term, the act did not deter the people of the diaspora from continuing to glorify the human head.

West African Head Coverings

Sieber finds hats to be "among the most wildly and wonderfully inventive elements of African dress . . .. Early descriptions indicate the fascination with which Europeans viewed the variety of unexpected forms of headgear they encountered" (53).[12] From the remarks made by the contributors to the *Narratives*, we gain a sense of the continuing fascination for head coverings held by the displaced people of African ancestry.

Just as the narrators noted that certain hat styles denoted varying degrees of status in the South, so too did some form of head ornamentation denote status in West Africa. And, just as Europeans remarked most often on the clothing worn by kings and other public officials, they also remarked most often on the head apparel worn by these important West African people. Anne Hilton cites an early report which noted: "In the late fifteenth century, [when] the governor of the north-west province of Sonyo . . . met the first European arrivals, he wore a cap embroidered with a snake . . ." (48). Hilton says that the investiture of the *mani Kongo* from the early sixteenth century included the following insignia: "a copper bracelet . . . a cap, called *mpu*, a fly whisk, and a throne . . ."(37).

Those who were closely associated with a king also wore special items of clothing that included special types of head coverings. Hilton writes that from the early sixteenth century and into the early seventeenth century, the *mani Kongo* invested the major provincial governors "in the public square, giving them a special cap, called *mpu* . . ." (40–41). Wargee (b. 1770s), a Tartar from the west shore of the Caspian Sea, describes the headgear of royal women in Timbuktu in the early nineteenth century: "On the head they (the king's wives) wore a kind of red cap, just covering the crown, which has some gold ornament, or gold lace on the top of it . . .. They also wear silver chains on their forehead . . ." (Wilkes, ed. in Curtin, 181).

Mungo Park, leaving Gambia and proceeding to Mali, 1795, describes the king's wives of Bondou: "They were ten or twelve in number, most of them young and handsome, and wearing on their heads ornaments of gold, and beads and amber" (Davidson, 364).

Though less often mentioned in early accounts, more ordinary West Africans, particularly those of the Islamic faith, also wore head coverings.

> Duarte Barbosa, Angoya (African east coast), ca. 1500: The natives thereof are some black and some tawny, they go bare from the waist up, and below are clad in silk and cotton cloths and they wear other cloths folded like cloaks on their shoulders; some wear turbans on their heads, and other caps made of squares of silk cloth (Davidson, 158).

> Uthman dan Fodio (d. 1817), a Hausa, says of the Niger and northern Nigerian Fulani Muslim reformers: One of the ways of their government is their forbidding

> to the worshippers of God part of that which is legal for them, such as the veiling of women, which is incumbent upon them, and turbans for men, which is *sunna* for them . . . (Davidson, 376).

D'Avezac paraphrases the description which Osifekunde, an Ijebu (between Oyo and Benin), reported in the 1810s. Osifekunde explores a full range of head gear regulated by a class system.

> Headdress is highly variable. The common people go bareheaded, or at the most contend themselves with the *botiboti*, a simple cap made in the country. The more well-to-do prefer the *akode* or brimless hat, or the straw hat, called *akoro*, both of them native to the country. Distinguished men require a red wool hat; and the rich, a felt hat with a wid brim, imported from Europe. The chief priest wears a kind of brimless cloth hat similar to our toque. As for the king, his headdress is raised up in the form of a tiara of great richness. It is made of coral beads mounted close together on a background of crimson leather; at the crest is a tuft or tassel of gold braid (Lloyd, ed., in Curtin, 264–265).

Osifekunde notes that by his time, rich Nigerian men had adopted a European hat style. Earlier evidence shows that important West African men began to embellish their heads with European gear almost from the beginning of the African-European trade. A Portuguese trading mission to Benin in 1512 brought various goods as presents to the officials who regulated trade with Europeans. Among them: "headgear, consisting of 37 caps dyed in grain and 12 coloured hats, [that] was clearly destined for the adornment of chiefs . . ." (Ryder, 40).

I close this chapter with a final example of continuities and discontinuities. As was noted, the enslaved Blacks in the Southern United States fashioned hats from a variety of plant materials, and early European descriptions make it evident that basket making was a firmly established craft form among many, if not all, West African social groups. Writing in the 1790s, Mungo Park said of the Bambarra and Kaarta (two eighteenth-century kingdoms located between the Senegal and Niger):[13] "The natives make very beautiful baskets, hats, and other articles, both for use and ornament, from *rushes*, which they stain of different colours . . ." (1954:219). Thomas Winterbottom wrote of the people in Sierra Leone, 1796: "Their mats show much neatness and ingenuity; they are composed of split bamboo or grass, and woven into a great variety of patterns, and are stained very beautiful and indelible colours . . ." (Davidson, 288).

In 1853, Heinrich Barth noted especially a type of hand-woven hat:

> [T]he whole house was filled with armed men, horse and foot, from Timbuktu, most of them clad in light blue togas, tightly girt round the waist with a shawl, and dressed in short breeches reaching only to the knees, as if they were going to fight, their head covered with a straw hat of peculiar shape of a little hut with regular thatch work, such as fashionable among the inhabitants of Masina and the provinces further west (Davidson, 396).

The evidence for hand-woven hats on both sides of the Atlantic offers persuasive evidence for the continuation of this crafting tradition from West African to the United States South. There is no evidence, however, for a continuation of particular West African hat types in the United States. Best accounting for the change is the fact that in any social group, clothing fashions fluctuate over time and because of place; that is, the Africans displaced to the Americas began to adopt the head gear worn by whites.

The early accounts about West African rulers who adopted European hats give a partial explanation for the reasons why the formerly enslaved narrators exhibited no conflict in admiring and wearing the same types of head coverings as those worn by their more powerful enslavers (Figure 23). After all, important African men had been wearing European hats for a long time. Yet another part of the explanation lies in that dimension of human nature that persuades us to conform to the status quo. But in wearing these non-African types of head coverings, the enslaved Black Americans once again demonstrated their less visible, but far deeper linkages, to West Africa. The most important part of the explanation lies in a fundamental aspect of West African worldview which places a decided emphasis on improvisation, of a worldview which allows for continuous manipulative play on the old and the new in order to create something that contains aspects of both but is not exactly either.

Notes

1. Scholarly and public interest in the fluctuations in African and African American hairstyles continues to the present. Of importance in this regard is the recent focus on women's hair grooming, a focus parallelled in the *Narratives* where little notice is given to men's hair grooming. Two examples illustrate that, today, contemporary African American women's hairstyles have become national news. Patricia McLaughlin, "Is Corporate America Really Ready for Braids?" (Oct 1993: E) argues that "Braids are about race as much as about culture, about different hair as much as different customs." Meanwhile, Rhonda B. Sewell finds that "the Afro is back from the '70s and it's proud" and being worn by a number of male

and female African American celebrities in "Another Fashion Flashback" (19 June 1994: 4E). The African American phrase "bad hair day" recently has entered white speech as when Bobbie Ann Mason writes a piece *for The New Yorker*, titled "Bad Hair Year" in which she discussed the 1994 hair-do problems of Hillary and Bill Clinton, Janet Reno, and other white politicos (1 August 1994:82). See also Noliwe M. Rooks, *Hair Rising: Beauty, Culture, and African American Women* (1996), for an recent analysis of the link between advertising and changes in Black women's hairstyles from the late nineteenth century to the present. An exhibition of photographs by Bill Gaskins, "Good and Bad Hair," at Syracuse University, "bring attention to the symbolic role of hair in contemporary African-American culture" (Gaskins, "The Symbolic Role of Hair," *The Chronicle of Higher Education*, 4 October 1996: B76).

2. Sylvia Boone notes that the Mende of Sierra Leone, among other West African communities, "admire a fine head of long, thick hair on a woman" (184).

3. Jean Fagan Yellin, editor of Jacobs' autobiography, glosses this passage by remarking that "the practice of shaving the head of a whore is grounded in Scripture; see Isaiah 4:24" (273).

4. See also Bessie Jones and Bess Lomax Hawes, *Step It Down*, 1987:55, for other hypotheses on the term and for lyrics and music to the old song. It is interesting to speculate on how much Stowe's use of "Jim Crow" in *Uncle Tom's Cabin* (1852) helped to insure the popular image of the singing and dancing African American in the white imagination. I refer to a scene in the book wherein the master of a black child, appropriately named Jim Crow, commands the boy to sing and dance for an audience of white men (44).

5. Shane and Graham White include a perceptive analysis of mutual hair-grooming and barbering among Blacks during the eighteenth and nineteenth centuries (1–3), making it evident that the African interest and concern for well-groomed hair remained a concern of African Americans. Devoting most of their analysis to male hair grooming, the authors demonstrate that hairstyles changed over time: American Blacks did not wear their hair in the same ways in the nineteenth century as they had in the eighteenth. The paper, "'His Hair is done up in the tastiest manner for his colour': Slave Hair and African-American Culture in the Eighteenth and Nineteenth Centuries," was unpublished at the time of this writing; therefore, I will not quote from it. I wish to acknowledge, however, the Whites' contribution to certain directions that my own thinking about African American hairstyles took. My thanks to Roger Abrahams for allowing me to read the Whites' article.

6. Anna Atkins Simkins offers a list of twenty-one "superstitions relating to hair management" gathered during her interviews with contemporary African American women (1982:150–151).

7. For a brief historical assessment of African American women's head ornamentation, see Anna Atkins Simkins, "Function and Symbol in Hair and Headgear Among African American Women" (1990:166–171).

8. Joan M. Jensen concludes *With These Hands: Women Working on the Land* (1981: 248ff) with a photo-essay of female agricultural laborers. Nearly all the women wear some form of head covering. Most of the images date from the 1930s and 1940s; however, the cloths, hats, and bonnets which cover their heads are comparable to those worn during the antebellum period.

9. A number of studies identify the African basketry techniques that survive in several Southern Black American communities today (Davis, 1983:234–257; Twining 1983:259–271; Vlach, 1990:7–19 and 1991:20–23).

10. Lena Williams describes the importance that contemporary African American women continue to place on wearing extravagant headgear for Sunday worship and suggests an historical link to African custom in "In Defense Of the Church Hat" (1996:1, 11).

11. Art historian Sylvia Ardyn Boone cogently argues for the significant meaning of the head in African worldview (1986). Boone proves that for contemporary Mende people of Sierra Leona, the head and face are the culminating factor in judging what is humanly beautiful, and she proves that their aesthetic has an historical past.

12. The Fowler Museum of Cultural History spotlighted this remarkable African affinity for elaborate headgear in a 1995 exhibition titled "Crowning Achievements: African Arts of Dressing the Head."

13. My sources for identifying historically named West African peoples and places are Boyd and van Rensburg (1965), Diop (1987), and Oliver and Fage (1988).

6

Crowning the Person

'Ogea, please get my head-tie, I am going out now' (Flora Nwapa, Nigeria, 1978:176).

. . . more than one gray hair . . . peeped from beneath the ample and graceful folds of [my grandmother's] newly ironed bandanna turban . . . (Frederick Douglass [1855:46].

Virginia wore a sweater over her dress and a bandana on her head. The ends of the bandana were tied in a tight little knot over her forehead (Ernest J. Gaines [1978] 1992:74).

Afterward, standing before the dim mirror in her bedroom, she would slowly and with a trace of vanity tie a white cloth around her head . . ..
A stained fedora, his also, sat at a rakish angle atop the spotless white cloth she had wound around her head (Paule Marshall [1969] 1984:25–26, 135).

Then she took a deep breath, as if to calm herself, adjusted the head rag on her head and sighed to herself: 'Well . . . stick wit me, Jesus' (Sylvester Leaks 1967:276).

The previous chapter covered hair grooming and various types of head coverings. One other type of headwear, the headwrap, was exclusive to Black Americans.[1] Pictorial evidence shows that through the antebellum period both men and women wore headwraps. Over time, however, the form gradually became a type of hair covering worn only by Black women. The headwrap is a piece of cloth fabric wound around the head, usually completely covering the hair and held in place either by tucking the ends of the fabric into the wrap or by tying the ends into knots close to the skull. This distinct head covering has been called variously "turban," "head rag," "head tie," "head handkerchief," or "headwrap." I use the latter term here.

Both by human nature and by the condition of enslavement, hair grooming and certain types of headgear had elements common to that found in contemporary white America. During the eighteenth century, however, headwraps specifically became legislated badges of servitude and poverty for Black women. A portion of the 1786 dress code issued by the governor of Louisiana (then a Spanish colony) forbade "females of color . . . to wear plumes or jewelry"; this law specifically required "their hair bound in a kerchief" (Crété, 80–81; also Gayarré, 178–179 and Wares, 135).

In the antebellum period, the concern of whites regarding the appropriate dress for African Americans continued. Citing one instance, Richard C. Wade writes that a Savannah editor bemoaned the "extravagant" dress of city Blacks. Wade says that the journalist, "[o]bserving that a turban or handkerchief for the head was good enough for peasants, . . . noted that 'with our *city* colored population the old fashioned turban seems fast disappearing'" (*Savannah Republican* 6 June 1849, quoted in Wade, 128–129).

As previously shown, in order to present Blacks for sale in the best possible way, whites often dressed them in better-than-usual clothing, albeit in attire fitting their class. For enslaved females, this costume might include a head wrap. The 12-year-old girl whom James Redpath saw on his visit to a slave auction in Richmond wore: "a small-checked tartan frock, a white apron and a light-colored handkerchief" (1859:5).

A Peculiar Silence

Two voluminous publications on southern culture include entries on antebellum African American clothing, and each features the female headwrap as an outstanding item (*Dictionary of Afro-American Slavery*, 119; *Encyclopaedia of Southern Culture*, 467). By contrast to an abundance of evidence in other types of sources, the *Narratives* contain but a smattering of terse references to the headwrap, such as

> Harre Quarls (male, 96 years): *No hat, just tie rag around our heads* (S2. 8. 7:3214 [MO, TX/TX]).
>
> Pernella Anderson (b. 1862): *We wore our hair wrapped and head rags tied on our head* (8. 1:129 [AR]).
>
> Mary Frances Webb: *The women wore a cloth tied around their head* (7. 1:314 [OK]).

Jacob Manson, 86 years): *Many of the slaves went bareheaded an barefooted. Some wore rags round dere heads and some wore bonnets* (15. 2:97 [NC]).

This disparity between known tradition and lack of textual evidence deserves a brief analysis. A folklorist in pursuit of references to a particular subject often finds only sparse primary evidence about the item because "folklore," by its very definition, is so commonplace, so mundane, so obvious, that it apparently merits little or no mention by the people who possess it – in this case, formerly enslaved African Americans. On the other hand, I uncovered references to headwraps in several contemporary texts written by whites. For instance, the New Orleans *Daily Picayune*, describes the dress of the Blacks assembled at Congo Square in 1846: "dressed in their holiday clothes, with the very gayest bandana handkerchiefs upon the heads of the females . . ." (quoted in Emery 1988:160).

In another instance, Frederick Law Olmstead noted the dress worn by a group of enslaved women during his travels through South Carolina in the 1850s. He says that most of the women, working alongside men repairing a road, "had handkerchiefs, only, tied around their heads; some wore men's caps, or old slouched hats, and several were bare-headed" (1959:110). In Mississippi, Olmstead observes field workers which included many women who wore "handkerchiefs, turban-fashion" (177). Enslaved Virginians, he writes, "are well supplied with handkerchiefs which the men frequently, and the women nearly always, wear on their heads" (92).

One of Elizabeth Botume's first physical descriptions of the people who greeted her as her boat docked at Beaufort contains an itemization of the women's clothes: "Some of the women had on old, cast-off soldier's coats, with 'crocus bags,' fastened together with their own ravellings, for skirts, and bits of sailcloth for head-handkerchiefs" (32). And the unnamed Mississippi planter who wrote "Management of Negroes Upon Southern Estates" (1851) notes: "I give to my negroes four full suits of clothes with two pairs of shoes, every year, and to my women and girls a calico dress and two handkerchiefs extra" (624). The supposition that the women wore their "two handkerchiefs extra" as headwraps is supported by J. C. Furnas who reports that among "[t]he annual issue for 200 slaves on the Coffin plantation on St. Helena Island, South Carolina . . . 100 turban handkerchiefs" were distributed (94). Two women noted that whites gave them their headwraps:

Unidentified woman: *My mistress would buy a handkerchief and tie around my head* (18:110 [VA/TN]).

> Annie Stanton: *At Christmas times de oberseer, he gib de women a dress a piece, a head-handkerchief, an' de mens a hat, a knife, an' a bottle of whiskey* (S1. 1:378 [AL]).

Besides the head handkerchiefs given by plantation "masters" to their servants, cloth for headwraps might be procured in other ways. Kemble relates that she was constantly asked by enslaved women on her husband's plantation for pieces of flannel (222). This fabric could have been used for a number of purposes, one of which might have been as a head covering.

It is possible to cover the head with a scrap of fabric eighteen inches square, although two feet square is more adequate for the purpose. This size is hardly enough to make a garment for a small child; therefore, fabric pieces leftover from domestic clothing production would be considered suitable only as "rags." These scraps then might be given to enslaved women for use as head coverings. Since most cloth was produced domestically, and quite often by Black women, scraps of fabric could be procured directly from weavers (see Chapter 2).

> Charlie Hudson (b. 1858, 80 years): *What yo' wore on yo' haid was a cap made out of scraps of cloth dey wove in de loom right dar on our plantation to make pants for de grown folks* (12. 2:224 [GA]).

African Origin?

> Second principle: people get used to a certain kind of reality and come to expect it, and if what they perceive doesn't fit the set of statements everybody's agreed to, either the culture has to go through a kind of fit until it adjusts . . . or they just black it out . . . (Suzette Haden Elgin 1984:140).

A number of modern historians make casual allusions to African origins for the headwrap, but they do so without corroborating evidence. For example, Edward Kamau Brathwaite notes:

> I have seen girls in the markets of Port-au-Prince who are Yoruba or Dahomean market girls, except for the lack of tribal marks. The headties persist, some of the hairstyles persist . . . ("Cultural Diversity and Integration in the Caribbean", paper presented 1973:38–39, quoted in Mintz and Price, 101).

Eugene Genovese writes:

> A curious historical irony surrounds the use of headkerchiefs or bandannas. Carried into the twentieth century in the rural South, it became a mark of servility . . . of everything to be exorcized, so far as militant blacks were concerned . . .. Yet originally, nothing so clearly signified African origins and personal pride. The whites transformed it into a badge of servility (558) . . .. The custom of wearing those headkerchiefs originated in Africa and appeared most strongly in those areas of the New World in which African values retained their greatest strength (559).

Likewise, Randall Miller and John David Smith state:

> Slave women wore kerchiefs as standard head coverings throughout the year. Headkerchiefs appear wherever black women were held in bondage throughout North and South America, the brightly colored material covering women's hair revealing culture ties to West African tradition (1987:119).

Similarly, Bill McCarthy notes: "Black women favoured a turban or bandana. In New Orleans this took the form of a *tignon*, an elaborately folded madras square worn around the head, reminiscent of African women's head coverings" (1989:466). And Kobena Mercer mentions "head-wraps" as "elements of 'traditional' African dress" (39); Charles Joyner writes, ". . . the custom of wearing headkerchiefs in the slave community reflected continuity with African tradition . . ." (1984:113); and Shane White says, "West Indian Blacks, who were either African-born or had lived in a culture heavily influenced by African patterns, were often noted for their distinctive appearance . . . the feature that attracted particular comment was the use of a handkerchief as a head covering" (1989:32).

Curious to find out exactly which Africans brought the headwrap to the Americas, I began to research early accounts that described the dress of West Africans. The earliest European pictorial representations of Africans show men wearing a variety of head coverings, including turbans; by contrast, women are bareheaded and their hair is usually shown close-cropped and unadorned. On a voyage to Senegal in 1468, Alvise de Cadamosta reported of the people: "They wear nothing on their heads: the hair of both sexes is fashioned into neat tresses arranged in various styles, though their hair by nature is no longer than a span" (Gunther, ed., 1978:10). Osifekunde (Ijebu, present-day Nigeria) recounted in the 1810's: *"Headdress is highly variable. The common people go bareheaded, or at the most content themselves with the 'botiboti', a simple cap made in the country"* (Curtin, 1967:264).

On the other hand, written accounts describe women wearing a variety of hairdos and hair decorations. Mungo Park, writing in the 1790s, summed up the attire of a variety of people he met on his journeys in West Africa. While he found clothing itself to be rather uniform throughout the region, "This account of their clothing is indeed nearly applicable to the natives of all the different nations in this part of Africa," Park adds, "a peculiar national mode is observable only in the head-dresses of the women" (15). His notes on women's head ornamentation are specific and illustrate the obvious care with which women adorned their heads. Park's continuing remarks on the subject are noteworthy because they point up the fact that no single type of hair ornamentation was standard. His comments make it apparent that in Africa, as in many other nations, one of the ways by which people marked themselves was by styling their hair or wearing head decorations in a manner unique to their particular social group.

> Thus, in countries of the Gambia [on the West African coast, between the Senegal and Gambia Rivers] the females wear a sort of bandage, which they call *falla*. It is a narrow strip of cotton cloth, wrapped many times round, immediately over the forehead. In Bondou [an area in the far western Sudan, east of the Niger River; Fulani people?] the head is encircled with strings of white beads, and a small plate of gold is worn in the middle of the forehead. In Kasson, the ladies decorate their heads in a very tasteful manner, with white sea-shells. In Kaarta and Ludamar, the women raise their hair to a great height by the addition of a pad (as ladies did formerly in Great Britain), which they decorate with a species of coral, brought from the Red Sea by pilgrims returning from Mecca, and sold at a great price (ibid.).

To date, after reading several hundred accounts, and in spite of the aforementioned historians' contention that the headwrap as worn by Black women in America is an African item, I have located only one reference which offers certain proof that some West African women were wearing headwraps by the mid-seventeenth century. This evidence appears in Richard Ligon's account, published in 1657. Ligon set forth from England to seek his fortune in the West Indies in the 1640s. On his way, he stopped at Cape Verde on the coast of present-day Senegal before proceeding to Barbados (Abrahams and Szwed, 420). While at Cape Verde in 1647, Ligon describes in detail the clothing of one particular woman whom, he says, "wore on her head a roll of green taffatie, strip't with white and Philiamont, made up in manner of a Turban, and over that a sleight vayle, which she took off at pleasure" (1657:12).

I uncovered no references to West African headwraps for the half-century following Ligon's account from Cape Verde; but by the early eighteenth century, evidence come from a variety of sources and from several geographical locations. Mungo Park's mention of the *falla* worn by Gambian women in the 1790s – "a narrow strip of cotton cloth, wrapped many times round, immediately over the forehead" – must be another example of the West African headwrap. Nearly 100 years earlier, West African women already had brought the custom across the Atlantic to the Caribbean. In 1707, Danish artist, Dirk Valkenburg, painted a group of newly arrived enslaved people on the Dómbi Plantation in Suriname. Each of the females wears a headwrap high on the forehead and above the ears.[2]

While Valkenburg's painting seems to support the general assumption that the headwrap made its way to the United States via the West Indies, an advertisement in the *Charleston South-Carolina Gazette and Country Journal* (25 April 1769) demonstrates that West African women also brought the custom of wearing headwraps directly from Africa to the colonies which later became the United States:

> RUN-AWAY from my Plantation at Goose-Creek a NEW NEGRO WENCH, she had on when she went away a new oznaburg coat and wrapper, and a black striped silk handkerchief round her head . . . she is a middle sized wench, about 24 years of age, of the Guiney country, has her country marks on her face, and speaks no English . . . (Windley 1983:644).

As did their eighteenth-century ancestors, West African women today wear a variety of head gear; but just when headwraps, as an item of head covering, became commonplace is unknown. Furthermore, the paucity of early literary or visual sources does not allow much supposition as to the origins of the headwrap as a type of head covering. An Arabic influence is possible, but if this is the case, it derives from the male turban. Park explains the difference between the dress of Moorish men and that of non-Islamic African men:

> The men's dress among the Moors (ie., Black Muslims) of Ludamar differs but little from that of the Negroes . . . except that they all adopted that characteristic of the Mohammedan sect the *turban* . . . (117).

In the fourteenth century, Ibn Battuta had this to say about the Iwàlàtan, people living west of Timbuktu: "With regard to their women, they are not modest in the presence of men, they do not veil themselves in spite of their perseverance in the prayers" (Hamdun and King, 1994:37–38). As described by Park in the eighteenth century, however, female Moors had adopted the veil as part of their religious faith:

> The head-dress is commonly a bandage of cotton cloth, with some parts of it broader than others, which serve to conceal the face when they walk in the sun; frequently, however, when they go abroad, they veil themselves from head to foot (ibid.).

Katie Brown of Sapelo Island, Georgia, was a daughter of Belali Mohomet who was enslaved on the plantation of Thomas Spalding (*Drums and Shadows*, 1972:152). Belali was a muslim, born in Africa, but Brown said that her grandmother came from the Bahamas. From Brown's description, however, it appears that her grandmother adapted Islam, wearing a veil just as Park reported earlier of African Muslim women:

> *She ain tie uh head up lak I does, but she weah a loose wite clawt da she trow obuh uh head lak veil an it hang loose on uh shoulduh* (154–155).

Similar to Katie Brown's description of her grandmother, Ben Sullivan of St. Simon's compared the head covering of another Muslim woman with that worn by Israel, an enslaved African Muslim:

> *I membuh a ole uhman [woman] name Daphne. He didn tie he head up lak ole man Israel. He weah loose wite veil in he head. [Israel] He alluz tie he head up in a wite clawt . . .* (ibid., 171).

Perhaps the African woman's headwrap derives from the male Muslim turban, but evidence suggests that most Muslim women veiled themselves both in Africa and in the United States. If some African Muslim women did adopt the turban rather than the veil, this does not account for women of other religions who wear headwraps today but not as part of Islamic belief. Furthermore, Sieber writes: "Quite possibly this type of dress appeared along the west coast [of Africa] as a costume of prestige rather recently" (29). Sieber bases his reasoning on eighteenth- and nineteenth-century European travelers who report seeing Black males who wear Muslim attire as being primarily inlanders.

I also question authorities who, by stating that the headwrap originated in Africa, thereby imply that it was commonly worn at very early dates by enslaved West Africans in the Americas. Rather, all evidence which I have uncovered to date points to the headwrap not becoming popular in either West Africa or in the Americas until the eighteenth century, that is, until sometime after European contact. At least three hypotheses may be made for Europeans introducing the headwrap in West Africa:

First, the women taken in bondage during the slave trade may have been forced or induced to cover their heads as a gesture to mark them as subservient. We know that headwraps served such a purpose in the Southern United States where legal codes actually enforced these measures.[3]

Second, it is possible that enslaved African women were forced to wear headwraps as a way to prevent infestations of lice in the inadequate African slave-holding pens, and later, in ship holds during the trans-Atlantic voyage. We know that sometimes the Africans' heads were shaven, presumably for hygienic purposes. In any case, it was to the traders' advantage to keep the Africans as healthy as possible for their eventual sale in the Americas. Later, in the quarters of enslaved people in the Americas, where bathing facilities were virtually nonexistent, headwraps no doubt continued to aid in combatting the ever-present lice as well as other scalp diseases such as ringworm (Morrow, 22–23).

> S. B. Adams (b. 1858): *Sunday was 'bout de onles time de mothers could clean up de chillun an' pick de lice from dere heads, my dey was bad, sometimes de most et us up* (S2. 2. 1:6 [TX]).

Another unsupported hypothesis is that of John Thornton who advances the unlikely interpretation that European missionaries introduced the headwrap to meet the Christian requirement that the female head be covered during mass. But women covering their heads is Muslim doctrine as well. Furthermore, Gus Pearson (ca. 79 years) said of southern Christian women, "*At de camp meetings de wimmens pulled off de head rags . . .*" (2. 2:62 [SC]).

These premises on the origins of the headwrap each point to Europeans imposing this type of cloth covering on West African women; yet the literary and visual evidence establishes an African source. The problem, then, is to chart the rise in the popular usage of the headwrap. It seems to me that it begins on the West African coast, perhaps even at the staging centres where human beings were traded for cloth. Both historical and cultural indicators suggest that the headwrap begins as a syncretic element of West African women's clothing: a combination of West African worldview with European material goods.

A perfect example of this comes from "a report to the committee on behalf of the African Prisoners" which describes the people taken from the slave ship, *Amistad* (see Chapter 1). Three of the Africans were young girls, about 13 years old. The prisoners received Western-style clothing, and the writer notes: "The girls are in calico frocks, and *have made the little shawls that were given them into turbans*" (9 September 1839, reprinted in Middleton Harris, *The Black Book*, 1974:15; emphasis mine).

Figural sculpture demonstrates that all tropical African cultures held a heightened regard for embellishing the head before European contact. This is manifested as well by early travelers' descriptions of the West Africans' penchant for ornamenting the human head. In the earliest period of contact, however, woven cloth was still scarce for all but the most wealthy and powerful. Therefore, instead of using cloth, most West Africans decorated their heads by a variety of alternative means such as elaborate hairstyles embellished with beads, shells, metal, and feathers. The influx of available and inexpensive cloth, imported with the coming of the Europeans, permitted a natural adoption of cloth to meet these aesthetic needs and personal choices. In addition, by the last-half of the eighteenth century, ready-made, foreign headwraps were being imported into West Africa. "Kerchiefs" are listed as a trade item to Benin in European merchant ship inventories; a "Cholet kerchief" and a "Nîmes silk kerchief" are listed for a French vessel in the early 1770s; a Portuguese ship's document of the same period lists "4 kerchiefs" (Ryder, 208, 210).

I hypothesize, therefore, that the woman's headwrap comes into being sometime after the start of the European trade expansion in Africa. This is brought home by Werner Gillon's statement concerning the adoption of outside patterns by West African weavers: " [T]he advent of Islam and the Europeans inspired new designs and colours. This mingling produced the splendid garments and *headscarves* of the women" (237, 239; emphasis mine).

The West African Headwrap as European High Fashion

> [W]e have to follow the things, themselves, for their meanings are inscribed in their forms, their uses, their trajectories (Arjun Appadurai 1986:5).

In the late eighteenth century, many travelers to the Near East brought back to Europe descriptions of the newly met peoples and their customs. Their accounts, which often stressed the exotic nature of these distant peoples, caught the European imagination. Napoleon's adventures into

North Africa (Egypt, 1798–1799) and the Near East (Syria, 1799) aided in propelling the European public's fancy which translated Napoleonic material objects into fashion statements. Thus, French women wore male military dress until an 1800 French law forbade them to wear the tricolour *concorde* hat. Napoleon's endeavors in North Africa and the Near East also propelled other types of objects to become fashionable and, quite rapidly, "things oriental" became a rage. This period of "orientalizing" included exotic forms of dress, particularly among fashionable French women who, in the late eighteenth century, sported their versions of a turban.[4] In France, the style was known as the "Directoire" period, reaching its height between 1795 and 1799.[5]

Aileen Ribeiro and Valerie Cumming, who analyze contemporary paintings and portraits for their fashion statements, note "a typical combination of the classical and oriental" in the attire and hairdo of an Italian woman's portrait of 1797 (161). Douglas Gorsline illustrates two types of turbans worn by fashionable European and white American women between 1800 and 1810(135). R. Turner Wilcox says that the fashion, known as the "French Consolate and Empire" styles, continued into the period between 1810 and 1815:

> Turbans were very popular, especially for evening, and were fashioned of brocaded, embroidered and spangled fabrics, moiré, satin, velvet, silvered gauze, fringed crêpe and knotted silk scarfs. Draped 'desert turbans' were open in back with curls tumbling out (1945:200).

Closer to home, and perhaps most fascinating for Americans, Dolly Madison wears a "fringed turban" in an 1812 portrait (illustrated in McClellan, n. p. n.). Slightly later, in the 1820s, Frances Trollope remarked on the white American infatuation with French fashions.

> If it were not for the peculiar manner of walking, which distinguishes all American women, Broadway might be taken for a French street, where it was the fashion for very smart ladies to promenade. The dress is entirely French; not an article (except perhaps the cotton stockings) must be English, on pain of being stigmatized out of fashion (310).

Caroline Howard Gilman described her American mother's costume for a ball in the early part of the last century: "I scarcely knew my dear, quiet, comfortable mother in the plume-coloured satin dress, exalted turban, and waving feathers, with which she was arrayed" (1834:134).

During the same period, African Americans also wore versions of the "turban." Samuel Jennings' oil painting of 1792, *Liberty Displaying the Arts and Sciences*, is an early allegorical work showing American Blacks. In the painting, Jennings portrays several African American women, all but one of whom wear a headwrap. A well-known, late eighteenth-century watercolour by an unidentified artist illustrates enslaved people dancing on an unknown plantation, probably in South Carolina. In the painting, African Americans of both sexes are either bareheaded or wear headwraps, and one man wears a hat.[6]

I believe, however, that it is more significant that among the earliest written and pictorial images of African women wearing a headwrap/turban in the Americas, many come from the French colonies. For example, Ligon's comments are about a woman at Cape Verde and Park's description is about women along the Gambia River; both are located in modern-day Senegal, which was a French colony. And, between 1770 and 1780, Agostino Brunias made several engraved variations based on his painting of a group of African Americans on Dominica, a French colony at the time. In one engraving, *Scene with Dancing in the West Indies*, several men wear hats and, again, members of both sexes are either bareheaded or wear headwraps. Centred prominently among the dancers is a tall, white female dancer, her head beturbaned; in the original painting, however, this figure is a Black woman.[7]

French women knew of the West African headwrap from written descriptions and from pictorial illustrations; but more important, they actually saw the headwrap being worn by African women brought to Europe. A fine example is Marie-Guilhelmine Benoist's *Portrait d'une négresse*. The portrait bust, painted and exhibited at the Paris Salon in 1800, is of an extraordinarily beautiful Black woman, her right breast bared, her hair surmounted by an intricately folded white cloth tied at the side of her head, the falling ends gently framing the left side of her face.[8] Some scholars believe the sitter was a servant, brought to France from the Antilles (Honour, 1989b:7–8). It is interesting that the painter, Benoist, was a woman.

Edouard Manet's *Olympia*, 1863, is arguably the most well-known European painting of an African woman in headwrap. Manet's work, however, contrasts starkly with Benoist's. In the Manet painting, the Black woman is fully clothed, while the 16-year-old white prostitute whom she serves is completely nude. Manet did a slightly earlier portrait sketch of the Black woman, *The Negress*, 1862–1863, in a differently styled headwrap. Her name was Laura, but nothing else is known of her at present (Reff, 93–94).[9]

Clearly, there is a connection between West African women's headwraps and French women's high fashion in the latter eighteenth century. Anna Atkins Simkins (1982) suggests the possibility that "the African significance accorded to headgear may have been augmented by exposure to the penchant for elaborate headdress which marked European costume from the Renaissance on through the latter part of the eighteenth century" (1985:30). Simpkins goes on to imply a counterpart to the African tradition of naming headwrap designs to the French fashion of transforming current affairs and events into symbolic hairstyles and headdresses (ibid.). While doing my own research, I recognized, as does Simpkins, a connection between late eighteenth-century French fashion and the elaborate headwraps worn by African women in French colonies of the time. This led me to the somewhat hasty conclusion that West African women had adopted the headwrap from French women. Once I read Ligon's 1647 journal entry, however, my hypothesis no longer held since the woman Ligon described wore a headwrap 150 years before the French female fashion for them.

We now need to rethink the route of exchange that placed turbans on the heads of French women in the late eighteenth century. It is possible that French women adopted this particular type of head covering either from North-African or East-Indian Muslim male dress. But in view of Ligon's first-hand account, I submit that it is more probable that French women actually adopted the style from West African women. Copying the French, other European and American women took up the fashionable trend. It appears that the white women wanted to wear the clothes of Black African women, just as the enslaved often remarked on their own desire to wear the fashions which whites wore. In both instances, the psychological impetus seems to have been the urge to wear articles of dress that were uncommon because they belonged to the other.

Functions

In order to examine the functions of African American women's headwraps specifically, we first need to focus more generally on the headgear worn by European and American white women in the nineteenth century. Women's hair coverings have had various functions over broad historical periods and places. They have been used as signifiers denoting religious beliefs and age, sex, marital, gender, and class status.

One aspect of acculturation for African women in America was customs associated with proper attire, including hair ornamentation and covering. According to the *Narratives*, Black women apparently took their cues from white women, just as white American women through the last century emulated their European counterparts by covering their hair for most public functions, as well as in the home. The *Narratives* demonstrate that enslaved women wore types of head coverings – from simple straw hats to the contemporary fashionable bonnets and mop caps (e.g., Phillis Wheatley frontispiece, 1773) – that were similar to those worn by white women. At certain events, however, neither white nor Black women were expected to cover their heads. The primary example being dances, where pictorial evidence shows both groups of women with only flowers adorning their hair.[10] On the other hand, an antebellum illustration portrays a dancing woman wearing a headwrap (Figure 28).

Dressing up for other occasions might also mean uncovering the hair. For example, Elsie Clews Parsons wrote that South Carolina Sea Islands' "[w]omen, old and young, quite commonly wear kerchiefs around the head and tied at the back" and the hair was wrapped in strings under the headwrap. Parsons significantly added that "often it will not be combed out until a person is 'going somewhere'" (ibid.). Similarly, Sylvia Boone's description of Mende women in modern Sierra Leone shows the headwrap may also serve to protect a well-groomed head of hair until it is time to expose it.

> Men find hair sexually seductive, and well-braided hair pleasing and attractive . . .. [A] woman always goes to a man's room with her hair neat; and if she wants to make a special impression, she will sport a new and elegant style well done. Since the woman would have left her quarters with her head under wraps so that other will not see her hair, the man will have the flattering feeling that she went through so much time and trouble to fashion herself for his eyes alone. Even in the *mawé* compound, when a wife has to walk only a few yards to her husband, she will follow the rituals of 'going to a man's room' and arrive in a head tie covering her coiffure (189).

Thus, when nineteenth-century enslaved African American women wore hats or bonnets or left their hair uncovered, they were not only conforming to normative customs prevalent for all Western women of the period, but to a West African aesthetic as well. What distinguished the Black woman, of course, was that at certain times she, alone, donned a headwrap. Although this form of hair covering came to be specifically associated with

Figure 28. Enslaved people dancing, or, "The Breakdown." *Harper's Weekly*, 13 April 1861:232–233.

African American women, no clear-cut, single reason accounts for this long-standing item in their dress.

Southern dress codes indicate that the headwrap at times served as a badge of servitude and as a way to differentiate the Black female from her white counterpart. In his 1890s reminiscences of plantation life, Alcée Fortier noted that on New Year's Day, the enslaved received "gifts" from the whites. The gifts included food and clothing which for the women meant "a dress and a most gaudy headkerchief or *tignon*, the redder the better" (1894:126, quoted in Jordan and de Caro, 1996:43). This and other instances suggests that by providing enslaved women with headwraps, whites purposely kept them supplied with items of dress associated with servants' uniforms.

On the other hand, the *Narratives* provide ample proof that Black women also wore hats and bonnets during the time of slavery, thus indicating the flexibility of the dress codes and suggesting that from the African American perspective, the headwrap served other purposes than merely as a white-enforced dress code denoting servitude.

The type of labor expected of enslaved women offers an explanation for the necessity of wearing the more easily acquired and simpler headwrap as a hair covering.

> Ebenezer Brown (80 years): *[My mammy] wrap her hair, and tie it up in a cloth. My mammy cud tote a bucket uf water on her head and niver spill er drap. I seed her bring dat milk in great big buckets frum de pen on her head an' niver lose one drop* (S1. 6. 1:249 [MS]).

Men also transported loads by balancing them on their heads, but they do not mention wearing a head cloth for this purpose.

> William Grimes (b. 1784, enslaved in Virginia and Georgia): *I sometimes went to town in order to procure something to eat with our common allowance, (a peck of corn a week) and have often carried on my head a bundle of wood, perhaps three miles weighing more than a hundred pounds* (reprinted in Bontemps, 93).

> Larence Holt (b. 1858): *My big brother he tote so many buckets of water to de hands in de field he wore all de hair offen de top he head* (4. 2:151 [TX]).

The descriptions given by Brown, Grimes, and Holt explain one reason why women might find the headwrap a necessity: a thick headwrap offered the protection Holt's brother did not take.[11]

The headwrap functioned to absorb perspiration in the same way that a bandana tied around the neck serves the same purpose. Headwraps also protect woman's hair from grime. In contemporary Europe, for example, peasant women continue to wear a piece of fabric to protect their hair while doing agricultural tasks. Similarly, testimony documents the lack of proper bathing facilities available to the enslaved African Americans as well as the lack of time necessary to keep themselves properly groomed and clean. By the same token, the headwrap kept the frequent infestations of lice and other scalp diseases in check and under cover. So prevalent were lice that they gave their name to a type of hand-woven cloth – "nits and lice" – because it resembled the ever-present pests.

> Clara Walker (111 years): *Den I weaves nits and lice. Wat's dat – well you see it was kind corse cloth de used for clothes like overalls. It was sort of speckeldy all over – dat's why dey called it nits and lice* (11. 7:22 [AR]).

> William Green (enslaved in Maryland): *for the winter they had one bare suit made of raw kersey apiece. This kersey is made of black and white wool, carded together and wove with cotton warp, which makes a kind of black and white, which we call nits and lice* (1853:7).

Depending on the function, the headwrap worn during the period of slavery could be a simple rag or bandana or handkerchief; or, it could be quite elaborate, made from 8 to 10 yards of fabric. Field workers wore simple rags to ward off the sun and to keep the hair more clean, and servants used headwraps for protection when carrying loads on their heads. Headwraps also represented status *within* the communities of Blacks; descriptions of house servants usually portray headwraps as part of the domestics' uniforms.

> Mary Graham (enslaved in Louisiana): *sides, fine folks dress up de waiter-gals in black dress an' white apern, wid a white kerchief on de haid* (Armstrong, 111).

Louis Hughes (b. 1843, enslaved in Mississippi and Virginia) noted: "*The cotton clothes worn by both men and women [house servants], and the turbans of the latter, were snowy white*" (43). After the family moved to the city, Hughes recalled, "*Each of the women servants wore a new, gay coloured turban, which was tied in differently from that of the ordinary servant, in some fancy knot*" (42) (Figure 17).

The headwrap served in another purely expedient capacity as an article of clothing which could be used to quickly cover the hair when there was not adequate time to compose it. Gloria Goode advances this argument in her recent dissertation on nineteenth-century African American women ministers wherein she includes a section on the costumes adopted by these women, all of whom were "free." Commenting on a biographical portrait of Hannah Tranks Carson (1864), Goode notes that Carson is shown "in a stereotypical manner in homely dress." Goode continues: "Obviously . . . if she [Carson] had possessed the strength, she would have discarded the head kerchief for a bonnet." Goode then presents her rationale for this argument: "The kerchief is an adaptation of the black woman's manner of dealing with her 'unpresentable' hair. It is tied in a traditional style covering the forehead" (388).

The headwrap as a conveniently serviceable item used to cover "unpresentable hair" or as merely a way to protect rural women's hair from grime, is advanced in the *Narratives* and other sources where a number of the interviews begin with the interviewer's own narrative "pictures" of the interviewees. These glosses provide evidence that in the 1930s some white Southerners still associated the headwrap as the most obvious piece of clothing by which to stereotype Southern Black women. Although the following depictions aid in assessing the iconography which American whites applied to African American women, they are of equal importance because they show that seventy years after emancipation, older, Southern Black women continued to wear some form of hair ornament or covering similar to that worn by women during the period of enslavement – and that the headwrap remained the most common form.

> Fashions come and go, but Sibby [Kelly] never changed from the old-fashioned method of tying up her head. A piece of white cloth folded smoothly above the forehead and tied in the back with the ends hanging down on the back of the neck was the proper method and she stuck to it (Cate, *Early Days*, 195, photograph on facing page).

> Her white hair was combed back off her fore-head, and held in place by side combs (11. 7. 8:27 [MO]).

> Ann Hawthorne's (b. 1851 or 1853) hair snow white [is] fixed in little pig tails and wrapped in black string (4. 2:118 [TX]).

> Mrs. Harriet Benton . . . is as one imagines an ex-slave woman to look. Her skin is dark, she wears a white cap upon her head . . . (S1. 3. 1:50 [GA]).

> 'Aunt Fannie Hughes' was seated on the narrow front porch with two small piccaninnies playing at her feet when we made our visit. Her tall, gaunt figure

was clothed in a neat plaid cotton dress . . .. On her head was a cloth sugar sack (S1. 3. 1:329 [GA]).

Alice [Green, 76 years] . . . wore a soiled print dress, and dingy stocking cap partly concealed her white hair (12. 2:39 [GA]).

Martha Everetts . . . was seated on the front porch of her son's home . . .. Her grizzled hair was covered by a white towel (S1. 3. 1:236 [GA]).

Tennis shoes, worn without hose, and a man's black hat completed her outfit [Rachel Adams, 78 years] (12. 1:2 [GA]).

The interviewer paraphrased Callie Bracey's description of her mother Louise Turrell: "Louise . . . never had a hat, always wore a rag tied over her head" (6. 2:26 [MS/IN]).

Seemingly the only real wid awake person on the place was Aunt Jemima, the housekeeper . . . brown of complexion, with her kinky hair entirely hidden by a bright bandana, she was truly a picture (S1. 3. 1:339 [GA]).

Hanna Fambro, a checked gingham turban wound about her head . . . presents the delightful picture of a real southern mammy (S1. 5. 2:332 [GA/OH]).

A white cloth, tied turban fashion about her [Georgia Baker, 87 years] head . . . completed her costume (12. 1:38 [GA]).

'Aunt Nicey' had on a blue dress, with a white head rag . . .. (S1. 1:297 [AL]).

Her [Chaney Moore Williams, b. ca. 1852, d. 1937] hair was grey and worn in small twists, her head was tied in a large 'head rag' (S1. 10. 5:2304 [MS]).

Her [Callie Elder, 78 years] crudely fashioned blue dress was of a coarse cotton fabric and her dingy head rag had long lost its original colour (12. 1:306 [GA]).

Camilla Jackson wears a white rag around her head and is always spotlessly clean (12. 2:295 [GA]).

Harriet Walker, [b. ca. 1852] . . . is about eighty-five years of age, and is a typical 'black mammy' type . . .. She wears a large cloth tied neatly and snugly around her head, which is called a "head rag" by the negroes (S1. 10. 5:2157 [MS]).

A large checkered apron almost covered her [Lulu Battle]dress and a clean white head cloth concealed her hair (12. 1:61 [GA]).

> Her [Julia Bunch, 85 years] head closely wrapped in a dark bandana, from which the gray hair peeped at intervals forming a frame for her face (12. 1:155 [GA]).

On a historical note, one Union officer wrote of Harriet Tubman's invaluable service "as a spy and scout . . .. Dressed as a freedwoman, with a *bandana on her head*, this short plain woman could travel anywhere in Rebel territory without arousing suspicion" (quoted in Sterling, 259; emphasis mine).[12]

And yet, one interviewer from Georgia added a note of ambiguity to the stereotype with this statement:

> In spite of what tradition and story claim, few of the older negroes of this district wear head clothes. Most often they wear their wooly hair "wropped" with string. The women often wear men's slouch hats (13. 4:352 [GA]).

In the American South, under specific conditions, headwraps also were worn as signifying additions to religious ceremonies. A New Orleans journalist reported on a "voodoo rite" that he witnessed in 1828: "Some sixty people were assembled, each wearing a white bandana carefully knotted around the head . . ." (Crété, 172). At a given moment in the ceremony, one of the women "tore the white handkerchief from her forehead. This was a signal, for the whole assembly sprang forward and entered the dance" (173).

Headwraps were included as one of the several special head coverings worn for Christian religious events.

> The interviewer paraphrased Edward Lycurgas: "Lycurgas recalls . . . the river baptisms! These climaxed the meetings . . .. All candidates were dressed in white gowns, stockings and towels would be about their heads bandana fashion" (17. 1:209 [FL]).

John Dixon Long (1857) remarked on a prayer-meeting held by enslaved people in Maryland.

> At a given signal of the leader, the men will take off their jackets, hang up their hats, and tie up their heads in handkerchiefs; the women will tighten their turbans, and the company will them form a circle around the singer, and jump and bawl to their heart's content . . . (Long, *Pictures of Slavery in Church and State . . .*, 383, quoted in Epstein, 1963:387).

Women might also wear headwraps for Sunday worship. Louis Hughes (b. 1832, enslaved in Mississippi and Virginia) remembered: "*once when*

Boss went to Memphis and brought back a bolt of gingham for turbans for the female slaves. It was a red and yellow check, and the turbans made from it were only to be worn on Sundays" (42). Fanny Kemble's description of the "grotesque" Sunday costume of the "poor" enslaved people on her husband's Georgia plantation included: "head handkerchiefs, that put one's very eyes out from a mile off . . ."(1863:93). But in certain areas, the custom of wearing a headwrap for the religious camp meetings apparently denoted the age of the women.

> Gus Pearson (ca. 97 years): *[De gals] took dey hair down out'n de strings fer de [camp] meeting. In dem days all de darky wimmens wore dey hair in string 'cep' when dey 'tended church or a wedding. At de camp meetings de wimmens pulled off de head rags, 'cept de mammies. On dis occasion de mammies wore linen head rags fresh laundered* (2. 2:62 [SC]).

In exploring functions, one final painting needs to be examined. The painting was done in New Orleans, a former French colony, which adds another bit of evidence for a French connection. Adolph Rinck painted a portrait whose subject some scholars believe to be Marie Laveau, the famous *voudon* priestess of New Orleans.[13] The painting serves as an example of another significant function which the headwrap served for African American women. The portrait dates from 1844 during the time when the New Orleans dress code legally required African American women (whether enslaved or "free") to wear some form of headwrap, but the subject of the painting took advantage of this supposed badge of degradation and transformed it into something else.

The portrait illustrates a woman who most certainly was quite aware of how to style her "tignon" away from her face and high up on her head so as to appear absolutely glorious. Marie Laveau's portrait shows that some African American women played with the white "code" and, by flaunting the headwrap, converted it from something which might be construed as shameful into something uniquely their own. That is, they developed an anti-style. If other Black women wore the headwrap with less self-conscious concern for fashion than did Laveau, and with more concern for its utilitarian functions, nevertheless, they continued to wear it in particularly innovative ways and always tied up and away from the face.

Roger Abrahams points out that in images portraying dancing African American women wearing a headwrap "the focus on the immbolized and statuesque head as amplified at least by the turban . . . strongly references the head as the source of display of order and respect-making."[14] This seems to be as true for the central dancer in the previously cited painting by Agostino Brunias (1770–1780) as it is for later images of Black women doing the cakewalk and the chalk line dance. As with the pronounced accent on the head of female dancers, the headwrap worn by Marie Laveau in her portrait appears to serve the same function. In all cases, the headwrap demanded respect for the head, and thus, for the person wearing it.

In his provocative article, Kobena Mercer, an African American, asks a pointed question: "Why do we pour so much creative energy into our hair?" (38). His answers concerning hairstyles also aid in answering questions about the exclusive use of headwraps by African American women. For instance, concerning Black American hairstyles, Mercer contends that neither Afros nor dreadlocks

> . . . were [ever] just natural, waiting to be found: they were stylistically *cultivated* and politically *structured* in a particular historical moment as part of a strategic contestation of white dominance and the cultural power of whiteness (40) . . . for "style" to be socially intelligible as an expression of conflicting values, each cultural nucleus or articulation of signs must share access to a common stock or resource of signifying elements (42).

The ornate headwrap appears to be West African and, in the way that it is worn, it relates to the ordinary, practical, Southern U.S. head rag. At its most elaborate, the African American woman's headwrap functioned as a "uniform of rebellion" that encoded resistance, but as a head rag worn by millions of enslaved women and their descendants, it also functioned as a uniform of communal identity.[15] The headwrap, therefore, acquired a paradox of simile: to the white overlords it was a badge of enslavement, but to the enslaved it was a helmet of courage that evoked an image of true homeland.

Continuity: Mammy in the Twentieth Century

> [T]here is no creation without tradition; the "new" is always a variation on a preceding form; novelty is always a variation on the past (Carlos Fuentes 1988:101).

At about the same time that the *Narratives* were being collected, William Faulkner sympathetically "pictured" one of the strongest personages in American fiction. Faulkner implants the African American, Dilsey, as the center, the true mother, in the household of the dysfunctional, white Compson family (*The Sound and the Fury*, 1929). By example, Dilsey has much to teach, and in two brief passages we learn from her the significance of specific types of head coverings; more especially, the scenes relate how various modes of African American dress continued to be gendered by sex and by age.

Dilsey is first viewed as she leaves her own house to go to the Compson's to prepare Sunday breakfast. Earlier she wore different clothes, but has changed because it is raining. Now, "Dilsey wore a stiff black straw hat perched upon her turban" (306). In the following passage, Dilsey has returned to her own home and changed her clothes for church: ". . . Dilsey emerged, again in the maroon cape and the purple gown, and wearing solid white elbow-length gloves and minus her head cloth now" (332). Accompanying her to church are her adolescent son, Luster, and her older daughter, Frony: "Luster returned, wearing a stiff new straw hat with a coloured band . . ." (333); Frony wears a dress of bright blue silk and a flowered hat (335). That Dilsey's conservative views about proper clothing are being displaced by a younger generation is made clear as Dilsey berates both of her children for their attire. She feels Luster should wear his simple "old hat" and not the dandy new straw one. And, concerning her daughter's expensive, new silk dress, Dilsey remarks, "You got six weeks' work right dar on yo back" (ibid.).

"Dilsey" is one of the best known, white literary conceptions of the Black "mammy," but the most circulated image of the "mammy," complete with headwrap, is the Quaker Oats Company's "Aunt Jemima."[16] Marilyn Kern-Foxworth documents the history behind the logo and the actual African American women who, beginning in 1893, served as its models. Kern-Foxworth notes that the inspiration for the advertising campaign came from a male, Black-face vaudeville team who "dressed in aprons and red bandanas" and were "reminiscent of traditional Southern cooks" (1989:18). Interestingly, when Edith Wilson, one of the better-known blues performers during the classic blues age, retired from the stage in the late 1940s, she "toured the United States raising funds for charities with Quaker Oat's 'Aunt Jemima' Pancakes" (Harrison, 1990:93). As described by Daphne Duval Harrison, Wilson did not see her portrayal to be "what some perceived as a negative 'mammy' stereotype . . .. She happily donned her bandana, white blouse, big checkered skirt and apron, and sang and flipped pancakes from coast-to-coast, raising upwards of three million dollars."

The "turbanned" female cook continued as a stereotype throughout the second-half of the last century (Figure 29).[17] The imaging comes not only from white stereotypes of the period. In his 1899 story, "The Sheriff's Wife," Charles W. Chesnutt gave a similar description of the cook in a white household; writing, "A turbaned coloured woman came to the door" (3).

I now trace the image of another character in American literature and the image of the actress who brought that character to stage and screen. The character, Berenice Sadie Brown, served much the same purpose as had Dilsey in the Compson household. Berenice offered stability for the two

Figure 29. The Cook in Turban. Illustration from David Hunter Strother, *Virginia Illustrated*, [1857]1871:236.

white children, Frankie and John Henry, in Carson *McCullers' The Member of the Wedding* (1946). Unlike Dilsey who wears a "turban" when she is at work in a white family's home, McCullers explicitly describes Berenice's hair as uncovered as she cooks for the white family. For example: "Her hair was parted, plaited and greased close to the skull" (3); ". . . the eleven greased plaits . . . fitted her head like a skull-cap . . ."(79). In spite of the specificity of McCullers' written descriptions, when Ethel Waters acted the role of Berenice in the 1950 Broadway adaptation of the novel and in the 1955 film version, her costume included a headwrap. This image compares to several images of a younger Waters during the early years of her career as singer and actress. While these images may be interpreted as racist and as white-directed, in the 1970s, when the older Waters performed for the Billy Graham Crusades, she often wore a headwrap. The headwrap at this time was certainly Waters' choice.

But lest we be persuaded that only white American authors, such as Faulkner, describe African American females with and without headwraps, some Black male authors have done the same (e.g., Charles W. Chesnutt, Ernest J. Gaines, and Sylvester Leaks). Furthermore, African American women writers sometimes portray their female characters wearing headwraps. A few noteworthy examples include: Zora Neale Hurston, *Their Eyes Were Watching God* ([1937] 1978:26, 87); Ann Petry, *The Street* ([1946] 1979:5 passim); Paule Marshall, *The Chosen Place, the Timeless People* ([1969] 1984:25–26, 135, 367–268); Sherley Anne Williams, *Dessa Rose* (1976:200, 258); and Alice Walker, *The Color Purple* (1982:21). And, in her autobiography, *Report From Part One* (1972), Gwendolyn Brooks not only includes the line ". . . the [Kenyan] women's hair and headdresses try to rebel – try *not* to 'abandon the hut'" (89), but she chooses for the author's photograph which boldly graces the outside of the dust jacket, an image of herself wherein her hair is covered by a simply-tied bandana. Finally, a full-page advertisement for the opening of a new Barnes and Noble bookstore in 1993 featured a portrait of Maya Angelou, her head crowned by an enormous African-inspired headwrap. For each of these women writers, the headwrap acts as an artistic devise towards character definition, but each writer uses the headwrap's symbolic potency for diverse meanings.

One of the items of slang recorded by Zora Neale Hurston in Harlem strongly suggests that by the early 1940s, the headwrap was already considered by some urban Blacks in the Northeast to be a symbol of servitude. Hurston notes that the term "handkerchief head" denoted a "sycophant Negro; also an *Uncle Tom*" (1942:95). In the South, rural women clung to the tradition longer. John Roberts, for instance, remarked that Black women commonly wore headwraps in South Carolina through the 1950s, but that they discarded it in the following decade.[18]

The 1960s was a period of intense communal-analysis by all African Americans. By then, the headwrap, evoking as it so often did the stereotypical "mammy" image of servitude to whites, represented one outward symbol that needed to be eliminated. But, even though older women had discarded the headwrap for public wear by the 1960s, towards the latter part of that decade, younger, urban African American women began wearing it outside the home. Today, Black women of all ages and from all regions wear it; and, like the writers mentioned above, these women invest the headwrap with diverse meanings.

Similar to Waters' later use of headwraps are the present-day African American women who purposely choose to enhance their public images by wearing them. Recent examples include publicity photographs of opera star Leontyne Price, gospel singer Marion Williams, and Jamaican reggae performer Judy Mowatt. Actress Ruby Dee and modern-dance choreographer Katherine Dunham wear headwraps in Brian Lanker's *I Dream a World: Portraits of Black Women Who Changed America*, 1989 (photos pp. 111 and 29). A difference between Waters' headwrap and those worn by contemporary women is that today's headwrap commonly carries "African" patterns and colours.

Public performers, however, are not the only African American women who wear some form of the headwrap today. For instance, in February 1992, the Uhuru Solidarity Center of Philadelphia advertised open community meetings by posting photocopies of Kentake Nzapa being harassed by Delaware police (Figure 30). Ms. Nzapa, a "black community leader" is wearing a modified headwrap reminiscent of those worn by women dubbed as "Black Radical," "Black is Beautiful," and "Black Militant" people during the late 1960s and 1970s. During that period a renewed concern with Africa as the motherland brought on a rash of hairstyles and clothing adopted by African Americans from what they understood to be historically authentic African clothing. That is, "Africa" was perceived as a static, transcendent foundation against which the displacement of American slavery and its aftermath could be based. During the 1960s, young Black women quite consciously began wearing headwraps as an expression of their historical link to Africa. By the 1980s and extending to the present, many more Black women have adopted headwraps for everyday as well

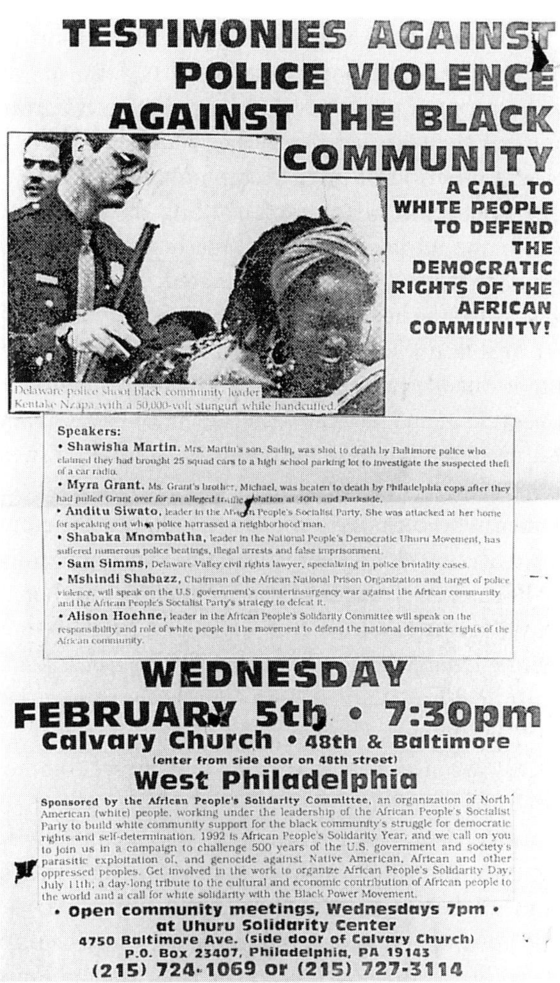

Figure 30. Kentake Nzape wears a modified headwrap. Philadelphia street poster, 1992. Collection of the author.

as for more formal or celebratory occasions. The headwrap as currently worn is not an historic retention, but one reintroduced or re-adopted. In some cases, it has become commercialized.[19]

Today, this item of dress signifies multiple meanings for Blacks as well as whites. Lest we assume that the mammy-with-headwrap stereotype is a thing of the past for all Americans, while in Louisiana in 1991, I purchased a pot holder imprinted with a turbaned "mammy" (Figure 31). Other items for sale included salt and pepper shakers, ashtrays, and numerous dolls representing bandana-wrapped Black women. Clearly this iconography explicitly reflects white racism, yet no single interpretation of the headwrap as worn by Black women in twentieth-century America is possible.

Further convoluting our usual notion of the headwrap as an item of attire worn by African American women is the recent adoption of the headwrap by men. In 1992, a publicity photo for the "Bluegrass, Blues and Bembe" concert in Columbus, Georgia, featured the head of African American, Eddie Kirkland, wrapped in a bandana, knotted at the front, and completely covering his hair. The more interesting phenomenon, however, concerns the head coverings worn by white males which replicate those formerly worn by enslaved Black women. We note, for instance, that some preppy, white fraternity males currently wear bandana headwraps, as do white male "Dead Heads"and country singer Willie Nelson. If there is an ambivalence to questions concerning survival and revival on the part of Black Americans, this ambivalence appears to be even more pronounced for white Americans.

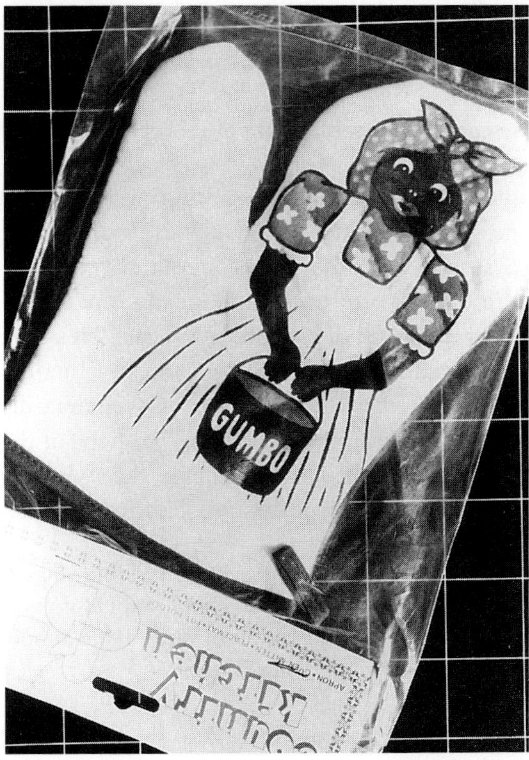

Figure 31. Pot holder bought in Louisiana, 1991. Collection of the author.

Figure 32. Cassandra Stancil, Philadelphia, 1992. Photograph by the author.

Interlude: An African American Woman's Voice, 1992

[A]ny kind of research has to start with the present (Linda Dégh [1962] 1988:49).

Cassandra Stancil was born in 1954, and grew up in Virginia Beach, Virginia. The most visible feature of Cassandra's dress is her headwrap which, as she says, she wears "more days out of the week than not" (Figure 32).[20] Cassandra uses two terms for the headwrap: if she purchases a finished scarf to wrap her head, she calls it a "scarf;" if she wraps with an unfinished cloth, she calls this a "rag." She notes: "Usually when people are talking to me about it, they call it a 'wrap.'" Cassandra calls the different ways she wears the headwrap "variations." The shape of the cloth is one determining factor for how she wears it; that is, the style of wrap depends on whether the fabric is "oblong or square." Fabric size is the other factor:

> It varies – you could just use a big bandana to get a look, you know, if you just want something like a headband around your head. Or, if you really want to wrap and have fun with it, at least a couple of yards. If it is a short oblong piece, say about a yard long, that is more limiting.

From her other remarks, I deduce three cultural influences that converge in Cassandra's choice of head covering. First, Cassandra consciously adopted the headwrap to mark her place as a modern African American and in recognition of Black women who wore it in the past; here, the influence is African American. Second, as Cassandra explained her rationale for not wearing the headwrap in certain situations, the influence is "American" and, again, conscious. Third, as she talked about how she styles her headwrap, it became evident that this is the African influence, but Cassandra is completely unaware of this. In the following, Cassandra voices these conscious and unconscious values.

First, the African American cultural values. The headwrap represents the most overt and visible material manifestation of Cassandra's decision to mark herself as an African American. Even as confrontations with other Black women have occurred concerning her headwrap, Cassandra maintains her own personal sense of self as she wears the headwrap no matter what negative connotations others may see in it.

> I remember my mother wrapping her head every night and when I'd come to her in the morning she had it wrapped. And when she's out in the yard, her hair is wrapped. But once she leaves the confines of that yard, the wrap's off.
>
> My mother is of a different generation and to her way of thinking to wear a headwrap is a kind of signal. She'll wear it in her house, not in public. It's not proper, more of a household thing. For her, it's not so formal, it would just be a rag tied around the head. Not respectable, not proper to go in the public eyes.[21]
>
> I've never cared about what people thought. And there are still fights today – my mother and I – about how I dress – not just about how I wrap my head – how I dress.
>
> For some women today, it's seems – let's begin with where I come from – *hats* on the *head* are the *thing* if you want to consider yourself *dressed*. And I've seen some older women wearing fancy headwraps on occasions where they generally in the past might have worn a hat – to church, to social functions.
>
> This is getting personal here – but one of the reasons – early on, and this is going way back in my history, say in the [early] 70s when I was wearing [headwraps], like college and high school – and I remember friends commenting to me, 'You look like Aunt Jemima' – and I guess that is what my mother might have had in mind, that that was what she thought other people were seeing, and she took that as a critique that she really did not want aimed at her, so that she did not wear them in public. Again, I never cared, number one, about how other people perceived it and number two, I never thought it was necessary to distance myself from Aunt Jemima. *I* never considered her to be a negative person, it's just a stereotype that she represents is [*sic*] negative, so I don't have that problem.
>
> It's more of a reclaiming of my Southern heritage, it's not necessarily going back to Africa. It's more valorizing the Southern women that I *know* and still know who did this. It's like putting myself in the same boat with them which I don't have a problem with.

Cassandra wore a headwrap "on and off" from the early 1970s until 1989, when she entered the University of Pennsylvania and decided to wear it anywhere, on any occasion, and most of the time. Earlier, she wore it depending on her jobs or on the particular circumstances. She mentioned that when she had a government job, a different sort of attire was expected. Here Cassandra acknowledges the second set of cultural standards which informed her decisions as to the appropriateness of wearing or not wearing the headwrap. These standards are "American", and perhaps ultimately derive from a different and Euro-centric system for coding dress.

> It's according to the kind of interactions. [Entering Penn] was the time I felt most free. Not confined by my work situation or the people that I would be encountering in the work situation.
>
> Where I've worked – I've been in rural parts of middle America – while on the one hand I could have chosen to play up the exoticism, I've never wanted to do that.

When I asked Cassandra why she always wears the headwrap tied up on her head, and not just tied under the chin, she clearly displayed a knowledge about the effect it produces in the way she styles it. Just as clearly, however, Cassandra's answers demonstrate that she is completely unaware of the fact that her particular style in applying the headwrap is decidedly African, the third cultural marker.

> It never occurred to me – but it wouldn't feel comfortable and I don't know – we don't wear – I'm thinking maybe – I mean, when you're a child you wear a hat tied under your chin to keep it on your head. Maybe that's apart of it. Ummmm. But it looks dressy to me, when, you know, it's all on my head. To me, it's the same effect as if I had elaborate braids on my head, if I had the headwrap tied up above my head and knotted above my head or had the ends worked into the actual wrap.

Black Style/White Style

> Laura Moore (86 years): *[Missus] like to see us dress up. We all wears hanches (handkerchiefs) on our heads. We had all colours. My sister only wore white on her head. De white folks would say, "I wishes I could wear hanches on my head 'cause they looks so pretty"* (S2. 7. 6:2744–2745 [TX]).

While headwraps, themselves, may be a very old form of adornment for African women, the styles they take cannot be understood as static. Although William Bascom noted that some Shango priests also braided their hair and some wore special forms of headdress, "[m]any of these religious styles are rapidly disappearing," significantly he added,

> . . . but in the years since World War II a whole series of new hairstyles for women have been introduced. Of equal importance to hair dress is the cloth head tied by which Yoruba women can often be recognized. This is a rectangular piece of cloth which is tied about the head in a number of imaginative ways, with new fashions still being created (101).

Several decades later, one of the characters in South African Can Themba's novel, *The Will to Die*, says: "We stood before the wardrobe mirror while my sisters helped tie Janet's *dock* [headwrap] in the current township fashion" (4).

Tying a piece of fabric around the head is not specific to any one cultural group. Men and women have worn and continue to wear some form of fabric head covering in many societies. What does appear to be culturally specific, however, is the way the fabric is worn; in other words, the *style* in which the fabric is worn is the ultimate cultural marker.

If we assume that the African American woman's headwrap was once a white-enforced way to stamp Black women as inferior and as servants, then one must ask several questions: Why have African American women always worn it in such a different manner than have American women of European descent? Why have African American women often twisted the fabric into so many varied arrangements? And why have African American women usually taken so much more care in wrapping it than have European and American white women when they have worn a similar headpiece? To answer these questions, careful note must be taken of the significant difference between the style of the headwrap as worn by white American women and by African American women.

To wrap her head, a European or white American woman simply folds a square piece of fabric into a triangular shape and covers her hair by tying the fabric under her chin (Figure 33) or, less often, by tying it at the nape of her neck. In either case, the untied points of fabric are left to fall down over the back of the head. The Euro–American style results in a headwrap which flattens against the head and encloses the face, and thus visually seems to pull the head down. This style mirrors, in effect, the way that European hair grows. The terms "scarf" or "kerchief" usually denote this style of headwrap, and while scarves are not particularly popular items of white American women's fashion today, when they are worn, they consistently will be arranged in the manner just described.[22]

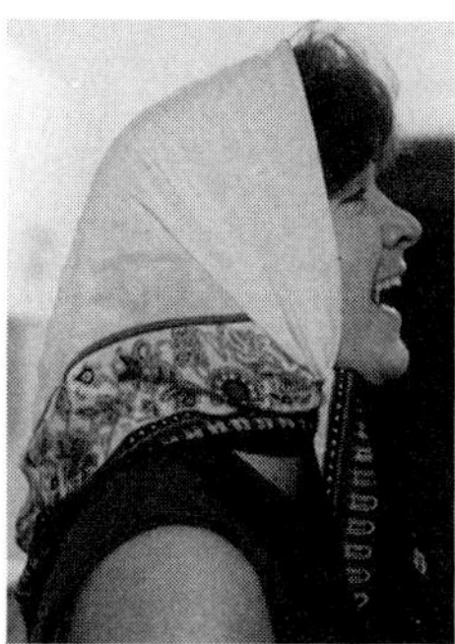

Figure 33. Euro-American style of wearing a head cloth, Baltimore, 1992. Photograph by the author.

In comparison to the Euro–American manner of folding the fabric into a triangle, a woman of African ancestry folds the fabric into a rectilinear shape. The African American woman then attaches the fabric to her head by wrapping it around her hair and then either tucking the ends into the wrapped fabric (Figure 34) or knotting the ends outside of the fabric. The

Figure 34. Unidentified woman wearing a head cloth in the African and African American style, Philadelphia, 1993. Photograph by the author.

most significant difference between the Euro–American and Afro-centric manner is that rather than tying the knot under her chin, the African American woman most often ties the knots somewhere on the crown of her head, either at the top or on the sides. Although the African American woman sometimes ties the fabric at the nape of her neck, her form of styling always leaves her forehead and neck exposed. By leaving her face open, the headwrap visually enhances the facial features. The African American headwrap thus works as a regal coronet, drawing the onlooker's gaze up, rather than down. An excellent example is the painting thought to be of Marie Laveau, who obviously donned her headwrap in a manner which exemplified her features. In effect, she, like many other African and African American women, wore the headwrap as a queen might wear a crown. In this way the headwrap compares toWest African women's manner of hair styling, wherein the hair is pulled so as to expose the forehead and is often drawn to a heightened mass on top of the head.

Another outstanding difference between the two ways of wearing the headwrap is that, in contrast to the singular manner by which white women wrap their hair in fabric, African American women exhibit a seemingly endless repertoire of elaborations on the basic mode. The evidence for this improvisation, on so simple an item as a squared swatch of cloth, is seen in one of the earliest group photographs of southern African Americans which shows that the headwraps as crafted by both Black women and men were far more ornamental than the simple Euro–American scarf. For, in the photograph, taken in 1862, twelve newly "freed" African Americans wear headwraps in twelve different ways; none, however, tied below the head (Figure 35).

A final note on the particular differences in style between white and Black American women: the only documented historical moment when white American women wore the headwrap in the Afro-centric manner after the brief orientalizing fad of the early 1800s, occurred during World War II when white women worked in industrial jobs usually reserved for males only (Figure 36). Four questions arise about this anomaly. First, why did the white woman adopt this style at that time? Second, rhetorically, could it be that as the white woman stepped into physical tasks traditionally off-limits to her gender, she unconsciously signified her bond with Black women who historically had been the American women best known for laboring at stereotypical "men's" tasks? Third, why, after the mid-1940s, did the white woman stop wearing the headwrap in the Afro-centric style? And fourth, rhetorically, if Cassandra Stancil's sense that a scarf tied under the

Figure 35. *Slaves of Rebel General Thomas F. Drayton, Hilton Head, South Carolina*, 1862. Henry P. Moore, photographer; albumen, 5 1/8″ × 8 3/16″. Collection of the J. Paul Getty Museum, Malibu, California.

chin is "child-like," does that explain why the white woman returned to the Euro–American way of wearing it after World War II?

Now we must ask again: What accounts for such pronounced differences between the way women of African descent set off their heads with the headwrap and the way white women wear the scarf? I propose that the answer lies in a return to Africa, particularly to African aesthetics.

Figure 36. During World War II, white women wore their scarves in the African style.

African Style

> At such times his mind searched the mystery of fate, groping in some imagined world where the spirits of his ancestors and that of his dead wife must be living, for a point of contact, for a line of communion.
>
> . . . Then he would face the world with renewed courage or with the reinforced secure knowledge that he was at peace with his relations, without whom he would be a nonentity, a withered twig that has broken off from its tree (Ezekiel Mphahlele, South Africa, 1964:136).

> It was the privilege of our generation to be the link between two periods in our history, one of domination, the other of independence (Mariama Bâ, Senegal, 1989:25).

An aesthetic of the human head is pronounced in all tropical African cultures. The style by which African American women wore and continue to wear a piece of fabric in such a way as to accentuate the head thus must be seen as a retention of African sensibilities. The next contributor probably married after emancipation, but her style, evident in her choice of *chapeau*, is encoded with an African aesthetic.

> Eliza Hasty (85 years): *My go-away-hat was 'stonishment to everybody. It was made out of red plush and trimmed wid white satin ribbons. In de front, a ostrich feather stood up high and two big turkey feathers flanked the sides* (2. 2:255 [SC]).

Botume offers further proof of a tradition that gives priority to the head and which extends in space and time from West Africa to the Southern United States when she describes a young girl who chose to glorify her head, while seeming to ignore embellishments to any other part of her body. As Botume reports, the girl's choice was highly successful:

> We patiently struggled to teach [Jane] to sew, and to bring about cleanliness and a degree of order . . .. About this time the cotton was sold, and she appeared in the classroom with an astonishing new hat on her head. It was a white straw, with a bunch of red, blue, and green rooster's tail-feathers standing up straight. Her feet were bare, and her frock ragged and dirty; but she walked into the room with the air of a queen (93).

The headwrap's style clearly emphasizes, accentuates, and heightens the head of the wearer. If Eliza Hasty's "go-away-hat," Marie Laveau's "tignon," Jane's "white straw," and Cassandra's "scarves" and "rags" are any indication, this style is meant to emphasize, accentuate, and "heighten" the wearer herself. Because the headwrap demonstrates that Africa is the source for the specific style worn by African American women, in the final analysis, the headwrap may be read as an African item. This deeper reading, however, will not be about the exact replication of a particular material object, rather it is about the item as African American material culture.

Robert Blair St. George argues persuasively that man-made objects can not be understood apart from the nonphysical intellectualizing of human beings; that is, he calls for the integration of "material life (the way we live) and the symbolic life (the way we think)" as academics use objects to construct other people's histories (1988:7 passim). Using St. George's logic, I understand the headwrap to be a physical object that signifies cultural worldview, a material manifestation of the metaphysical foundation that guides members of a particular social group. As such, the headwrap expresses in material form many of the most deeply rooted attitudes that comprise African/African American worldview and by which Africans and African Americans express themselves in other, more overt behaviours.

For example, numerous scholars recognize improvisation as a hallmark of both African and African American performative achievement. In fact, improvisation is fundamental to the African and African American concept of successful communication in all its forms – from speech, to song, to instrumental music, to dance, to dress.

> Cassandra Stancil: No, I never asked another woman how she tied it. I always figured I could do it. I could try and experiment and if not get *that*, get something that I liked.
>
> It's more an aesthetic thing, I've never looked it up. As I'm wrapping, I'm looking in the mirror to see what it looks like. And sometimes I'll go for something symmetrical, sometimes asymmetrical. Sometimes I'll let the ends be out, sometimes I'll tuck them up, sometimes I'll braid them so that they have some kind of a design and then I'll tuck them under, sometimes I'll want to hide how I've made them so I make sure everything's tucked under, and then sometimes I don't care, I want them out, and like, when I have a really short piece that will really just barely go around my head, I'll just go with the Aunt Jemima look and just let the knot be there – If it's up in front it's the Aunt Jemima look.

Thus, the seemingly limitless ways of attaching a piece of cloth to the head may be read as yet another expression of improvising.

Another primary characteristic of African and African American performative style is call-and-response wherein no clear lines are drawn between the roles of "performer" and "audience" as is often the expectation in Eurocentric performance. A successful African American performance demands audience response all through the event, and the response is often expected to be loud and to include bodily motion as well as vocalization (Allen, 1991:85 ff). This expectation for both performer and audience to play roles is as true for a Black Baptist preacher's sermonic performance (Davis, 1987:16 ff.) as it is for an Aretha Franklin concert performance, and as it is for the wearing of a particular item of clothing. That is, when Eliza Hasty, Marie Laveau, and Jane ornamented their heads they were performing; and, in the African American way, they expected a response.

> Cassandra Stancil: I do get positive responses – and I don't know if I could categorize them. Yah – and it's generally in cultural settings, I guess, or at Penn I get a lot of responses, or when I go to other events where other people are dressed accordingly. But you know, if I'm in an environment where there's a greater "division" in points of view, then I don't get the responses at all. Having worn them so often, other women asked me how to wear them.

Eliza's, Marie's, Jane's, and Cassandra's expectations mirror those of the going-to-church women whom Fanny Kembla said wore "head handkerchiefs that would put one's eyes out from a mile off," and they mirror as well Caroline Wright's worldview when she emphatically stated for herself and many other Black women: "Us sho' did come out looking choice some." By a quirk of historical documentation, Fanny Kembla and those who responded to Eliza, Marie, and Jane were white Americans, but significantly, their inscribed responses tell a great deal about their own culture's sense of style.

The headwrap encodes at least one pronounced aspect of African cosmological view: an absolute belief in the power of the ancestors and the belief that universal order can only be maintained through ritualistically honouring those who came before.[23] This belief continues to be embedded in African American society, and thus, may be taken to represent yet another African-entered approach to life (John Roberts, 1990:75). The retention of the headwrap by some African American women, even to the present, denotes this commitment to those who came before. For, as the Black communities of the South were broken asunder with emancipation, the Reconstruction, and the great migration, the headwrap became, however consciously or unconsciously, one material link by which those women who came after could bond with and acknowledge those who preceded them.[24]

> Cassandra Stancil: It's kinda like the way we have, in the 60s, re-appropriated the term "Black" which was once pejorative, and once we reclaimed it and wore it as our banner, it became okay for us to call *ourselves* "Black." Similarly, I see the same thing happening with headwraps and it may happen with braids, we've sort of taken back those, those, like – to have a "napped head" is how we use to call having dreadlocks now, and it was very negative.[25] To have braids, that was something that only a child wore, but now it's something that older Black women wear, and it's something we realize that it's something we *have* done in the past with our hair, whether or not it was the Southern past or the African past, and it's something that is conducive to the way our hair is (Figure 26). So that now we wear it with those things in mind, sort of reappropriated it and used it to signify something different. And I guess that's how I would categorize how I see most people wearing them now. We have reappropriated it from the stereotypic views of it – we've reappropriated it from those who would say 'it's primitive' and so forth – and we valorized it, I think.

Today, the headwrap as emblematic of this bond seems to encompass not only the enslaved American ancestors, but those who were left on the shores of Africa as well. When I asked Cassandra if there were occasions, such as African American festivals, where any Black woman might wear a headwrap, she responded:

> Definitely. Definitely. I mean those are the parts, I mean those are the ways that we have to re-incorporate the African dress into our everyday or fun-type dress . . ..

American Tradition: Paradox and Meanings

The African American headwrap holds a distinctive position in the history of clothing for both its longevity and for its potent significations. It endured the travail of slavery and never passed out of style. The headwrap has its origin in Africa, but in America it gained a complex of subtle functions not traditional to the ancestral continent. The preceding has been an unfinished history of the multilayered meanings acquired by the headwrap over several centuries. My intent has been to show that the headwrap is African in style, but as worn by African American women, the traditions could only have been forged in the crucible of American slavery and its continuing legacy.

During the period of enslavement, men as well as women wore cloth head coverings, but gradually the headwrap became an exclusively female item. For the enslaved woman, the headwrap acquired significance as a form of self- and communal identity and as a badge of resistance against the servitude imposed by whites. This represents a paradox in so far as the whites misunderstood the self-empowering and defiant intent and saw the headwrap only as the stereotypical "Aunt Jemima" image of the Black woman as domestic servant.

In their published narratives, the formerly enslaved people put into words their thoughts on the headwrap's three basic functions. One purpose was purely practical: the cloths covered hair when there was lack of time to prepare it for public view, the material absorbed perspiration and kept the hair free of grim during agricultural tasks, and the headwrap offered some protection against lice.

Although whites sometimes enacted codes which legally required Black women to cover their heads with cloth wrappings, these codes do not explain two other functions for the headwrap which the African Americans, themselves, devised. These additional functions – fashion and symbol – often overlapped. The headwrap denoted age, sex, and the sexuality of the wearer. It marked the social status of the wearer within the larger American society as well as the wearer's status within the Black communities. For example, the quality of fabric and the manner in which it was arranged on the head often distinguished a domestic servant from a field laborer. Enslaved African American women practiced customs wherein they wore certain types of headwraps for special social events such as dances, and for religious events such as worship services, baptisms, and funerals. In these usages, African American women demonstrated their recognition that they alone possessed this particular style of head ornamentation, and thereby, donning the headwrap meant they were acknowledging their membership in an unique American social group.

After emancipation, the headwrap became a much more private matter possessing closely held meanings that were evident but mostly subconscious. In the past four decades, the headwrap reemerged as an item of clothing worn publicly by many Black women. When the headwrap reappears, a white audience senses the true contradiction in the original paradox: it evokes the whites' role in the system of racial slavery. While the headwrap still bears this metaphor for modern African Americans, it also represents a symbolic embrace of their enslaved American forebears, and it now serves yet another function as an emblem of their West African ancestry. Thus, over time, the headwrap displays a dynamic quality in acquiring new meanings without shedding the older nuances.

* * * * *

I recently observed an African American woman from Philadelphia wearing African jewelry and an African-patterned robe and headwrap. When I complimented her on her "costume," she corrected me saying, "We call it traditional dress."

* * * * *

Concluding one story, Zora Neale Hurston wrote that "time and place have had their say," but for the story of the headwrap, the times and places are ever changing, just as the questions we ask and the answers we receive about those times and places change and never have their final say.

The headwrap means more than a textile wrapped around the head. It relates to the precious cloth woven by uncountable Black women after they grew, harvested, cleaned, combed, and spun the fibres. The headwrap must be seen *on* a body, for it is merely a length of cloth without the head that it enfolds. And the African American woman's headwrap must be seen as but one piece of a whole ensemble, not as a single item of clothing. It relates to the shirts and shifts, the undergarments and outer garments, the brogans and boots that covered other bodily parts. It relates to protecting the human body and to ornamenting that body and to celebrating that body. And it relates to all those items of clothing that were inadequate and to all those articles of dress that were denied.

The headwrap is part of still other ensembles, encoding meanings that go beyond an examination of the clothing of African Americans in the antebellum South. Forever, these other meanings circulate back-and-forth through space and time, undulating between the dream and the reality of Africas and Americas, between actual presents and remembered pasts. The hand-woven cloth and the items of dress may have meant new raiments – but it must never be forgotten that the cloth, the headwrap, and all the other articles of clothing will always be interwoven, as well, with the older raiments of self.

Notes

1. Under my former name, portions of this chapter have appeared in "The West African Origin of the African-American Headwrap" (Griebel, 1995a) and "The African American Woman's Headwrap: Unwinding the Symbols" (Griebel, 1995b).
2. The painting illustrates the cover of Richard Price's *First-Time* (1983).
3. An interesting parallel to whites forcing Black women to wear the headwrap

which then is assumed to be historically "African" is suggested by Bernard S. Cohn who traces the English colonial insistence that Sikh Indians serving in the military wear turbans. Eventually, this type of headwrap became a "national costume" presumed to have been always the traditional dress of Sikh men (1989:304–309).

4. Earlier, Dutch gentlemen donned turbans during their leisure, presumably a by-product of Dutch ventures in Africa and India. Witness, for example, Rembrandt's several portraits from the 1670s of himself in a turban.

5. R. Turner Wilcox, however, gives another culture credit for the trend:

> The late eighteenth and the early nineteenth centuries witnessed a decided vogue for that most wearable and artistic headdress, the Oriental turban, especially for evening wear. The fashion of the turban, supposedly inspired by Napoleon's Egyptian campaign, is said really to have originated in London where the draped headpiece was seen on the heads of visiting Indian nabobs (1945:189–190).

6. The painting, known as *The Old Plantation*, was found in Columbia South Carolina. Beatrix Rumford dates the costumes to the last quarter of the eighteenth century (1975:333–335). The work is owned by the Abby Aldrich Rockefeller Folk Art Center, Williamsburg, Virginia.

7. I am discussing the illustration from Abrahams and Szwed which is a print made from an engraving by Brunias from his original painting made ca. 1770–1778. The original painting (whereabouts currently unknown) is illustrated in Hugh Honour, 1989a:33. Brunias made several engravings of this painting, none exactly like the original. In the engraving reprinted in Abrahams and Szwed, Brunias borrowed certain elements from the painting to make new compositions; rearranged or completely altered details include certain figures, costumes and landscape. Most interesting is that the tall dancing figure in the engraving is shown as a white female, not Black as in the original painting. Honour says Brunias painted the original of this particular scene on Dominica (1989b:32); Abrahams and Szwed label it a scene on St. Vincent.

8. A white woman is pictured wearing the identical head gear in 1802–1804, as "Empire Style" in Braun and Schneider, plate 85, n.p.n.

9. In his monograph on Manet, Timothy J. Clark discusses the Black figure in *Olympia* in the same vein as have most critics: she is viewed only as a contrast, in both color and exotica, to the white, European prostitute (1985:79ff.).

10. Lewis Miller's watercolor, *Lynchburg-negro dance*, 1853, is an African American example.

11. Transporting objects on the head was apparently not only done by Blacks. Elizabeth Fox-Genovese quotes a woman who observed a southern, white "yoeman" woman in 1827 "with an infant in her arms and a large bundle on her head" (210).

12. Dorothy Sterling publishes two photos of Tubman, in one she wears a hat, in the other, she wears a headwrap (398 and 399).

13. The work is in the collection of the University of Southern Louisiana Art Museum.

14. Personal communication, 19 February 1993.

15. Bernard S. Cohn uses the phrase "uniform of rebellion" in his argument for the meaning of the turban to contemporary Indian Sikhs (304).

16. In a similar manner, "Uncle Ben," complete with tall chef's hat, serves as the stereotypical Black male counterpart for another commercial food product.

17. For example, Don Yoder includes three illustrations that portray nineteenth-century Black cooks with bandana-wrapped heads (1971:19, 22, 27). Two of the illustrations were originally published in *Virginia Illustrated*, New York, 1857; the other illustration is from *Willson's Second Reader*, a school text published in 1864.

18. Conversation, 23 March 1992.

19. See, for example, Leon E. Wynter, "Stores Have Different Ideas on African Style," an article exploring the ways in which Montgomery Ward and J. C. Penney market this type of merchandise (*Wall Street Journal*, 26 October 1993, "Business & Race" column).

20. This and the following quotations are excerpts from a taped interview with Cassandra Stancil on 27 March 1992, Philadelphia.

21. When I asked Ella Williams Clarke, age 70, who was reared in North Carolina about wearing a headwrap she said, "We always wore hats and gloves to church when I was growing up. When you were a teenager you wore a hat – not everywhere, but always to church." Conversation, 10 Sept 1992.

22. Although they are less often seen in the United States at present, European peasant women engaged in agricultural tasks, as previously noted, continue to wear such a hair covering. And, in Greece, it is still customary for widowed, rural women to cover their hair in public with a dark-colored scarf. For whatever purposes, when white women wear head scarves today, they always tie them in the Eurocentric style.

23. Sterling Stuckey writes: "Respect for age is the basis of much black African culture and the principle inspiration for its art (333) . . . The core of African culture . . . is based on respect for the ancestors and elders . . ." (334).

24. While this is an explicit or implied theme in all contemporary African American women's literature, perhaps the strongest and most extended written reflection on the meaning of the ancestors in African American culture is Alice Walker's *In Search of Our Mother's Gardens*, 1983.

25. In Ghana, Maya Angelou describes her similar reaction when a local woman gave her a Ghanaian hairstyle: "It was a fashion worn by the pickaninnies whose photographs I had seen and hated in old books. I was aghast" (1986:37).

7

Clothing as the Weft of a Folk History

> Aunt Permahoule, for whom marvels and folklore were the warp and woof of her life, had a different explanation (Stratis Myrivilis 1959:82).

> '. . . *but the half was never told.*'
> '*No, half of it ain't been told*' (Charlotte Brooks in Alberts [1890] 1988:29).

> Truth uncompromisingly told will always have its ragged edges (Herman Melville, 1970:405).

These astute observations about our desire to know the past by way of others' individual memories of the past, even while acknowledging that our understanding will never be complete, certainly apply to the *Narratives*. That being said, I turn to the written words of the two most articulate African American spokesmen of the nineteenth century: Frederick Douglass and Booker T. Washington, both born before the American Civil War. Douglass freed himself by escaping from the South at about age 21; Washington was legally emancipated at age 9. Both became teachers with a national audience, telling stories with strong didactic appeal.

I cited above several of their autobiographical experiences concerning clothing in particular. A last story related by Booker T. Washington concerns a head covering. Upon first entering school, Washington learned that "*all the other children wore hats or caps upon their heads, and I had neither hat nor cap*," implying that he had not worn a head covering up until this experience. "*But, of course, when I saw how all the other boys were dressed, I began to feel uncomfortable.*" Washington asked his mother to buy him a "'*store hat,' which was a rather new institution at that time among members of my race and was considered quite the thing for young and old to own*" (33). But Washington's mother explained to him that she had no money to buy him one. Instead, his mother "*got two pieces of 'homespun' (jeans) and sewed them together and I was soon the proud possessor of my first cap.*"

> *The lesson that my mother taught me in this has always remained with me, and I have tried as best as I could to teach it to others . . .. [T]hat my mother had strength of character enough not to be led into the temptation of seeming to be that which she was not – of trying to impress my schoolmates and other of the fact that she was able to buy me a "store hat" when she was not* (ibid.).

To stress the lesson, Washington concludes:

> *[S]everal of the boys who began their careers with "store hats" and who were my schoolmates and used to join the sport that was made of me because I had only a "homespun" cap, have ended their careers in the penitentiary, while others are not able now to buy any kind of hat* (34).

Booker T. Washington directs his instructions at African Americans, whereas Frederick Douglass uses clothing to reach a white audience. In describing slavery as he remembered it on an Eastern Shore plantation in Maryland during the antebellum period, Douglass punctuates his moral with this oft-quoted observation: "*Children from seven to ten years old, of both sexes, almost naked, might be seen at all seasons of the year*" (28). When Douglass is sent as a servant to Baltimore, one of the benefits is that he is outfitted with his first pair of trousers: "*The thought of owning a pair of trousers was great indeed!*" (44). These memories no doubt account for all the photographs of the adult Douglass which show that though his long life he remained highly attentive to his personal appearance, particularly noticeable in his choice of dress (Figure 37).

Later, Frederick Douglass teaches another lesson, developed around another theme: the ugly change in personality of Mrs. Ault, his Baltimore "mistress," once she wedded a slaveholder. Mrs. Ault's "*angelic face gave place to that of a demon*" (49). Earlier in his autobiography, Douglass remembered that weaving was among the several industries that "*were all performed by the slaves*" (30). Subtly connecting the enslaved weavers on the rural plantation with his urban mistress, Douglass writes that Mrs. Ault

> *. . . had never had a slave under her control previously to myself, and prior to her marriage she had been dependent upon her own industry for a living. She was by trade a weaver; and by constant application to her business, she had*

been in a good degree preserved from the blighting and dehumanizing effects of slavery (48).

Figure 37. *Frederick Douglass, Abolitionist Orator, Cazenovia, New York*, 1850. Ezra Greenleaf Weld, daguerreotypist. Collection of the J. Paul Getty Museum, Malibu, California.

This study involved two tasks: the recovery of a record about clothing as it pertains to African American experiences, and the giving of a reality to the voices of the many African Americans in the *Narratives* and in other sources. This objective has allowed me to carefully document their vast technical knowledge. It has also led to a clear sense of the spirit behind the African Americans' particular aesthetic sensibilities. The forced diaspora from Africa to America changed much of the enslaved peoples' material world, while at the same time it placed them in a society which allowed them little control over most aspects of their physical living conditions. Thus, over the years, as Africans became Americans, transformations occurred in the fabrication and the procuring of their clothing, as well as in the modes of their dress.

In addition to the symbolic codes inherent in the clothing itself, articles of dress, or absence of them sometimes caused personal joy or humour or pride, but clothes were often also the stuff of hellish realities. Overcoming the emotional and political distortions created by the institution of racial slavery led to very real material changes in their way of life. But this was tempered by creative retention of the African heritage coupled with an adaptive manipulation of the remnants of their African material culture.

John Roberts correctly perceives the male folk heroes in African American oral narrative as being on an odyssey in search of empowerment: "[T]hose possessing physical power and those not possessing it were equally endowed with mechanisms for protecting their well-being and survival" (36). The people of the *Narratives* also expressed their inner and communal sources of empowerment by spinning the theme of clothing as the weft of their own songs, beliefs, tales, and legends.

This history ends with another form of folklore wherein actual material objects function as "memory objects" around which to tell a story (Barbara Kirschenblatt-Gimblett, 1989). Woven into these final narratives are descriptions of clothing so precious that they became the tangible memorials of past experiences. Patricia Darish gives an example from the Kuba in Zaire.

> I was shown a short overskirt . . . which had a border much older than its central panel. The informant explained that the original central panel had been detached from the border and buried with a family member a number of years previously. The older border (which had been made approximately fifty years earlier by her great-grand-mother) had been kept because of its age and the quality of workmanship. She also kept the border because she wanted to show her children and her grandchildren how finely embroidered textiles used to be (131).

Flora Nwapa, a Nigerian writer, includes this passage in her novel, *Efuru*:

> She bought them many years ago and whenever there was a festival or the second burial of a relative, the cloths served very well. She knew that to buy some cloths in the market for the occasion would not do. The older the cloth the better (1978:19).

The West African customs concerning a reverence for aged clothing compare with what is found in the *Narratives* when contributors opened their old trunks full of memories.

> Lina Hunter (ca. 90 years): *I'se still got one of my old weddin' petticoats; I wore out four bodies on it.* "Lina excused herself and went inside the house for a moment. She returned to the porch with an old-fashioned suitcase . . .. She opened it and took out a petticoat that was yellow with age. It was several yards wide and was encircled with numerous embroidered ruffles. The skirt was sewed on

to a tight, straight body-waist that was much newer than the skirt and this waist was topped by a rose-coloured crocheted yoke." *Mrs. Fannie Dean made dat for me . . .. Dat's what I used to wear for a wrop on church days 'fore I ever had a coat* (12:271 [GA]).

Clara Walker (111 years): *[O]l' miss . . . give us lots of good clothes. Thos clothes and my mother's clothes burned up in de fire I had few years ago right on dis farm. Lawdy I hated loosin' dose clothes I had when I was a girl more den anything I lost* (11. 7:22 [AR]).

Mary Colbert (84 years): *I was laughing at myself just the other day about those homespun dresses and sleeveless aprons I wore as a child. I reckon that was a sign you were coming to ask me about those things. I kept one of those dresses of mine until my own baby girl wore it out, and now I am sorry I let her wear it, for it would be so nice to have it to show you* (12. 1:217 [GA]).

Scott Bond (84 years): *My mother had a large chest, which, in those days, was used as a trunk. I had often seen her going through the things in that old chest. She would take out her calico dresses, which we people called "Sunday Clothes." She would hang them out to air on Sundays. Among the things she would take from the chest was a pair of little red shoes and a cap, and would say to me: "These are the shoes your father gave you." Being only a child, I thought she referred to my step-father* (S2. 1:32 [AR/AZ]).

Scott Bond learned later that the man who had presented the red shoes was his mother's master.

Calvin Moye (b. 1842): *We was married bout 18 years . . .. I bought a new shirt fer de weddin and she bought a new calico dress. Calico was high den, a calico dress cost almost as much as a silk dress does now . . .. I is still got some of her clothes too, I jus keeps dem in my trunk to remembah her as she was when she wore dem* (S2. 7. 6:2870 [GA, TX/TX]).

Ferebe Rogers was over 100 years old when interviewed By Ruth Chitty. In the following sensitive narration about what happened during the interview in Rogers' home we have a glimpse of the two separate worlds of the Black and white women. But we also have a sense that this separation could be bridged by a common understanding about the meaning of long-ago clothing.

I still got de fus' dress my husband give me. Lemme show it to you.

"Gathering her shawl about her shoulders, and reaching for her stick, she hobbled across the room to an old hand-made chest."

My husband made dis ches' for me. "Raising the top, she began to search eagerly through the treasured bits of clothing for the 'robe-tail muslin' that had been the gift of a long-dead husband. One by one the garments came out – her daughter's dress, two little bonnets all faded and worn (*'my babies' bonnets'*), her husband's coats."

And dat's my husband's mother's bonnet. It use to be as pretty a black as you ever see. It's faded brown now. It was dyed wid walnut.

"The chest yielded up old cotton cards, and horns that had been used to call the slaves. Finally the 'robe-tail muslin' came to light. The soft material, so fragile with age that a touch sufficed to reduce it still further to rags, was made with a full skirt and plain waist, and still showed traces of a yellow colour and a sprigged design" (13. 3:211 [GA]).

Epilogue

> To want to understand is an attempt to recapture something we have lost (Peter Høeg 1994:37).

> . . . the end is in the beginning . . . (Ralph Ellison 1952:5).

A personal item of our cumulative cultural material started me on this journey to find both Mimi and answers to questions I did not know how to formulate in my childhood. Questions which, in the 1940s and 1950s, when Mimi cared for my family, she would not and could not have answered even had I known what to ask. The item I refer to is a small, black-and-white snapshot of myself (Figure 38), taken in the back yard of our home in Annapolis, Maryland, where I lived until I was five. A corner of the white-clapboard house and the bottom edge of an open shuttered window are visible behind me, as is the lower trunk of one of the huge oak trees that shaded the lawn where a portion of the grass can be seen between the house and me. "November 3, 1943" is stamped on the back of the photo; I was nearing my third birthday then. A can of white paint and a potted geranium rest on a sheet of newspaper spread on a low wooden table. I am seated before the table holding a paintbrush which touches the geranium pot.

I found the snapshot in 1982 while sorting through a box of my parents' old photographs at my father's request. My father was dying of cancer and, I surmise, his request was interwoven with that. Mimi had died in New Jersey, her childhood home, less that a year before.

In the photo, I look at the camera. My eyes squint, perhaps a sign that in time I will become very nearsighted.

In the photo, I am wearing a jacket, buttoned from my waist to my neck, and corduroy pants just visible before the photo cuts off.

In the photo, my hair is completely covered by a patterned bandana wrapped around the back of my neck and tied in a knot above my forehead. The ends of the knot stick out and cast a shadow over my brow. And as I studied that picture in 1982 as Daddy lay dying and as I continued to grieve

Figure 38. Snapshots from a Maryland childhood.

and yearn for Mimi, of all the details in that photo, it was my head wrapped in a bandana that brought back absolute recall of that late-Autumn day in 1943 of my almost-three self.

I remember that Mimi and her husband, Clarence, and their son, Earl Humphrey, were living at our home and caring for me at the time because my father was stationed at an army camp in Indiana and my mother had gone to be with him. I remember that on that day Mimi let me help paint the geranium pots in preparation for their removal from the yard to the house for the winter. I remember that before I could paint, she changed me into old clothes and I remember that she tied the bandana on my head so that I would not get paint in my hair. I remember I was thrilled about the bandana because up until then I had always worn children's caps and bonnets and that was the first time I had ever worn a scarf like a grownup woman.

In all the years that I knew her, I do not remember ever seeing Mimi herself wear a headwrap. Hats, oh my yes! And later, the last time I saw her before she died, when her hair had turned snow white, she wore a jet-black wig. But never a headwrap. And yet she tied one around my head in exactly the style that women of African descent have used for centuries.

Why did Mimi wrap it that way instead of in the manner that white women do? Was it purely cultural instinct on her part? Or, was she mocking the little white child whom she had tended since the girl's birth? I choose to believe instead that her act had another significance: She did it to bind me to her. She needn't have; for she would have remained my beloved anyway, binding me to her forever with my other memories of her countless loving gestures and deeds. But by that particular act, and because the photograph which Clarence took of me on that long ago day survived, I was compelled to set upon a delayed journey in an attempt to understand our lost pasts, and through understanding, to recapture at the end what was always there at the beginning.

Appendix I: Glossary of Selected Trade-Cloth Terms Used by Europeans

Definitions from:

Alice Baldwin Beer, *Trade Goods*, 1970.
J. W. Mollett, *Dictionary of Art and Archaeology*, 1883.
Florence M. Montgomery, *Textiles in America 1650–1870*, 1984.
Webster's Third New International, 1963.
R. Turner Wilcox, *The Dictionary of Costume*, 1945.

baize – coarsely woven woolen or cotton fabric napped to imitate felt and dyed in solid colors

Bajudepants (also bejutapauts, *baju*, *badjoo*, *badju*) – a Malay short jacket Note: Brigitte Menzel, a German anthropologist who works among Asante in Ghana, says the term designates an Indian trade textile (personal communication).

brocade (also boysades?) – luxurious fabric, loom woven in an allover pattern with contrasting colors on a background of satin or twill weave

brocardels – a brocade made in combination of yarns; design in high relief of silk or linen on plain or satin ground

cambay, cambaye – a coarse cotton cloth made in India

camelot, camlet – 1) a: medieval Asiatic fabric of camel's hair or Angora wool, b: European imitation of this fabric of silk and wool, c: fine lustrous woolen of plain weave usually dyed bright red; 2) a garment made of camlet

chints, chintss, chintz – a printed or spotted cotton cloth

clout – a cloth for household use (as a towel or cover); an article of clothing (as for infants, i.e., diaper)

cuttenee, (Hindi, *kattani*) – piece goods of fine linen or of silk and cotton made in India damask – rich fabric woven of silk or linen; flat pattern

Ells (green), perhaps ell – an old European measurement of cloth, different lengths in different countries; an English unit of length chiefly for cloth equal to about 45" but no longer used; Dutch or Flemish equal 27"

frisé – a late nineteenth-century pile fabric usually mohair, of uncut loops

frieze – course napped woolen cloth

frize (red) (archaic version of *frizz*) – refers to tightly curled hair; French: *friser*, to curl (hair), raise a nap on cloth

fustian – originally Asian; stout cotton or flax cloth; solid color, usually grey or brown, tufted or striped

Gregorie, perhaps grége – any fabric in untreated condition as it comes from the loom before bleaching, dyeing, and finishing

Guinea stuff – no definition found

kanneken – white cotton cloth with a red stripe at an end

lungee handkerchiefs – no definition found

micanees (fine & coarse), Necanees, Nankee, nicanees, (*Webster's* offers nankeen, nankin, nanking) – 1) a durable fabric hand-loomed in China from local cottons that had naturally a yellowish color; also a firm twilled cotton fabric dyed to imitate the Chinese fabric; 2) nankeens – trousers made of nenkeen

neganipaut (Hindu, *lungi* or *lungyi*) – 1) an usual cotton cloth used especially in India, Pakistan and Burma for articles of clothing (as sarongs, skirts and turbans); 2) a piece of cotton cloth usually 2½ yards long worn folded about the body and tied at the waist by men in Southern India

patna – of or from the city of Patna, India; of the kind or style prevalent in Patna

perpetuana, perpetuan, perpéta – a kind of serge

plathilios (Dutch); *platilhas* (Portuguese) – white linen cloths

pullicat handkerchiefs (Pulicat, a town of southeast coast of India) – bandana

romberges – no definition found

Rumal, romal (Hindu) – 1) a usually silk plain woven Indian fabric used for dresses and handkerchiefs; 2) an often checked cotton or silk kerchief used as a scarf and in India as a headdress by men
Note: Capt. John Adams mentions: abbaphotoe or Tom Coffee romal, tape romal, abang romal, quaducher romal, Ashantee ramal, hair romal "a common piece of handkerchiefs, but cheap and useful"; Red Dane romal

sarry, sari, saree – a garment worn chiefly by Hindu women that consists of a light weight cloth 5 to 7 yards in length and draped gracefully and loosely so that one end forms a skirt and the other a head or shoulder covering

Note: standard West African woman's cloth equals 6 yards. Did they adapt and transform Indian cloth to create their own style?

says – a hard wearing worsted

Sepatero (also sempiternum, sempiterne, sepiternille?) – a twilled woolen stuff, resembling serge, deriving its name from its durable qualities

Silesia (also sinen) – a linen cloth of Silesian (former Prussian provence) origin

studilha – no definition found

Taffaty, taffeta, taffeties – rich, thin silk; luxurious fabric of plain weave and several finishes

touca, toucas – Turkey work?

velvet – originally made in India; luxurious, thick-bodied, close-napped, soft type of cloth with a face finish

Welsh plain, perhaps Welsh flannel – fine hand-woven cloth from the wool of Welsh mountain sheep

Appendix II: Annotated Glossary of Terms Related to Textile Manufacture and Clothing taken from the Narratives

Definitions from:

Georgina O'Hara, *The Encyclopedia of Fashion*, 1986.
Webster's Third New International, 1963.
R. Turner Wilcox, *The Dictionary of Costume*, 1945.
Doreen Yarwood, *The Encyclopedia of World Costume*, 1978.

Augusta cloth – of or from Augusta, the capital of Maine; of the kind or style prevalent in Augusta
Note: The reference is from a person formerly enslaved in Georgia, and therefore, it more likely refers to a kind of cloth prevalent in Augusta, Georgia.

baggin' – no definition found, but contributors used this to describe the fabric from which their clothing was made. The term probably refers to the large cloth sacks in which commercial grains were sold. Other similar terms used by the contributors include: "meal sack," "croker sack," and "crocus sack."

balmorals – refers to either an oxford-type shoe or a round, flat cap
Note: In the *Narratives*, balmorals referred to a woman's winter dress.

bandana/bandanna (from Hindu, a tie and dye process from the verb "to tie") – a large cotton or silk handkerchief.that usually has a solid background of red or blue with simple figures or geometrical forms in white

banyan (Hindu) – a loose shirt, gown, or jacket that is worn in India
Note: Ann Perry (82 years) of South Carolina was the only narrator who used this word, describing the garment thus: *Dey mek banyans for de chillen. Sleebe bin cut in de cloth, and dey draw it up at de neck, and call um bayan* (3.3:252). Shad Hall referred to the "binyan" he wore as a young boy (Parrish, 131); Parrish noted that it was "apparently an African word."

bat (also batt) (n) – a continuous sheet of cotton or wool fiber prepared for carding

bonnet – a woman's head covering of cloth or straw usually tied under the chin with ribbons or strings and made with or without a brim
Note: Contributors often describe a slat bonnet or sunbonnet that is made of cotton fabric with a brim or poke held in shape by stitched sleeves holding thin wooden slats; or, the poke could be straw. Popular between 1800 and 1870.

brake – an instrument or machine for separating out the fiber of flax or hemp by breaking up the woody parts

broach (n) – a spindle on which newly spun yarn is wound

brogan – a heavy shoe, especially a course leather shoe; from Gaelic "brogue shoe" made originally of half-dressed or untanned leather; a heavy shoe often having a hob-nailed sole.
Note: Overwhelmingly, the most common type of shoe referred to by the contributors.

calico, also calycot (from *Calicut*, a city in India from which it was first imported) – cotton cloth, usually figured; chintz

card (n) – a hand instrument for cleaning, disentangling and ordering animal and vegetable fibers preparatory to spinning, usually consisting of bent wire teeth set closely in rows in a thick piece of leather fastened to a back

card (v) – act of using a card, as above

cursey cloth – see "kersey"

cut (n) – 1) a unit indicating yarn size based on the number of fixed-length hanks per pound (a 1-cut woolen yarn has 300 yds. per lb.; a 6-cut has 1800 yds. per lb.); 2) a length of cloth cut from a loom varying from 40 to 100 yards in length

Dolly Varden – a dress style named after the heroine in Charles Dickens' *Barnaby Rudge* (1841); flower-sprigged with a tight bodice, panniered overskirt, bustle, different colored underskirt
Note: Two narrators referred to this dress style. Alice Hutcheson (b. 1862): *One time dey was Dolly Vardens, and dey was so pretty us kep'*

'em for Sunday bes' dresses. Dem Dolly Vardens was made wid overskirts what was cotched up in puffs (GA.12.2:285).

Matie Stenson probably also mentioned the style when she referred to a "dolly fodden" dress with "long tails" (S1.10.5:2038 [MS]).

draw – one complete outward and inward run of a mule carriage in spinning (see "mule")

drill or drilling (n) – strong durable cotton fabric in twill weave made in various weights for clothing

Note: George W. Harmon (b. 1854) spoke of "drillin'" for cold weather underwear (S1.12:141 [TX/OK]).

duck – a durable plain closely woven fabric now usually made of cotton (cf. canvas), but formerly of cotton, linen or hemp and used in the gray or with various finishes

Note: One contributor called it "duckling." Another referred to "ducking cloth similar to khaki cloth" (S2.4.3:1099 [TX]).

flannel – soft twilled fabric with a loose texture and a slightly napped surface made in various weights of wool or worsted yarns and often in combination with cotton

Note: Contributors often specifically mentioned red flannel.

flax (genus *Linum*) – a plant cultivated for its long silky bast fiber which, when freed from the stem by retting and mechanical processes, is used in textile manufacture and is the source of linen

gin (Middle English from Old French *engin*, mechanical contrivance) – a cotton gin or any similar device used for separating seed or foreign matter from fiber to be used commercially

gingham – plain woven clothing fabric usually yarn-dyed in solid colors, checks, plaids, or stripes

hackle (n) (sometimes "hatchel", "heckle") – a comb or board with long metal teeth for dressing flax, hemp, or jute

hackle (v) – to separate the long fibers of flax, hemp or jute from waste material and from each other by combing with a hackle

hair strings – no definition found; probably colloquial and meaning small pieces of string tied to the hair

hand – a unit of measure equal to 4 inches

hemp (*Cannabis sativa*) – plant with tough bast fiber used for making cloth, floor covering and rope; also the useful fiber from plants other than hemp (e.g., jute)

hickory checks, hickory shirts, hickory stripes – mentioned by the contributors, but no definition found; one meaning for "hickory" is "marked by firmness or toughness" and thus the folk term may refer to the durability of the cloth. Hickory bark was used as a dye, and the term may refer to this.

homespun – loosely woven, usually woolen or linen fabric hand loomed in the home from uneven hand-spun yarns (see "kersey")

indigo (*genus Indigofera*) – a plant that yields indigo blue dye; one species, *I. tinctoria*, is native to Africa

jean – durable twilled cotton cloth (denim), usually in solid colors or stripes; American blue jeans invented in 1853 by Levi Strauss. Also called dungaree, from the Hindu word, *dugri*, meaning coarse cloth.

Jenny Lind – Swedish singer, nicknamed "the Swedish Nightingale," became a popular celebrity during her U.S. concert tour in 1850 to 1852.
Note: Lou Smith (female, b. 1854) said, *My mother....went around with her hair and clothes all Jenny-Lynned-up [sic] all the time...* (7:303 [TX/OK]).

kerchief – a square of cloth worn usually folded by women as a head covering

kersey – course ribbed woolen cloth for hose and work clothes woven first in medieval England; heavy wool or wool and cotton fabric made in plain or twill weave with a smooth finish (obsolete synonym for homespun)

lawn – a sheer, plain-woven cotton or linen fabric that is given in several finishes when used for clothing

linsey or linsey-woolsey (Middle English) – course sturdy fabric with cotton warp and woolen weft (formerly linen and wool)
Note: Contributors mentioned "mixed cotton and flax" cloth and "mixed cotton and wool" cloth.

lowell cloth – a cheap cloth made in Lowell, Massachusetts in the nineteenth century
Note: A few contributors spoke of home-spun "lowell" cloth. Several Texas contributors referred to "loyal cloth" or "royal cloth." Neither term was found in the dictionary. "Loyal" may be the way "lowell" was heard, and thus, "royal."

lowering – dark or threatening; cf., "lower" – situated or regarded as being situated below the lower part of another part or place.
Note: Neither definition explains the contributors' use of the term, except perhaps, symbolically: Andrew Goodman (97 years) said, *Our shirts was made of lowerings – that's the same as cotton sacks was made out of* (4.2:75 [TX]).

moccasin (Algonquian origin) – heelless shoe of a single piece of soft leather that is the distinctive footwear of Native Americans; the sole is brought up the sides of the foot and over the toes where it is joined with a puckered seam to a U-shaped piece by lying on top of the foot

mother Hubbard – also known as a wrapper, dressing gown, or tea gown according to its fabric and use
Note: Anderson Furr (87 years) likened the boy's shirt to this style, *Boys wore long blue stripped shirts in summer and nothin' else a t'all. Dem shirts was made jus' lak mother hubbards* (12.1:347 [GA]).

mule – a machine having a moving carriage for simultaneously drawing and twisting a sliver into yarn or thread and winding it; originally for cotton but now limited mostly to wool (also called "mule-jenny")

nigger cloth – no definition found, this term was mentioned by the contributors to indicate a strong, durable, but usually uncomfortable clothing fabric. Antebellum advertisements use the term "Negro cloth" expressly to mean durable fabric suitable for making garments for enslaved peoples.
Note: One definition given for "nigger" is "cotton spinner."

nine-stitch dress – Mary Johnson said girls wore a dress made from cottonade that *we called a nine-stitch dress* (S2.6.5:2026 [MS/TX]). No definition found.

osnaburg or osnaberg – rough course durable cotton fabric in plain weave made originally of flax and used in the gray for bagging and industrial purposes
Note: Footnote to one narrative reads, "osnaberg, the cheapest grade of cotton cloth" (7.2:24 [MS]).

pine straw – dried pine needles
Note: Contributors mention weaving pine straw, and also wheat, rye and oat straw, oak leaves, grass, cane corn stalks, and [corn?] shucks into hats and bonnets.

piqué – a durable clothing fabric of cotton or silk originally woven with crosswise ribs obtained by the interlacing of a fine surface warp and a heavy back warp

reel (n) (from Greek *krekein*, to weave) – a revolving device used in winding yarn or thread into hanks or skeins

ret – to soak or expose flax or hemp to moisture in order to promote the loosening of the fiber from the woody tissue by bacterial action

roundabout – No definition found. George Womble (b. 1843) mentioned a one-piece garment made by sewing a pair of pants and a shirt together (2.4.284 [GA]).

russet – 1) of, or relating to, or constituting leather that is finished except the coloring and polishing; the color varies from brown to rust-red; 2) a strong twilled woolen cloth for clothing and shoes.

Note: The "russet" shoes mentioned so often by the contributors refer to the first definition. Two contributors spoke of "russel shoes," perhaps a corruption of "russet."

scutch – to separate the woody fiber from flax or hemp by beating the stems

serge – a durable twilled fabric having a smooth clear face and a pronounced diagonal rib on the front and on the back, made in various weights in worsted, wool, cotton, or silk and used especially for suits, coats, and dresses

shimmy – alternate for chemise

Note: An unidentified female contributor said, *We always went in our 'shimmy tails' in the summer* (18:136 [TN]).

size (v) – to make a proper or suitable size.

Note: Rachel Cruze reported, *They would first size the thread by dipping it in some solution...* (S1.5.2:297 [GA]).

spinning – the act of twisting fibers into strong strands. There are two types of spinning tools: hand spindle (Africa) or spinning wheel (North America).

starch – a substance used especially to stiffen textile fabrics.

Note: Contributors mentioned flour, rice, hominy, and corn meal as starch bases.

tarlaton or tarelton – a sheer cotton fabric in open plain weave, usually heavily sized for stiffness and used for dresses, costumes, and trimmings

Note: Used by contributors to describe a woman's dress.

thrum – loom waste consisting of warp thread left on the loom after the cloth has been removed

tignon – a local, New Orleans word for the headwrap; "tignon" is a variation of the French word "chignon," a smooth knot or twist or arrangement of hair that is worn at the nape of the neck; originally meaning chain, collar, nape of the neck.

tow – short broken fiber removed from flax, hemp or jute during the scutching or hackling and used for yarn, twine, or stuffing

Note: Several contributors noted their clothing, especially undergarments and shirts, were made of tow.

turban – a fashionable headdress for women, especially in the nineteenth century

Note: "Turban" derives from the French from a Turkish word meaning a headdress worn chiefly by Muslims.

warp – the threads or yarns set up and extending lengthwise on a loom through which the filler threads (weft) are woven to produce cloth
weft – a filling thread or yarn that crosses the warp when weaving cloth and extends from salvage to salvage
worsted – smooth compact yarn spun with average to hard twist from long wool fibers that have been carded and combed and used especially for napless fabrics or knitting wools
yank (hank?) – four spun cuts of yarn

Appendix III: Cloth Dyes Reported in the Narratives

PLANT	MORDANT (setting agent)	COLOR	SOURCE
bamboo	*chamber lye	turkey red	wild
bay leaves	chamber lye	yellow	home-grown?
beech bark	**copperas	slate	wild
blackjack oak			wild
butternut (American tree)	copperas		wild
cedar moss		yellow	wild
cherry bark	cold salt water		wild?
cinnamon bark			wild?
current bush root		yellow	cultivated?
copperas		yellow	bought?
crocus		yellow	cultivated?
dogwood bark		blue	wild
elder berry		red	wild
elm (& red elm)		red	wild
elm (slippery)			wild
gallberry (eastern U.S. holly)			wild
green dye		green	store
hazel nut bush			wild
hickory bark	chamber lye	yellow	wild
indigo	***alum myrtle seed	blue, all shades	wild; cultivated; druggist
ink balls			
maple bark	copperas	yellow	wild

PLANT	MORDANT (setting agent)	COLOR	SOURCE
michael tea	copperas		
peach tree		red	wild
pecans		black	cultivated?
pine bark			wild
pine straw	chamber lye	purple	wild
poison ivy	copperas	black	wild
poke berry, or poke berry root		red	wild
red bud			wild?
red dirt, red mud, or red clay		red	gathered; cloth buried in clay
red oak bark or "chips"	salt	pink, red, brown, yellow	wild
red shank (root?)			wild?
sumach	copperas	tan, black, red	wild
sweetgum bark	chamber lye/ copperas	purple, black	wild
sycamore bark		pink or red	wild
tobacco	copperas		cultivated
walnut hull, green		black, brown, all shades	wild
walnut hull, ripe		black	wild
"Yellow Root"		yellow	wild

*chamber lye – urine

**copperas – green ferrous sulfate heptahydrate
Milton Marshall (82 years) spoke of clothes of "copper straw" cloth and "white" cloth (3.3:172 [SC]); perhaps the comparison is between cloth dyed with copperas and undyed cloth.

***alum – double sulfate of aluminum, naturally occurring as potash

Also mentioned as mordants:
salt (S2.8.3131 [AL/TX]) and cold salt water (S1.4.3:1389 [GA/TX])
"indigo t' hol' d' udder colors" (2.7.6:2728 [TX])

Bibliography

Abrahams, Roger D. 1968. "Trickster, the Outrageous Hero." In Tristram Potter Coffin, ed., *Our Living Traditions: An Introduction to American Folklore*, NY and London: Basic Books, 170–178.

——. 1992. *Singing the Master: The Emergence of African American Culture in the Plantation South*. NY: Pantheon Books.

Abrahams, Roger D. and John F. Szwed, eds. 1983. *After Africa*. New Haven and London: Yale University Press.

Achebe, Chinua. [1958] 1988. *Things Fall Apart*. Oxford: Heinemann.

——. 1967. *A Man of the People*. Garden City, NY: Doubleday.

——. [1967] 1989. *Arrow of God*. NY: Anchor Books/Doubleday.

Adams, Monni. November 1978. "Juba Embroidered Cloth." *African Arts* 12 (1):6; cited in Eli Leon, *Who'd A Thought It: Improvisation in African-American Quiltmaking*, San Francisco Craft and Folk Art Museum [exh. cat.], 1978, 26.

Adams, Captain John. [1822] 1966. *Remarks on the Country Extending from Cape Palmas to the River Congo with An Appendix Containing an Account of the European Trade with the West Coast of Africa*. London: Frank Cass & Co.

A Friend, as given to him by Brother Jones. 1857. *The Experience of Thomas H. Jones who was a Slave for Forty-three Years*. Reprint, Wilmington, DE: Scholarly Resources.

Albert, Octavia V. Rogers. [ca. 1890] 1988. *The House of Bondage or Charlotte Brooks and Other Slaves*. Reprint with Introduction by Frances Smith Foster, NY and Oxford: Oxford University Press.

Allen, Ray. 1991. *Singing in the Spirit: African-American Sacred Quartets in New York City*. Philadelphia: University of Pennsylvania Press.

A Mississippi Planter. June 1851. "Management of Negroes Upon Southern Estates." *De Bow's Southern and Western Review*, 621–625.

Anderson, Jervis. 17 January 1994. "The Public Intellectual." *The New Yorker*, 39–47).

Andrews, William L. 1988. *Six Women's Slave Narratives*. NY and Oxford: Oxford University Press.

Angelou, Maya. 1986. *All God's Children Need Traveling Shoes*. NY: Random House/Vintage Books.

Appadurai, Arjun. 1990. "Introduction: Commodities and the Politics of Value." In Appadurai, ed., *The Social Life of Things*, Cambridge and NY: Cambridge

University Press, 3–63.

Armstrong, Orland Kay. 1931. *Old Massa's People: The Old Slaves Tell Their Story*. Indianapolis: Bobbs-Merrill.

Arnoldi, Mary Jo and Christine Mullen Kreamer. 1995. *Crowning Achievements: African Arts of Dressing the Head*. Exh. cat., Fowler Museum of Cultural History University of California, Los Angeles.

Aronson, Lisa. 1990. "Women in the Arts." In Margaret Jean Hay and Sharon Stichter, eds., *African Women South of the Sahara*, London and NY: Longman, 119–138.

——. 1991. "African Women in the Visual Arts." *Signs: Journal of Women in Culture and Society* 16 (31), 550–574.

Asa-Asa, Louis. [1831] 1993. *Narrative of Louis Asa-Asa, a Captured African. Appended to The History of Mary Prince, A West Indian Slave Related by Herself*, Moira Ferguson, ed., Ann Arbor: University of Michigan Press, 121–124.

Ascher, Robert and Charles H. Fairbanks. 1971. "Excavation of a Slave Cabin: Georgia, U.S.A." *Historical Archaeology*, Volume V, 3–17.

Austin, Allan D. 1984. *African Muslims in Antebellum America: A Sourcebook*. NY & London: Garland.

Bâ, Mariama. 1989. *So Long a Letter*. London: Heinemann.

Baker, Houston A., Jr. 1984. *Blues, Ideology, and Afro-American Literature: A Vernacular Theory*. Chicago: University of Chicago Press.

——. 1991. *Workings of the Spirit: The Poetics of Afro-American Women's Writings*. Chicago and London: University of Chicago Press.

Baldwin, James. [1948] 1967. "This Morning, This Evening, So Soon." From *Going to Meet the Man*, reprinted in Langston Hughes, ed., *The Best Short Stories by Negro Writers*, Boston: Little, Brown.

Barber, Elizabeth W. 1994. *Women's Work: The First 20,000 Years: Women, Cloth, and Society in Early Times*. NY: W.W. Norton.

Barbot, John A. 1746. *A Descriptions of the Coasts of Nigritia, vulgarly called North-Guinea*. In A. and J. Churchill, eds., *A Collection of Voyages and Travels*, London, V, 77–78; reprinted in Leslie H. Fishel, Jr. and Benjamin Quarles, *The Negro American: A Documentary History*, Glenville, OH: Scott, Foresman and William Morrow, 1967:14–16.

Bascom, William. 1969. *The Yoruba of Southwestern Nigeria*. NY: Holt, Rinehart and Winston.

Bassett, John Spencer. 1925. *The Southern Plantation Overseer: As Revealed in His Letters*. Westport CT: Negro Universities Press.

Beatty, Bess. Feb 1987. "Lowells of the South: Northern Influences on the Nineteenth-Century North Carolina Textile Industry." *Journal of Southern History* LIII (1), 37–61.

Beer, Alice Baldwin. 1970. *Trade Goods: A Study of Indian Chintz in the Collection of the Cooper-Hewitt Museum of Decorative Arts and Design Smithsonian Institution*. Washington, D.C.: Smithsonian Institution Press.

Bentley, Rosalind. 27 September 1993. "Cornel West: A Closer Look." [Minneapolis] *Star Tribune*, 1E-2E.

Biobaku, S. O. 1973. *Sources of Yoruba History*. Oxford: Clarendon Press.

Blassingame, John W. 1972. *The Slave Community: Plantation Life in the Antebellum South*. NY and Oxford: Oxford University Press.

——. Nov 1975. "Using the Testimony of Ex-Slaves: Approaches and Problems." *The Journal of Southern History* XLI, 473–492.

——. 1977. *Slave Testimony: Two Centuries of Letters, Speeches, Interviews, and Autobiographies*. Baton Rouge and London: Louisiana State University.

Bledsoe, Michael. 21 February 1994. "In the Mail." *The New Yorker*, 8.

Blier, Suzanne Preston. Sept 1993. "Imaging Otherness in Ivory: African Portrayals of the Portuguese ca. 1492." *The Art Bulletin* LXXV 3, 375–396.

Bontemps, Arna. 1971. *Five Black Lives*. Middletown, CT: Wesleyan University Press.

Boone, Sylvia Ardyn. 1986. *Radiance from the Waters: Ideals of Feminine Beauty in Mende Art*. New Haven and London: Yale University Press.

Botkin, B.A., ed. 1940. *Slave Narratives: A Folk History of Slavery in the United States From Interviews with Former Slaves*. Washington, D.C.

——. [1945] 1989. *Lay My Burden Down*. Athens and London: University of Georgia Press.

Botume, Elizabeth Hyde. [1893] 1968. *First Days Amongst the Contrabands*. NY: Arno Press and the New York Times.

Bovill, E. W. 1968. *The Golden Trade of the Moors*. London: Oxford University Press.

Boser-Sarivaxevanis, Renée. 1980. *West African Textiles and Garments From the Museum für Vöikerkunde Basel*. Minneapolis-St. Paul: University Gallery and Goldstein Gallery, University of Minnesota (exh. cat.).

Boyd, Andrew and Patrick van Rensburg. 1965. *An Atlas of African Affairs*. NY and Washington: Frederick A. Praeger.

Bradley, Keith R. 1989. *Slavery and Rebellion in the Roman World 140 B.C.–70 B.C.* Bloomington and Indianapolis: Indiana University Press.

Bracciolini, Poggio and Ludovico de Varthema. [1510] 1963. *Travelers in Disguise: Narratives of Eastern Travel by Poggio Bracciolini and Ludovico de Varthema*. English Translations by John Winter Jones; Revised and Introduced by Lincoln David Hammond, Cambridge, Mass.: Harvard University Press for the Department of Romance Languages and Literatures.

Brathwaite, Edward Kamau. April 1973. "Cultural Diversity and Integration in the Caribbean." Paper presented to the Schouler Lecture Symposium, Johns Hopkins University; cited in Sidney W. Mintz and Richard Price, *The Birth of African-American Culture*, Boston: Beacon Press, 1992, 101–102, fn. 37.

Braudel, Fernand. 1979. *The Structures of Everyday Life: Civilization and Capitalism 15th-18th Century, Volume 1*. Translation from the French revised by Sian Reynolds, NY: Harper & Row.

Braun and Schneider. 1975. *Historic Costume in Pictures*. 1975. NY: Dover.

Brooks, Gwendolyn. 1972. *Report From Part One*. Detroit: Broadside Press.

Bronner, Simon J., ed. 1985. *American Material Culture and Folklife: A Prologue and Dialogue*. Ann Arbor: UMI Research Press.

Brown, Ina Corinne. 1965. "What Shall We Wear?" In Mary Ellen Roach and Joanne Bubolz Eicher, eds., *Dress, Adornment and the Social Order*, NY: John Wiley & Sons, 9–10.

Brown, William Wells. [1847] 1968. *Narrative of William W. Brown*. Reprinted in William Loren Katz, ed., *Five Slave Narratives: A Compendium*, NY: Arno Press and The New York Times.

Burns, A. R. 1983. "Introduction." *Herodotus: The Histories*, NY: Penguin, 7–37.

Burton, Annie L. [1909] 1988. *Memories of Childhood's Slavery Days*. Reproduced in William L. Andrews, *Six Women's Slave Narratives*, NY and Oxford: Oxford University Press.

Cable, Mary. 1977. *Black Odyssey: The Case of the Slave Ship Amistad*. NY: Penguin Books.

Cade, John B. 1935. "Out of the Mouths of Ex-Slaves." *Journal of Negro History* 20, 294–337.

Campbell, Edward D.C., Jr., ed. 1991. *Before Freedom Came: African-American Life in the Antebellum South*. Charlottesville: University of Virginia Press and Museum of the Confederacy, Richmond (exh. cat.).

Casely-Hayford, Adelaide. 1964. In Ellis Ayitey Komey and Ezekiel Mphahlele, eds., *Modern African Stories*, London: Faber and Faber, 50–59.

Cate, Margaret Davis. 1955. *Early Days of Coastal Georgia*. St. Simons Island, Ga: Fort Frederica Association and NY: The Gallery Press.

Catterall, Helen Tunnicliff, ed. 1926. *Judicial Cases Concerning American Slavery and the Negro*. Vol 1. Washington, D.C.: Carnegie Institution.

——. 1929. *Judicial Cases Concerning American Slavery and the Negro*. Vol 2. Washington, D.C.: Carnegie Institution.

Chesnutt, Charles W. [1899] 1967. "The Sheriff's Children." From *The Wife of His Youth*, reprinted in Langston Hughes, ed., *The Best Short Stories by Negro Writers*, Boston: Little, Brown, 1–16.

Clark, Timothy J. 1985. "Olympia's Choice." *The Paintings of Modern Life: Paris in the Art of Manet and His Followers*. NY: Alfred A. Knopf, 79–146.

Clinton, Catherine. 1982. *The Plantation Mistress: Woman's World in the Old South*. NY: Pantheon Books.

Coffin, Tristram Potter, ed. 1968. *Our Living Traditions: An Introduction to American Folklore*. NY and London: Basic Books.

Cohn, Bernard S. 1991. "Cloth, Clothes, and Colonialism: India in the Nineteenth Century." In Annette B. Weiner and Jane Schneider, eds., *Cloth and the Human Experience*, Washington and London: Smithsonian Institution Press, 304–353.

Connah, Graham. 1992. *African Civilizations: Precolonial Cities and States in*

Tropical Africa: An Archaeological Perspective. NY and Cambridge: Cambridge University Press.

Conneau, Captain Theophilus. [1853] 1977. *A Slaver's Log Book or 20 Year's Residence in Africa*. Introduction by Mabel M. Smythe. NY: Avon Books.

Conover, Ted. 1987. *Coyotes*. NY: Random House/Vintage Books.

Cordwell, Justine M. and Ronald A Scwarz. 1979. *The Fabric of Culture: The Anthropology of Clothing and Adornment*. The Hague, Paris, NY: Mouton.

Crawley, Ernest. 1965. "Wedding Garments." In Mary Ellen Roach and Joanne Bubolz Eicher, eds., *Dress, Adornment and the Social Order*, NY: John Wiley & Sons, 53–56.

Crayon, Porte (pseudonym for David Hunter Strother). [1857] 1871. *Virginian Illustrated: Containing a Visit to the Virginia Canaan*. NY: Haper & Brothers.

Crété, Liliane. 1981. *Daily Life in Louisiana 1815–1830*. Translated by Patrick Gregory, Baton Rouge and London: Louisiana State University Press.

Curtin, Philip D., introduction and annotation. 1968. *Africa Remembered: Narratives of West Africans from the Era of the Slave Trade*. Madison, Milwaukee & London: University of Wisconsin Press.

Darish, Patricia. 1991. "Dressing for the Next Life: Raffia Textile Production and Use Among the Kuba of Zaire." In Annette B. Weiner and Jane Schneider, eds., *Cloth and the Human Experience*, Washington and London: Smithsonian Institution Press, 118–140.

Davidson, Basil. 1991. *African Civilization Revisited*. Trenton, NJ: Africa World Press.

Davis, Gerald L. 1983. "Afro-American Coil Basketry in Charleston County, South Carolina: Affective Characteristics of an Artistic Craft in a Social Context." In Ferris, *Afro-American Folk Art and Crafts*, 234–257.

——. 1987. *I Got the Word in Me and I Can Sing It, You Know: A Study of the Performed African-American Sermon*. Philadelphia: University of Pennsylvania Press.

Davis, Noah. 1859. *A Narrative of the Life of Noah Davis. A Colored Man*. Reprint, Wilmington, De: Scholarly Resources.

Deetz, James. 1967. "The Analysis of Form." In Deetz, *Invitation to Archaeology* Garden City, NY: Natural History Press, 43–52.

Dégh, Linda. [1962] 1988. *Folktales and Society*. Bloomington and Indianapolis: Indiana University Press.

Delaney, Lucy A. [189?] 1988. *From the Darkness cometh Light or Struggles for Freedom*. Reproduced in William L. Andrews, *Six Women's Slave Narrative*, NY and Oxford: Oxford University Press.

de Negri, Eve. June 1960 "Hairstyles of Southern Nigeria." *Nigeria Magazine* 65, 191–198.

de Tocqueville, Alexis. [1835] 1954. *Democracy in America*. Richard D. Heffner, ed.,NY: Vintage Books.

Disraeli, Benjamin. [1845] 1954. *Sybil or the Two Nations*. Middlesex, GB:

Penguin.
Diop, Cheikh Anta. 1987. *Precolonial Black Africa*. Brooklyn: Lawrence Hill Books.
Douglass, Frederick. [1845] 1968. *Narrative of the Life of Frederick Douglass: An American Slave*. NY: Signet.
——. [1855] 1969. *My Bondage and My Freedom*. NY: Dover.
Du Bois, W. E. B. 1924. *The Gift of Black Folk: Negroes in the Making of America*. Boston: The Statford Co.
Dupuis, Joseph. [1824] 1966. *Journal of a Residence in Ashantee*. Edited by W. E. B. Ward, London: Frank Cass.
Egharevba, Jacob. [1934] 1968. *A Short History of Benin*. Ibadan: Ibadan University Press.
Eicher, Joanne Bubolz. 1976. *Nigerian Handcrafted Textiles*. Ile-Ife, Nigeria: University of Ife Press.
——. 1995. *Dress and Ethnicity: Change Across Space and Time*. Oxford and Washington, D.C.: Berg.
Ellison, Ralph. 1952. *Invisible Man*. NY: Random House.
——. 1972. *Shadow and Act*. NY: Vintage.
Elgin, Suzette Haden. 1984. *Native Tongue*. NY: Daw Books.
Ekwensi, Cyprian. [1961] 1982. *Jagua Nana*. London: Heinemann.
Emery, Lynne Fauley. 1988. *Black Dance: From 1619 to Today*. Princeton: Princeton Book Company.
Epstein, Dena J. Summer 1963. "Slave Music in the United States Before 1860. A Survey of Sources (Part 2)." Music Library Association *Notes* 20, 377–390.
Equiano, Olaudah. [1789, 1837] 1969. *The Life of Olaudah Equiano or Gustavus Vassa the African*. NY: Negro Universities Press.
Fanon, Franz. 1963. *The Wretched of the Earth*. NY: Grove Press.
Faulkner, William. [1929] 1987. *The Sound and the Fury*. NY: Vintage.
Ferris, William, ed. 1983. *Afro-American Folk Art and Crafts*. Jackson and London: University Press of Mississippi.
Fishel, Leslie H., Jr. and Benjamin Quarles. 1967. *The American Negro: A Documentary History*. Glenview, IL: Scott, Foresman and William Morrow.
Fitzgerald, Sharon. Oct/Nov 1992. "Negro Burial Ground." *American Visions*, 18–19.
Flanders, Ralph Betts. 1933. *Plantation Slavery in Georgia*. Chapel Hill: University of North Carolina Press.
Forbath, Peter. 1979. *The River Congo*. NY: E. P. Dutton.
Fox-Genovese, Elizabeth. 1988. *Inside the Plantation Household: Black and White Women in the Old South*. Chapel Hill and London: University of North Carolina Press.
Fuentes, Carlos. 1983. *The Death of Artemio Cruz*. NY: Farrar, Straus and Giroux.
——. 1988. "How I Started to Write." Republished in Rick Simpson and Scott Walker, eds., *The Greywolf Annual Five: Multi- Cultural Literacy*, Saint Paul,

MN: Greywolf Press, 83–111.

Furnas, J. C. 1956. *Goodbye to Uncle Tom*. NY: William Sloane Associates.

Fry, Gladys-Marie. 1990. *Stitched From the Soul: Slave Quilts from the Ante-Bellum South*. NY: Dutton Studio Books in association with the Museum of American Folk Art.

Gaines, Ernest J. [1978] 1992. *In My Father's House*. NY: Random House/Vintage.

——. 1993. *A Lesson Before Dying*. NY: Alfred A. Knopf.

Gaskins, Bill. 4 October 1996. "The Symbolic Role of Hair." *The Chronicle of Higher Education*, p. B76.

Gates, Louis Henry, Jr. [June 1976} 1993. "Portraits in Black." Originally in *Harper's Magazine*; reprinted in Henry Louis Gates, Jr., ed., *Voices in Black & White*, NY: Franklin Square Press.

Gayarré, Charles. 1885. *History of Louisiana: The French Domination*, Vol. III. New Orleans: Armand Hawkins.

Genovese, Eugene. 1974. *Roll, Jordan, Roll*. NY: Pantheon.

Georgia Writers' Project. 1972. *Drums and Shadows*. Garden City, NY: Anchor Books.

Gillon, Werner. 1986. *A Short History of African Art*. London: Penguin.

Gilman, Caroline Howard. 1838. *Recollections of a Southern Matron*. NY: Harper & Brothers.

Glassie, Henry. 1977. "Meaningful Things and Appropriate Myths: The Artifacts Place in American Studies." *Prospects* 3, 1–48.

Goode, Gloria. 1990. "Preachers of the Word and Singers of the Gospel: The Ministry of Women Among Nineteenth Century African-Americans." Dissertation: University of Pennsylvania.

Gorsline, Douglas. 1952. *What People Wore: A Visual History of Dress from Ancient Times to Twentieth-Century America*. NY: Bonanza Books.

Grandy, Moses. [1844] 1968. *Narrative of the Life of Moses Grandy, Late a Slave in the United States of America*. Reproduced in William Loren Katz, ed., *Five Slave Narratives*, NY: Arno Press and The New York Times.

Graybeal, Jay. 1991. *Visitor's Guide: The Sherman-Fisher-Shellman House*. Westminster, Md.: Historical Society of Carroll County, Maryland.

Green, William. 1853. *Narrative of Events in the Life of William Green (Formerly a Slave)*. Reprint, Wilmington, DE: Scholarly Resources.

Griebel, Helen Bradley. 1995a. "The West African Origin of the African-American Headwrap." In Joanne B. Eicher, ed., *Dress and Ethnicity: Change Across Space and Time*. Oxford and Washington, D.C.: Berg, 207–226.

——. 1995b. "The African American Woman's Headwrap: Unwinding the Symbols." In Mary Ellen Roach-Higgins, Joanne B. Eicher, and Kim K. P. Johnson, eds., *Dress and Identity*, NY: Fairchild, 445–460.

Grimes, William. [1855] 1971. *Life of William Grimes, The Runaway Slave, Brought Down to the Present Time*. Reprinted in Arna Bontemps, *Five Black Lives*, Middletown, Mass.: Wesleyan University Press.

Gundersen, Joan Rezner. August 1986. "The Double Bonds of Race and Sex: Black and White Women in a Colonial Virginia Parish." *The Journal of Southern Culture* LII (3), 351–372.

Gunther, Lenworth. 1978. *Black Image: European Eyewitness Accounts of Afro-American Life*. Port Washington, NY: National University Publications.

Hall, Radclyffe, [1928] 1990. *The Well of Loneliness*. NY: Anchor Books.

Hammond, Lincoln Davis, revisor. 1963. *Travelers in Disguise: Narratives of Eastern Travel by Poggio Bracciolini and Ludovico de Varthema*. John Winter Jones, English translator, Cambridge, Mass.: Harvard University Press for the Department of Romance Languages and Literatures.

Hamdun, Said and Noël King. 1994. *Ibn Battuta in Black Africa*. Princeton: Markus Wiener.

Hansberry, William Leo. 1958. "Indigenous African Religions." In *Présence Africaine*, special issue, *Africa from the Point of View of American Negro Scholars*, France, 83–100.

Harris, Middleton. 1974. *The Black Book*. NY: Random House.

Harrison, Daphne Duval. 1990. *Black Pearls: Blues Queens of the 1920s*. New Brunswick, NJ, and London: Rutgers University Press.

Hay, Margaret Jean and Sharon Stichter. 1990. *African Women South of the Sahara*. London and NY: Longman.

Hayden, William. 1846. *Narrative of William Hayden. Containing a Faithful Account of His Travels for a Number of Years, whilst a Slave in the South*. Reprint, Wilmington, Del.: Scholarly Resources.

Herskovits, Melville J. 1958. *The Myth of the Negro Past*. Boston: Beacon Press.

Higginbotham, A. Leon. 1980. *In the Matter of Color: Race and the Legal Process*. Oxford and NY: Oxford University Press.

Hildreth, R. ed. 1852. *The White Slave: A Story of Life in Virginia*. London: Ingram, Cooke, & Co.

Hilton, Anne. 1985. *The Kingdom of Kongo*. Oxford: Clarendon Press.

Hoebel, E. Adamson. 1965. "Clothing and Ornament." In Mary Ellen Roach and Joan Bubolz Eicher, eds., *Dress, Adornment and the Social Order*. NY: John Wiley & Sons, 15–27.

Høeg, Peter. 1994. *Smilla's Sense of Snow*. NY: Dell.

Hollen, Norma, Jane Saddler, Anna L. Langford and Sara J. Kadolph. 1988. *Textiles*. NY: MacMillan.

hooks, bell. May 1992. "My 'Style' Ain't No Fashion." *Z Magazine*, 27–29.

Honour, Hugh. 1989. *The Image of the Black in Western Art: IV. From the American Revolution to World War II*. Part 1 [a] and Part 2 [b]. Cambridge, Mass., and London: Harvard University Press.

Hughes, Langston and Milton Meltzer. 1963. *A Pictorial History of the Negro in America*. NY: Crown.

Hughes, Langston, ed. 1967. *The Best Short Stories by Negro Writers*. Boston: Little, Brown.

Hughes, Louis. [1897] 1969. *Thirty Years a Slave: From Bondage to Freedom.* NY: Negro Universities Press Reprint.

Hurston, Zora Neale. [1935] 1963. *Mules and Men.* Bloomington: Indiana University Press.

——. 1942, "Story in Harlem Slang." *The American Mercury*, 84–96.

——. [1937] 1978. *Their Eyes Were Watching God.* Urbana and Chicago: University of Illinois Press.

——. 1981. "Characteristics of Negro Expression." Originally In Nancy Cunard, *The Negro*, 1934; reprinted in *The Sanctified Church.* Berkeley: Turtle Creek.

Idiens, Dale. 1980. "An Introduction to Traditional African Weaving and Textiles." *Textile History* 11:5–21.

Isaac, Rhys. 1982. *The Transformation of Virginia: 1740–1790.* Chapel Hill: University of North Carolina Press for the Institute of Early American History and Culture, Williamsburg, Virginia.

Jackson, Andrew. 1847. *Narrative and Writings of Andrew Jackson of Kentucky.* Reprint, Wilmington, Del.: Scholarly Resources.

Jackson-Brown, Irene V. 1985. "Black Women and Music: A Survey from Africa to the New World." In Filomina Chioma Steady, ed., *The Black Woman Cross-Culturally*, Rochester, Vt.: Schenkman Books, 383–402.

Jacobs, Harriet A. [1861] 1987. *Incidents in the Life of a Slave Girl: Written By Herself.* Jean Fagan Yellin, ed., Cambridge, Mass., and London: Cambridge University Press.

Jensen, Joan M. 1981. *With These Hands: Women Working on the Land.* Old Westbury NY: The Feminist Press, NY: McGraw-Hill.

Jernegan, Marcus W. Jan 1920. "Slavery and the Beginnings of Industrialism in the American Colonies." *American Historical Review* 25 (2), 220–240.

Jones, Bessie and Bess Lomax Hawes. 1972. *Step It Down: Games, Plays, Songs and Stories from the Afro-American Heritage.* Athens and London: University of Georgia Press.

Jones, Jacqueline. 1985. *Labor of Love, Labor of Sorrow: Black Women, Work and the Family, From Slavery to the Present.* NY: Vintage.

Jones, John Winter, English translator. 1963. *Travelers in Disguise: Narratives of Eastern Travel by Poggio Bracciolini and Ludovico de Varthem.* Lincoln Davis Hammons, revision, Cambridge Mass.: Harvard University Press for the Department of Romance Languages and Literatures.

Jones, Norrece T., Jr. 1990. *Born a Child of Freedom, Yet a Slave: Mechanisms of Control and Strategies of Resistance in Antebellum South Carolina.* Hanover, NH and London: Wesleyan University Press, University Press of New England.

Jordan, Rosan and Frank de Caro. Winter 1996. "'In This Folk-Lore Land': Race, Class, Identity, and Folklore Studies in Louisiana." *Journal of American Folklore* 109 (431), 30–59.

Joyner, Charles. 1984. *Down By the Riverside: A South Carolina Slave Community.* Urbana and Chicago: University of Chicago Press.

Katz, William Loren. 1968. *Five Slave Narratives: A Compendium*. NY: Arno Press and The New York Times.

Kane, Cheikh Hamidou. 1985. *Ambiguous Adventure*. London: Heinemann.

Keckley, Elizabeth. [1868]. 1985. *Behind the Scenes*. Salem NH: Ayer.

Kelso, William M. Sept/Oct 1986. "Mulberry Row: Slave Life at Thomas Jefferson's Monticello." *Archaeology*, 28–35.

Kemble, Frances Anne. 1863. *Journal of a Residence on a Georgia Plantation in 1838–1839*. N.Y.: Harper & Brothers.

Kern-Foxworth, Marilyn. January/February 1989. "Aunt Jemima" Part I. *Black Ethnic Collectibles*, 18–22.

——. March/April 1989. "Aunt Jemima" Part II. *Black Ethnic Collectibles*, 18–19.

King, Martin Luther, Jr. 16 April 1963. "Letter from Birmingham Jail."

Kirschenblatt-Gimblett, Barbara. 1983. "The Future of Folklore Studies in America: The Urban Frontier." *Folklore Forum* 16 (2), 175–233.

——. 1989. "Objects of Memory: Material Culture as Life Review." In Elliott Oring, ed., *Folk Groups and Folklore Genres: A Reader*, Logan: Utah State University Press, 329–338.

Kroll, Carol. 1981. *The Whole Craft of Spinning: From the Raw Material to the Finished Yarn*. NY: Dover.

Kytle, Elizabeth. 1993. *Willie Mae*. Athens and London: University of Georgia Press/Brown Thrasher.

Lanker, Brian. 1989. *I Dream a World: Portraits of Black Women Who Changed America*. NY: Stewart, Tabori and Chang.

Lauer Jeanette C. and Robert H. Lauer. 1989. "Fashion." In Charles Reagan Wilson and William Ferris, eds., *Encyclopedia of Southern Culture*, Chapel Hill and London: University of North Carolina Press, 612–613.

Leaks, Sylvester. 1967. "The Blues Begins." From *Trouble, Blues, n' Trouble*, reprinted in Langston Hughes, ed., *The Best Short Stories by Negro Writers*, Boston: Little, Brown, 275–287.

Leon, Eli. 1978. *Who'd A Thought: Improvisation in African-American Quiltmaking*. San Francisco Craft and Folk Art Museum [exh. cat].

Levine, Lawrence W. 1978. *Black Culture and Black Consciousness: Afro-American Folk Thought From Slavery Through Freedom*. Oxford, London and NY: Oxford University Press.

Levtzion, Nehemia. 1973. *Ancient Ghana and Mali*. London: Methuen.

Ligon, Richard. 1657. *A True and Exact History of the Island of Barbadoes*. London.

Lloyd, P. C., introduction and annotation. 1968. "Osifekunde of Ijebu" [Originally published by Marie Armand Pascal d'Avezac-Macaya, *Mémoires de la Société Ethnologique*, 1845]. In Philip D. Curtin, ed., *Africa Remembered: Narratives of West Africans from the Era of the Slave Trade*, 217–289.

Logan, Rayford W. 1958. "The American Negro's View of Africa." In *Présence*

Africaine, special Issue, *Africa From the Point of View of American Negro Scholars* [*Africa Seen By American Negroes*], France, 217–246.

Malcolm X (assisted by Alex Haley). 1966. *The Autobiography of Malcolm X*. NY: Grove Press.

Malcolm X. 1970. *Malcolm X On Afro-American History*. NY: Pathfinder Press.

Mainardi, Patricia. 1973. "Quilts: The Great American Art." *The Feminist Art Journal*, Winter, 17–22.

Marks, Bayly E. Nov 1987. "Skilled Blacks in Antebellum St. Mary's County, Maryland." *Journal of Southern History* LIII (4), 537–564.

Marshall, Paule. [1969] 1984. *The Chosen Place, The Timeless People*. NY: Vintage/Random House.

Mason, Bobbie Ann. 1 August 1994. "Bad Hair Year." *The New Yorker*, 82.

McCarthy, Bill. 1989. "Clothing." In Charles Reagan Wilson and William Ferris, eds., *Encyclopaedia of Southern Culture*, Chapel Hill and London: University of North Carolina Press, 466–468.

McClellan, Elisabeth. 1977. *Historic Dress in America 1607–1870*. NY: Arno Press.

McCullers, Carson. [1945] 1986. *The Member of the Wedding*. NY: Bantam Books.

McLaughlin, Patricia. 27 Oct 1993. "Is Corporate America Really Afraid of Braids?" [Minneapolis] *Star Tribune*, reprinted from *Philadelphia Inquirer*, 2E.

Melville, Herman. [incomplete manuscript] 1970. "Billy Budd, Sailor." In Harold Beaver, ed., *Billy Budd, Sailor and Other Stories*, 317–409.

Mercer, Kobena. 1987. "Black Hair/Style Politics." *New Formations* 3, 33–54.

Miller, Randall M. and John David Smith, eds. 1987. *Dictionary of Afro-American Slavery*. NY and Westport, Conn.: Greenwood Press.

Miller, Ronald. 1954. *Travels of Mungo Park*. London: J. M. Dent and NY: E. P. Dutton.

Mintz, Sidney W. and Richard Price. 1992. *The Birth of African-American Culture: An Anthropological Perspective*. Boston: Beacon Press.

Mollett, J. W. 1883. *Dictionary of Art and Archaeology*. London.

Montgomery, Florence M. 1984. *Textiles in America 1650–1870*. NY: W. W. Norton.

Morris Richard B., Jr. ed. 1953. *Encyclopedia of American History*. NY: Harper & Brothers.

Morrison, Toni. 1992. *Playing in the Dark: Whiteness and the Literary Imagination*. Cambridge, Mass., and London: Harvard University Press.

Morrow, Willie L. 1984. *Four-hundred Years Without a Comb*. NY: Cosmetology Pub.

Morton, Patricia. 1991. *Disfigured Images: The Historical Assault on Afro-American Women*. NY; Westport, Conn., and London: Greenwood Press.

Mphahlele, Ezekiel. 1964. "Greig on a Stolen Piano." In Ellis Ayitey Komey and Mphahlele, eds., *Modern African Stories*, London: Faber and Faber, 129–147.

Mullin, Michael. 1992. *Africa in America: Slave Acculturation and Resistance in the American South and the British Caribbean, 1736–1831*. Urbana and

Chicago: University of Illinois Press.

Myrivilis, Stratis. 1959. *The Mermaid Madonna*. Athens: Efstathidis Group.

Naipaul, Shiva. 1984. *North of South: An African Journey*. Middlesex: Penguin.

National Museum of African Art. 1987. *The Art of West African Kingdoms*. Washington DC: Smithsonian Institution Press.

Niane, Djibril T. 1965. *Sundiata: An Epic Tale of Old Mali*. Translated by G. D. Pickett, London: Longman.

Nordquist, Barbara K. 1990. "African Traditional Dress and Textiles: Material Form." In Nordquist, et. al., eds., *African American Dress and Adornment*, Dubuque, IA: Kendall/Hunt, 19–38.

Northup, Solomon. [1853] 1968. *Twelve Years a Slave*. Baton Rouge and London: Louisiana State University Press.

Nwapa, Flora. 1978. *Efuru*. Portsmith, NH: Heinemann.

Offley, Rev. G. W. [1860] 1971. *A Narrative of the Life and Labors of the Rev. G. W. Offley, A Colored Man, and Local Preacher*. Reprinted in Arna Bontemps, *Five Black Lives*, Middletown, Conn.: Wesleyan University Press.

O'Hara, Georgina. 1986. *The Encyclopedia of Fashion*. NY: Harry N. Abrams.

Oliver, Roland and J. D. Fage. 1988. *A Short History of Africa*. New Edition. London: Penguin.

Olmsted, Frederick Law. [1861] 1984. *The Cotton Kingdom: A Travellers Observations on Cotton and Slavery in the American Slave States*. NY: Modern Library.

——. 1959. *The Slave States*. Harvey Wish, revisor and editor. New York: Capricorn Books.

Oring, Elliott, ed. 1989. *Folk Groups and Folklore Genres*. Logan: Utah State University Press.

Otten, Charlotte M, ed. [1971] 1990. *Anthropology and Art: Readings in Cross-Cultural Aesthetics*. Austin: University of Texas Press.

Oxford Classical Dictionary. 1989. "Herodotus." Oxford: Clarendon Press, 507–509.

Page, Thomas Nelson. [1892] 1994. *Social Life in Old Virginia: Before the War*. Sandwich, MA: Chapman Billies.

Park, Mungo. 1954. *Travels of Mungo Park* [1795–1797]. Edited by Ronald Miller, London: J. M. Dent & Sons and NY: E. P. Dutton.

Parrington, Michael and Janet Wideman. 1986. "Acculturation in an Urban Setting: The Archaeology of a Black Philadelphia Cemetery." *Expedition* 28 (1):55–62.

Parrish, Lydia. 1942. *Slave Songs of the Georgia Sea Islands*. NY: Creative Age Press.

Parsons, Elsie Clews. 1923. *Folk-Lore of the Sea Islands, South Carolina*. Memoirs of the American Folklore Society, NY: G. E. Stechert.

——. 1936. *Mitla: Town of the Souls*. Chicago and London: University of Chicago Press.

Pennington, James W. C. [1849] 1968. *The Fugitive Blacksmith; or, Events in the History of James W. C. Pennington*. Reproduced in William Loren Katz, ed.,

Five Slave Narratives, NY: Arno Press and The New York Times.

Perdue, Charles L., Jr., Thomas E. Barden and Robert K. Phillips. 1980. *Weevils in the Wheat: Interviews with Virginia Ex-Slaves*. Bloomington and London: Indiana University Press.

Petry, Ann. [1946] 1974. *The Street*. Boston: Houghton Mifflin.

Picton, John and John Mack. 1979. *African Textiles: Looms, Weaving and Design*. London: British Museum Publications.

Picton, John. 1995. *The Art of African Textiles: Technology, Tradition and Lurex*. London: Barbicon Art Gallery/Lund Humphries Publishers.

Plumer, Cheryl. 1971. *African Textiles: An Outline of Handcrafted Sub-Saharan Fabrics*. East Lansing: Michigan State University.

Postell, William Dosite. [1950] 1970. *The Health of Slaves on Southern Plantations*. Gloucester, Mass.: Peter Smith.

Présence Africaine. 1958. *Africa From the Point of View of American Negro Scholars [Africa Seen by Negroes]*. France.

Preyer, Norris W. April 1961. "The Historian, the Slave, and the Ante-bellum Textile Industry." *Journal of Negro History* XLVI (2), 68–81.

Price, Richard. 1983. *First-Time: The Historical Vision of an Afro-American People*. Baltimore and London: Johns Hopkins University Press.

——. 1990. *Alabi's World*. Baltimore: Johns Hopkins University Press.

Prince, Mary. [1831] 1991. *The History of Mary Prince, A West Indian Slave Related by Herself*. Moira Ferguson, ed., Ann Arbor: University of Michigan Press.

Randolph, Peter. 1855. *Sketches of Slave Life: or, Illustrations of the 'Peculiar Institution'*. Reprint, Wilmington, Del.: Scholarly Resources.

Rawick George P. 1972. *From Sundown to Sunup: The Making of the Black Community*. Volume 1, *The American Slave: A Composite Autobiography*. Westport, Conn.: Greenwood Publishing.

——. General Ed. 1972 and 1979. *The American Slave: A Composite Autobiography*. Westport, Conn.: Greenwood Publishing.

Redpath, James. [1859] 1968. *The Roving Editor: or, Talks with Slaves in the Southern States*. Reprint, NY: Negro Universities Press.

Reed, Ishmael. 1967. *The Free-Lance Pallbearers*. London: Allison and Busby.

Reff, Theodore. 1977. *Manet: Olympia*. NY: Viking Press.

Ribeiro, Aileen and Valerie Cumming. 1989. *The Visual History of Costume*. London: B.T. Batsford.

Roach, Mary Ellen and Joanne Bubolz Eicher. 1979. "The Language of Personal Adornment." In Justine M. Cordwell and Ronald A Schwarz, eds., *The Fabrics of Culture: The Anthropology of Adornment*, The Hague, Paris, NY: Mouton, 7–21.

——. eds. 1965. *Dress, Adornment and the Social Order*. NY: John Wiley & Sons.

Roach-Higgins, Mary Ellen, Joanne B. Eicher, and Kim K. P. Johnson, eds. 1995. *Dress and Identity*. NY: Fairchild.

Roberts, John W. 1990. *From Trickster to Badman: The Black Folk Hero in Slavery and Freedom*. Philadelphia: University of Pennsylvania Press.

Roberts, Robert. 1827. *The House Servant Directory, etc.* Reprint, Wilmington, Del.: Scholarly Resources.

Roberts, Warren. 1988. *Viewpoints on Folklife: Looking at the Overlooked*. Ann Arbor: UMI Press.

Rooks, Noliwe M. 1996. *Hair Raising: Beauty, Culture, and African American Women*. New Brunswick, NJ: Rutgers University Press.

Roper, Moses. 1838. *A Narrative of the Adventures and Escape of Moses Roper From American Slavery*. Reprint, Wilmington, Del.: Scholarly Resources.

Rountree, Cathleen. 1993. *On Women Turning 50*. San Francisco: Harper Collins.

Rumford, Beatrix. February 1975. "Folk Art in America: A Living Tradition." *Antiques*, 333–335.

Ryder, A. F. C. 1969. *Benin and the Europeans 1485–1897*. NY: Humanities Press.

Scarborough, William Kauffman. 1984. *The Overseer: Plantation Management in the Old South*. Athens: University of Georgia Press.

Schwartz, Jack. 1965. "Men's Clothing and the Negro." In Mary Ellen Roach and Joanne Bubolz Eicher, eds., *Dress, Adornment, and the Social Order*, NY: John Wiley & Sons, 164–174.

Sellers, James Benson. 1950. *Slavery in Alabama*. University, Ala.: University of Alabama Press.

Sewell, Rhonda B. 19 June 1994. "Another Fashion Flashback." *[Minneapolis] Star Tribune*.

Sieber Roy. 1972. *African Textiles and Decorative Arts*. N.Y.: Museum of Modern Art (exh. cat).

Simkins, Anna Atkins. 1982. "The Functional and Symbolic Roles of Hair and Headgear Among African American Women: A Cultural Perspective." Dissertation: University of North Carolina at Greensboro.

——. 1990. "Function and Symbol in Hair and Headgear Among African American Women." In Nordquist, et al., eds., *African American Dress and Adornment*, Dubuque, Ia.: Kendall/Hunt, 166–171.

Singleton, Theresa A. 1985. *The Archaeology of Slavery and Plantation Life*. NY: Academic Press.

——. 1991. "The Archaeology of Slave Life." In Campbell, ed., *Before Freedom Came*, 155–175.

Smith, James L. [1881] 1971. *Autobiography of James L. Smith*. Reprinted in Arna Bontemps, *Five Black Lives*, Middletown, Conn.: Wesleyan University Press.

Spillers, Hortense J. Summer 1987. "Mama's Baby, Papa's Maybe: An American Grammar Book." *Diacritics* 17 (2), 65–81.

Spradley, James P. and David W. McCurdy, eds. 1980. *Conformity and Conflict: Readings in Cultural Anthropology*. Boston: Little, Brown.

Starke, Barbara M. 1990. "U.S. Slave Narratives: Accounts of What They Wore." In Starke, et al., eds., *African American Dress and Adornment: A Cultural*

Perspective.

Starke, Barbara M., Lillian O. Holloman and Barbara K. Nordquist, eds. 1990. *African American Dress and Adornment: A Cultural Perspective*. Dubuque, Ia.: Kendall/Hunt.

Starobin, Robert S., ed. 1974. *Letters of American Slaves*. NY: New Viewpoints.

Stavisky, Leonard. Oct 1947. "The Origins of Negro Craftsmanship in Colonial America." *Journal of Negro History* 32 (4), 417–429.

Steady, Irene Chioma, ed. 1985. *The Black Woman Cross-Culturally*. Rochester, Vt.: Schenkman Books.

Stedman, Captain John Gabriel. [1796] 1971. *Narrative of a Five Year Expedition Against the Revolted Negroes in Surinam*. Amherst: University of Massachusetts Press.

Sterling, Dorothy, ed. 1984. *We Are Your Sisters: Black Women in the Nineteenth Century*. NY and London: W. W. Norton.

St. George, Robert Blair, ed. 1988. "Introduction." *Material Life in America 1600–1860*. Boston: Northeastern University Press, 3–13.

Stowe, Harriet Beecher. [1852] 1984. *Uncle Tom's Cabin or, Life Among the Lowly*. Ann Douglas, ed., and "Introduction," NY: Penguin.

Strobel, Margaret. 1990. "Women in Religion and In Secular Ideology." In Margaret Jean Hay and Sharon Stichter, ed., *African Women South of the Sahara*, London and NY: Longman, 87–101.

Stroyer, Jacob. [1898] 1968. *My Life in the South*. Reprinted in William Loren Katz, ed., *Five Slave Narratives*, NY: Arno Press and The New York Times.

Stuckey, Sterling. 1987. *Slave Culture: Nationalist Theory and the Foundations of Black America*, NY: Oxford University Press.

——. 1994. *Going Through the Storm: The Influence of African American Art in History*. NY and Oxford: Oxford University Press.

Styron, William. [April 1965] 1993. "This Quiet Dust." Originally in *Harper's Magazine*; reprinted in Henry Louis Gates, Jr., ed., *Voices in Black and White*, NY: Franklin Square Press.

Szwed, John. 1975. "Race and the Embodiment of Culture." *Ethnicity* 2:19–33.

Themba, Can. 1983. *The Will to Die*. London, Ibadan, Nairobi: Heinemann.

Thornton, John. 1992. *Africa and Africans in the Making of the Atlantic World 1400–1680*. NY: Cambridge University Press.

Trollope, Frances. [1832] 1984. *Domestic Manners of the Americans*. Richard Mullen, ed., Oxford and NY: Oxford University Press.

Truth, Sojourner. 1878. *Narrative of Sojourner Truth*. Battle Creek, MI: Published for the Author.

Twining, Mary. 1963. "Harvesting and Heritage: A Comparison of Afro-American and African Basketry." In William Ferris, ed., *Afro-American Folk Art and Crafts*, Jackson and London: University Press of Mississippi, 259–271.

Venture. [1798] 1897. *A Narrative of the Life and Adventures of Venture A Native of Africa*. Reprinted in Arna Bontemps, *Five Black Lives*, Middletown, Conn.:

Wesleyan University Press, 1–34.
Virginia Writers' Project. [1940] 1960. *The Negro in Virginia*. Reprint, NY: Arno Press and *The New York Times*.
Vlach, John Michael. 1990. *The Afro-American Tradition in the Decorative Arts*. Athens and London: University of Georgia Press.
——. 1991. *By the Work of Their Hands: Studies in Afro-American Folklife*. Charlottesville and London: University of Virginia Press.
——. 1993. *Back of the Big House: The Architecture of Plantation Slavery*. Chapel Hill and London: University of North Carolina Press.
Wade, Richard C. 1964. *Slavery in the Cities: The South 1820–1860*. NY: Oxford University Press.
Wahlman, Maude Southwell. 1986. "Religious Symbols in Afro-American Art." *New York Folklore* 12 (1–2), 1–24.
Walker, Alice. 1970. *The Third Life of Grange Copeland*. NY: Harcourt Brace Jovanovich.
——. 1982. *The Color Purple*. NY: Harcourt Brace Jovanovich.
——. 1983. *In Search of Our Mothers' Gardens*. San Diego, NY and London: Harcourt Brace and Jovanovich.
Wares, Lydia Jean. 1981. "Dress of the African-American Woman in Slavery and Freedom:1500–1935." Dissertation: Purdue University.
——. 1990. "African Dress." In Nordquist, et al., *African American Dress and Adornment*, Dubuque, Ia.: Kendall/Hunt, 39–47.
Washington, Booker T. [1901] 1986. *Up From Slavery*. NY: Penguin Books.
Waters, Ethel. 1978. *I Touched a Sparrow*. Minneapolis, Minn.: World Wide Publications for the Billy Graham Evangelistic Association.
Weiner, Annette B. and Jane Schneider, eds. 1991. *Cloth and the Human Experience*. Washington and London: Smithsonian Institution Press.
West, Cornel. 1993. *Race Matters*. Boston: Beacon Press.
Wheatley, Phillis. [1773] 1989. *The Poems of Phillis Wheatley*. Julian D. Mason, Jr., ed., Chapel Hill and London: University of North Carolina Press.
White, Shane. Jan/March 1989. "A Question of Style: Blacks in and Around New York City in the Late 18th Century." *Journal of American Folklore*, 23–44.
White, Shane and Graham White. Unpublished. "His Hair is done up in the tastiest manner for his colour": Slave Hair and African-American Culture in the Eighteenth and Nineteenth Centuries."
Wiggins, David Kenneth. 1979. "Sport and Pastimes in the Plantation Community:The Slave Experience." Dissertation: University of Maryland.
Wilcox, R. Turner. 1945. *The Mode in Hats and Headdresses*. NY: Charles Scribner's & Sons.
——. 1969. *The Dictionary of Costume*. NY: Charles Scribner's & Sons.
Willett, Frank. [1968] 1990. "Ife in Nigerian Art." Reprinted in Charlotte M. Otten, ed., *Anthropology and Art: Readings in Cross-Cultural Aesthetics*, Austin: University of Texas Press, 354–365.

——. 1993. *African Art*. NY: Thames and Hudson.

Williams, Isaac D. 1885. *Sunshine and Shadow of Slave Life: Reminiscences As Told to "Tege."* East Saginaw, Mich.: Evening News Printing and Binding House.

Williams, James. n.d. *Narrative of James Williams*. Reprint, Wilmington, Del.: Scholarly Resources.

Williams, Lena . 12 May 1996. "In Defense Of the Church Hat." *New York Times*, Section 13:1, 11.

Williams, Sherley Anne. 1987. *Dessa Rose*. NY: Berkeley Books.

Wilks, Ivor, introduction and annotation. 1968. "Sâlih Bilâli of Massina" and "Wargee of Astrakhan." In Philip D. Curtin, ed.,*Africa Remembered: Narratives by West Africans from the Era of the Slave Trade*, Madison, Milwaukee and London, 145–151 and 170–192.

Wilson, Charles Reagan. 1989. "Jim Crow." In Wilson and William Ferris, eds., *Encyclopedia of Southern Culture*, Chapel Hill and London: University of North Carolina Press, 213–214.

Wilson, Charles Reagan and William Ferris. 1989. *Encyclopedia of Southern Culture*. Chapel Hill and London: University of North Carolina Press.

Windley, Lathan. 1983. *Runaway Slave Advertisements: A Documentary History from the 1730s to 1790*, Volume I, VA and NC. Westport, Conn.: Greenwood Publishing.

Woodson, Carter G. [1926] 1969. *The Mind of the Negro As Reflected In Letters Written During the Crisis 1800–1860*. NY: Negro Universities Press.

Woolf, Virginia. [1928] 1981. *Orlando*. London: Granada Publishing Ltd.

Writers Program, Louisiana. 1945. *Gumba Ya-Ya*. Boston: Houghton Mifflin.

Wynter, Leon E. 26 October 1993. "Stores Have Different Ideas on African Styles." *Wall Street Journal*.

Yarwood, Doreen. 1978. *The Encyclopedia of World Costume*. London: B. T. Batsford.

Yetman, Norman R. Fall 1967. "The Background of the Slave Narrative Collection." *American Quarterly* XIX, 534–553.

Yoder, Don. Spring 1971. "Historical Sources for American Traditional Cookery: Examples from the Pennsylvania German Culture." *Pennsylvania Folklife*, 16–29.

Index